Korean

In this accessible survey, two leading specialists introduce a broad range of topics in Korean linguistics, including the general historical background of the language, its phonetics, phonology, morphology, syntax, semantics, pragmatics, and sociolinguistics, and the interfaces between those areas. Expertly written and drawing on the authors' many years of experience, the book answers questions such as what languages Korean is related to, what is unique about the Korean sound system, and how "subject" and "topic" are distinguished in Korean. It guides the student through the major issues in Korean linguistics in a theory-neutral way, at the same time discussing the latest research on the language, and exploring its unique writing system, which has long been a topic of interest to linguists and to those interested in writing systems in general. It is the ideal introduction for students both at the beginning of their studies and at a more advanced level.

Sungdai Cho is professor of Korean Linguistics and director of the Center for Korean Studies at State University of New York at Binghamton. He is internationally renowned in Korean linguistics and its pedagogy, including his main research interest in syntax, morphology, learning motivation, and testing.

John Whitman is professor and current chair of the Department of Linguistics at Cornell University. He has published extensively on Chinese, Japanese, and Korean – their history, relations, and structure. His theoretical foci are syntax and historical linguistics.

Korean

A Linguistic Introduction

Sungdai Cho

State University of New York, Binghamton

John Whitman

Cornell University, New York

CAMBRIDGE
UNIVERSITY PRESS

CAMBRIDGE
UNIVERSITY PRESS

Shaftesbury Road, Cambridge CB2 8EA, United Kingdom

One Liberty Plaza, 20th Floor, New York, NY 10006, USA

477 Williamstown Road, Port Melbourne, VIC 3207, Australia

314–321, 3rd Floor, Plot 3, Splendor Forum, Jasola District Centre, New Delhi – 110025, India

103 Penang Road, #05–06/07, Visioncrest Commercial, Singapore 238467

Cambridge University Press is part of Cambridge University Press & Assessment, a department of the University of Cambridge.

We share the University's mission to contribute to society through the pursuit of education, learning and research at the highest international levels of excellence.

www.cambridge.org
Information on this title: www.cambridge.org/9781009325400

DOI: 10.1017/9781139048842

First published 2020
First paperback edition 2022

A catalogue record for this publication is available from the British Library

Library of Congress Cataloging-in-Publication data
Names: Cho, Sungdai, 1958– author. | Whitman, John, 1954– author.
Title: Korean : a linguistic introduction / Sungdai Cho, State University of New York, Binghamton; John Whitman, Cornell University, New York.
Description: Cambridge ; New York, NY : Cambridge University Press, 2020. | Includes bibliographical references and index.
Identifiers: LCCN 2019006489 | ISBN 9780521514859 (alk. paper)
Subjects: LCSH: Korean language.
Classification: LCC PL908 .C435 2019 | DDC 495.7 dc23
LC record available at https://lccn.loc.gov/2019006489

ISBN   978-0-521-51485-9   Hardback
ISBN   978-1-009-32540-0   Paperback

Contents

Figures

Tables

Preface

As linguists both working on Korean, we have often encountered the need for a textbook on Korean linguistics for advanced undergraduates, graduate students, and instructors who teach Korean language and Korean linguistics. We bring different perspectives to the task: one as a teacher of Korean and specialist on Korean second-language learning, one as a researcher in comparative syntax and historical linguistics. This textbook has grown out of the lecture notes for the "Structure of Korean" courses that we have taught over the past few decades.

Korean linguistics attracts the interest of not only students, researchers and teachers working on the language, but of students and scholars of general linguistics. Korean is well known for such features as its three-way distinction among obstruents without a voicing distinction, case stacking, and multiple nominative and accusative constructions. The Korean writing system has long been a topic of interest to linguists and to those interested in writing systems in general. We have written this book with such a broad audience in mind, but in particular for students in linguistics wishing to focus on Korean as well as Korean studies students wishing to know more about the language. We have not attempted to "dumb down" the linguistic content of the book; for students coming to the subject for the first time, an introductory course in linguistics may be beneficial. Among those working with Korean from a practical standpoint, we hope to be of use not only to Korean-language teachers and specialists in different areas of Korean studies, but also to English speakers learning Korean as a foreign language.

This book provides a detailed survey of Korean linguistics, covering the general historical background of the language, phonetics, phonology, morphology, syntax, semantics, pragmatics, sociolinguistics, and interfaces between these areas. We attempt to take the student through most of the major issues in Korean linguistics in a theory-neutral way: thus phonological issues such as the status of the obstruent series or consonant-cluster reduction are presented in a manner useful and comprehensible to a student conversant with the basics of phonological description; syntactic issues such as scrambling and *wh*-questions presuppose no background in or commitment to a specific syntactic theory.

All errors in the book are entirely ours. The first author had main responsibility for Chapters 5–10 and the second author for Chapters 2–4. We owe a particular intellectual debt to the following texts, which we have used in teaching Korean Linguistics and East Asian Linguistics:

> Martin, Samuel. 1992. *A Reference Grammar of Korean*. Rutland, VT: Charles Tuttle.
>
> Sohn, Ho-min. 2001. *The Korean Language*. Cambridge and New York: Cambridge University Press.
>
> Sun, C. 2008. *A Linguistic Introduction: Chinese*. Cambridge and New York: Cambridge University Press.
>
> Tsujimura, N. 1996. *An Introduction to Japanese Linguistics*. Malden, MA: Blackwell Publishing.

We use the McCune–Reischauer (MR) Romanization system in the body of the text for proper names and titles, and Yale Romanization (YR: see Martin 1992: 8–12) for linguistic data, with two important exceptions. Both follow current informal practice among many Korean linguists. First, we do not employ the graph <q> used in YR to mark reinforcement in contexts such as *kal kil* (YR *kalq kil*) [kal.ki̱l] 'the road to be taken'. Second, we represent the high back rounded vowel /u/ as <wu> in all environments. Standard YR writes only after labial consonants. In addition to these two romanization systems, we use the International Phonetic Alphabet (IPA) in Chapters 3 and 4 where phonetic accuracy in representing the sounds of Korean is important. IPA transcriptions of Korean are always set off by slash brackets / / or square brackets [ ], or by an asterisk * in the case of reconstructed sounds of earlier Korean.

Acknowledgments

We would like to express our sincere appreciation to our colleagues, friends, and students whose helpful comments and encouragement have been invaluable to us in the preparation of this book. This work was supported by the Laboratory Program for Korean Studies through the Ministry of Education of the Republic of Korea and the Korean Studies Promotion Service of the Academy of Korean Studies (AKS-2016-LAB-2250004).

We would like to thank Helen Barton at Cambridge University Press for her careful work, support, and encouragement in the preparation of this book, Jiseon Kim for editorial feedback, and William O'Grady of the University of Hawaii for reading and commenting on the manuscript. The first author would like to express his appreciation for the support and input of several colleagues at State University of New York at Binghamton. The second author would like to thank Naomi Enzinna, Christina Kim, Hankyul Kim, Michelle Troberg, and colleagues in the Linguistics Department at Cornell University for theoretical, descriptive, and editorial feedback. Both authors would like to express our appreciation to Haley Deibel for her exceptionally skillful and careful work editing both English and Korean.

Abbreviations

*	ungrammatical
%	acceptability variable depending on speaker
=	clitic boundary
-	verbal suffix boundary
+	compound boundary
ACC	Accusative case particle
ADJ	Adjective adnominal suffix
ADJM	Adjective marker
ADN	Adnominal marker
ADV	Adverb suffix
A/M	Aspect/Modality
APP	Appositive marker
AUX	Auxiliary
BCE	Before Common Era
BNDN	Bound noun
CAUS	Causative suffix
CE	Common Era
CK	Contemporary Korean
CLSF	Classifier
COM	Comitative particle
COMP	Complementizer
CON	Connective
CONJE	Conjective suffix
DAT	Dative case particle
DEC	Declarative suffix
DEF	Deferential speech level suffix
DEFDEC	Deferential declarative suffix
DIR	Directional particle
DIS	Discourse marker
DISJ	Disjunctive suffix
DPRK	Democratic People's Republic of Korea
EMK	Early Middle Korean

EMoK	Early Modern Korean
EXCLAM	Exclamatory
FUT	Future tense suffix
FUTADN	Future adnominal suffix
GEN	Genitive case particle
GER	Gerundive suffix
HON	Honorific suffix or particle
IMP	Imperative suffix
INF	Infinitive suffix
INST	Instrumental suffix
INT	Intimate speech level suffix or particle
INTEN	Intentional suffix
IPA	International Phonetic Alphabet
ISO	International Standardization Organization
LMK	Late Middle Korean
LOC	Locative particle
MASCSG	Masculine singular
MOD	Modulator
NEG	Negative
NOM	Nominative case particle
NOMNL	Nominalizing suffix
NPI	Negative polarity item
OECD	Organization for Economic Cooperation and Development
OK	Old Korean
PASS	Passive suffix
PAST	Past tense suffix
PERF	Perfective suffix
PL	Plural marker
PLN	Plain speech level suffix or particle
POL	Polite speech level suffix or particle
POSS	Possessive particle
PRED	Predicate suffix
PRENOM	Prenominal
PRES	Present tense suffix
PRESADN	Present adnominal suffix
PROC	Processive
PROG	Progressive suffix
PROP	Propositive suffix
PRT	Particle
PSTADN	Past adnominal suffix
PURP	Purposive suffix
Q	Question marker

QWH	*Wh*-question marker
QYN	*Yes–No* question marker
RET	Retrospective suffix
ROK	Republic of Korea
RTR	Retracted tongue root
SK	Sino-Korean
SUSP	Suspective suffix
TAM	Tense/Aspect/Modality
TOP	Topic particle
UNGEGN	United Nations Group of Experts on Geographical Names
VOT	Voice onset time
WALS	World Atlas of Language Structures
YR	Yale Romanization

1 Introduction

Korean has emerged as an important world language not only for learners and teachers of Korean as a foreign or second language but also for scholars and students of general and Korean linguistics. Thousands of heritage schools, elementary, intermediate, and high schools, colleges and universities, private institutes, and government agencies around the world offer Korean language instruction at a range of levels. The number of institutions offering Korean, and consequently the number of students learning Korean, is constantly on the increase in Australia, Europe, China, Japan, New Zealand, the former Soviet Union, and the United States. Ever-growing numbers of general and Korean linguists, linguistics students, and language educators are interested in the structure and use of Korean and its universal and typological features from diachronic, synchronic and dynamic perspectives.

This volume, *Korean: A Linguistic Introduction*, meets the immediate needs of linguists working on linguistic universals and typology as well as students interested specifically in the structure of Korean. The volume is designed for a general audience of readers who desire to learn about Korean language and linguistics as professionals (graduate students and instructors) or as upper-level undergraduates who have had a basic linguistics course.

Two features of the book distinguish it from previous linguistic overviews of Korean. First, in almost all cases we have presented contemporary Korean linguistic data in Korean script, Hangul, as well as in romanization. Learners of Korean as well as native speakers agree that Hangul is easier to learn and recognize than the various systems of romanization. We hope that presenting Korean data in Hangul will make the discussion more user-friendly to them. Second, wherever possible, we have introduced crosslinguistic data that either contrast with or are similar to the facts of Korean under discussion. This is part of our effort to place Korean in a broader context, both among the world's languages and within the Northeast Asian region where Korean is a central presence.

The book consists of nine chapters, following this introduction, on the history of the language, writing, phonology and phonetics, morphology, morphosyntax, syntax, syntax and its interface with semantics, language and society, and language and gender.

Chapter 2 outlines the history of the Korean language, starting from the internal reconstruction of proto-Korean through Old Korean, Middle Korean, Modern Korean, and Contemporary Korean. Old Korean designates the language of Silla up until the end of the Unified Silla period in the tenth century. Middle Korean covers the Koryŏ (Early Middle Korean) and Chosŏn (Late Middle Korean) periods up until the end of the sixteenth century. Early Middle Korean (EMK) is characterized by the substantial influx of Chinese loans and the establishment of largely fixed Korean readings for Chinese characters around the end of the Old Korean and the beginning of the EMK period. Late Middle Korean coincides with the invention and promulgation of Hangul writing in the fifteenth century, which makes Korean, heretofore attested only through the imperfect medium of Chinese characters, suddenly one of the most carefully recorded languages of its period. Modern Korean, from the seventeenth century to the end of the nineteenth century, gradually comes to reflect contact with foreign languages and the final establishment of Hangul as the primary means of writing Korean, in combination with Chinese characters. Contemporary Korean spans the language of the twentieth century up to the present. This relatively brief period has also seen events of great linguistic importance: the Japanese colonial period (1909 to 1945), which saw the importation of Japanese loans and loans from Western languages through Japanese; the Korean War, resulting in the division of the two Koreas; and finally the turbulent postwar period, which has seen the final disappearance of Chinese characters in the Democratic People's Republic of Korea and their near-complete disappearance in the Republic of Korea, and ever greater impact of neologisms and loans from electronic media and the Internet.

Chapter 3 covers the way the Korean language is and has been written. The primary topic of this chapter is Hangul, the writing system invented in the fifteenth century and now a symbol of Korean culture and language wherever it is used. The Hangul system is renowned among linguists and specialists on writing systems for the elegance and rationality of its design. Alone among national writing systems in the world, it combines features of an alphabetic and syllabic writing system. We cover the background and controversies surrounding the invention of Hangul and describe the important linguistic features of the system. But we also stress the continuities between Hangul and the writing technologies that preceded and surrounded it. These include the system known as *kugyŏl*, which was devised by Koreans in the Silla period as a way of glossing a Chinese text to read it in Korean. Like *kugyŏl*, the Hangul alphabet was originally devised to make texts in Chinese characters accessible to Korean readers. Although far superior to *kugyŏl* and, unlike its predecessor, designed as an all-purpose writing system, Hangul retained a central design feature – the ability to write the sounds of Korean as a syllabic block, thus occupying graphic space in the same way as other written languages of the region.

Chapter 4 introduces the phonetics and phonology of Korean. In this realm as well, Korean is frequently cited as an unusual example of a language with a three-way distinction among obstruents without a contrast in voicing. In recent years this property has attracted renewed attention, as the aspiration contrast appears to be giving way to a prosodic or tonal distinction. Korean is thus a rare example of an intensively studied, major world language undergoing the process of tonogenesis. Korean is also notable for its processes of consonant cluster reduction, which give rise to striking differences between underlying and surface forms in many environments. Finally, many dialects of Korean have lexical pitch accent. We discuss the differences between these varieties and the prosody of standard Korean.

Chapter 5 describes word formation in Korean. We focus on three major aspects of Korean morphology: morphological types and properties, affixation, and compounding. We introduce the approach of Korean grammarians in classifying major parts of speech. They distinguish Category 1 (nominals: nouns, pronouns, and numerals), Category 2 (predicatives: verbs and adjectives, which can function in Korean as predicates on their own), and Category 3 (modifiers: determiners, adnominals, adverbials, and particles). We go on to examine bound morphemes, including the bound stems in Category 2, particles in Category 3, and dependent nouns. We also discuss affixation and compounding processes, distinguishing derivational and inflectional affixation and surveying co-compounding and sub-compounding.

Chapter 6 focuses on the interface between morphology and syntax. The five sections in this chapter deal with case (nominative, accusative, and genitive), postpositions, delimiters, nominalization, and numerals. In the section on case, we describe the distribution and allomorphy of the three cases, and devote special attention to contexts where the usage of nominative and accusative is interchangeable or nearly so. We introduce the postpositions: dative, locative, direction, goal, source, conjunctive, and disjunctive. The three most common delimiters – particles marking association with focus – are introduced with their properties: =*man* 'only', and the exceptive =*pakkey* plus negation; =*to* 'also'; and =*kkaci/mace/cocha/ilato*, all expressing 'even'. We discuss three nominalization processes, derived from four distinct parts of speech. We present constructions related to numerality, including cardinal numbers, ordinal numbers, numeral classifier phrases, and the marking of plurality. As Korean speakers have been using Chinese characters from early in the Common Era, the Sino-Korean stratum has heavily impacted Korean morphosyntax, and we see this impact particularly in numerality. We describe the well-known "ubiquitous" nature of the Korean plural marker *tul*, which appears not only on pluralized NPs, but on other parts of speech as well.

Chapter 7 deals with syntax proper. In this chapter, we discuss Category 2 (verbal and adjectival) formation, basic sentence structure, and the passive and causative patterns. We describe five basic patterns of predication: verbal predicates, adjectival predicates, nominal (copular) predicates, auxiliaries, and irregular predicates. We begin with basic sentence patterns, then introduce "scrambling" phenomena (that is, variations in word order), clausal embedding, and other complex sentence patterns. For both passive and causative constructions, we describe the basic shape of the patterns, the three-way distinction of lexical, morphological and syntactic passives and causatives, and major syntactic characteristics of each. For lexical passives, the lexical predicates themselves specify a "passive" meaning, with the canonical or thematic object in subject position. Korean morphological passives involve an additional passive morpheme, but the allomorphy is not completely predictable: there are four allomorphs of the passive suffix, conditioned by the final of the stem. Syntactic passives are formed with the passive auxiliary -ci-. These passives have a number of distinctive syntactic properties, including disallowing accusative case. Korean causatives fit the expected typological pattern in that a new subject is introduced and the causee marked with non-nominative case, while the underlying direct object remains in the accusative. As with lexical passives, lexical causatives are underived. Morphological causatives involve seven allomorphs, four homophonous with the suffixes of the morphological passive. We survey the four patterns of syntactic causatives, and explain the major syntactic differences between morphological and syntactic causatives. We show that from an areal/typological perspective, Korean fits the North Asian pattern of primarily causativizing (transitivizing) languages.

Chapter 8 examines the syntax/semantics interface in Korean. In this chapter, we focus on the following five interface areas: negation, topic/focus marking, tense/aspect/modality (TAM), pronouns and anaphora, and ellipsis. We discuss lexical, morphological, and syntactic negation. We illustrate the differences in the semantic scope of pre- and postverbal negation. We discuss the syntax and interpretation of Negative Polarity Items (NPIs). We investigate the marking of topic and focus, examining prosodic, morphological, and syntactic devices for marking information structure. In the section on TAM, we demonstrate properties and features of tense and aspect marking and also examine the relation between modality and evidentiality in Korean. Korean distinguishes past, present, and future tense, with the latter arguably a modal. For aspect, we introduce two major types which are sometimes construed as a portmanteau expression. For mood, we introduce three major patterns, indicative, conjectural, and retrospective, the latter sometimes argued to be an evidential. We then turn to the syntax and semantics of nominal reference, surveying personal and deictic as well as anaphoric pronouns. In the final section of the chapter, we discuss ellipsis and zero anaphora patterns.

Chapter 9 discusses the relationship between language and society. We describe five areas of sociolinguistic variation: regional variation (regional dialects), speech style, honorifics, terms of address, and language policy. Six major regional dialects are described in terms of lexicon, phonology, and morphosyntax: four of South Korea and two of North Korea. We introduce four different speech styles and their usage, together with two now archaic forms. The honorific system is one of the unique features of the Korean language. We discuss the three basic patterns of honorification in Korean, involving the relationship between the speaker, hearer, and referent. We also introduce two patterns that stand aside from the canonical honorific patterns: *Apjonpŏp* and indirect honorifics. "Terms of address" refers to how the addressee in a context of social communication is designated. Term of address choice can be extremely complicated in Korean. We discuss second person pronouns, titles with proper names, and kinship terms. Finally, we present four major issues that have been the focus of language policy in the Koreas: use of Hangul, language standardization, general language policy. and romanization.

Chapter 10 examines the interaction between language and gender. In this chapter, we describe how language and gender interact in Korean, in the realms of lexicon, phonology, syntax, and discourse. We distinguish five categories of lexical distinction: non-male terms, non-female terms, male-only terms, female-only terms, and terms for both male and female. In terms of phonological differences, women's speech is characterized by a rising intonation with increased tensing and aspiration, while men tend to use falling intonation with less pronounced tensing or aspiration. With regard to syntactic differences between men and women, men use more declarative sentences and deferential speech style, while women use more interrogative sentences, polite speech style, tag questions, adverbials, and deixis. For discourse differences between men's and women's style, women use more indirect speech style, hedges, obscure expressions, and cooperative communication, while men use more direct speech style, a difference which may be related to differences in power status in society.

Part I

Background

2 Historical Background

2.1 Introduction and Periodicization

This chapter summarizes what we know about the historical development of Korean from proto-Korean through the present. Our knowledge of earlier Korean is based on written sources, in Korean and other languages, and the techniques of comparative and internal reconstruction. The main periods of Korean language history in (1) are based on Lee (1961, 1998) and Lee and Ramsey (2011).

(1)   Historical Periods of Korean

      a. Three Kingdoms: from the earliest records (approximately the end of the third century CE) to 668.
      b. Old Korean (OK): 668–918
      c. Early Middle Korean (EMK): 918–1392
      d. Late Middle Korean (LMK): 1392–1600
      e. Early Modern Korean (EMoK): 1600–1900
      f. Contemporary Korean (CK): twentieth, twenty-first century

Although some of the periods in (1) correspond to periods in Korean political history, there is never an exact correspondence between linguistic history and political or cultural history. Early Middle Korean, for example, coincides with the period of the Koryŏ dynasty and the shift of the capital from Kyŏngju to Kaesŏng, but these political and geographic changes do not mark a sharp break in the language. Many important features of EMK carry over from Old Korean (Section 2.6). Languages do not change overnight with the coronation of a new ruler or relocation of the capital. Likewise, features of Old Korean are already evident in the linguistic material associated with the region of what became Silla in the Three Kingdoms period, to the extent we can tell from the limited sources (Section 2.4). For the oldest period of Korean history recorded in Chinese records, the state of Chosŏn (conventionally known as Kojosŏn "Old Chosŏn"), we simply have no sources. As we see in Section 2.2, linguists do have techniques for reconstructing forms of a language older than any written records. But unfortunately, these reconstructions do not usually come with information about where and by whom they were spoken.

Conventionally "Old" (as in Old Korean, Old English) refers to the oldest reasonably well-attested stage of a language. In designating the language of Silla as OK we are implicitly stating that the Silla language is the immediate ancestor of the stages designated as (Early and Late) Middle Korean and ultimately Contemporary Korean.

2.2   Comparative and Internal Reconstruction

One of the great accomplishments of modern linguistics is the development of techniques to reconstruct linguistic forms and patterns for which we have no written records; in effect, to go back to the prehistory of languages. These techniques have been successfully applied to Korean as well.

Comparative reconstruction uses information from related languages to reconstruct features of their common parent. As we see in Section 2.4, we have very little information about the language or languages of Paekche, but some of the information we do have allows us to reconstruct some features of proto-Korean, the common parent of the language in the Paekche materials and Late Middle Korean, as well as the ancestor of LMK, OK. In an eighth-century Japanese source, the Paekche word for 'island', CK *sem* 섬 is written in phonograms as /sjema/. This is a good match with LMK *syěm* 셤 'island', except that the second syllable is absent in LMK. LMK Hangul orthography adds an additional piece of information. As we see in Section 2.7, LMK was a word-tone or pitch-accent language, which distinguished words by which syllables were pronounced high, and which low. Fifteenth-century Hangul texts carefully marked the pitch of each syllable with a system of *pangchŏm* 'side dots' (see Section 3.3). The two side dots written on the left side of LMK *syěm* :셤 'island' in the fifteenth century indicated that the vowel was pronounced long and with rising pitch. We show this in romanization by marking the vowel with an inverted wedge *ě*, indicating that it starts out low and then rises. Until some time in the twentieth century, speakers of Seoul Korean still pronounced the vowel in 섬 *sem* 'island' as long. The length is still prescribed in CK dictionaries, which indicate the long vowel with a colon :섬 *se:m*, even though for most speakers of contemporary Seoul Korean the vowel is not long anymore. Linguists know that long vowels often come from the merger of two short vowels. Given this background, comparison of the Paekche and LMK forms suggests that the proto-Korean word for 'island' was close to the Paekche word *sjema.

Internal reconstruction examines the systematic relations between forms in a single variety of a language to arrive at hypotheses about ancestral forms. Consider the rising (low-high) tone in LMK words like *syěm* :셤 'island' and similar words such as *kwǒm* :곰 'bear'. Comparative reconstruction based on the Paekche form suggested that such words originally had two syllables; internal reconstruction suggests that the tone of those two syllables was low-high, because a low-pitched vowel and a high-pitched vowel combined into one syllable would give rising tone. This piece of internal reconstruction is confirmed by fifteenth-century textual evidence. The early Hangul text *Yongbi ŏch'ŏn ka* (*Songs of the Dragons Flying to Heaven*, 1445) attests the place name *Kwòmá noro* 'Bear River' as the name for Kongju (here the grave accent *wò* indicates low pitch, and the acute accent *á* high pitch). When Kongju was the capital of Paekche, its name was recorded with the Chinese characters 'bear' and 'river' (熊川). The name survived into the fifteenth century, with 'bear' pronounced in Paekche style, with a low-tone vowel followed by a high-tone vowel.

A proto-language is the reconstructed ancestor of the attested daughter languages. Proto-Korean is reconstructed by applying internal and comparative reconstruction to all Koreanic languages and dialects, including contemporary Seoul Korean, the dialects of Hamgyŏng-do and the Yanbian Korean Autonomous Prefecture in China, and the language of Cheju-do, as well as the language of the fifteenth-century Hangul texts. Where data is available, earlier Koreanic languages may be included in this comparative research.

Through comparative and internal reconstruction, we know that proto-Korean had the same inventory of plain consonants as modern standard Korean. It appears not to have had a distinction between voiced and voiceless consonants. The aspirated and reinforced consonants of modern Korean appear to have developed after proto-Korean (Section 2.5). The vowel system of proto-Korean was similar to the system of seven primary vowels in LMK, but there is evidence that proto-Korean had an eighth vowel, high front IPA *e, corresponding to some instances of modern Korean *ye* ㅖ after a consonant. This would explain both the high frequency of /Cye/ in the Korean lexicon, and the frequent violation of the rules of vowel harmony by initial syllables of this shape. See Section 2.5 and Whitman (2015) for details.

2.3   Genetic Affiliation and Areal Status

Perhaps the most fascinating question for anyone interested in the history of Korean is: what other language or languages is Korean related to? During the second half of the twentieth century, the most widespread answer to this question was Altaic, the putative language phylum made up of the Turkic, Mongolic, and Tungusic language families, and according to some linguists, Koreanic and Japonic (Japanese and the languages of the Ryūkyūs). The distinguished scholar Ki-moon Lee (1961, 1998) has been a leading proponent of the Altaic hypothesis, as have many other Korean historical linguists. There are two major problems with the hypothesis that Korean is related to Altaic.

The first is the status of Altaic itself. Since the 1970s, the weight of comparative linguistic research has tended to disfavor the idea that the core Altaic languages, Turkic, Mongolic, and Tungusic, are descended from a common ancestor, proto-Altaic. The debate continues to this day; for a sober assessment see Georg et al. (1999).

It is not possible to prove that Altaic is NOT a valid proto-language, but as long as its status is in doubt, we cannot conclude that Korean is descended from it. What about the possibility that Korean shares a common ancestor with one or more of its neighbors? A plausible candidate is Tungusic, which includes nearly extinct Manchu, the language of the founders of the Qing, the last imperial dynasty of China, and languages such as Evenki, spoken across a wide expanse of Siberia. Scholars such as Ki-moon Lee (1958) and Kim (1981) have attempted comparative studies of Korean and Tungusic (in Lee's case, Manchu alone). But as researchers such as Jahnunen and Kho (1982) and Vovin (2013) point out, many of the most convincing cognates on the Tungusic side tend to be found only in Manchu or other Southern Tungusic languages. This heightens the possibility that the lexical items in question are the result of contact: that they are loans from Korean to Tungusic or vice versa. A further problem is that more careful internal analysis often shows that two lookalike words cannot be related, at least in the straightforward way linguists have proposed.

Take, for example, the widely cited comparison Korean *pwulk-* 붉- 'red' : Manchu *ful-giyan* 'red'; also Mongolian *hula-yan* 'red'. This comparison looks good, but Ki-moon Lee (1991) points out that the Korean adjective is derived, from *pwul* 불 (LMK 블) 'fire', plus the same adjectivalizing suffix -*k* found in *mwulk-/malk*- 묽-/맑- (LMK *mulk-/molk-* 几-) 'clear, pure', from *mwul* 'water' + -*k*. This indicates that the meaning 'red' is secondary, casting doubt on the comparison. Of course it could be that the Tungusic and Mongolic words also embed a basic root for 'fire'. But until this is shown by careful historical work on those languages, the comparison cannot be accepted.

Similar problems obtain with attempts to show that Korean shares a common ancestor with another of its neighbors, Japanese. Japanese has a moderate amount of basic vocabulary items which show an interesting correspondence with their Korean counterparts. These are cases where Korean nouns ending in a sonorant consonant correspond to proto-Japanese-Ryūkyūan (pJR) nouns ending in *j, such as *pwul* 불 'fire' : pJR *pəj 'fire'; *mom* 몸 'body' : pJR *muj 'body'. But the correspondence runs into counterexamples: for example, we would expect Korean *mwul* (LMK *múl* 믈) 'water' to give pJR *məj, but instead the reconstructed pJR form for 'water' is *me. Proto-Tungusic *mo: (traditionally reconstructed as *mö:) 'water' and Mongolian *moren* 'river' (traditionally *mören*) also have been proposed as good matches with Korean *mwul* 'water'. Tungusic and Mongolic distinguish /r/ and /l/, while Korean and Japanese do not. Could the shape of the "Altaic" final consonant explain the aberrance of the Korean–Japanese correspondence? Until details like these are worked out, we must reserve judgment on the possibility of a genetic relation between Korean and any of its neighbors.

This does not mean that Korean is a language isolate, however. At the start of this section we used the term "Koreanic." This points to the fact that the various varieties of Korean form what linguists call a small language family. Traditionally these varieties – Seoul, North and South Kyŏngsang, Cheju, North Hamkyŏng, etc. – are referred to as dialects (*pangŏn* 방언). The distinction between dialect and language is mostly a political, not a linguistic matter. But one fairly objective measure for distinguishing language and dialect is the "dialect chain" criterion of Hockett (1958). The dialects of South Chŏlla and Yanbian in China are mutually unintelligible: two speakers of these dialects would not understand each other if they spoke their native dialects. (Of course they could understand each other if they spoke standard Seoul, or even standard Seoul and P'yŏngyang Korean.) But we hypothesize that there is a chain of localities all the way from Chŏlla-do to Yanbian across the Chinese border, where speakers of the local dialect in one locality can understand the dialect in the neighboring locality. On the other hand, the variety spoken by native speakers of Cheju Korean – a severely endangered language – is not comprehensible even to speakers of South Chŏlla. This conjecture has been confirmed by linguists William O'Grady, Changyong Yang, and Sejung Yang (2019), who conducted an experiment in which speakers of Cheju, South Chŏlla, and South Kyŏngsang were asked to evaluate their own comprehension of a recorded narrative in the Cheju language. Speakers of all three mainland dialects reported a low level of comprehension of the Cheju spoken narrative.

On the basis of this important fact – the status of Cheju as a language in its own right – we are justified in speaking of the Koreanic language family. Extinct and poorly attested Koreanic languages, such as the language of Paekche, which are related to but distinct from OK (Silla), give us further justification for referring to the Koreanic language family. In the remainder of this book we will use the more familiar term "Korean." But speakers and learners of Korean should be aware that Korea's place in the world is as a language family, not as a single, isolated language.

One final point should be made about the relation between Korean and its neighbors in Northeast Asia. While the matter of genetic affiliation is still very much under debate, there is no question that Korean is a prime representative of the Northeast Asian linguistic area. Typological traits shared by Korean and its neighbors include head-final word order, almost complete predominance of suffixes, and a high degree of morphological agglutination. Another striking trait is vowel harmony based on the position of the tongue root, as described in

Section 2.7. In the past, some linguists have looked to traits like these as evidence for genetic relatedness. But we now know that features such as tongue-root harmony are areal features that spread across language boundaries in a way similar to (but separate from) loanwords. Tongue-root harmony turns out also to be an areal feature in central Africa, and possibly in northwestern North America. In Northeast Asia, it is found not just in Korean, Mongolic, and Tungusic, but vestigially in Nivkh, and possibly Ainu and Japanese, as well as the unrelated language families Yukaghiric and Kamchukotic (see Ko et al. 2014 for details). Shared traits like these show us that Korean has long been part of the interchange of languages and peoples in its geographic region.

Within the Northeast Asian linguistic area (Figure 2.1), Korean occupies a central and in some ways transitional position. It shares the property of relatively robust tongue-root harmony with other "continental" languages such as Tungusic and Mongolic. On the other hand it shares the lack of a distinction between voiced and voiceless consonants with the "eastern" languages Ainu and Japanese. Korean also shares with these languages the property of having a tone- or pitch-accent system. The co-occurrence of tone with the absence of a voicing distinction seems unlikely to be coincidental.

Finally, Korean shares with Japanese and Manchu the property of intensive contact with Chinese. All three languages share traits such as absence of

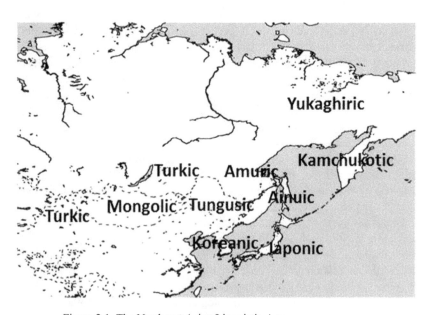

Figure 2.1 The Northeast Asian Linguistic Area

agreement, and the pervasive use of devices for turning Chinese verbs borrowed as nouns back into verbs again.

2.4   Three Kingdoms

The dates for the founding of the Three Kingdoms given in the *Samguk sagi*, a twelfth-century history of Korea, are 57 BCE for Silla, 37 BCE for Koguryŏ, and 18 BCE for Paekche, but we do not find any appreciable amount of Korean linguistic data in historical records until the *Wei shu* section of the *Sanguo zhi* in the late third century CE, where local toponyms and a few other lexica are transcribed in Chinese characters. This and other Chinese sources report some linguistic diversity in the Korean peninsula around the third century. The *Wei shu* depicts Koguryŏ in the North as a fully formed state. In contrast, the Samhan (Three Han) polities in the southern part of the peninsula do not yet bear the names by which they are later known in the Three Kingdoms period, Paekche and Silla. The *Wei shu* reports that the language of Chinhan (the predecessor of Silla) was "not the same as that of Mahan" (the predecessor of Paekche). We discussed one such difference in Section 2.2: some words of two syllables in Paekche correspond to words of one syllable in LMK, which is presumably descended from the language of Silla. This correspondence has been confirmed by the study of Samhan toponyms in Toh (2008). Other than place names and a few words preserved in Japanese sources such as *syema* 'island', our knowledge of the Paekche language is sparse.

The language of Koguryŏ has been the subject of considerable debate. The *Wei shu* compares the Koguryŏ language to the language of Puyŏ, Koguryŏ's predecessor polity in Manchuria, not with the southern Han languages. The *Wei shu* and other Chinese sources give very little concrete information about the Koguryŏ language, but the *Samguk sagi* records a large number of Koguryŏ place names using Chinese characters for their sound – so-called phonograms – and for their meaning. Korean, Japanese, and Western linguists have pointed out that some of the sound/meaning pairs resemble words in Korean, Japanese, and in a few cases Tungusic languages. It has been suggested that Koguryŏ is a "missing link" language related to all three. But given the very great linguistic distance between these three language groups, that seems unlikely. We know that Koguryŏ was a multiethnic state, ultimately controlling the territory associated with many languages. It is more likely that Koguryŏ conquerors borrowed the placenames used by the original inhabitants, just as Europeans adopted Native American placenames throughout the Americas. This explains why there are two completely different words for "three" in the Koguryŏ place names. One is transcribed using the phonogrammatic Chinese character 蜜. This is read as *mir* or *mit* and resembles Japanese *mi(t)-* 'three'. But the *Samguk sagi* also gives the phonograms 悉 *sit/sir* and 史 *sʌ/sriX* for the word 'three' in the first morpheme of the name for present-day Samch'ŏk-si on the border of Kangwŏn and Kyŏngsang-bukdo. This region was originally Sillan before passing under Koguryŏ control, so it is no surprise that the transcription is a good fit with LMK *séyh* 'three'. In other words, the Koguryŏ place names do not tell us very much about the language of Koguryŏ, but they tell us something about the languages of the peoples Koguryŏ conquered.

2.5   Old Korean (668–918 CE)

Old Korean (OK) is the language of Silla, the conqueror of Paekche and Koguryŏ in the seventh century. The Unified Silla period (668–935) is conventionally given as the period of Old Korean, although sometimes the term is extended to the Sillan language prior to unification. Sources for OK include inscriptions on stone as well as on wooden tablets known as *mokkan*. Chinese characters used as phonograms to transcribe Korean are referred to as *ch'aja* 借字 'loan characters'. Loan character writing (*ch'aja p'yogibŏp*) can be divided into proper name transcription (*koyu myŏngsa p'yogibŏp*), where all the Chinese characters are used for their sound; *idu* 吏讀 (literally 'clerk readings'), where Chinese characters are used primarily for their meaning but some bound morphemes are written phonogrammatically; and *hyangch'al* 鄉札, the mixture of phonograms and logograms used to transcribe the twenty-five *hyangga* songs.

Idu texts show the adaptation of Chinese characters to write Korean. Typically they consist of Chinese characters read for their meaning in Korean word order. An early example that gives us some insight into the language of Koguryŏ is the Chungwŏn Koguryŏ stele (中原高句麗), tentatively dated to 495 and considered to be a monument erected by Koguryŏ near the southern limits of its territorial expansion. The stele text has a number of features that can only be Korean, not Chinese:

(2)　　　建立　處　　用者　賜　　之　　(side 1, lines 4-5)
　　　　　build　place　use-r　give　this
　　　　　'(I) give the place (where this is) built to the users.'

Nam (2009: 182) observes that both the direct and the indirect object precede the verb, showing Korean rather than Chinese word order.

Hyangch'al texts give us information about OK syntax, morphology, and phonology, because they use Chinese characters both as logograms to be read in Korean (*hun* or vernacular readings) and sound (*ŭm* or Sino-Korean readings). We can find examples of both in the *hyangga Hŏnhwaga* 獻花歌 recorded in the *Samguk yusa* (thirteenth century) but dated to the period of King Sŏngdŏk (702–732).

(3) 紫布   岩乎   过希
     Tolpwo(y)   *pahwo(y)*   *kos-oy*
     azalea   crag   side-LOC
     執音   乎   手   母牛   放教遣
     Cap-om   *h-wo(-n)*   *swon* *amsywo*   *noh-i-si-kwo*
     hold-NOM   do-MOD-ADN   hand   cow   put-CAUS-HON-GER
     吾肹   不喩 慚肹伊賜   等
     Na-lol   *anti* *puskuli-so(-n)*   *to(-n)*
     me-ACC   not   ashamed-HON-ADN   fact-TOP
     花肹   折叱可   獻乎理音如
     Kwoc-ol   *kesk-e*   *pat-wo-li-m(-s)-ta.*
     flower-ACC pluck-INF   present-MOD-NOM-DEC
     'By the side of the azalea crag/if it is not the case that you find me shameful,/
     and allow the hand that was holding it to leave the cow/I must pluck the flowers
     and present them to you'

Our interpretation follows Nam (2010a). The spelling of the nominalized verb
cap-om 'holding' in line 2 is a clear example of the two ways in which Chinese
characters were used to write Korean. The character 執 'hold' has the vernacular reading *cap-* 'grab, hold', while the next character 音 is read for its
sound /um/ to represent the verbal nominalizing suffix *-u/om*. The pattern
V-(*u/o*)m ho- 'do V-ing' is not found in LMK Hangul texts, but it is found in
EMK *kugyŏl* glosses (see Section 2.6). Similarly, negative 不喩 *anti* in line 3 is
used in EMK *kugyŏl* texts to negate nominal predicate sentences. Here it
indicates that negation takes scope over the whole adnominal clause: "if it is
not the case that you find me shameful."

It used to be believed that the OK vowel inventory involved a [±back]
harmonic opposition, but more recent work has discredited the hypothesis
that Korean underwent a "vowel shift" in EMK (see Ko 2019 for a thorough
discussion of tongue-root harmony in the history of Korean). The loan pronunciations for Chinese characters known as Sino-Korean were established late
in the OK period. We can infer the OK pronunciations based on Middle
Chinese, giving us the OK vowel inventory in (4).

(4) Old Korean vowel inventory with LMK correspondences (based on Itō
     2007: 267)

OK		LMK	OK		LMK	OK		LMK
*i	>	i [i]	*ɨ	>	u [ɨ]	*u	>	wu [u]
*e	>	e [ə]	*ə	>	o [ʌ]	*o	>	wo [o]
			*a	>	a [a]			

We do not have direct philological evidence that OK had vowel harmony, but if
it did, it cannot have been of the [±back] (palatal) type, because, based on the
harmonic oppositions preserved in LMK, *i would have to alternate with *ə,

and *u with *o, but these vowels do not differ in backness. They do contrast, however, in height and with respect to the feature [±retracted tongue root].

Phonological features referring to the position of the root of the tongue may be less well known than features such as [±back] or [±labial], but they play a crucial role in the vowel harmony systems of many of the world's languages, including languages belonging to many different families in a band across the center of the African continent, some languages in northwestern North America, and many languages in Northeast Asia, including the Tungusic and Mongolic languages neighboring Korean. We see in Chapter 3 that King Sejong was aware of the phonological contrast based on retraction of the tongue root in the fifteenth century. Speakers of English can get a sense of the contrasts associated with the position of the tongue root from the articulation of the English tense vowels /i/ and /u/ in *seat* and *suit* versus the lax vowels /ɪ/ and /ʊ/ in *sit* and *soot* /sʊt/. For tense /i/ and /u/, the root of the tongue is advanced, while for /ɪ/ and /ʊ/ it is relatively retracted. In languages with tongue-root harmony, this kind of contrast pervades the vowel system, so that all or most vowels can be classified as advanced tongue root [ATR] or retracted tongue root [RTR].

The OK vowel inventory in (4) can be rearranged as a retracted tongue root (RTR) system as in (5), where the [coronal] high front vowel *i is neutral with respect to the RTR feature, but all the other vowels are classified as [+RTR] or [−RTR]:

(5)

[+coronal]		[+back]			
			[+round]		
*i	*e	*ɨ	*u	[−RTR]	
	*a	*ʌ	*o	[+RTR]	

Most of the Sino-Korean evidence for the OK vowels in (4) is straightforward, and their reconstructed value is close to their value in Late Middle Korean. But the case of the OK vowel corresponding to LMK /e/ 어 [ə] is more complex. Middle Chinese and other external evidence pointing toward a front vowel such as *e in (4) comes from syllables where this vowel is preceded by a palatal glide, as in Paekche *sjema, LMK *syĕm* 'island'. In syllables where no palatal glide is present, the evidence for *e is less clear. This suggests that OK – strictly speaking, what we should call pre-OK – might have had two vowels which merged to give a single vowel in LMK and later Korean. One is the vowel *e reconstructed in (4) on the basis of Sino-Korean. The second was a vowel which we will reconstruct as *ɛ, a nonhigh front vowel which was the harmonic opposite of [+RTR] *a. These two vowels merged to give LMK /e/ [ə], but the two earlier vowels left distinct traces. Pre-OK *e left a trace in the form of palatalization (written as /ye/ 여) of the preceding consonant and agreement in vowel harmony with [+RTR] *a, *ʌ, and *o. We see this trace both in LMK *syem*섬 'island' and in Paekche *sjema. The second vowel *ɛ surfaces in LMK simply as /e/ [ə] ㅓ, and agrees in vowel harmony with *e, *ɨ, and *u. On this view, the Pre-OK vowel system can be reconstructed as in (6). We should emphasize that (6) is a reconstruction: it is based on a number of linguistic considerations which enable us to take a step further back in time than OK written records.

(6)

Pre-Old Korean Vowel Inventory with LMK Reflexes
*i > LMK i [i]   *ɛ > LMK e [ə]   *ɨ > LMK u [ɨ]   *u > LMK wu [u]
*e > LMK ye [jə]   *a > LMK a [a]   *ʌ > LMK o [ʌ]   *o > LMK wo [o]
[−RTR]
[+RTR]

OK had a simpler consonant system than the modern language. OK appears not to have developed the voiced spirant series [β], G [ɣ], /z/ of LMK (Chapter 3), and the reinforced or tense obstruents of Modern Korean did not come into existence as a phonemically distinct series until around or after LMK. There is controversy as to whether OK had developed a distinct aspirated series corresponding to LMK /ph/ /th/ /kh/ /ch/. Sino-Korean does not regularly reflect Middle Chinese /kʰ/, and correspondences for /pʰ/ are sporadic. Correspondences for aspirated coronals and the alveopalatal affricates are somewhat better, but as we see in Section 2.6, aspirates in the native Korean lexicon, like the reinforced consonants, appear to have resulted from consonant clusters.

The *hyangga* example (3) shows us that OK had the honorific suffix *-u/osi-* and causative *-(h/k)i-*. Like the humble suffix, LMK *-zoW-*, these morphemes are often written logographically, but we see functional morphemes such as the nominalizing suffix *-u/om* written with phonographs.

2.6   Early Middle Korean (918–1392 CE)

Early Middle Korean (EMK) corresponds to the language of the Koryŏ Dynasty. Two different sources of data show us that EMK retains many features of OK which are not present in the Hangul texts of the fifteenth century. The *Jīlín lèishì* (*Kyeylim yusa* 鷄林類事, 1103) is a description of Koryŏ written by a Chinese author. Surviving fragments include a list of Korean words transcribed by Chinese characters used as phonograms. Although recent research indicates that the vowel system was little changed from OK, *Jīlín lèishì* transcriptions show us that aspirated and reinforced initial consonants in the native Korean lexicon result from consonant cluster formation through syncope. Thus the tense obstruent /ss/ ㅆ in *ssal* 쌀 'uncooked rice' is written *psól* in LMK, and as two syllables, 菩薩 *posol*, in the *Jīlín lèishì*. Similarly, aspirated obstruents such as LMK *khu-* 'big' and *tho-* (CK *tha-*) 'ride' were transcribed as disyllabic with an initial /h/, *huku-* and *hoto-* in the *Jīlín lèishì*.

These sources for initial tense and aspirated consonants are shown schematically in (7):

(7)   Sources for Korean tense and aspirated consonants
       Tensed: EMK C_1o/uC_2V > LMK C_1C_2V > CC_2V
       Example: EMK *posol* 'rice'   > LMK *psól*   > CK *ssal* 쌀
       Aspirated: EMK ho/uC_2V > LMK Ch$_2$V   > Ch$_2$V
       Example: EMK *huku-* 'big'   > LMK *khu-*   > CK *khu-* ㅋㅡ-

The LMK onset clusters have a skewed distribution: there are only the s-initial clusters sp, st, sk; p-initial clusters pt, pth, ps, pc; and the triple clusters pst and psk. The absence of coronals and velars in the C_1 position suggests that these consonants may have been weakened to /s/ and /h/ in clusters resulting from syncope, preserving the sonority hierarchy. If this supposition is correct, clusters involving a velar and another oral stop gave aspirates, while initial coronals in clusters were fricativized to /s/.

Our primary source for EMK morphosyntax, in addition to *idu* materials, are *kugyŏl* glossed texts, which have recently been the object of intensive study. *Kugyŏl* is a system for glossing Chinese texts to be read in Korean. The practice dates back to the Silla period, and EMK *kugyŏl* texts retain many OK features. A text fully glossed in *kugyŏl* is a Korean text, to be read in Korean. This form of vernacular reading of Chinese texts had an impact on the later development of Korean writing, as we see in Chapter 3. Although the quantity of *kugyŏl* glossed texts is not large, they are our richest pre-Hangul source for the syntax and morphology of earlier Korean. The example in (8) is from the Nakchang-bŏn *Kuyŏk Inwang-gyŏng* 落張本 舊釋仁王經 (*Humane King Sutra*). This text is a fragment of the Humane King Sutra discovered in 1973 in the belly of a bronze Amitābha image in a temple in Ch'ungch'ŏng Nam-do. The glosses, inscribed in *kugyŏl* characters, were written in the thirteenth century, but the Korean text preserves many features of OK syntax. The *kugyŏl* characters are underlined in (8), and words written with Chinese characters used as logograms are glossed in small capitals (to indicate that we are not completely sure how they were pronounced). In the original text, *kugyŏl* characters were written in a smaller hand next to the main line of Chinese characters (see Chapter 3 for a fuller description of *kugyŏl* writing).

(8)   他方叱   量乎音   可叱爲隱   不知 是飛叱   衆   有叱在彌
       THAPANG-*s* RYANG*h-wo-m* *cisho-n*   *anti i-no-s*   CYUNG *is-kyə-myə*
       opposite-GEN measure do-MOD-NOM act do-ADN not be-PRES-GEN masses be-PERF-
       CON
       'and there were the masses on the other side whose numbers were not to be counted'

In (8), -*n* ADNOMINAL marks a clausal or propositional nominalization, which functions as the complement of the nominal predicate negator *anti*. In contrast, the nominalizer -(*u/o*)*m* derives an event nominalization from RYANG 'measure' plus *h-wo* 'do-MODULATOR', meaning 'measuring, to measure'. Adnominal -*(u/o)l* and -*(u/o)n* lose their nominalizing function in LMK, but EMK uses the same "verbal noun" form for nominalization and noun modification. This use of adnominal affixes as nominalizers is a widespread typological feature in Northeast Asia, and based on the patterns in other Northeast Asian languages, it seems likely that the nominalizing function was primary, or at least as old as the adnominal or modifying function. We can see something similar with so-called participles in English and many other languages. The present participle *wrapping* can be a modifier, modifying another noun, as in *wrapping paper*. Or it can be a nominalization, functioning as a noun on its own, as in *Pass me the wrapping*. In LMK the future adnominal suffix -*(u/o)l* (CK -*ul* -을) forms noun modifiers, as in *nip-ul wos* 니블 옷 (CK *ip-ul os* 입을 옷) 'the clothes (one) will wear'. The existence of fossilized nominalizations such as LMK *nipul* 니블, CK *ipwul* 이불 'blanket = thing to wrap oneself in' confirms the *kugyŏl* evidence that adnominal -*(u/o)* *l* was a kind of nominalizer, like a participle. The disappearance of the nominalizing function was surely gradual, but its near-complete absence by LMK is a clear difference between this stage of the language and EMK.

In terms of lexicon, an important development in EMK is expansion of the Sino-Korean stratum of the Korean lexicon. This too is best seen as a gradual process, beginning with contact with speakers of Old Chinese during the period of the Han commanderies (108 BCE–313 CE), continuing through the promulgation of Chinese-style two character place names in the eighth century, and the establishment of a relatively fixed set of Sino-Korean readings at the end of the OK period. The strengthening of the *kwagŏ* national examination system in the Koryŏ period further spread Chinese literacy among the elites. Sino-Korean terms in the *Jīlín lèishì* for vocabulary such as the higher numerals and cultural items like 'tea' and 'bottle' indicate that the SK stratum was in the process of becoming established for the general populace.

2.7   Late Middle Korean (1392–1592 CE)

With the invention of Hangul in the fifteenth century, we suddenly obtain extraordinarily detailed information about Late Middle Korean (LMK). Because much of what we know about the LMK sound system is bound up with Hangul writing, we discuss it in Chapter 3. LMK morphosyntax has most of the features of Contemporary Korean, including the basic case-marking system, nominalizations in -*u/om*, and complementation using bound nouns such as *kes* 'thing'. Only two centuries after the *kugyŏl* text in (8), nominalizations involving adnominal -*(u/o)l* and -*(u/o)n* are no longer a productive part of the language, but grammaticalized patterns based on -*(u/o)l* and -*(u/o)n* nominalizations remain. An example is concessive -*kenul*, shown in (9) with its LMK allomorph -*nanol*:

(9) *ku cip=s*   *stol=i*   *psol kacy-e*   *na*   *wo-na-n=ol*
     that house=GEN daughter=NOM rice take=INF exit come-PROC-PSTADN=ACC
     PPALAMWON=i   *pwo-ko*   *kisk-e*
     brahman=NOM   see-GER   rejoice-INF
     'The brahman rejoiced seeing when the daughter of the house brought out the rice'
     'The brahman rejoiced seeing that the daughter of the house brought out the rice'

In CK -*kenul* 'but, since, it being the case that' has a literary flavor, but its source is the effective aspect -*ke* plus adnominal -*n*, followed by accusative -*u/ol*. In (9) -*na* is the allomorph of effective -*ke* after *wo*- 'come', and -*ol* is the [+RTR] form of the accusative marker. The example in (9) shows this ending just as it was becoming grammaticalized; as Martin (1992: 933) points out, (9) can be interpreted either as a concessive adjunct 'while' or as a nominalized complement of the verb 'see'. Either way, the loss of adnominal -*u/on* as a productive nominalizer triggered the grammaticalization.

Example (9) also shows some of the developments that take us from EMK (and earlier) to Contemporary Korean. The words *stol* 'daughter' and *psol* 'uncooked rice' were two syllables in EMK, but by the fifteenth century the first syllable vowel has been lost resulting in the consonant clusters /st/ and /ps/. Sometime after the sixteenth century the clusters become tense consonants, resulting in the CK forms *ttal* 딸 and *ssal* 쌀.

Another future change evinced by these two words is the development of the vowel /o/ [ʌ], known as *arae-a* 아래아 'lower a'. In LMK this vowel was the [+RTR] counterpart of /u/ [ɨ] 으, whose value as a high mid unrounded vowel was essentially the same as CK /u/ [ɯ] 으. In Yale Romanization, *arae-a* is transcribed as /o/, contrasting with the round back [+RTR] vowel which is written as /wo/ [o] 오. In the centuries after LMK, *arae-a* was lost in all varieties of Koreanic except the language of Cheju-do. In initial syllables it eventually merged with /a/ 아, giving the CK pronounciations of *ttal* 딸 'daughter' and *ssal* 쌀 'rice'. In noninitial syllables it merged with /u/ [ɨ] 으. These changes contributed to the breakdown of the vowel harmony system. In LMK, the full set of [+RTR] vowels inherited from OK, /a/ [a], /o/ [ʌ], /wo/ [o] contrasted with the same number of [−RTR] vowels, /e/ [ə], /u/ [ɨ], and /wu/ [u]. But the loss of *arae-a* meant that only /a/ 아 and /wo/ 오 remain from the first set. This is why in CK the only trace of vowel harmony involves verbs and adjectives whose stem contains the vowels /a/ 아 and /wo/ 오, such as *cap-a* 잡아 'grab-INF' and *coh-a* 좋아 'good-INF' or *cap-ass* 'grab-PAST' 잡았- and *coh-ass* 좋았- 'good-PAST'. All other verbs take the infinitive in -*e* -어 and the past tense in -*ess* -었. Merger with /u/ [ɨ] 으 in noninitial syllables had an even bigger effect. In LMK, [+RTR] *arae-a* and [-RTR] /u/ [ɨ] were the most common vowels in suffixes and postnominal particles. Nominal and verbal stems with a [+RTR] vowel selected suffixes with *arae-a*. The accusative suffix in *wo-na* *-n-ol* in (9) was pronounced with *arae-a*, =<u>ol</u>, to harmonize with the [+RTR] vowel /a/ in the preceding processive suffix *-na-*. But following the merger of *arae-a* and /u/ [ɨ] ⌒, in CK only /u/ ⌒ occurs in particles such as the accusative or topic marking =*(n)nun* and suffixes such as adnomimal *-ul* and *-un*. Most vowel harmony alternations are lost.

Grammatical features of LMK still present in CK include the basic structural case particles, =*i* nominative, =*(u/o)y* genitive, =*e/a/u/oy* locative/allative, =*(lu/o)l* accusative, and =*(u/o)lwo* instrumental, as well as the topic particle =*(nu/o)n*. As we have seen, in the fifteenth and sixteenth centuries the particles containing *arae-a* /o/ [+RTR] and /u/ [−RTR] still alternated depending on the vowel of the preceding syllable, but there were already exceptions in LMK texts. After a preceding consonant, the vowel-initial allomorph appears. After a vowel, the consonant-initial allomorph appears, as in CK, but we also find the short allomorphs *-y* genitive/locative and *-l* accusative.

The topic particle =*(nu/o)n* marked contrast, much as in CK:

(10) *Ne=non*   *kisk-e-two*   *na=non*   *kis-ti*   *ani*   *ho-mye*
       you-TOP   happy-INF-even   I-TOP   happy-SUSP   not   do-and
       'Even if you are happy, I am not happy.' (*Kumkang kyeng samka-hay*
       1482 2:5b)

The genitive allomorph =*y* could only be distinguished from nominative *-i* after a vowel by its accent.

(11) ZYÈLŎY   *kyèsí-l*   *ccèk-úy=nón*   [[*wúlì[-y] hò-n-wò-n*]   *ìl*] =*òl*
       tathâgata be(HON)-ADN   time-at-TOP   we-GEN do-PROC-MOD-ADN   thing=ACC
       kŭmcì   *hóy-á*
       proscribe do-INF
       'When the tathâgata was alive, he proscribed the things that we did and ...'
       (*Sekpo sangcel* 1447, 23: 41b)

In (11) genitive =*(ú/ó)y* elides completely with the second syllable of *wuli* 'we', but the exceptional low tone on this syllable shows that the subject is marked genitive, rather than nominative. We see from this example that subjects of adnominal clauses in LMK could be marked with genitive case. In adnominal subject or possessive function, genitive was marked with =*s* for inanimates or targets of honorification such as the Buddha, and =*(ú/ó)y* for others.

LMK verbal morphology shows a number of differences with CK. As in analyses of the modern language, Korean specialists on LMK distinguish between final and prefinal endings. Prefinal endings produce bound derived stems: they must combine with final endings to stand alone. The prefinal endings include status (honorific), aspect, and some modal suffixes, ordered as shown in (12) following Lee and Ramsey (2011: 213):

(12)   Prefinal endings Lee and Ramsey (2011: 213)

(1)	(2)	(3)	(4)	(5)	(6)
DEFERENTIAL	EFFECTIVE/ RETROSPECTIVE	HONORIFIC	PROCESSIVE/ AORIST	VOLITIVE	FUTURE
V -zoW-	-ke- -a/e- -te-	-(u/o)si-	-no- -(u/o)ni-	-wu/wu-	-(u/o)li-

(7)	(8)
EMOTIVE	POLITE
-two(s)-	-ngi-

In adnominal clauses, LMK distinguished future *-(u/o)l(q)* and nonfuture *-(u/o) n-*. As we saw in Section 2.6, these were nominalizers in EMK; through their original nominalizing function, they contribute the only tense categories in LMK: aorist *-(u/o)ni-* and future *-(u/o)li-*, which were derived by combining nominalizing *-(u/o)n* and *-(u/o)l* with the copula *-i*. At some earlier period, Korean was a tense language only in nominalized clauses; in other contexts, only aspect and mood were distinguished. Some of the aspectual endings in (12) are likely derived from verbs: thus processive *-no-*, expressing ongoing action, may be a reflex of the verb *na-* 'emerge' with a weakened vowel, while effective *-ke-* and its lenited variants *-a/e-*, expressing change of state, may be a reflex of *ka-* 'go'. This could help explain the irregular allomorph of the effective after *wo-* 'come', *wo-na-*, if *na-* suppleted for 'go' in this context. Such etymologies are also consistent with another distinctive property of LMK: the ability to derive verb–verb compounds by combining two verb stems directly, as in *kul-talh-* 'boil it down' from *kulh-* 'boil it' (vt) + *talh-* 'get worn down'. This contrasts with CK, where productive V–V compounds are derived by attaching V_2 to the infinitive form of V_1 in *-e/a*.

The LMK deferential and polite endings survive only in the CK formal ending *-(su)pni-*: the first syllable comes from deferential *-zoW-* and the second from polite *-ngi-*. Volitive *-wu/wo-* has disappeared in the modern language. Many questions remain unanswered about this suffix, as its uses were highly diverse. It appears in adnominal clauses where nonsubjects are relativized. In LMK it was obligatory in *-m* event nominalizations: thus *sălòm* derives the concrete nominalization 'person' from *săl-* 'live'; *sàlwóm* 'living' is the event nominalization. In other contexts, *-wu/wo-* expresses the volition of discourse participant subjects, with other subjects, irrealis mood.

Final endings include matrix clause and coordinate and adjunct suffixes. Declarative *-ta* alternates with lenited *-la*. Interrogative *-ko* [+wh] and *-ka* [−wh] follow only nominal forms; in the case of verbs and adjectives, these are derived by adnominal *-(u/o)lh* and *-(u/o)n*. The contrast between [+/−wh] forms of the interrogative survives in modern Kyŏngsang dialects. Matrix endings do not alternate for vowel harmony, nor, in general, do coordinate and adjunct suffixes.

We mentioned earlier in this chapter that LMK was a pitch-accent or what some linguists call a word-tone language. This contrasts with tonal languages such as most varieties of Chinese, where in principle every syllable may have its own pitch. In LMK, words were distinguished by the location of an accent, the syllable in the word where pitch distinctively rises or falls. The dialects of Kyŏngsang-do, parts of Kangnŭng-do, Hamgyŏng-do, and the Yanbian Korean Autonomous Prefecture in China have similar systems. The location of accent has shifted in Kyŏngsang-do varieties, but Ramsey (1978) showed that Hamgyŏng-do has a system similar to LMK, including the location of accent. Correspondences for monosyllabic words are shown in (13). Low-pitched vowels are marked by grave /è/ for LMK and unmarked in the modern dialects. In fifteenth-century Hangul texts, a single side dot as in *kúl* ·글 'writing' marked high pitch.

(13)   Pitch accent correspondences for LMK, Kyŏngsang Nam-do and
        Hamgyŏng-do, based on Ramsey (1978)

	LMK		Hamgyŏng-do	Kyŏngsang Nam-do	
a.	Low		Low	Low	
	kyèth	곁	*ceth*	*ceth*	side
	kwòc	곳	*kkoc*	*kkoch*	flower
b.	High		High	Low	
	kálh	·갏	*khál*	*khal*	knife
	kúl	·글	*kúl*	*kul*	writing

We can see in (13) that while the LMK and Hamgyŏng patterns are the same, modern Kyŏngsang Nam-do has low pitch for both classes of monosyllabic nouns (Ramsey 1978 shows that the two classes are still distinguished in Kyŏngsang-do in certain contexts).

The words in (13) reveal other changes that have taken place between LMK and CK. In monosyllabic uninflecting stems – basically nouns – such as *khal* 칼 'knife' that ended in /h/ in LMK, the aspiration associated with /h/ has migrated back to the initial stop of the syllable: LMK *kálh* 갏 > CK *khal* 칼. This is one of the sources of aspirated stops in CK.

A different kind of change is the source of the tense consonant in the onset of *kkoch* 꽃 'flower'. In LMK, nouns modifying nouns (including some cases of possession) were marked by the postnominal particle =*s* =ㅅ, subsequently referred to as *sai-sios* 사이 시옷 'medial s'. We see an example of this in (9), where *ku cip* 'that house' is marked by =*s* as a possessive modifier of *stol* 'daughter'. In most environments in CK, *sai-sios* is realized as the tensed variant of the following obstruent consonant (see Section 4.2.6 for a description of *sai-sios* in CK). Because of the tendency for words such as 'flower' or 'blossom' to occur in a compound, preceded by a nominal modifier – rose of Sharon blossom, plum blossom – speakers took the tensed form *kkoch* 꽃 to be the basic form for 'flower'.

2.8   Early Modern Korean

During and immediately after the catastrophe of the Imjin Wars (1592–1598), publication in Hangul ceased. When it resumed in the early seventeenth century, the language appeared much changed: tones were no longer recorded, and the LMK voiced spirant series had disappeared. These are not changes that happened overnight: instead, the loss of the highly prescribed orthographic standards laid down in the fifteenth century allowed developments already underway in the spoken language to emerge in Hangul texts. The merger of *arae-a* /o/ with /u/ in non-initial syllables was already underway in the sixteenth century. By the end of the seventeenth century, /o/ in initial syllables begins to merge with /a/.

We can tell by orthographic confusions that initial clusters have become homorganic tense obstruent consonants by the seventeenth century, resulting in the tense consonant series of CK. Tense stops do not result only from clusters: we have seen the example of *kkòch* 'flower' (< LMK *kwòc*), while *kkoma* 'little one' (< LMK *kwòmá*, itself a Mongolian loan) exemplifies reinforcement as an intensifying device, probably in this case with a diminutive effect. We have also seen that the aspirated series expands in the EMoK lexicon through processes such as final /h/ shifting to an initial stop in the same syllable as in LMK *kálh* 'knife' > *khal*.

A major change in the typology of EMoK was the development of a tense system in matrix verbs. CK past *-e/ass-* results from contraction of the infinitive endings *-e/a* with the verb of existence LMK *is-* > *iss*. LMK processive *-nó-* is the source for CK present *-(nu)n-*. CK future *-keyss-* probably results from adverbative *-key* plus *iss-*.

A kind of cyclic change is observable in the development of new nominalizing forms. The LMK bound nouns *tó* and *só* disappear in EMoK, while the role of *kes* '(thing) that' expands. In modern Korean, *kes* + copula *-i* has reintroduced some of the patterns produced prior to LMK by adnominal *-(u/ol)* and *-(u/o)n* plus copula, such as the future ending *-(u)l kkey* < *(u)l kes=i-*.

Finally, the expansion of the Sino-Korean stratum of the lexicon, a process that has unfolded over two millennia, accelerated during the EMoK period. Native LMK words such as *năyh* 'river' and *mŏyh* 'mountain' have been replaced in CK by their SK counterparts *kang* (江) and *san* (山). The importation of Western scholarly, religious, and technical vocabulary took place through the medium of Sino-Korean, first in the form of loans from Chinese, later from Japanese.

2.9 Contemporary Korean

In the twenty-first century Korean has emerged as an important world language not only for Koreans worldwide but for the growing number of learners of Korean as a foreign language. Korean is a language with approximately seventy-eight million speakers, including fifty million in South Korea, twenty-three million in North Korea, and five million outside of Korea.

Despite the relatively small size of the Korean peninsula (about 85,563 square miles, approximately the size of Indiana), scholars recognize six or seven geographically based varieties, including the endangered language of Cheju. Kyŏngsang and Hamgyŏng retain the tonal distinctions recorded in LMK texts. The Hamgyŏng tonal system is quite close to LMK, while Kyŏngsang shows regular correspondences with the LMK and Hamgyŏng patterns. Dialects to the west of the Sobaek Mountains do not have word tone, but the retention of length corresponding to LMK rising tone in the Seoul dialect until recently indicates that it too once had lexical tone.

The Korean language has diverged considerably in North and South Korea since the division of the country at the end of World War II. Acceleration of linguistic divergence is due mainly to three interrelated factors: the physical isolation of North and South since 1945; polarized political, ideological, and social distinctions; and the different language policies implemented by the two governments. The most significant cause of the divergence related to policy differences is that North Korea has instituted the P'yŏngyang-based Munhwaŏ (Cultured Language) as its standard speech, as against the traditional Seoul-based P'yojunmal (Standard Language). Cultured Speech in the North and Standard Speech in the South have evolved separately, causing divergences in orthography, lexicon, phonology, grammar, and usage, with the lexicon being affected most significantly.

Furthermore, different policies in North and South Korea have been carried out in regard to the use of Chinese characters. After changing its policy several times, the South Korean government now calls for 1,800 Chinese characters to be taught in secondary schools for reading and writing. Based on its *chuch'e* 'self-reliance' ideology, which rejects foreign cultural influence, the North Korean government banned the use of Chinese characters from 1945 to 1964. Since 1964, a revised policy was adopted whereby Chinese characters are taught in schools for reading purposes only.

In the remainder of this book our focus is on the Seoul standard, but we occasionally refer to facts from other varieties. The history of the Korean language does not end with the twentieth century. As we see in the following chapters, Korean continues to be characterized by changes in progress, and the complex history of Korea suggests that this will continue to be the case in the future.

2.10   Summary

In this chapter, we introduced the historical periods of Korean and described how internal and comparative reconstruction can recover information about the Korean language before writing. We saw that while no genetic relation between Korean and any other language family has been proven, Koreanic itself constitutes a small language family. Finally, we briefly reviewed the phonological and morphosyntactic changes revealed by earlier written records.

Further Readings

Huh, Woong. 1975. *Wuli Yeys Malpon: Hyengthalon* [Middle Korean morphology]. Seoul: SaynMunhwasa.

Kang, Sinhang. 1980. *Kyeylim yusa kolye pangen yenkwu* [A study of Koryŏ dialect in the *Jīlín Lèishì*]. Seoul: Sungkyunkwan University Press.

Ko, Seongyeon. 2019. Vowel harmony. In Sungdai Cho and John Whitman (eds.), *The Handbook of Korean Linguistics*. Cambridge University Press.

Lee, Ki-moon and S. Robert Ramsey. 2011. *A History of the Korean Language*. Cambridge and New York: Cambridge University Press.

Martin, Samuel E. 1992. *A Reference Grammar of Korean*. Rutland, VT: Tuttle.

Nam, Phunghyun. 2010b. Hankwukŏ-sa e issŏ ŭi kukyŏl charyo [Kukyŏl materials in the context of the history of Korean]. *Kukyŏl yŏnku* 124: 5–36.

Nam, Pung-hyun. 1999. *Kwuke-sa lul wihan kwukyel yenkwu* [Research on Kwukyel for Korean language history]. Seoul: Tayhak-sa.

Nam, Pung-hyun. 2012. Old Korean. In Nicholas Trantner (ed.), *The Languages of Japan and Korea*, 41–72. Milton Park, UK: Routledge.

O'Grady, William, Changyong Yang, and Sejung Yang. 2019. Jejueo: Korea's other language. In Sungdai Cho and John Whitman (eds.), *The Handbook of Korean Linguistics*. Cambridge University Press.

References

Georg, Stefan, Peter A. Michalove, Alexis Manaster Ramer, and Paul J. Sidwell. 1999. Telling general linguists about Altaic. *Journal of Linguistics* 35, 65–98.

Hockett, Charles. 1958. *A Course in Modern Linguistics*. Toronto: MacMillan.

Ito, Chiyuki. 2007. *Chōsen Kanjion Kenkyū* [Research on Sino-Korean]. Tokyo: Kyūko shoin.

Janhunen, Juha and Songmoo, Kho. 1982. Is Korean related to Tungusic? *Hangŭl* 177, 179–190.

Kim, Tong-so. 1981. *Hangugŏ wa TUNGUS-ŏ ŭy ŭmun pikyo yŏnku* [A comparative study of Korean and Tungusic phonology]. Taegu: Hyosŏng yŏja taehakkyo ch'ulp'anbu.

Ko, Seongyeon, John Whitman and Andrew Joseph. 2014. Comparative consequences of the tongue root harmony analysis for proto-Tungusic, proto-Mongolic, and proto-

Korean. In Martine Robbeets and Walter Bisang (eds.), *Paradigm Change in the Transeurasian Language and Beyond*. Amsterdam: John Benjamins.

Lee, Ki-moon. 1958. A comparative study of Manchu and Korean. *Ural Altaische Jahrbücher* 30: 104–120.

Lee, Ki-moon. 1961. *Kugŏ-sa kaesŏl* [Outline of the history of the Korean language]. 2nd ed. 1972. Seoul: T'ap ch'ulp'an-sa.

Lee, Ki-moon. 1991. *Kugŏ ŏhwi-sa yŏngu* [Research on the history of the Korean lexicon]. Seoul: T'ap ch'ulp'an-sa.

Lee, Ki-moon. 1998. *Kugŏ-sa kaesŏl*. Revised ed. of Lee 1961/1972. Seoul: Taehaksa.

Nam, P'ung-hyŏn. 2009. *Kodae Hangugŏ yŏngu* [Research on ancient Korean]. Seoul: Sigan ŭi Mulle.

Nam, Phunghyun. 2010a. *Hŏnhwaga* ŭi haedok [The interpretation of the Hŏnhwaga]. *Kukyŏl yŏnku* 124: 5–36.

Ramsey, Samuel Robert. 1978. *Accent and Morphology in Korean Dialects: A Descriptive and Historical Study*. Seoul: Tower Press.

Toh, Soo-hee. 2008. *Samhan ŭy yŏnku* [Research on the Samhan language]. Seoul: Che-i-aen-ssi.

Vovin, Alexander. 2013. Why Korean is demonstrably not related to Tungusic. Proceedings of the conference Comparison of Korean with Other Altaic Languages: Methodologies and Case Studies, November 15, 2013, Gachon University, Seongnam, Republic of Korea.

Whitman, John. 2015. Old Korean. In Lucien Brown and Jae Hoon Yeon (eds.), *The Handbook of Korean Linguistics*, 422–438. London: Wiley-Blackwell.

3   Writing System

3.1   Introduction

Hangul 한글, the name by which the Korean script is known in the Republic of Korea and internationally, is a relatively recent term. It appears to have been coined by the pioneering Korean linguist Chu Sigyŏng (주시경 周時經, 1876–1914) at the beginning of the twentieth century. Prior to that time, the script was known as *ŏnmun* 언문 (諺文 'vernacular writing'). *Han* in Hangul can be interpreted in two ways. In the late Chosŏn dynasty the Chinese character *Han* 韓, which was used in the pre-Three Kingdoms period to refer to the Three Han (Samhan 三韓) polities in Southern Korea, was put into use again as Chosŏn came to refer to herself as the Korean Empire *Tae Han Cheguk* 대한제국 (declared in 1897 by King and subsequently Emperor Kojong [1852–1919, who reigned 1863–1897 as King, 1897–1907 as Emperor]). By the beginning of the twentieth century, the Chinese character *Han* 韓 had come to designate Korea in Sino-Korean compounds, for example *Han-Mi* 'Korean-American', *hanbok* 'Korean clothing'. At the same time, *Han* 'Korean' is homophonous with *ha-n*, the adnominal form of the adjective *ha-* 'great, multitudinous'. It was therefore natural for Chu to compound *han* 'Korean/great' with *kŭl* 'writing' to replace the somewhat pejorative term *ŏnmun* 'vernacular writing' that had been in use since the fifteenth century. But because the same *Han* 韓 is also used in the name of the Republic of Korea, *Tae Han Minguk*, the term Hangul cannot be used in the Democratic People's Republic of Korea. Instead the Korean writing system is called *Chosŏn'gŭl* in the DPRK. For many speakers of Korean outside the DPRK, Hangul denotes not just the Korean writing system, but the Korean language itself.

In this chapter we introduce the basic properties of Hangul. We describe the structure of the system and why it has attracted the admiration of specialists on writing systems the world over. We recount the remarkable history of the invention of Hangul. Then we take a step back and examine the history of writing in Korea prior to that invention. Contrary to standard accounts, we emphasize the continuity between Hangul and earlier forms of writing. Finally, we examine the use of Hangul today.

3.2   The Structure of the System

A ready way to understand Hangul is to consider the Hangul representation for each of the basic speech sounds, or phonemes, of Korean that we discuss in Chapter 4. The phonemes are given in Yale Romanization in Tables 3.1 and 3.2 with their Hangul counterparts.

Table 3.1 and Figure 3.1 immediately reveal a number of design features of the Hangul system. First, the shape of the graphs is iconically linked to place of articulation, the place in the vocal tract, from the larynx to the lips, where the articulators (larynx, tongue, velum, lips, etc.) come together to make the distinctive articulation of a sound. The labial stops, oral and nasal, formed with the lips, all involve an enclosure such as ㅁ <m> or ㅂ <p>. The alveolar stops, formed by touching the alveolar ridge just behind the upper teeth with the tip of the tongue, all involve a horizontal line joined on the left by a vertical or diagonal, such as ㄴ <n> and ㄷ <t>. The velar stops, formed by raising the body of the tongue to the velum at the back of the mouth, all include a horizontal line joined on the right by a vertical line, such as ㄱ <k>. These result from deliberate design decisions made by the inventor(s) of the system to represent the configuration of labials, alveolars, and velars in the vocal tract. Manner of articulation is also iconically represented: for example, the aspirates all involve an increase in graphic complexity, capturing the intuition that aspirates are stronger than plain stops and affricates through the metaphor "quantity = strength."

This representation of place of articulation and manner of articulation in the shape of its graphs has led linguists such as Sampson (1990) to describe Hangul

Table 3.1 *Consonants of Korean and their Hangul representations*

	Labial	Alveolar	Alveopalatal	Palatal	Velar	Glottal
Nasal stops	m ㅁ	n ㄴ			ŋ ㅇ	
Lax stops/ Affricates	p ㅂ	t ㄷ	c ㅈ		k ㄱ	
Tense	pp ㅃ	tt ㄸ	cc ㅉ		kk ㄲ	
Aspirates	ph ㅍ	th ㅌ	ch ㅊ		kh ㅋ	
Lax fricative		s ㅅ				h ㅎ
Tense fricative		ss ㅆ				
Liquid		l ㄹ				
Approximants	w ㅜ/ㅗ			y		

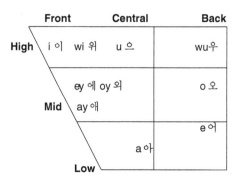

Figure 3.1 Vowels of Korean and their Hangul representations

as a **featural** writing system. The idea is that phonological features such as [labial] and [aspirated] are represented by specific components of the graphs. Featural iconicity is also present in the design of the vowel graphs (Kim-Renaud 1997b). For example, in the original *Hunmin chŏng'ŭm* 'Correct Sounds for the Instruction of the People' the contrast between [+Retracted Tongue Root] /o/ [ʌ] in Middle Korean and [−Retracted Tongue Root] /u/ [ɨ] was represented by a dot <•> for the former and a horizontal line <—> for the latter. The explanatory text in the 1446 *Hunmin chŏng'ŭm haerye* (훈민정음해례 訓民正音解例 'Explanations and Examples of the Correct Sounds for the Instruction of the People') gives what appears to be a metaphysical explanation: the dot is associated with Heaven, and the horizontal line with Earth. But as Kim-Renaud makes clear, this is part of an iconic representation of the MK tongue-root harmony system. The other [+RTR] vowels /a/ ㅏ and /wo/ ㅗ are grouped with /o/ [ʌ] by placing a dot (in modern Hangul fonts represented as a short line) on the right or above the central axis of the graph: "positive" placements that correlate with the traditional classification of [+RTR] vowels as *yang* 양 陽 or "light." The [−RTR] vowels /e/ ㅓ and /wu/ ㅜ are represented by placing the dot to the left or below: "negative" placements that correlate with classification of the [−RTR] vowels as *in* 인 陰 or "dark." The neutral vowel /i/ is represented by no dot, only a vertical line.

How the consonant graphs are used embodies another revolutionary aspect of the Hangul system. A sophisticated understanding of traditional Chinese phonological theory played a major part in the design of the system. But the basic elements of traditional Chinese phonology were limited to onset (the initial consonant of the syllable) and rime (the vowel, its tone, and coda or final consonants). The fact that onset and coda consonants can involve the same sound segments was not part of the traditional understanding. But the system promulgated in the *Hunmin chŏng'ŭm* is based on the insight that onset and

Table 3.2 *Representation of [+RTR] "light"
and [−RTR] "dark" vowels in Hangul*

Neutral	[+RTR] "light" *yang* 양	[-RTR] "dark" *in* 인
ㅣ	• /o/ [ʌ]	― /u/ [ɨ]
	ㅗ /wo/ [o]	ㅜ /wu/ [u]
	ㅏ /a/ [a]	ㅓ /e/ [ə]

coda consonants are the same segments. As stated concisely in the *Hunmin chŏng'ŭm haerye*, "the coda consonant sounds reuse the initial sounds":

(1)   終   声   復   用   初   声
       final sound again use initial sound

This is the aspect in which Hangul is an **alphabetic** system. The same consonant (and vowel) graphs are used regardless of where they occur in the syllable.

Finally, the basic unit of Hangul writing in most of the applications to which it has been put is the syllable. Although the graphs of the system are alphabetic, from its invention in the fifteenth century through the present, Hangul have almost always been written by combining the graphs into syllabic blocks of shape (C) V(C). Thus the word *hankul* is composed of six graphs, which, arranged horizontally in the manner of Roman or Greek writing, would have the form in (2a). But conventional Hangul writing arranges them into two syllabic units, with the onset graph written to the left of vowels with a vertical graph and above vowels with a horizontal graph (2b). The vowel – the nucleus – is written in the middle, and the coda consonant, if any, is written underneath. This is shown in (2c). The hangul graphs corresponding to 한 *han* are composed as the first syllable on the left, and the graphs corresponding to the second syllable, 글 *gul*, are composed on the right, spelling the word 한글 *hangul* (YR *hankul*).

(2)   a. ㅎ ㅏ ㄴ ㄱ ㅡ ㄹ
          h a n k u l
       b. 한 + 글
          h a + k u
          n   l
       c. ㅎ₁ ㅏ₂ ㄱ₁ ㅡ₂
             ㄴ₃   ㄹ₃
          h₁ a₂ k₁ u₂
          n₃   l₃

This order of arrangement of onset, nucleus, and coda graphs is also an iconic representation of the temporal sequence in which the corresponding phoneme is pronounced, based on the principles of Chinese calligraphy (see Lee 1997 for the role of calligraphy in the creation of the Hangul graphs). These principles dictate that the brush moves from left to right, up to down, so that first strokes are on the left, the next, moving to the right, on the top, and finally down. Because Hangul were designed to be written in syllabic blocks like this, Hangul can also be said to function as a **syllabic** system.

It is often said, and surely the case, that a major motivation for the syllabic arrangement of Hangul is the fact that throughout most of the history of Hangul writing, it has been used in combination with Chinese characters, which also represent syllables. It has also been argued that syllabic arrangement facilitates reading, since the basic graphs are simple, symmetrical, and few, and reuse the same basic components. But beyond that, the basic sequence left – top – bottom is simply the way that writing was done in the Sinographic world at the time Hangul were invented. As we see in Section 3.3, the inventor of Hangul was deeply knowledgeable about Chinese writing and phonology. He was well aware of the component parts of Chinese characters and their order of arrangement. One facet of his genius was to substitute for those component parts units of sound – that is, phonemes, represented by Hangul graphs arranged by order of pronunciation.

From the late nineteenth through the late twentieth century, when typewriter and moveable metal type were the basic technologies for reproducing written language, the syllabic arrangement of Hangul was occasionally characterized as a shortcoming, and experiments were made in writing Hangul in purely linear fashion, as in (2a). But Hangul were invented at a time when handcarved wood block printing was the dominant technology and labor for typeface carving was cheap. At the end of the twentieth century, the issue of coding the syllabic representation of Hangul writing came full circle. Two approaches emerged for graphic encoding of Hangul into syllables: the 3-set keyboard devised by Kong Pyeong U in 1949, and the 2-set keyboard which has become dominant since the 1990s. The 3-set keyboard puts the burden on the user, requiring her to select between syllable-initial consonants, vowels, and final consonants. In effect this arrangement fails to capture the original **alphabetic** genius of the system: the insight that initial and final consonants are the same basic sounds. The 2-set keyboard distinguishes only consonants and vowels, like the original *Hunmin chŏng'ŭm*. The burden of deciding whether to place a consonant in coda or onset position is put on the word-processing application, which figures out by context which position a consonant graph occupies. But with improved efficiency and lowered cost of word-processing software, this has once again become a nonissue, just as it was in the fifteenth century. Most younger users of Hangul keyboards have likely never seen a 3-set keyboard.

In its combination of featural, alphabetic, and syllabic properties, the Korean alphabet is unique. Most who have learned to use it feel a certain reluctance toward using Roman letters to write Korean. Hangul, once mastered (and mastery comes very quickly), are easier to use to write Korean than several of the most prominent romanization systems, for reasons discussed in Section 3.7. Hangul combine flexibility, elegance, and easiness to learn with the sophistication of design that we have outlined in this section. In the Section 3.3 we will see how it came to be that Hangul are considered one of the most important cultural monuments in the history of Korea.

3.3   The Invention of the System

The new writing system is first mentioned in the official history of the reign of King Sejong (1397–1450, ruled 1418–1450), the *Sejong sillok*, in the twelfth month of the twenty-fifth lunar year of his rule. When converted to the Gregorian calendar, most of the twenty-fifth year falls into 1443, but most of the twelfth month falls into January 1444. Thus one sees both 1443 and 1444 as the date for invention of the alphabet, but as the actual invention surely preceded the record, we will use the more commonly given date, 1443. The official promulgation of the new system took place in 1446 with the publication of the *Hunmin chŏng'ŭm yeŭibon* (훈민정음예의본, 訓民正音例義本) "The Correct Sounds for the Instruction of the People." This text is written in seven brief pages of classical Chinese and begins with the following famous passage.

國之語. 音異乎中國與文字
不相流通. 故愚民 有所欲言
而終不得伸其情者. 多矣. 予
爲此憫然. 新制二十八字. 欲
使人人易習. 便於日用矣

The sounds of the nation's language are different from those of China, and are not mutually compatible with their characters. Thus it is often the case that unschooled commoners have something to say but are unable to express their feelings. Grieved by this, I have newly created twenty-eight characters. I wish to have everyone learn them easily, and use them at their convenience in everyday life.

A Korean translation, the *Hunmin chŏng'ŭm ŏnhae* (훈민정음언해 訓民訓 音諺解) appeared in 1451. The *Hunmin chŏng'ŭm* was published in 1446 together with a longer text, the *Hunmin chŏng'ŭm haerye* (훈민정음해례, 訓 民正音解例) "Explanations and Examples of the Correct Sounds for the Instruction of the People," also in classical Chinese, compiled by a commission of scholars from the Chiphyŏnjŏn, the "Academy of Worthies," assembled by Sejong to advise him, and often implicated both in the creation of the system and subsequent elite opposition to it. The *Hunmin chŏng'ŭm haerye* gives examples of how the newly created twenty-eight letters are to be used, and also explains the linguistic thinking that went into their creation. The postface, written by Chŏng Inji, gives the first ten days of the ninth month of 1446 as the date of promulgation. This converts to October 9 in the Gregorian calendar, which is celebrated as a national holiday, Hangul Day (Hangŭl Nal 한글 날) in the Republic of Korea. The DPRK celebrates Chosŏn'gŭl Day on January 15, commemorating the date that Hangul are first mentioned in the *Sejong sillok*.

The *Sejong sillok* states in literary Chinese: "In this month, His Highness personally created (*ch'inje* 친제 親製) the twenty-eight letters of the vernacular script (*ŏnmun* 언문 諺文)." Most subsequent commentators have assumed that the phrase "personally created" was a form of royal flattery, and that the system was created, albeit under Sejong's direction, as a team effort, involving scholar-officials close to the king. However Ki-Moon Lee (1997) argues forcefully that, in large part, the invention of the writing system was the personal invention of King Sejong, exactly as the *Sejong sillok* states. Lee points out that the expression *ch'inje* is not used in the *Sejong sillok* to describe any of Sejong's many other inventions, and that the language used by Ch'oe Malli, the vice-director of the Chiphyŏnjŏn, uses deferential language that implies creation by the king, in his famous memorial attacking the new writing system. It is well known that Sejong was deeply interested and profoundly read in the contemporary scholarship on Chinese writing and the phonological principles behind it. But the majority of scholars have found it impossible to believe that an active and effective king could find the time to invent a writing system of the brilliance that we described in Section 3.2.

Lee's most compelling argument is a linguistic one. In most of the texts printed in the fifteenth century, the writing system introduced in the *Hunmin chŏng'ŭm*, the document that promulgated it, is a **phonemic** system. The *Hunmin chŏng'ŭm* system provides a separate graph for every phoneme of the language, and it combines them in syllabic units, as we have seen. But it does not represent the morphological structure of the language. This is in contrast to modern Hangul writing. For example, the end of the second sentence in the Korean text of the *Hunmin chŏng'ŭm* contains the expression *nom=i ha-n i-la* 'people are many (who cannot enounce their thoughts)'. In modern Korean orthography, this would be written as in (3a), with *nom* 놈 'guy, person' a single morpheme, written as a single syllabic unit. But the *Hunmin chŏng'ŭm* orthography ignored morphology. Instead, it followed what Ledyard (1966/1998) calls "the principle of consonantal acrography": consonants that function as syllable onsets are written at the beginning of the syllable, even if the result breaks up a morpheme, as in (3b).

(3)   a. 놈이 하니라
        nom=i   ha-n i-la
        person=NOM   many-ADN be-DEC
        'persons are many'

b. 노 미 하 니 라
no.mi ha.ni.la

In contrast, modern Hangul orthography is **morphophonemic**: morphemes are written as a unit. In the pronunciation of (3), the coda consonant /m/ ㅁ of *nom* 'person' is pronounced as the onset of the next syllable, but modern Hangul spelling groups it with the other phonemes of the noun *nom* 놈. However 'standard' orthography at the time of the *Hunmin chŏng'ŭm* in the fifteenth century ignored morpheme boundaries and represented only purely phonological information.

Lee points out that there is a trace of morphophonemic writing in some fifteenth-century Hangul texts. Allophonic rules of Middle Korean merged the affricates /c/ ㅈ and /ch/ ㅊ with /s/ ㅅ in coda position (in contrast with Modern Korean, which merges the affricates, and /s/, with /t/). As in Modern Korean, aspirates merge with the corresponding plain stops in coda position. The *Hunmin chŏng'ŭm haerye* specifies that the outputs (what we would call today the surface forms) of these allophonic rules are what should be reflected in spelling. Thus a word like *kwoc* 곶 'flower' was to be spelled <kwos> 곳 in phrase-final position, where /c/ ㅈ is in the coda and merged with /s/. But there are two salient fifteenth-century texts where words of this sort are spelled morphophonemically rather than phonemically: that is, the "underlying" or basic form of the morpheme *kwoc* 'flower' is written <kwoc> 곶 even when /c/ is in coda position, regardless of how it was pronounced.

The first of these texts is the *Yongbi ŏch'ŏn ka* (飛御天歌 용비어천가 'Songs of the Dragons Flying to Heaven', 1445). This is the canonical poetic epic, in Korean and Chinese, commissioned by King Sejong to celebrate the establishment of the Chosŏn dynasty and praise his ancestors and forebears "the dragons," the founders of the dynasty. The *Yongbi ŏch'ŏn ka* was published two years after the announced invention of the new writing system, but before it was officially promulgated in the *Hunmin chŏng'ŭm*, perhaps as a demonstration of what Hangul could do. As Lee points out, we know that King Sejong was intimately involved in the composition of this work. The third line of the *Yongbi ŏch'ŏn ka* reads <kwoc tyo-khwo> 곶 됴코 'the flowers were good and', with the coda consonant of *kwoc* 'flower' written morphophonemically: this final consonant is written <c> ㅈ instead of phonemically with <s> ㅅ. The second text with this kind of morphophonemic writing is the *Wŏrin ch'ŏn'gang chi kok* 'Songs of the Moon's Imprint on a Thousand Rivers', a poetic text composed by Sejong himself. Lee argues that this partially morphophonemic writing must have been Sejong's own choice, and that it is hard to imagine that the king controlled this level of detail without having played a direct role in devising the script. It might further be pointed out that morphophonemic writing comes naturally to those who have experience actually using a script, whereas phonemic writing is more characteristic of those who are mechanically following the spelling rules. Lee's argument not only shows that King Sejong was centrally involved in inventing Hangul writing, but that he anticipated the morphophonemic adaptation chosen by modern Koreans centuries later.

The *Hunmin chŏng'ŭm* system has twenty-eight graphs, seventeen graphs for initials and eleven graphs for medials. The system is laid out in the *Hunmin chŏng'ŭm haerye*, which gives a phonetic explanation in Chinese of the sounds corresponding to each Hangul graph.

The seventeen initials are given in Table 3.3. The consonant values are shown in Yale Romanization. /q/ [ʔ] is a glottal stop.

Vertically, the sounds corresponding to the Hangul graphs are classified by place of articulation. The five classes of sounds use categories from traditional Chinese phonology. These correspond quite well to places of articulation in modern phonology. Velar consonants are termed *aŭm* 아음, literally 'molar sounds', referring to a position in the back of the mouth. This category correctly groups together the velar stops ㄱ k, ㅋ kh, and ㆁ ŋ. Alveolar sounds are termed *sŏlŭm* 설음 'tongue sounds', and group ㄷ t, ㅌ th, and ㄴ n. In traditional Chinese phonology, alveolar and palatal sounds were grouped together in two subcategories of *sŏlŭm* 설음 'tongue sounds', but in the *Hunmin chŏng'ŭm* ㅈ c and ㅊ ch were grouped together with ㅅ s as *ch'iŭm* 치음 'dental sounds'. This is because /s/ was classified as dental in both Chinese phonology and the Indian tradition it drew from, and in Middle Korean ㅈ c and ㅊ ch were not alveopalatal affricates but alveolar fricative affricates [ts] and [tsʰ], as they are in many northern varieties to this day. Labial *sunŭm* 순음 are straightforward: ㅂ p, ㅍ ph, and ㅁ m, but the laryngeal *huŭm* 후음 'throat sounds' contain two graphs no longer used in modern Hangul: ㆆ, representing the glottal stop [ʔ], and ㅇ, used at the beginning of words that nowadays we would recognize as beginning with a vowel. Some scholars believe that this is what it represented in the fifteenth century as well, but Ki-moon Lee has argued that it represented the voiced laryngeal fricative [ɦ].

Table 3.3 *The 17* Hunmin chŏng'ŭm *initials* 초성 *(初声)*

5 Classes of Sounds	Letter Shape	전청 [Plain]	차청 [Aspirated]	불청불탁 [-Plain,-Aspirated]
Velar 아음 牙音	Tongue root closing throat	ㄱ k	ㅋ kh	ㆁ ŋ
Alveolar 설음 舌音	Tongue touching upper jaw	ㄷ t	ㅌ th	ㄴ n, ㄹ l
Labial 순음 唇音	Shape of lips	ㅂ p	ㅍ ph	ㅁ m
Dental 치음 歯音	Shape of teeth	ㅈ c, ㅅ s	ㅊ ch	ㅿ z
Laryngeal 후음 喉音	Shape of throat	ㆆ q [ʔ]	ㅎ h	ㅇ ɦ

The *Hunmin chŏng'ŭm* system distinguished ㅇ and ㆁ /ŋ/, but as /ŋ/ does not occur in onset position in native Korean words, and ㆁ was not written in final (coda) position, over time the slight graphic distinction between them came to be ignored, and ㅇ came to have two functions: representing a vowel-initial syllable in initial position, and /ŋ/ in coda position.

In addition to the seventeen initials in Table 3.3, the *Hunmin chŏng'ŭm haerye* adds *kabyŏun piŭp* 가벼운비읍 'light p' ㅸ, representing a voiced bilabial fricative /β/. This seems to have been omitted from the original inventory of initials because it was viewed as a combination of basic initial graphs, ㅂ <p> plus ㅇ, where the latter represents a "light" sound; in traditional Chinese phonology "light labials" are labial continuant initials, labiodental /f/ and the labial glide /w/. Only ㅸ was used to write native Korean words, such as the example in the *Hunmin chŏng'ŭm haerye*, *saWi* 사ᄫᅵ 'shrimp', modern Seoul Korean *saywu* 새우. This example gives us a sense of the fate of the Middle Korean voiced spirants /z/, represented by ㅿ <z>, known as *panch'iŭm* 반치음 'half dental sound', and ㅸ <β >, Yale Romanization /W/ . Neither of these graphs are used in modern Korean, as the phonemes /W/ [β] and /z/ have disappeared. In *saywu* 'shrimp', /W/ [β] was deleted, but not before labializing the following vowel. We can tell that the sequence of events was: (i) umlaut of the first syllable vowel to /ay/ 애, triggered by the final vowel /i/; (ii) labialization of final /i/ to /wu/ [u], triggered by labial /W/ [β]; (iii) deletion of /W/ [β]. The *Hunmin chŏng'ŭm haerye* example for ㅿ <z> is *azo* 아ᅀᆞ 'younger brother', modern Seoul *awu* 아우. Once again, the MK voiced spirant has been lost, but the labialization of the final vowel results from epenthetic /w/ inserted to break up the vowel-vowel sequence.

Horizontally, in Table 3.3 the graphs are classified by manner of articulation using the terms *chŏnch'ŏng* 전청 'completely clear', *ch'ajŏng* 차정 'secondary clear', and *pulch'ŏng pult'ak* 불청불탁 'neither clear nor muddy', which come from traditional Chinese phonology. 전청 'completely clear' corresponds to plain obstruents (*yesa sori* 예사소리 in modern Korean), 차정 'secondary clear' to aspirated stops and affricates (*kŏsen sori* 거센소리), and *pulch'ŏng pult'ak* 'not clear not muddy' to sounds that were neither plain nor aspirated. For the most part, the latter are sonorants (*ullim sori* 울림소리), but the voiced spirant ㅿ <z> is also included here. Setting up a [-plain, -aspirated] category was perceptive on the part of Sejong and his collaborators. The traditional Chinese category of voiced or "muddy" initials (*chŏnt'ak* 전탁) was reserved for spelling the sounds of (Middle) Chinese, where voicing was contrastive.

The *Hunmin chŏng'ŭm haerye* also explains that the five 전청 'completely clear' (plain) initials <k> ㄱ, <t> ㄷ, <p> ㅂ, <c> ㅈ, <s> ㅅ plus the 'secondary clear' initial ㅎ can be doubled to write ㄲ, ㄸ, ㅃ, ㅉ, ㅆ, ㆅ (doubled ㅇㅇ < ㆀ> was also used in a small number of derived verb stems).

These digraphs are called *pyŏng sŏ* 병서 竝書 'doubled writing'. It explains that the *pyŏng sŏ* are *chŏn t'ak* 전탁 (全濁) 'completely muddy', the traditional Chinese designation for voiced consonants. In the *Hunmin chŏng'ŭm haerye* they are not used to write native Korean words, but only Chinese characters whose initials were originally voiced. However the use of doubled graphs to write the reinforced consonants of modern Korean is already prefigured in fifteenth-century Hangul writing. As Lee and Ramsey (2011) point out, there is an alternation between two ways of writing a consonant preceded by the future adnominal suffix *-lq* [lʔ]. One spelling represents this sequence as <lʔ+C>, e.g. *h-o-lq kes* 'thing to be done'. The other spelling omits the glottal stop <ʔ> ㆆ and doubles the following consonant, e.g. *swum-wul kkwumk-i* 수물꿈기 'hole to hide in' (examples from Lee and Ramsey 2011: 118). This can be understood as another example of morphophonemic versus phonemic spelling. The morphophonemic spelling includes the glottal stop as part of the adnominal suffix, but the actual pronunciation assimilated the glottal stop to the following consonant, producing a geminate or doubled consonant. Reinforcement of the following consonant after the future adnominal suffix continues in Korean to this day.

Aside from restricted contexts like these, the LMK ancestors of reinforced obstruents in modern Korean were written as consonant clusters. Writing two different consonants together is referred to in the *Hunmin chŏng'ŭm haerye* as *hapyong pyŏngsŏ* 합용병서 合用並書 'combined use doubled writing'. The *Hunmin chŏng'ŭm haerye* gives examples such as *stah* 'earth, ground', modern *ttang* 땅; and *pcak* 'pair', modern *ccak* 짝. There are nine well-attested onset clusters in fifteenth-century writing: <pt>, <pth>, <ps>, <pc>, <sp>, <st>, <sk>, <pst>, <psk>; a tenth, <sn> occurs as the clear result of syncope (vowel loss): *snahoy* < *sonahoy-i* 'man-GEN'. Some scholars such as Ki-moon Lee hold that at least some of the sC clusters already represented a reinforced consonant or geminate, not a heterorganic cluster, so that <sp> was meant to spell /pp/, <st> /tt/, and <sk> /kk/. This would leave <pC(C)> as the only true clusters in LMK, which raises the question of what happened to the other clusters that we might expect to arise from vowel syncope. One answer to this question might be that original *tC clusters fell together with *sC clusters, and were spelled the same way, while original *kC clusters merged with *hC, both prior to the invention of Hangul.

The *Hunmin chŏng'ŭm* system distinguishes eleven medial sounds, as shown in Table 3.4.

Of these eleven medials, seven are simple vowels, while <yo> ㅛ, <ya> ㅑ, <yu> ㅠ, and <ye> ㅕ are combinations with the glide /y/ [j], written by adding an additional stroke to the simple vowel. In LMK, the precursors of the modern vowels /ey/ 에 and /ay/ 애 were diphthongs made up of the vowels /e/ 어 and /a/ 아

Table 3.4 *The 11* Hunmin chŏng'ŭm *medials* chung song 중성 *(*中声*)*

Ŭm or Yang	Shape	Basic	+1 Stroke	+2 Strokes
양성 陽性	天 heaven	·	ㅗ, ㅏ	ㅛ, ㅑ
음성 陰性	地 earth	ㅡ	ㅜ, ㅓ	ㅠ, ㅕ
중섬 中性 (neutral)	人 person	ㅣ		

plus a palatal glide. They are written in exactly this way, adding ㅣ to the right of the nuclear vowel.

As we have seen, the *Hunmin chŏng'ŭm haerye* states that no special graphs are made to represent finals; instead the initials are reused for this purpose: the brilliant insight that makes the system phonemic.

We have seen already some of the *Hunmin chŏng'ŭm haerye* provisions for graphic combinations in writing. The examples in (4)–(6) below lay them out explicitly:

(4) *Yŏn sŏ* 연서 'linked writing' (連書): ㅂ+ㅇ > ㅸ /β/

(5) *Pyŏng sŏ* 병서 'doubled writing' (竝書): 각자병서

합용병서 ㅅtype – ㅺ, ㅼ, ㅽ, (ㅻ)
ㅂ type – ㅲ, ㅄ, ㅳ, ㅶ, ㅷ
ㅄtype – ㅴ, ㅵ

(6) *Kajŏm* 가점 'adding dots' (加点) is the system of *pangjŏm* 방점 'side dots' (傍点) used to mark the tone of each syllable, for the language of fifteenth-century Hansŏng, the name of the capital Seoul in that period, was a word-tone or pitch-accent language, like modern Kyŏngsang or Hamgyŏng, as we saw in Chapter 2.

3.4 Korean Writing before Hangul

As we saw in Chapter 2, pre-Hangul devices for writing Korean were based on Chinese characters, specifically *ch'aja* 'loan characters' used to write Korean. Forms of writing based on *ch'aja* are traditionally divided into three types: *hyangch'al, idu*, and *t'o/kugyŏl*.

Hyangch'al 향찰 鄕札 'local letters', is a term dating from 967 (Ledyard 1966/1998: 44). This term designates the system used to write the twenty-five surviving *hyangga* 'native songs', written between 600 and 967 and broadly comparable to the orthography in the *Man'yôshû*, the oldest surviving Japanese poetic anthology, which dates from approximately the same period (around the seventh or eighth century). Much discussion has centered on the issue of whether there is an historical relation between the two genres. Many more examples are attested in the Japanese source, which includes over 4,500 songs, but this is an accident of history. Large poetic anthologies existed in Korea as well, such as the *Samdaemok* 삼대목 (三代目 'Collection of the Three Eras'), compiled in 888, but it was lost in the thirteenth-century Mongol invasion.

In comparing the two systems, it should be kept in mind that Korean precursors for Japanese writing of this kind are more likely to have come from Paekche. One of the *hyangga*, the *Song of Sŏdong* (*Sŏdong yo*), composed around 600 CE, is credited to King Mu of Paekche, but there is no evidence that this song preserved original Paekche orthography. Specific similarities between the Korean and Japanese systems include the fact that both used a combination of Chinese characters as phonograms, representing sounds of the vernacular language (Korean or Japanese), and logograms, which represent vernacular words based on the meaning of the character. For example, in the *hyangga Hŏnhwaga* cited in Chapter 2, whose first two lines are repeated below, the verb stem *cap-* 잡- 'grab, hold, seize' in line two is represented by the Chinese character with that meaning, 執, modern Mandarin *zhí*, Sino-Korean *cip* 집, used as a logogram to represent the native Korean verb.

(7) 紫布   岩乎   过希
     Tolpwo(y) *pahwo(y)* *kos-oy*
     azalea   crag   side-LOC
     執音   乎   手   母牛   放教遺
     Cap-om   *h-wo(-n)*   *swon* *amsywo* *noh-i-si-kwo*
     hold-NOM   do-MOD-ADN   hand   cow   put-CAUS-HON-GER

As we saw in Chapter 2, the next character, 音, is used as a phonogram, unrelated to its meaning 'sound', to spell the syllable *-om*, the pronunciation of the nominalizing suffix *-o/um*. The pronunciation of the phonogram is very close to this character's modern Sino-Korean reading, *-um*, but in fact we do not know for sure how it was read in the eighth century. If readers followed the rules of RTR vowel harmony, as in fifteenth-century Late Middle Korean, the word was read *cap-om*.

The Japanese *Man'yôshû* also used a combination of logographs and phonographs, but differences between the two languages were reflected in the choice of phonograms. For instance, since Japanese lacked closed (CVC) syllables, phonographs such as 音 <o/um> were not used. However the two systems were similar in that the inventory of phonographs was quite economical. In general a single sound was represented by a single phonogram, although the size and heterogeneity of the surviving Japanese corpus creates the impression of more variation.

Furthermore, many of the phonographs overlapped. It should be kept in mind here that one reason for this is that many shared a common source: Chinese characters used in China to transcribe the sounds of foreign languages, especially in Buddhist translations of Sanskrit.

Idu 이두 吏讀 'clerk reading', a term commonly used for all of the systems of writing Korean using Chinese characters, in its narrow sense refers to a style of writing that uses Korean syntax (particularly word order) and writes content words with standard Chinese characters, but uses phonograms to write Korean functional morphemes. In both *hyangch'al* and *idu* there are two types of phonograms. The first type uses the Sino-Korean pronunciation of the character to represent a native Korean sound. These are referred to as *kaja* 가자 (假字) 'temporary characters'. The second type, known as *hunja* 훈자 (訓字) 'meaning characters', uses the vernacular reading of the character in Korean, based on its meaning, to represent a native Korean sound. All of the examples in Table 3.5 are of the first type. But some very common *ch'aja* are of the second type. For example, the character 等 (Sino-Korean *tung* 등, Middle Chinese *təŋ^X*) is used as a phonogram for the syllable *tol*, based on its vernacular reading as the plural marker, MK =*tol*, Modern Korean =*tul* 들.

In contrast to the small *hyangga* corpus, *idu* (which is sometimes taken to include *hyangga* as a subtype) was used continuously through the Chosŏn dynasty; in some cases entire Chinese texts were translated into *idu*. We saw an example of fifth-century Koguryŏ period *idu* in (2) of Chapter 2.

T'o/kugyŏl 토/구결 吐/口訣 'oral embellishment' (Lee and Ramsey 2011: 51), is a primary source for Early Middle Korean morphosyntax, in addition to *idu* materials. *Kugyŏl* is a system for glossing Chinese texts to be read in

Table 3.5 *Common* Hyangch'al/Idu *phonograms and their Chinese and Japanese usages*

Phonograph	Korean	Japanese	Middle Chinese	Example used to spell Sanskrit word
阿	a	a	a	阿羅漢 *āluóhàn*, spells /a/ in Sanskrit *arhat*.
伊	i	i	iᵢ	伊師迦 *yīshījiā*, *spells /i/ in Sanskrit iṣīkā 'arrow'*.
烏	u	u	uo	烏仗那 *wūzhàngnà*, spells /u/ in Sanskrit *Udyāna*.
加	ka	ka	kʸa	加蘭頻伽 *jiālánbīnqié*, spells /ka/ in Sanskrit *kalaviṇka*, a mythical bird.
豆	tu	du, tu	dəu^H	婆藪槃豆 *pósŏupándòu*, spells /dhu/ in Sanskrit *Vasubandhu*.
羅	la [l/ra]	ra	lɑ	鳩摩羅什 *jiūmóluóshí*, spells /ra/ in Sanskrit *Kumārajīva*.
尼	ni	ni	ŋʲiᵢ	釋迦牟尼 *shìjiāmóuní*, spells /ni/ in Sanskrit *Sakyamuni*.

Korean. The practice dates back to the Silla period, and EMK *kugyŏl* texts retain many OK features. A text fully glossed in *kugyŏl* is a Korean text, to be read in Korean. Although the quantity of *kugyŏl* glossed texts is not large, they are our richest pre-Hangul source for the syntax and morphology of earlier Korean. We saw an example of *kugyŏl* in (8) of Chapter 2, repeated here as (8).

(8)   他方ヒ   量ハ ヲ 可ヒ 爲隱   不ヲ   リ ヒ ヒ   衆   有ヒ ナ ふ
       THAPANG-S   RYANGh-wo-m cisho-n   anti   i-no-s   CYUNG   is-kyə-myə
       opposite-GEN measure do-MOD-NOM act do-ADN not be-PRES-GEN masses be-PERF
       -CON
       'and there were the masses on the other side whose numbers were not to be
       counted'

This example illustrates the use of *kugyŏl* characters or *chat'o* 자토 'character glosses'. *Kugyŏl* glosses are of two types. *Chat'o* involve the same phonographs used in *idu*, but abbreviated by using just two or three of its strokes. For instance, the character 尼 in Table 3.5, used to write the syllable /ni/ in *hyangga* and *idu*, is abbreviated to its two lower right-hand strokes (see [10] in Figure 3.2). Like the *idu* phonograms they are derived from, some *chat'o* are *kaja*, used to represent their Sino-Korean reading, while others are *hunja*, used to represent the sound of their vernacular (Korean) reading. The *kugyŏl* character derived from 尼 in (10) of Figure 3.2 is an example of the former, based on the Sino-Korean pronunciation / ni/. The *kugyŏl* character derived from 飛 in example (8) of Chapter 2 is a *hunja*. It is based on the vernacular Korean reading of the character 飛 'fly' as MK *nol-* (Modern Korean *nal-* 날-). In example (8), this *kugyŏl* character is used to spell *-no-*, the processive suffix. In this context the processive suffix has nothing to do with the verb 'fly'; the character read as *no-* 'fly' is being used purely for its sound. Figure 3.2 provides a partial inventory of *kugyŏl* graphs.

Many scholars have noted the similarity in form and function between *kugyŏl* characters and Japanese *katakana*. Their origin and function are the same: both were formed by abbreviating Chinese characters by reducing them to a few strokes, and both were used to gloss Chinese texts to be read in the vernacular. The similarities have led some scholars to suggest that the Japanese *katakana* syllabary is based on the *kugyŏl* syllabary. This is not implausible, since *katakana* developed in Japan in the late eighth and early ninth century for the purpose of glossing texts associated with the Huayan (Avatamsaka, Korean Hwaŏm) Buddhist tradition, which in large part was imported from Silla to the Japanese capital of Nara in the eighth century. But the Korean *kugyŏl* inventory in Figure 3.2 is derived from the inventory of *idu* and *hyangch'al*

Kugyŏl	Hangul	Source character	Kugyŏl	Hangul	Source character
1. 朩	거 ke	去	13. ﾉ	리 l	尸
2. ﾅ	겨 kye	在	14. ㄲ	라 la	羅
3. ㅁ	고 kwo	古	15. ⋯	로 lwo	以
4. 仒	금 kum	爾	16. ﾄ	며 mye	彌
5. 人	괴/와 (k)wa	果	17. ﾜ	면 myen	面
6. ハ	ㄱ/기 k/ki	只	18. ﾞ	사 sa	沙
7. ㅌ	ㄴ no	飛	19. 入	샤 sya	舍
8. ㄱ	ㄴ n	隱	20. ﾝ	셔 sye	立
9. ﾄ	누 nu	臥	21. ﾌ	소 swo	所
10. ㄷ	니 ni	尼	22. ﾆ	시 si	示
11. |	다 ta	多	23. ㄷ	ㅅ s	叱
12. ㄴ	리/룰 l(ol)	乙	24. ﾉ	아 a	良

Figure 3.2 Partial inventory of *kugyŏl* graphs

phonograms, while the Japanese *katakana* syllabary is based on Japanese *man'yōgana* phonograms. These older systems themselves have links, with the direction of influence moving from Korea to Japan, but those links are older than *kugyŏl* or *katakana*. It remains quite possible that the idea of abbreviating Chinese characters, as convenient devices for glossing Chinese texts to read them in the vernacular, was borrowed in Japan from Korea. And it is even more likely that the entire practice of reading Chinese texts in the vernacular (local) language, Korean *hundok* 훈독, Japanese *kundoku* 訓読, was a major cultural borrowing from Korea to Japan.

A second type of *kugyŏl* glossing is called *chŏmt'o* 'point glosses'. These involve dots or points, and occasionally other symbols such as lines, inscribed around the Chinese character to indicate the suffixes and particles that should be attached to it in its Korean vernacular reading. In Korea, surviving examples of *chŏmt'o* were inscribed using a stylus (a bamboo or metal tool for making a small impression on paper), so they are referred to as *kakp'il* 각 필 'stylus written' glosses. *Chŏmt'o* inscribed by stylus are attested as early as a tenth-century printed manuscript of the *Hwaŏm-gyŏng* (*Avatamsaka sutra*).

Chat'o and *chŏmt'o* refer to the form of the glosses used to make it possible to read a Chinese text in Korean. We can also distinguish the form of the vernacular Korean reading produced by the glosses. The vernacular reading exemplified in (8) is called *sŏktok kugyŏl* 'translation *kugyŏl*', because it generates more or less complete vernacular Korean sentences (although much Sino-Korean vocabulary remains). By the late thirteenth century, after the Mongol invasion of Korea, *sŏktok kugyŏl* began to be replaced by a different kind of vernacular reading, *sundok kugyŏl* 순독 구결 '*kugyŏl* read in order'. Unlike translation *kugyŏl*, this type of glossing did not convert the Chinese text into more or less acceptable Korean. Instead, it left the Chinese word order largely intact, connecting complete phrases in the Chinese texts with forms of the Korean copula =*i*- or the verb *ha*- 'do'. The following example is taken from a late–Koryŏ period (fourteenth-century) *sundok kugyŏl* glossed text, the *Pŏmmang-gyŏng Posal-gye* (the Chapter on the Bodhisattva Precepts of the Bhramajala-sutra). This text is glossed in as many as five different versions from the late Koryŏ period.

(9) Excerpt from the Kyemyung University text of the *Pŏmmang-gyŏng Posal-gye*

此 是 佛　行　處 ㅣ ㅌ　　聖主 ㅌ　　所 稱 歎 ㅣ ㅌ ㅅ

    this is   Buddha go place is-CONJ holy lord=GEN what call lament is-CONJ is.DEC
    'This is where the Buddha went, and what the holy lord named and lamented.'

Glosses in small capitals represent Chinese characters read in Sino-Korean. The first five characters are a full sentence in Chinese, 'This is where the Buddha went.' The *sundok kugyŏl* reading treats this Chinese sentence as a block, and connects it to the next clause with the inflected native Korean verb *i-ni* 'is and'. Literally, this is equivalent to saying, '(It being) [this is the place where the Buddha went] it is [this is what the holy lord named and lamented]'.

Why did Koreans read like this? It is important to remember that the glossed text in question is a religious text, so it should come as no surprise that preserving the form of the Chinese original text was of prime importance to the glossators, who were Buddhist monks. But more importantly, *kugyŏl* glossing allows us to understand how Koreans read and understood Chinese before and even after the invention of Hangul. Through the end of the nineteenth century, the bulk of textual production in Korea was in (literary) Chinese. It is often said that Korean literati, officials, and aristocrats through this period were diglossic; that is, that they used two languages, Korean and literary Chinese. But this is misleading. Not only were the vast majority of Koreans who were trained to read and write literary Chinese unable to speak any form of Chinese, the norms of Korean linguistic behavior proscribed "speaking" Sino-Korean, the only way to vocalize Chinese characters that all but a very few specialists knew, except in very limited Buddhist or Confucian ritual circumstances. To make the reading of a text like (9) an acceptable Korean speech act, the vocalized text had to be put in Korean, even if this meant only adding a few Korean function words to link clauses together.

This is important in understanding Korean literary production before the twentieth century. Aside from the Hangul texts published under official auspices in the fifteenth and sixteenth centuries, which were mostly vernacular renditions – actually very much like *sŏktok kugyŏl*, and probably influenced by earlier *sŏktok kugyŏl* readings – of Chinese texts, either Buddhist or Confucian, Hangul writing remained, in the form of letters and diaries written by men and women, largely in the realm of personal production until novels such as Kim Man-jung's *Ku un mong* ('The nine cloud dream') began to appear by the eighteenth century in Hangul. Nowadays Koreans read classic Korean literature such as Pak Chiwŏn's (1737–1805) *Yŏlha ilgi* ('Jehol diary') in Hangul. Vanishingly few people can read it in the original literary Chinese. Is something lost by reading in Hangul "translation"? The answer is no. Reading practice in Pak's own time involved borrowing a copy from one of the lending libraries increasingly active in the late Chosŏn period, and having an expert reader read the text aloud to a group of family or friends. Reading was in Korean, following the practice of vernacular reading embodied in *kugyŏl* glossing and established in Korean literary practice centuries before.

As a final example of the continuity of Korean writing before and after the invention of Hangul, consider the first two pages of the *Hunmin chŏng'ŭm* in Figure 3.3.

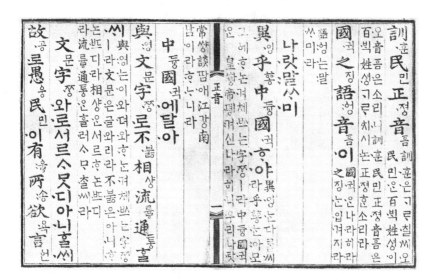

Figure 3.3 The *Hunmin chŏng'ŭm*
Source: https://bit.ly/2BvtiQO

The first line contains the title in Chinese characters with the pronunciation of each character in Hangul, followed by two lines giving a detailed definition of each character in Korean, mixing Hangul and Chinese characters. The third line begins with the famous opening line, "The language and sound of the country . . .," apparently in Chinese, with each character defined in line four in Korean. However the Chinese 國之語音 'language and sound of the country' is followed by the Korean nominative particle =*i* 이. In fact, this line is not really in Chinese. Line five gives the vernacular Korean counterpart, "The speech of the country . . . ." But line six once again prints out four large-font Chinese characters, 異乎中國 'different from China', followed by the Hangul 하야 'doing'. Lines three and six are standardly interpreted as the first two lines of the "Chinese" version of the *Hunmin chŏng'ŭm*. But this is not quite right. These lines provide a *sundok kugyŏl* version of the text, preserving phrase-level chunks of Chinese in their Chinese word order, but connecting them with Korean morphemes. King Sejong intended for even the "Chinese" portions of the *Hunmin chŏng'ŭm* to be vocalized, but he intended for them to be vocalized in Korean.

3.5   After the Fifteenth Century

Hangul were used continuously from the fifteenth century on, but primarily for what we might characterize as "private" writing: letters, diaries, journals. As in all of East Asia, "public" writing – dynastic histories, published laws and proclamations, "higher" literary writing – continued to be in Chinese. The Vernacular Script Commission or *Ŏnmun Ch'ŏng*, 언문청 (諺文廳), established by King Sejong as the *Chŏng'ŭm Ch'ŏng* 정음청 'Correct Sounds Commission', was abolished during the reign of King Chungjong in 1507. The General Directorate for the Publishing of Religious Texts or Kan'gyŏng Togam 간경도감 (刊經都監), established in 1457 under Sejong's second son Sejo, was responsible for the publication of many Buddhist texts in vernacular translation using Hangul, but was abolished in 1471. "Public" publication of vernacular texts using Hangul continued with the publication in the last decades of the fifteenth century of a vernacular version of the *Samgang haengsil to* 삼강 행실도 'The Three Bonds and Actual Examples of their Practice, with Illustrations' (三綱行實圖), a collection of tales set in China and Korea exemplifying Confucian virtues.

In the sixteenth century the locus of "public" production of Hangul texts can be found in the government Interpreters' School, the Sayŏkwŏn 사역원 司譯 院. The remarkable teacher, scholar, and interpreter Ch'oe Sejin, affiliated there, produced two important Korean–Chinese bilingual texts intended to train interpreters, the *Pŏnyŏk Pak T'ongsa* 번역박통사 'The Translated Interpreter Pak' (飜譯朴通事) and *Pŏnyŏk Nogŏltae* 번역노걸대 'The Translated Old Cathayan' (飜譯老乞大). Ch'oe also compiled the famous

Hunmong Chahoe 훈몽자회 訓蒙字會, a compilation of Chinese characters with Sino-Korean and vernacular Korean readings in Hangul. The *Hunmong Chahoe* was designed as a textbook for learning Chinese characters, and widely used for that purpose in Korea and later Japan. Its innovations included the orderly arrangement of Chinese characters and the introduction of the alphabetic order of Hangul still used today: <k> ㄱ, <n> ㄴ, <t> ㄷ, <l> ㄹ, <m> ㅁ, <p> ㅂ, <s> ㅅ, <ng> ㆁ, <kh> ㅋ, <th> ㅌ, <ph> ㅍ, <c> ㅈ, <ch> ㅊ, <z> ㅿ, <Ø/fi> ㅇ, <h> ㅎ; and for vowels, <a> ㅏ, <ya> ㅑ, <e> ㅓ, <ye> ㅕ, <wo> ㅗ, <ywo> ㅛ, <wu> ㅜ, <ywu> ㅠ, <u> ㅡ, <i> ㅣ, <o> ㆍ. From a linguistic standpoint, the *Hunmong Chahoe* is important because it records the pronunciations of Sino-Korean actually used in the fifteenth century, as opposed to the artificial and prescriptive pronunciations recorded in the *Tongguk chŏng'un* 동국정운 東國正韻 Chinese character dictionary compiled in 1448 at King Sejong's behest and in other official Hangul publications of the fifteenth century.

From the sixteenth century onward, Hangul underwent the natural evolution of a writing system actually used to write down a language. *Pangjŏm* 방점 'side dots' ceased to be used to mark tone or pitch accent. This does not necessarily indicate that Korean speakers in Seoul lost distinctive pitch accent in the sixteenth century. Rather, it was a step in the practical evolution of Hangul writing. Pitch accent or word tone is a property of words that native speakers can predict as soon as they recognize the word; they are no more likely to record it in writing than native speakers of English are to mark stress, unless they have a special reason for doing so.

By the late nineteenth century, various political and social factors began to combine to undermine the still unquestioned predominance of Chinese writing. These included the repression of *sŏwŏn* (Confucian academies, where classical Chinese was taught) and the abolition of the *kwagŏ* government examination system as part of the Kabo reforms in 1894.

In an edict of November 1894, the Imperial Korean government decreed that thenceforth government documents were to be issued in Hangul. In 1907, the Ministry of Education set up an Institute for Research on the National Language (Kugŏ Yŏnguso 국어연구소 国語研究所), with the mission of establishing an official orthography for Hangul. The imposition of the Japanese colonial government in 1910 interrupted these official efforts, but in 1921 the colonial government issued a directive on Hangul orthography titled "An Outline of Vernacular Orthography for Use in Public Schools" (*Pot'ong hakkyoyong ŏnmun ch'ŏljabŏp taeyo* 보통 학교용 언문 철자법 대요 普通学校用諺文綴字法大要). This system advocated a mixture of phonemic and morphophonemic spelling.

Meanwhile the linguistic research of Chu Sigyŏng and his followers continued apace, even under the increasingly oppressive strictures of the colonial regime. One very important part of Chu's legacy was a preference for morpho-phonemic spelling. In 1921, the Korean Language Research Society (Chosŏnŏ Yŏnguhoe 조선어 연구회 朝鮮語研究会) – the precursor of today's Korean Language Society (the Hangul Hakhoe 한글 학회) – was founded, and members of the Society became actively involved in devising a systematic ortho-graphy for Hangul.

Concurrent with these official and semi-official developments was the emer-gence of Korea as a modern nation, with a clear sense of national language. The establishment of Hangul as the national writing system was not truly imposed from above. The efforts of numerous private citizens and the spread of Hangul literacy combined to make the establishment of Hangul an irresistible force.

One such development was the emergence of "public" writing in Hangul from nongovernmental sources, beginning with newspapers. The *Tongnip sinmun* 독립신문 ('Independent') is generally considered the first Korean newspaper, and the first to be published in Hangul. The *Tongnip sinmun* (Figure 3.4) was published three times a week. Each issue was four pages. The first three pages were printed in Korean and the last page in English. The newspaper ran editorials, local Seoul news, government bulletins, and short pieces of overseas news.

The *Tongnip sinmun* also ran and charged for advertisements. It was founded by Seo Jae-pil, who came from an aristocratic family and passed the *kwagŏ* civil service exam at age eighteen, one of the youngest people ever to do so. He participated in the failed Kapsin Coup in 1884 and fled to the United States as a number of his family members were executed. He returned to Korea in 1895–1898, after coup participants were pardoned, and joined the Kaehwap'a (개화파) reformist faction, also serving as an unofficial advisor to the govern-ment. Seo believed in the importance of independent newspapers using Hangul and contemporary language so as to reach the masses. Seo obtained a printer and typeface from abroad and printed the newspaper in a government-owned building in Seoul. The first issue was published in April 1896. Average circulation was 2,000–3,000 readers.

As shown in the enlarged image in Figure 3.5, the *Tongnip sinmun* was published entirely in Korean, with no Chinese characters. Seo's practice on the issue of morphophonemic versus phonemic writing is interesting: Sino-Korean words, which in fifteenth-century Hangul orthography would have been written using Chinese characters, are written morphophonemically, with Sino-Korean morphemes preserved as graphic units and never broken up. Native Korean words, in contrast, are sometimes written phonemically, so for example *ssu-non kes=un* write-PRESADN COMP=TOP is written SSU.NON KE.S-UN. Word spacing is largely as in contemporary usage.

In 1931, the Chosŏnŏ Yŏnguhoe changed its name to the Chosŏnŏ Hakhoe. Meeting over one hundred times over the next few years, the Society issued its

Figure 3.4 The *Tongnip sinmun* 독립신문

Hangŭl mach'umbŏp t'ongil an 'Proposal for the Unification of Korean Orthography' on October 9, 1933, the date at that time of Hangul Day. The Society proposed a thoroughgoing morphophonemic orthography. Its proposal

Figure 3.5 Close-up of the *Tongnip sinmun*

forms the basis for Korean spelling both in the Republic of Korea and the Democratic People's Republic of Korea. The proposal was revised in 1940, 1946, and again in 1948, even under the vicissitudes of the colonial suppression of teaching and learning Korean, war, liberation, and the division of Korea into North and South. The DPRK issued its own orthographic guidelines in 1948 under the title "New Orthography for the Spelling of Korean" (*Chosŏnŏ sin ch'ŏljabŏp* 조선어 신철자법), but this was soon abolished due to the purge of its main author Kim Tu-bong, linguist, first chairman of the Workers' Party, and designer of the DPRK flag. A second official DPRK orthography was promulgated in 1954 and subsequently in 1966 and 1987. It is perhaps ironic to note that although the DPRK rejected the use of Chinese characters from the start, the official titles of their orthographic directives, like DPRK government directives in general, are entirely in Sino-Korean, while the 1933 proposal and subsequent ROK directives use vernacular Korean expressions such as *mach'um* 'spelling'.

In the ROK, the 1933 *Hangŭl mach'umbŏp t'ongil an* continued to guide orthography. Revisions in 1949 and 1958 by the Ministry of Education mandated terms for grammatical markers and other terminology. In 1988, a revised *Hangŭl mach'umbŏp* was issued as directive 88–1 of the Ministry of Education and continues in effect today. Differences, especially as regards word division and the spelling of Sino-Korean words, have developed over time between the DPRK and ROK systems, but both systems are firmly based on the morphophonemic principles advocated by Chu Sigyŏng and enshrined in the 1933 proposal.

3.6   Modern Writing

Korea North and South today report almost universal literacy. This is sometimes attributed to the simplicity and rationality of Hangul's design that we have described in this chapter. But there are dissenting voices. An OECD report (2005) caused a minor furor when it ranked the ROK twenty-seventh out of 182 countries in adult functional literacy, behind such countries as Japan (tenth), the USA (thirteenth), and Hong Kong (twenty-fourth). Functional literacy refers to reading and writing skills required to handle work and daily life beyond a basic level of literacy. Advocates of reintroducing Chinese characters in the ROK seized on this result to argue that ignorance of Chinese characters, combined with the high proportion of Sino-Korean vocabulary in the Korean lexicon, leads to difficulties in comprehension and writing.

But this argument seems dubious. As in Korean, the proportion of borrowed vocabulary in English is high, as much as 80 percent of entries in a standard dictionary, less in everyday life and nontechnical writing. Just as Korean neologizes using a borrowed lexical stratum, Sino-Korean, English neologizes with Latin. Both English and Korean writing is alphabetic, giving no hint as to the borrowed or native identity of morphemes other than their spelling. In fact, it could be argued that the syllabic clustering of Hangul orthography gives a better indication of Sino-Korean morphemes and their components derived from Chinese characters than English spelling does of Latinate roots.

Whatever the case, Hangul are a deserved point of national pride North and South, and arguably an important part of the ROK's extraordinarily vibrant internet culture. The design features of Hangul lend themselves to graphic practices that go beyond Roman letter internet "slang." Some of these partake of (and also contribute to) graphic conventions used in *manhwa* (comics). Examples are given in (10).

(10)   Hangul   Pronunciation   Meaning
      a. ㅋㅋㅋ <kh kh kh>   khu khu khu ㅋㅋㅋ   snicker
      b. ㅎㅎㅎ <h h h>   ha ha ha 하하하   laughter
      c. ○ ○ <Ø Ø>   ung ung 응·응   yes (from ung 응 'yes')
      d. ○ ㅋ <Ø kh>   okheyi 오케이   okay

These writings playfully and ingeniously make use of many facets of a literate writer's knowledge. For example, (c) uses the name of the letter ○, ung 응, while (d) plays on the visual similarity of ○ and Roman letter <o>.

We conclude this section with an interesting example of how pride in the virtues of Hangul plays out on the international stage. In 2008, the mayor of the Indonesian city of Baubau in southeast Sulawesi signed a memorandum of understanding with the Hunminjeongeum Society to promote the use of Hangul as a writing system for Ciacia, or Butonese, the endangered local language. The Hunminjeongeum Society was founded that same year to promote scholarly research on Hangul, and also to promote the visibility of the Korean writing system on the world stage. One idea that occurred to members of the society was to explore the utility of Hangul as a writing system for endangered languages.

The Ciacia Hangul project attracted international attention. A Ciacia-speaking elementary school teacher went to Korea to receive Korean language training, and collaborated in the production of a textbook for writing Ciacia in Hangul, and a Korean teacher was later sent to Baubau. The authors of the textbook made several interesting orthographic decisions. They chose to represent Ciacia voiced stops using the Hangul for Korean plain stops, e.g. ㅂ <p> for Ciacia /b/. Ciacia voiceless stops were represented with the Hangul for Korean reinforced stops, e.g. ㅃ <pp> for /p/. The Hangul for Korean aspirated stops were reserved for the Ciacia implosives, e.g. ㅍ <ph> for /ɓ/. Associating the Ciacia voiced (and unaspirated) stops with Hangul plain consonants might have been inspired by the ROK government's 2000 revised romanization system discussed in Section 3.7, but associating the Hangul for aspirated obstruents with Ciacia implosives is a very different decision, since the latter are voiced, and Korean aspirated obstruents are not voiced in any context. The Hangul Ciacia orthography also made use of original graphs from the *Hunmin chŏng'ŭm* no longer in use in modern Hangul, ㆆ <ʔ> for the Ciacia glottal stop /ʔ/ and ㅸ <β> for the Ciacia voiced labiodental fricative /v/.

Ultimately the project did not succeed. There had originally been a suggestion of economic support from the Seoul Metropolitan Government, but this fell through with a change of administration. The Indonesian government expressed mild concern about the project, with the Indonesian ambassador to Korea commenting in an interview with the Korea Times that "people shouldn't use the language as a promotional tool."[1]

From a linguistic standpoint, it is hard to decide whether Hangul were truly superior to Roman letters for writing Ciacia. Hangul naturally express a three-way manner distinction for stops and affricates, while Roman letters capture only a two-way distinction. On the other hand, the assignment of Hangul to manner of articulation types in Ciacia was not particularly natural. Ultimately political and economic factors determined the fate of the project. We revisit the issue of Hangul versus romanization in Section 3.7.

3.7   Romanization

As we remarked at the outset of this chapter, users of Hangul often experience a certain level of frustration with the various systems of romanization for Korean. This is not unrelated to the issue mentioned at the end of Section 3.6: the Hangul graphic distinction between plain, aspirated, and tense (in modern Hangul spelling, doubled) consonants naturally represents the three-way manner distinction among stops and affricates in modern Korean. In contrast, the Roman distinction between "soft" /b/ and "hard" /p/ etc. can represent the distinction between voiced and voiceless consonants, as in French, or unaspirated and aspirated consonants, as in Chinese pinyin, but when a language has a third manner distinction, either a diacritic, such as the raised ^{h} used to indicate aspiration in the International Phonetic Alphabet (IPA), e.g. p^h for Korean ㅍ <ph>, or a digraph, a combination of two letters, such as Yale Romanization ph for ㅍ <ph>, must be used. Table 3.6 gives five of the best known romanization systems for Korean.

Of these systems, ISO TR 11941 is a transliteration system for Hangul that was agreed upon by the ISO experts of the Democratic People's Republic of Korea and the Republic of Korea in a provisional technical report. The ISO is the International Organization for Standardization. This system was never officially adopted by any organization or state and has probably never been used. The UNGEGN Working Group on Romanization (2013) adopted the order of Hangul in this report (duplicated in Table 3.6) because the DPRK and the ROK have otherwise never been able to agree on an order.

DPRK 1992 is the system adopted in the North in 1992. It combines features of the McCune–Reischauer and Yale systems. The ROK adopted the new romanization system in column 4 in 2000 and now enforces its use in government publications. This system has become increasingly widely used

---

[1] I am indebted to Mr. Jong Wook Bae for this and other information about the Ciacia Hangul orthography project. Mr. Bae collected the information in a very fine Cornell University class paper.

Table 3.6 *Romanization systems for Korean, based on UNGEGN Working Group on Romanization (2013)*

Hangul	ISO TR 11941	DPRK 1992	ROK 2000	McCune–Reischauer	Yale
ㄱ	k/g	k	g, k	k/g	k
ㅋ	kh/k	kh	k	k'/k	kh
ㄲ	kk/gg	kk	kk	kk	kk
ㄷ	t/d	t	d, t	t/d	t
ㅌ	th/t	th	t	t'/t	th
ㄸ	tt/dd	tt	tt	tt	tt
ㅂ	p/b	p	b, p	p/b	p
ㅍ	ph/p	ph	p	p'/p	ph
ㅃ	pp/bb	pp	pp	pp	pp
ㅈ	c/j	j	j	ch/j	c
ㅊ	ch/c	ch	ch	ch'/ch	ch
ㅉ	cc/jj	jj	jj	tch	cc
ㅅ	s	s	s	s	s
ㅆ	ss	ss	ss	ss	ss
ㅎ	h	h	h	h	h
ㅇ	-, ng	-, ng	-, ng	-, ng	-, ng
ㄴ	n	n	n	n	n
ㄹ	l, r	r	r, l	r, n, l	l
ㅁ	m	m	m	m	m
ㅏ	a	a	a	a	a
ㅓ	eo	ŏ	eo	ŏ	e
ㅗ	o	o	o	o	o
ㅜ	u	u	u	u	wu
ㅡ	eu	ŭ	eu	ŭ	u
ㅣ	i	i	i	i	i
ㅐ	ae	ae	ae	ae	ay
ㅔ	e	e	e	e	ey
ㅚ	oe	oe	oe	oe	oy
ㅑ	ya	ya	ya	ya	ya
ㅕ	yeo	yŏ	yeo	yeo	ye
ㅛ	yo	yo	yo	yo	yo
ㅠ	yu	yu	yu	yu	yu
ㅒ	yae	yae	yae	yae	yay
ㅖ	ye	ye	ye	ye	yey
ㅘ	wa	wa	wa	wa	wa
ㅝ	weo	wŏ	wo	wŏ	we
ㅟ	wi	wi	wi	wi	wuy

internationally. This book uses two systems, the McCune–Reischauer system for Korean words other than linguistic examples, and the Yale system for linguistic examples. Despite its defects, McCune–Reischauer continues to be used by organizations such as the U.S. Library of Congress and by scholarly publications, especially in the English-speaking world.

In evaluating a romanization system, the following factors come into play: (i) Is it phonemic (that is, does it represent all and only the phonemes of the language)? (ii) Does it provide a one-for-one transliteration of the graphs of the language (one Roman letter or digraph for one graph in the language)? (iii) Does it avoid diacritics? (iv) Does it avoid digraphs? (v) Are the Roman letters used in familiar ways? (vi) Are the Roman letters used in consistent ways?

Factors (i) and (ii) are not necessarily compatible; depending on how close the native writing system is to being phonemic itself, a phonemic representation of a language and a transliteration of its writing system can be very different. But modern Hangul orthography is very close to being an accurate phonemic representation of contemporary Korean; therefore a romanization system that transliterates Hangul comes close to being an accurate phonemic representation. Discrepancies occur when Hangul are not completely phonemic. One such example is the writing of /wu/ after a labial consonant. Yale Romanization (YR) was devised to implement the allophonic rule that labializes /u/ after a labial consonant. Thus YR writes 'fire' 불 as <pul>, not *<pwul>, because the /wu/ is predictable after /p/. (Earlier, in LMK, 'fire' was 블 [pɨl]). In this case, Hangul spelling represents a subphonemic property. On the other hand, users of YR who transliterate 불 as <pwul>, rather than transcribing the word as <pul>, are not all wrong. In the loan stratum of contemporary Korean there are many words such as *swuphulley* 수플레 'souffle' that do not labialize /u/ for all speakers, and in terms of Hangul spelling, write 으 rather than <wu> 우 after a labial. The emergence of such contrasts justifies writing *pwul* for 'fire' in contrast to *swuphulley* for the French dish.

Among the systems in Table 3.6, only YR and DPRK 1992 come close to satisfying (1) and (2). The ROK 2000 and McCune–Reischauer romanization systems are neither transliterations of Hangul nor phonemic. Let us take a simple example. The word *Hanguk* 'Korea' (in the ROK) is romanized in the four main systems as follows:

(11)   a. 한국 'Korea'
        b. *Hankwuk* (Yale)
        c. *Hankuk* (DPRK 1992)
        d. *Hanguk* (ROK 2000)
        e. *Han'guk* (McCune–Reischauer)

In this word, the phoneme /k/, spelled as Hangul ㄱ, occurs in intersonorant position (between two sonorants) at the beginning of the second syllable, and in coda (syllable-final) position at the end of the same syllable. The ROK 2002 system Romanizes ㄱ as <g>, and aspirated ㅋ <kh> as <k>. This is not an unreasonable choice; Chinese pinyin also represents plain stops as "soft" <b>, <d>, <g> and aspirated stops as "hard" <p>, <t>, <k>. But pinyin is phonemic: the same phoneme is romanized the same way no matter where it occurs. The

ROK 2002 system is not phonemic: the ㄱ that appears at the end of *Hanguk* spells the same phoneme that appears before it, but it is written differently. Because the final /k/ in this word does not appear between two sonorants, it is not voiced.

A truly phonemic (or transliterational) application of the choice to Romanize ㄱ as <g> would spell 'Korea' as *Hangug*. But the architects of the ROK 2002 system, like the Anglophone missionaries McCune and Reischauer, did not make this choice. Were they concerned that spellings like *Hangug* would look too deviant to English speakers? We cannot answer this question, but it is the case that, with respect to factor (5) above, the ROK 2000 system may make more "familiar" letter choices than YR, which includes romanizations such as <lywu> for the syllable 류.

We use YR for linguistic examples in this book because it is important for readers to be able to recover Hangul spellings from the romanization, and because YR is phonemic, and phonemic analysis is the foundation of all further linguistic analysis. In real life, the final choice between romanization systems will probably be determined by practical factors such as keyboard utility. It is a striking fact that in the case of the other major languages of East Asia, Chinese and Japanese, Roman (qwerty) keyboards are the rule. The writing systems of these languages are much more complex and much less elegant than Hangul, but the combination of Roman input plus intelligent word processing applications that allow users to select from a menu of choices when the Roman input is ambiguous make the Roman keyboard adequate. The twenty-six letter keys on a standard qwerty keyboard suffice to write the fourteen non-doubled Hangul consonant graphs and fourteen of the vowels and diphthongs; doubled (reinforced) consonants are written by using the shift key, and the remaining diphthongs are written using shift keys or key combinations. But the keyboard is not Roman: there is no match between Roman and Hangul letter values. Any of the systems in Table 3.6 could be adopted for Roman input for Hangul word processing; which eventually wins out for this purpose will probably determine the romanization system of the future.

3.8   Summary

In this chapter we discussed the salient characteristics of Korean writing, in particular the features of Hangul that have made it a writing system admired the world around. We introduced the background behind the invention of Hangul, and the argument that the system was indeed personally invented by King Sejong. We showed how Hangul is at once a featural, an alphabetic, and a syllabic system. We showed how Hangul orthography shifted from being primarily phonemic in the fifteenth century to the morphophonemic systems in use in the North and South today, following the 1933 Proposal for the Unification of Korean Orthography.

We discussed pre-Hangul writing and highlighted certain aspects of continuity between pre-Hangul and the system promulgated in the *Hunmin chŏng'ŭm*. Finally, we briefly discussed issues surrounding Korean writing today, in particular the problem of romanization.

Further Readings

Lee, Ki-moon. 1997. The inventor of the Korean alphabet. In Kim-Renaud (ed.), 1997a, 11–30.

Lee, Ki-moon. 1998. *Kugŏ-sa kaesŏl*, new revised ed. Seoul: T'aehak-sa.

Lee, Ki-moon and S. Robert Ramsey. 2011. *A History of the Korean Language*. Cambridge and New York: Cambridge University Press.

Lee, SangOak. 1997. Graphical ingenuity in the Korean writing system: With new reference to calligraphy. In Kim-Renaud (ed.) 1997a, 107–143.

Nam, P'ung-hyŏn. 1991. *Kugŏ-sa lŭl wihan kugyŏl ŭi yŏngu* [Research on *Kugyŏl* for the history of Korean]. Seoul: T'aehak-sa.

OECD and Statistics Canada. 2005. *Learning a Living: First Results of the Adult Literacy and Life Skills Survey*. Paris: OECD.

References

Kim-Renaud, Young-Key (ed.). 1997a. *The Korean Alphabet: Its History and Structure*. Honolulu: University of Hawai'i Press.

Kim-Renaud, Young-Key. 1997b. The phonological system reflected in the Korean writing system. In Kim-Renaud (ed.), 1997a, 161–192.

Ledyard, Gari. 1966. The Korean Language Reform of 1446: The origin, background, and early history of the Korean alphabet. Unpublished Ph.D. dissertation, University of California, Berkeley. Published as National Language Research Center monograph 2, Shingumunhwa-sa, Seoul (1998).

Sampson, Geoffrey. 1990. *Writing Systems*. Stanford University Press.

UNGEGN Working Group on Romanization. 2013. *Report on the Current Status of United Nations Systems for Geographical Names*. New York: UNGEGN (United Nations Group of Experts on Geographical Names).

Part II

Language Structure

4   Phonology and Phonetics

Korean has attracted the attention of theoretical phonologists and phoneticians for much of the past century. This is due to three factors: features that are either relatively unusual or are textbook examples of theoretically important phenomena; the fact that Korean is a well-documented, major world language; and the existence of remarkable changes in progress that phoneticians and phonologists have been able to document as they develop. We will introduce all these in this chapter.

The chapter is organized as follows. Section 4.1 introduces the basic phonemic inventory. Section 4.2 discusses allophony: the processes that map from underlying phonological form to surface pronunciation. Section 4.3 discusses prosody and suprasegmental phenomena. Section 4.4 discusses important changes in progress, including tonogenesis and denasalization. Section 4.5 concludes the chapter.

4.1   Phonemic Inventory

One of the first things a linguist learns is that the sounds of a language must be represented in different ways depending on what facet of a speaker's knowledge she wants to focus on. For example, the way that the word 꽃 *kkoch* 'flower' is spelled in Hangul and Yale Romanization does not directly represent how a native speaker of Korean pronounces this word in isolation. The McCune–Reischauer spelling *kkot* is closer to the pronunciation in isolation, but to represent the actual pronunciation using a standardized system adaptable to all the world's languages, we adopt where possible the conventions of the International Phonetic Alphabet (IPA). We transcribe 'flower' as it is pronounced in isolation as [k̥ot]. The square brackets indicate that this is a **phonetic** representation: a representation as close as practicable to what comes out of a speaker's mouth. The diacritic ̥ is proposed by Ladefoged and Maddieson (1996: 56) to represent [stiff] consonants. Over the years a variety of different symbols have been used to mark the Korean tense or fortis (strong) consonants, as we see in Section 4.1.1.1.

The phonetic representation [ḳot] represents what a speaker actually says, but it does not represent everything that she knows about how this word is pronounced. YR *kkoch* and Hangul 꽃 are more helpful for this purpose. They are **morphophonemic** representations of the word, representing all the information that a speaker needs to pronounce the word in any context, in combination with her knowledge of the morphological (word structure) and phonological or phonemic (sound structure) rules of the language. For example, a native speaker knows that if the word occurs followed by the nominative particle =*i*, together they are pronounced 꽃이 [ḳotɕʰi], with the consonant ㅊ /tɕʰ/ fully released as an affricate, and aspirated (followed by a puff of air). She also knows that if the word is followed by the comitative particle =*kwa* 'and', the combination is pronounced [ḳotḳwa], with ㅊ /tɕʰ/ realized as the unreleased stop [t], and the following initial consonant of 'and' pronounced as a tense [ḳ]. Since morphophonemic representations underlie the actual pronunciations produced in combination with various rules, they are sometimes called underlying representations. Underlying morphophonemic representations make good dictionary entries, and in languages with good spelling systems, like Korean, they are what good dictionaries use. Thus the dictionary entry for 'flower' is Hangul 꽃 and YR *kkoch* in Martin, Lee and Chang's (1967) dictionary. Our approach in this chapter is to follow IPA conventions as much as possible to represent the sounds of Korean, so we will use the morphophonemic representation /ḳotɕʰ/. The convention in linguistics is to enclose morphophonemic representations in slash (//) brackets, and phonetic representations in square brackets. Throughout this chapter, Korean forms will be given in Hangul and italicized YR, with morphophonemic representations in slash brackets and phonetic representations in square brackets.

Our discussion in this section presupposes a basic background in phonology and phonetics, at the level presented in an introductory course in linguistics. Readers desiring a more pedagogically oriented approach or more in-depth coverage of the linguistic background are recommended to consult Choo and O'Grady (2003) or Shin, Kiaer, and Cha (2013).

4.1.1   The Consonant Inventory of Korean

The nineteen consonants of modern standard (Seoul) Korean can be represented in terms of their place of articulation (where they are pronounced in the vocal tract) and manner of articulation (how they are pronounced) as in Table 4.1.

As Table 4.1 shows, Korean, like English, has a three-way distinction between labial, coronal, and velar stops, and a single position for affricates (consonants combining a stop and a fricative). There are only two positions for fricatives, coronal (involving the tongue blade), and glottal. Korean has only

Table 4.1 *The consonant inventory of Korean*

		Labial	Coronal	Alveopalatal	Velar	Glottal
Stop/ Affricate	**Plain**	p ㅂ	t ㄷ	tɕ ㅈ	k ㄱ	
	Tense	p̚ ㅃ	t̚ ㄸ	t̚ɕ ㅉ	k̚ ㄲ	
	Aspirated	pʰ ㅍ	tʰ ㅌ	tɕʰ ㅊ	kʰ ㅋ	
Fricative	**Plain**		s ㅅ			h ㅎ
	Tense		s̚ ㅆ			
Nasal		m ㅁ	n ㄴ		ŋ ㅇ	
Liquid			l ㄹ			
Approximant		w ㅗ/ㅜ		j ㅣ		

a single liquid /l/, realized as lateral [l] in coda position and as alveolar flap [ɾ] elsewhere.

4.1.1.1 Laryngeal Contrast Among phonologists and phoneticians, Korean is best known for the fact that it has a three-way contrast among stops and affricates represented as "plain," "tense," and "aspirated" in Table 4.1. Laryngeal contrasts result from the configuration of the larynx during the articulation of the consonant. According to the *World Atlas of Language Structures* (*WALS*) Online (Dryer and Haspelmath 2013), the nineteen consonants of Korean rank it as "average" in consonant inventory size. Most of the languages in the *WALS* sample with this consonant inventory size have a contrast in voicing for stops (sixty-seven languages) or both stops and fricatives (seventy-one languages). But as we explain below, the three-way contrast among Korean stops and affricates does not involve voicing. Only 49 in the *WALS* sample of 543 languages (9.01 percent) have average consonant inventory size and no voicing contrast for stops and fricatives.

The Korean consonants are thus unusual among the world's languages. Absence of a voicing contrast for stops and fricatives per se is not unusual in Northeast Asia: as shown in *WALS*, a voicing contrast is absent in the Tungusic languages in the database: Manchu, Evenki, Even, and Nanai, as well as Ainu and Yukaghir. The three Mongolic languages in *WALS* geographically closest to Korean – Khalkha, Dagur, and Mangghuer – also have a contrast between aspirated and plain consonants, but no voicing contrast, like Korean. What distinguishes Korean from these other Northeast Asian languages is that it has a three-way laryngeal contrast among stops and affricates (and a two-way distinction among fricatives).

Laryngeal contrasts depend on what the vocal cords or folds housed in the larynx are doing during the articulation of a sound. During the articulation of English voiced /b d g/, the vocal folds are in contact with one another and vibrating. During the articulation of English voiceless /p t k/ at the beginning of a word or Korean aspirated /pʰ tʰ kʰ tɕʰ/ ㅍ ㅌ ㅋ ㅊ, the vocal folds are spread apart. Voicing of Korean plain /p t k tɕ/ ㅂ ㄷ ㄱ ㅈ is variable and predictable. In word initial position, they are voiceless and somewhat aspirated, like English voiceless /p t k/. But between sonorant sounds, vowels and the sonorant consonants /m n l w j/, they are voiced, like English /b d g/. The reader can confirm this by placing her hand over her voicebox and pronouncing the name of the dish 비빔밥 *pipimpap* [pibimpap]. The vocal cords will start to vibrate at the first vowel /i/ and stop just before the tense stop /p/, which is tensed for reasons we discuss in Section 4.2.7. In between, the vowels and the second ㅂ /p/ are voiced, but the initial and final ㅂ /p/ are not, while the third ㅂ /p/ is tense. In contrast, in the English word *Beelzebub* [biːɛlzɪbʌb], the vibration of the vocal cords (voicing) starts with the first /b/ and ends with the final /b/.

There are other languages in the world, such as Burmese and Thai, that have a three-way contrast among consonants including a distinction between plain and aspirated consonants. But in these languages, the third series is voiced. Languages with a three-way contrast not involving voicing also exist, but the most common such pattern involves plain, aspirated, and ejective consonants. Ejective consonants are formed by closing the glottis and then raising it, building up air pressure in the vocal tract which is then released at the point of articulation. Ejectives are found throughout the Western Hemisphere, as in Tlingit (Na-Dene) and Nisga'a (Tsimshian), spoken on the northwest coast of North America; Nasa Yuwe (isolate), spoken in Columbia; and Jaqaru (Aymaran), spoken in Peru. The IPA diacritic for ejectives, apostrophe ◌', has sometimes been used for the Korean tense consonants. However Korean tense consonants are phonetically quite distinct from ejectives. Ejectives involve complete closure of the glottis, while Korean tense consonants involve constriction, but not complete closure. Ejectives often lower the pitch ($f0$) of the following vowel, but Korean tense consonants raise the pitch of the following vowel. Ejectives typically have a long time lag, or long voice onset time (VOT), before voicing begins after release of the consonant, but Korean tense consonants have the shortest VOT among the three sets of Korean stops and affricates. This is probably why the doubled graph Hangul spelling ㅃ <pp> ㄸ <tt> ㄲ <kk> ㅉ <cc>, now used for tense consonants, was originally used in the fifteenth century to represent the voiced consonants of Middle Chinese, and why Hangul loanword spellings in the twentieth century often represented voiced initial consonants in other languages as tense consonants, e.g. 뻬쓰 *ppesu* 'bus', still the approved spelling in *Munhwa'e*, the DPRK standard.

The Korean tense consonants /p̚ t̚ s̚ tɕ̚ k̚/ ㅃ ㄸ ㅆ ㅉ ㄲ have been variously described as stiff, fortis (strong), or reinforced. We have many good descriptions of the articulatory and acoustic properties of the Korean tense consonants. In the 1970s, electromyography, a technique that measures the electrical activity in muscles, showed that the muscles around the larynx are tensed in the production of these consonants, resulting in stiffness of the vocal folds, and tension in the walls of the vocal tract above the larynx as well. The stiffness of the vocal cords appears to inhibit their vibration and thus block voicing, even though the glottis is narrowed. Using an MRI imaging technique that allowed them to simultaneously view tongue position and configuration of the larynx, Kim et al. (2005) suggest that two articulatory variables are relevant for the three-way laryngeal distinction: oral closure, which can condition the height of the glottis, and glottal width. Tense consonants have a heightened glottis and narrowed glottal width, and their oral closure is longest among the Korean consonants, with this effect clearest in medial position between vowels.

Despite our good understanding of the phonetics of the three-way laryngeal contrast, there is still dispute as to how the contrast should be represented in the phonological inventory. The source of the approach we adopt here, Ladefoged and Maddieson (1996) associate Korean tense consonants with the articulatory feature [stiff], and propose the diacritic ̣ for this feature. Other well-studied cases of [stiff] voiceless consonants include the tense stops of Javanese, a major language of Indonesia. Brunelle (2010) summarizes the acoustic properties of Javanese tense and lax stops and suggests that a heightened glottis is at least one of the articulatory mechanisms responsible for these properties. Like Korean tense stops, Javanese tense stops have a shorter VOT and higher pitch on the following vowel. Based on these similarities, we will adopt the feature [stiff] and the diacritic ̣ for our phonetic characterization of the Korean tense consonants.

Various attempts have been made to assimilate the Korean laryngeal contrasts to more familiar systems. The most influential is to treat the tense consonants as geminates, clusters of two identical consonants. Yale Romanization (Martin 1954) represents tense consonants as sequences of two identical consonant graphs, following the way they are represented in modern Hangul. Because of this, Martin's (1951) phonemic analysis of the tense consonants is sometimes interpreted as a geminate analysis (Jun 1994, Ahn and Iverson 2004), but this is not the case: Martin (1951) analyzes tense consonants as sequences of /p t c s k/ and an abstract (placeless) phoneme /q/ representing glottal tension. The geminate analysis was made explicit by Han (1996), who accounts for the greater duration of tense consonants in intervocalic position by appealing to the inadmissibility of consonant clusters in onset and coda position: on this analysis, tense consonants are underlyingly geminates, but reduced to singleton consonants in onset and coda position due to these constraints. Ahn and Iverson (2004) adopt similar geminate analyses, but Kim (2005) and Yu Cho (2011) marshal the phonetic and phonological arguments against the geminate analysis.

The biggest difficulty for the geminate analysis is the lack of evidence that tense consonants involve the extra prosodic unit of timing expected of two consecutive consonants. This contrasts with true geminates in Korean in words such as 엄마 *emma* 'mother' and 알리다 *allita* 'inform', where speakers have a clear intuition that /mm/ and /ll/ take up "two beats"; that is two units of phonological timing.

In favor of the geminate analysis, Jun (1994) gives an ingenious prosodic argument based on mimetic words such as 빵 *ppang* /paŋ/ 'bang'. These words reduplicate without a tensed consonant in the second syllable: 빠방 *ppapang* /papaŋ/ 'bang'. The same is true of mimetic words beginning with an aspirate, which reduplicate the consonant without aspiration in the second syllable: 팡 *phang* /pʰaŋ/ → 파방 *phapang* /pʰapaŋ/ 'bombing sound'. Jung argues that the loss of tenseness and aspiration in the second syllable of the reduplicated mimetic can be explained if tense and aspirated consonants are analyzed as sequences of two consonants, /pp/ and /ph/ (as in Yale Romanization); reduplication is then constrained to consist of a light (CV) and a heavy (CVC) syllable: CVCVC *ppa.pang* 'bang'. On this analysis, if the second syllable retained tense or aspiration, the outcome of reduplication would be **ppap.pang* (or in the case of aspiration, **phah.pang*), violating the constraint.

But Jung's approach is not the only way to explain the reduplication facts. Many linguists analyze reduplication as a form of affixation, where the reduplicant (in this case, the second syllable) has the status of an abstract affix RED, spelled out according to the rules of the language. Korean has a general constraint against tense or aspirate-initial suffixes in their basic or underlying form. For example, the quotative complementizer *-ko* originates from LMK *ho-ko* do-GER 'doing, saying', and is reduced through syncope of the first syllable vowel to 코 *hko*, but after reanalysis as a suffix, aspiration was lost. This general constraint against tense and aspirate-initial suffixes may account for the loss of tense and aspiration in reduplication. See Yu Cho (2011) for an alternative account of the reduplication facts.

Direct comparison with the behavior of true geminates argues against the geminate analysis of tensed consonants. Tak and Davis (1994: 410–411) point out that umlaut (1), a process which fronts a back vowel in the syllable preceding front /i/, applies across singleton consonants (1a, b), but is blocked by true geminates (1c, d). Crucially, it is not blocked by tense or aspirated consonants (1e, g):

(1)   Korean umlaut (based on Tak and Davis 1994)
        a. 아기 *aki* 'baby'   [agi] or [ɛgi]
        b. 어미 *emi* 'mother'   [ʌmi] or [emi]
        c. 알리 *-alli-* 'inform'   [alli] not *[ɛlli]

   d. 언니 *enni* 'older sister'   [ʌnni] not *[enni]
   e. 아끼 *-akki-* 'cherish'   [aki̧] or [ɛki̧]
   f. 토끼 *thokki* 'rabbit'   [tʰoki̧] or [tʰøki̧]
   g. 막히 *-makhi-* 'be blocked'   [makhi] or [mɛkhi]

A different approach to accounting for the three-way laryngeal contrast is developed by Kim and Duanmu (2004), who propose that the plain stops be analyzed as voiced, tense stops as voiceless, and the aspirates as aspirated (making Korean look like Burmese or Thai). On this view, the underlying voiced character of the plain stops surfaces only in intersonorant position; in other positions they are devoiced. There are problems with this approach as well. First, as we discuss below, intersonorant voicing in Korean is variable and gradient. This is not predicted if plain stops are underlyingly voiced. Second, the tense stops are the most marked among the three sets of consonants: they are disallowed in stem-final position, and, as we have seen, in suffix-initial position. This is unexpected if these are merely plain unaspirated stops. Finally, the analysis of Korean plain stops as voiced and the tense stops as voiceless and unaspirated fails to capture differences between Korean and languages which have a true three-way contrast involving voicing. For example, in Burmese, voiceless unaspirated stops undergo intervocalic voicing. But in Korean, the supposedly corresponding series of stops (tense stops analyzed as voiceless unaspirated) is exactly the series that does not undergo medial voicing.

Because of these issues, we will adopt the mainstream view that Korean has a three-way laryngeal contrast for stops and affricates, and associate tense consonants with the feature [stiff]. Cho, Jun, and Ladefoged (2002) adopt a proposal due to Lombardi (1991) that uses the features [spread glottis] and [constricted glottis] (Halle and Stevens 1971) to account for the three-way contrast. While in languages with a voicing contrast [(+)constricted glottis] is used to pick out voiced consonants, Lombardi proposes that in Korean [constricted glottis] picks out tense consonants, [spread glottis] picks out aspirated consonants, and plain consonants are unspecified for laryngeal features. This approach captures nicely the articulatory and acoustic properties of the tense aspirated stops, as well as the unmarked character of the plain stops. Cho, Jun, and Ladefoged then propose a Korean-particular redundancy rule which specifies that both tense and aspirated consonants have the feature [stiff vocal folds].

4.1.1.2 Plain and Tense Fricatives   Since there is only a two-way distinction between the fricatives ㅅ /s/ and tense ㅆ /s̞/, it is theoretically possible that ㅅ /s/ could pattern with the plain or the aspirated obstruents. Contrary to what Hangul orthography might suggest, it has been proposed that ㅅ /s/ be classified as aspirated, because it is usually described as not undergoing medial or intersonorant voicing (for example, 남산 *Namsan* 'Mt. Namsan' is transcribed <Namsan>, not <Namzan> in McCune–Reischauer), and because it is associated with raised pitch on the following vowel. However Cho, Jun, and Ladefoged (2002) found that a majority of tokens of intervocalic /s/ showed some degree of voicing in their experimental tokens, and they also found that while *f*0 on the vowel after ㅅ /s/ is higher than with plain stops, it is lower than with aspirated stops. On this basis we follow the standard view that ㅅ /s/ should be classified as plain rather than aspirated.

4.1.1.3 Affricates ㅈ /tɕ/, ㅉ /t͈ɕ/, and ㅊ /tɕʰ/   The Korean affricate series has traditionally been analyzed as alveopalatal, meaning that they are formed from an alveolar stop component comparable to /t/, and a palatal fricative component represented as IPA /ɕ/. However Kim (1999) argues that the affricates should be analyzed as alveolar in both their stop and fricative component. Subsequent researchers have arrived at conflicting results about the alveopalatal or purely alveolar nature of the Korean affricates. Most of this research has not taken dialectal or idiolectal variation into account, although it has long been reported that some North Korean varieties have a purely alveolar articulation, /ts/. Schertz et al. (2014) investigate two North Korean varieties and contrast them with the articulation of the plain affricate in Seoul Korean. They confirm the traditional view that the Seoul affricate has a less anterior articulation, although they also demonstrate gender-based variation in Seoul. To capture this contrast with North Korean purely alveolar articulations, we will maintain the traditional alveopalatal representation of the affricate.

4.1.1.4 Glides /w/ and /j/   Table 4.1 includes the labial glide or semivowel /w/ in words such as 왕 *wang* /waŋ/ 'king' and 활 *hwal* /hwal/ 'bow', and the palatal glide /j/ in words such as 여덟 *yetelp* /jʌtʌlp/ 'eight' and 형 *hyeng* /hjʌŋ/ 'older brother'. Hangul orthography represents the glides as vowels, directly in the case of the labial glide /w/, which is represented as 오 <o> or 우 depending on the identity of the following vowel, and indirectly in the case of the palatal glide /j/, which is represented by the addition of a stroke, originally associated with ㅣ, to the graph for the following vowel, e.g ㅣ + ㅏ <a> giving ㅑ for /ja/.

Perhaps for this reason, some linguists have analyzed the glides as vowels. One ostensible argument for this analysis might be that glides can occur as medials between an initial consonant and the nuclear vowel; analyzing the glides as consonants makes examples like 활 *hwal* /hwal/ 'bow' and 형 *hyeng* /hjʌŋ/ 'older brother' the only instances of consonant clusters in the same syllable in Korean. But languages allowing only consonant-glide clusters are not uncommon (e.g. Burmese).

A trickier issue for the consonant analysis of glides is capturing the contrast between the initial element in 위사 *wisa* 'weft' and 의사 *uysa* 'doctor'. While some approaches would posit a third glide, /ɰ/, the semivowel counterpart of the high back unrounded vowel 으 /ɯ/, giving /ɰisa/ for 의사 *uysa* 'doctor', a more economical treatment is to follow the lead of Yale Romanization and recognize glide counterparts of the high cardinal vowels only, /w/ for /u/ and /j/ for /i/. 의사 *uysa* 'doctor' may then be analyzed as vowel plus offglide, /ɯjsa/.

The complete set of rising diphthongs in Korean are 위 /wi/, 웨 /we/, 워 /wʌ/, and 와 /wa/ for the labial glide, and ㅠ /ju/, 예 /je/, 여 /jʌ/, ㅛ /jo/, and ㅑ /ja/ for the palatal glide. /ɯ/ does not occur as the nuclear vowel of rising diphthongs (nor did it at earlier attested periods of the language). The distinctively rounded vowels /u/ and /o/ do not occur after labial glide /w/ and the distinctively coronal vowel /i/ does not occur after the palatal glide /j/.

4.1.1.5 Features for Korean Consonants   Since the mid twentieth century, linguists have attempted to classify the speech sounds of natural languages using a set of **distinctive features**, combining **manner** features such as [continuant] with **place** features such as [labial]. The consonant features in Table 4.2 are those commonly used for Korean. Rather than specifying binary values, + or – for each feature for each consonant, we have attempted to treat the features in Table 4.2 as privative, meaning that a feature is either relevant for the classification of a consonant, indicated by *, or not. Thus, as discussed in Section 4.1.2, the Korean tense consonants are specified as [constricted glottis], the aspirated stops and affricates as [spread glottis], while their plain counterparts are unspecified for either of these laryngeal features.

4.1.2   The Vowel Inventory of Korean

Modern Seoul Korean has been analyzed as having as few as seven and as many as ten vowels. Table 4.3 shows the maximal inventory of ten, but the two front rounded vowels /y/ and /ø/ exist only in the speech of older speakers, and most younger speakers have merged the two nonhigh front vowels /e/ and /ɛ/ (Shin 2015: 4).

Some linguists represent the high back unrounded vowel ― /ɯ/ as central /ɨ/ and the nonhigh back unrounded vowel ㅓ /ʌ/ as /ə/. We also adopted this approach for LMK in Chapter 2. For CK, we follow IPA convention and represent these vowels as the unrounded counterparts of the rounded back vowels. For younger Seoul speakers, what were attested as the front rounded vowels /y/ and /ø/ in the previous generation are now realized as the diphthongs /wi/ and /we/ respectively. The diphthongal realizations are suggested by the Hangul spellings 위 <ui> and 외 <oi>, but it seems unlikely that the current diphthongal realizations are spelling pronunciations; instead, they

Table 4.2 *Distinctive features for Korean consonants*

	p	p͈	pʰ	t	t͈	tʰ	k	k͈	kʰ	tɕ	tɕ͈	tɕʰ	s	s͈	h	m	n	ŋ	l	w	j
Consonantal	*	*	*	*	*	*	*	*	*	*	*	*	*	*	*	*	*	*	*		
Sonorant																*	*	*	*	*	*
Spread glottis			*			*			*			*			*						
Constricted glottis		*			*			*			*			*							
Continuant													*	*	*				*	*	*
Delayed release										*	*	*									
Sibilant										*	*	*	*	*							
Lateral																			*		
Nasal																*	*	*			
Labial	*	*	*													*				*	
Coronal				*	*	*				*	*	*	*	*			*		*		
Dorsal							*	*	*									*			*
Front	*	*	*	*	*	*				*	*	*	*	*		*	*		*		*
Back							*	*	*									*		*	

Table 4.3 *The vowel inventory of Korean*

	Front		Back	
		(Round)		Round
High	i	(y)	ɯ	u
	e	(ø)	ʌ	o
Low		(ɛ)		a

were probably generalized in the last half of the twentieth century by younger speakers from environments where even older speakers have a diphthongal pronunciation.

Yu Cho (2016-10-26) summarizes the distribution of the front rounded vowels /y/ and /ø/ for speakers who have them in their grammars, versus the diphthongs /wi/ and /we/ which take their place in the speech of younger speakers. Even for older speakers, diphthongal /wi/ occurs instead of /y/ in onset (absolute initial) position and after /k/, while diphthongal /we/ occurs instead of /ø/ in these two positions and also after /t/ and /n/. Yu Cho presents an argument for an underlying monophthong, at least in the case of /y/, based on words such as 쉽다 *swip-ta* 'easy-PLN' and 쉬다 *swi-ta* 'rest-PLN', where speakers palatalize the initial fricative to [ʃ]. This is easy to explain if the following segment is the front /y/, but not if it is the back labial glide /w/. However the pronunciation of these words by younger speakers is not [ʃypta], [ʃyda] but [ʃɯjpta], [ʃɯjda], or, if we admit the existence of a glide /ɰ/, [ʃɰipta], [ʃɰida]. If such speakers have underlying monophthongs in their grammars, we would have to claim that in their grammars, palatalization precedes diphthongization. As we observe in Section 4.2.7.3, palatalization of /s/ is usually regarded as a low-level phonetic process that does feed, or provide, an output referenced by phonological processes. It therefore seems likely that younger speakers have simply phonologized palatal /ʃ/ in these words.

The four features [high], [low], [round], and [back] suffice to distinguish the seven vowels of contemporary Seoul Korean (Table 4.4). We have added the feature [coronal] in Table 4.4 because it is useful to characterize the distinctive behavior of /i/ described in Section 4.2 with respect to phenomena such as palatalization and umlaut. Because /a/ is the only /low/ vowel, it is not strictly speaking necessary to specify this vowel as [back]. But it is useful to represent /ʌ/ and /a/ as differing with respect to only one feature, because these two vowels are involved in alternation in the shape of the past and infinitive suffixes and in the mimetic stratum.

Distinctive features for the glides /w/ and /j/ could be given with the vowels, or, as we have chosen, with the consonants in Table 4.2. As we see in that table,

Table 4.4 *Distinctive features for Korean vowels*

	i	ɯ	u	e	ʌ	o	A
Coronal	*						
High	*	*	*				
Low							*
Round			*			*	
Back		*	*		*	*	*

glides differ from the other consonants in not being specified as [consonantal]; they differ from vowels (but pattern like consonants) in not being specified as [syllabic]. If we were to use vowel features for the glides, [w] would have the same place features as /u/, and /j/ would have the same place features as /i/.

4.2   Allophony

As we saw in Section 4.1, the underlying forms of Korean morphemes, as represented in Hangul and in slash (//) brackets, can differ considerably from how they are actually pronounced in specific contexts. Different realizations of underlying phonemes are called **allophones**, and the rules or generalizations mapping from underlying forms to the way morphemes and words are actually pronounced are called **allophonic rules**. In this section, we describe some of the main allophonic rules in Korean.

4.2.1   Coda Neutralization

We saw in Section 4.1 that the word 꽃 *kkoch* 'flower' is pronounced in isolation as [kot̚]. This is part of a general rule: all of the affricates ㅈ /tɕ/, ㅉ /t͈ɕ/, and ㅊ /tɕʰ/ are pronounced [t] in syllable-final or **coda** position. More exactly, affricates in this position are pronounced [t̚], where ◌̚ is the IPA diacritic for an **unreleased** consonant – a consonant with no stop burst or release of air. And this is part of a still broader generalization: ㅅ /s/ and tense ㅆ /s͈/ are also pronounced [t̚] in final positions. But the generalization is broader still: the tense stops /p t k/ ㅃ ㄸ ㄲ and the aspirated stops /pʰ tʰ kʰ/ ㅍ ㅌ ㅋ are pronounced as their plain counterparts, again with an unreleased articulation, [p̚] [t̚] [k̚]. The overarching generalization is that all obstruents in this position must be unreleased: not only the frication associated with affricates and fricatives, but the aspiration associated with the aspirate stops may not be realized in final position. This generalization applies to the plain stops as well: while /p/ /t/ /k/ are released (and aspirated) in initial position, they are unreleased in final position. This pattern of coda nonrelease is called coda neutralization

Table 4.5 *Patterns of coda neutralization*

Obstruent	p	p͈	pʰ	t	t͈	tʰ	k	k͈	kʰ	tɕ	t͈ɕ	tɕʰ	s	s͈	H
Allophone in final position	p̚	p̚	p̚	t̚	t̚	t̚	k̚	k̚	k̚	t̚	t̚	t̚	t̚	t̚	(t)

because all obstruents in coda position neutralize to the allophones [p] [t] [k], as in the lower row of Table 4.5.

Examples are given in (2). In the phonetic transcriptions in (2) we specify unreleased coda consonants with the diacritic ̚, but elsewhere in this chapter we write them just as plain consonants unless being precise about nonrelease is crucial for the discussion.

(2)   Coda neutralization (nonrelease)
            Underlying form   In final position
          a. 옆 *yeph* /jʌpʰ/ 'side'   옆도 *yeph+to* [jʌp̚to] 'side too'
          b. 밭 *path* /patʰ/ 'field' 밭도 *path+to* [pat̚to] 'field also'
          c. 맛 *mas* /mas/ 'taste' 맛도 *mas+to* [mat̚to] 'taste also'

English speakers can get a sense of the unreleased pronunciation of final stops by contrasting the normal unreleased pronunciation of final [t] in *cat* [kæt] as [kæt̚] in a sentence like *Feed the cat*, versus an exaggerated pronunciation with a released (and aspirated) [tʰ] in *Feed the CATTTuh!* Either an unreleased or an artificial but possible released pronunciation can be used in English, but Korean allows only an unreleased pronunciation in coda position.

In addition to the phonetic effect of nonrelease, the realization of final obstruents has a phonological aspect. Intuitively speaking, inherently released obstruents (such as the affricates and fricatives) become the potentially unreleased obstruent closest in place of articulation. This obstruent is /t/ (pronounced as [t̚]) in the case of the affricates and fricatives because they all share the place feature [coronal]. We discuss the glottal fricative /h/ in Section 4.2.2. Another way of thinking of this is that the manner features for consonants – the laryngeal features [constricted glottis] and [spread glottis], but also the features [continuant], [delayed release], and [sibilant] – are **neutralized**, or not realized, in final position. Removing [continuant] and [sibilant] from /s/ and /s͈/ and [delayed release] from /tɕ/, /t͈ɕ/, and /tɕʰ/ results in them having the feature specifications of /t/, which describes exactly how they are realized in final position.

4.2.2   *Assimilation of /h/*

The glottal fricative /h/ does not occur in stem-final position in independent stems in modern Korean. It did in Late Middle Korean. We know this because words like 코 *kho* 'nose' were originally written 고히 [ko.hi] *kwoh=i* 'nose=NOM' when followed by a particle in LMK. In other words, the underlying representation for 'nose' was /kwoh/, and the stem-final ㅎ /h/ surfaced when followed by a vowel. But already in LMK, the /h/ was dropped in word-final position, so in isolation 'nose' was spelled 고 *kwo* (recall here that LMK ㅗ is romanized as /wo/ in YR). Later, in monosyllabic words where the initial consonant had an aspirated counterpart, aspiration migrated to that consonant: LMK *kwoh* > Modern Korean *kho*. This is the source of the initial aspirates in words like those in (3):

(3)   LMK coda /h/ > Modern Korean initial aspiration
    a. /kalh/   >   /k^{h}al/ 'knife'
    b. /polh/   >   /p^{h}al/ 'arm'
    c. /kwoh/   >   /k^{h}o/ 'nose'

We can imagine that as /h/ was lost in final position, the aspiration associated with /h/ became associated with breathiness on the preceding vowel, and eventually was reinterpreted as a property of the preceding consonant. But while coda /h/ was lost in independent stems, it survives in bound stems such as 좋- *coh-* 'be good' and 닿- *tah-* 'touch, come into contact with'. When coda /h/ in a bound stem is followed by an obstruent with an aspirated counterpart, the obstruent becomes the aspirated counterpart:

(4)   Coda /h/ assimilation
    a. 좋다 *coh-ta* 'be good-PLN' [tɕot^{h}a]
    b. 닿고 *tah-ko* 'touch-GER' [tak^{h}o]

The segment /h/ disappears, but the following obstruent **assimilates** in manner of articulation to /h/: more precisely, the feature [spread glottis] shifts to the following obstruent. Where coda /h/ cannot be realized as aspiration on the following consonant, there is good reason to hold that it, like the other plain fricative /s/, neutralizes to /t/. We return to this issue in Section 4.2.4.

Coda /h/ assimilation is an example of **progressive** assimilation: the following segment takes on the [spread glottis] feature of /h/. But /h/ also triggers **regressive** assimilation: stops in coda position become aspirated when followed by /h/:

(5)   Coda assimilation to /h/
    a. 맛하고 *mas=hako* 'taste=and' [mat^{h}ago]
    b. 먹히다 *mek-hi-ta* eat-PASS-PLN 'be eaten' [mʌk^{h}ida]
    c. 약하다 *yakha-ta* 'weak' [jak^{h}ada]

Note that what undergoes coda assimilation to /h/ follows from final nonrelease in Section 4.2.1. Thus the final /s/ in 맛 *mas* 'taste' in (5a) becomes /t/ in coda position by coda neutralization, and this /t/ is aspirated by assimilation to the following /h/ in 맛하고 *mas=hako* 'taste=and' [mat^{h}ago]. In traditional generative phonology, this would have been treated as a case of **rule ordering**: first the rule of final nonrelease applies, and then coda assimilation to /h/ applies to the output of that rule. More recent approaches eschew the idea of phonological rules applying in a sequenced order, but it is still useful to keep in mind how the processes described in this chapter interact with one another.

4.2.3   Intersonorant Voicing

In Section 4.1 we discussed the fact that plain obstruents in Korean become voiced between sonorants, as shown in (6):

(6)   Intersonorant voicing

Voiceless
a. 밥과 *pap=kwa* 'rice=and' [pap̚kwa]
b. 밭과 *path=kwa* 'field=and' [pat̚kwa]
c. 밭이 *path=i* 'field=Nominative' [patɕʰi]

Voiced
d. 밥이 *pap=i* 'rice=Nominative' [pabi]
e. 손도 *son=to* 'hand=also' [sondo]
f. 밤과 *pam=kwa* 'night=and' [pamgwa]

As we see in (6e) and (6f), voicing happens not only between vowels, but between any pair of sonorants, including sonorant consonants such as /n/ (6e) and /m/ (6f). Intersonorant voicing is another instance of assimilation, because in Korean all sonorant consonants are voiced. The result of this process is that the voicing associated with the preceding and following segment continues through the intervening plain consonant.

Recall that the feature [voiced] is not one of the distinctive features that we used to distinguish Korean consonants in Table 4.1; instead we associated the feature [constricted glottis] with tense consonants. The nonprimacy of the feature [voiced] can be related to the status of intersonorant voicing as a gradient, phonetic process rather than a true phonological rule, as argued by Silva (1992) and Jun (1993). These linguists point out that intersonorant voicing stands apart from (and, in traditional terms, applies after) phonological processes such as final nonrelease or coda assimilation to /h/. We saw in Section 4.2.2 that the latter two processes interact, but no such interaction with other phonological processes can be found with intersonorant voicing. More importantly, degree of voicing is affected by typically gradient factors such as speech rate and position in the phrase. We saw in Section 4.1.1 that traditionally linguists have claimed that /s/ is not subject to intersonorant voicing, but that Cho, Jun, and Ladefoged showed that it is, if at a lower rate than stops and affricates. Silva (1992) shows that intersonorant voicing is part of a more general pattern of medial **lenition**, where lenition or weakening may be defined as processes by which a segment becomes less distinct from its environment. Thus /k/ between vowels in a word like 먹었다 *mek-ess-ta* eat-PAST-PLN 'ate' may not only be voiced but lenited to a velar fricative [mʌɣʌtta] in rapid speech. In sharing not only the [voiced] feature but the [continuant] feature of the preceding and following segments, /k/ becomes less distinct from them.

4.2.4   Place Assimilation

Further examples of progressive assimilation are provided by processes which assimilate coda consonants to the place of articulation of the following consonant.

4.2.4.1   Coda Coronal Assimilation   Coda coronal stops, including those that are the product of coda neutralization, assimilate to the following obstruent in faster speech, as shown in (7).

(7)   Coda coronal assimilation
   a. 곧고 *kot-ko* straight-GER 'be straight and' [kotk̚o] or [kokk̚o]
   b. 신문 *sinmwun* 'newspaper' (SK) [ʃinmun] or [ʃimmun]
   c. 문법 *mwunpep* 'grammar' (SK) [munpʌp] or [mumpʌp]
   d. 옷감 *oskam* 'fabric' [otk̚am] or [okk̚am]
   e. 곧바로 *kot+palo* 'straight' [kotp̚aɾo] or [kopp̚aɾo]
   f. 좋소 *coh-so* 'be good-BLUNT' [tɕoss̬o]

Note that the following obstruents in (7) undergo post-obstruent tensification, discussed in 4.2.5. Coda coronal assimilation is often treated as a casual speech phenomenon; that is, it is not obligatory. Prescriptive grammar sources such as the web page of the National Institute of Korean Language specifically pro-scribe assimilated pronunciations such as [okk̚am] for 옷감 *oskam* 'fabric' and [mumpʌp] for 문법 *munpep* 'grammar' (https://bit.ly/2Gq30U6).

Linguists such as Iverson and Kim (1987) have argued that coda consonant assimilation is related to the fact that /t/ is the least specified, or maximally **underspecified**, consonant in Korean. On this view, segments that are least **marked**, that is, most likely to appear in an environment where a specific con-sonant is not required, have the fewest distinctive feature specifications. This approach would hold that /t/ is specified, for example, only as [consonantal]. In most positions, other features associated with /t/ are filled in by default, but in coda position /t/ copies the features from the following obstruent. For expository purposes, we have not adopted this approach in the features for Korean consonants in Table 4.4, but the approach gains support from the coda realization of /h/ in examples like (7e). Notice that /h/ is distinctively specified only as [spread glottis] and [continuant] in Table 4.4. If these features are eliminated in coda position by final nonrelease, /h/ becomes specified only as [consonantal], the same as /t/ on the view that /t/ is the maximally underspecified consonant. Coda /h/ then would be subject to coda coronal assimilation, as we see in (7e). See Yu Cho (2016), however, for a recent careful discussion of the challenges for a thoroughgoing account of /t/ as the least marked, or maximally underspecified, consonant in Korean. One basic challenge is that, in the coda position of independent stems such as nouns, /t/ is actually quite rare in Korean independent (noun) stems. We would normally expect unmarked segments to be relatively high in frequency.

4.2.4.2 Labial Assimilation to Velars   This is also identified as a casual speech phenomenon, and may also be affected by frequency factors; that is, (8a) [ʌk̡ko] 'not exist', involving a higher frequency verb, is more acceptable than (8b).

(8)   Labial assimilation to velars
         a. 없고 *eps-ko* not.exist-GER 'not exist and' [ʌpk̡o] or [ʌk̡ko]
         b. 덥고 *tep-ko* hot-GER 'hot and' [tʌpk̡o] or [tʌk̡ko]
         c. 감기 *kamki* 'cold (illness)' [kamgi] or [kaŋgi]

Once again, the National Institute of Korean Language expressly proscribes the assimilated pronunciation [kaŋgi] for 'cold'.

4.2.5   Post-obstruent Tensification

We saw in the Section 4.2.4.1 that /p/, /t/, /k/, /s/, and /c/ after another obstruent (non-sonorant) consonant tensify to [p̚], [k̚], and [s̚]. This exemplifies the general phenomenon of post-obstruent tensification (POT): obstruent consonants become their tense counterparts after another obstruent (cf. Kim-Renaud 1974, who labels this phenomenon Post-Unreleased Fortition). Examples are given in (9):

(9)   Post-obstruent tensification (POT)
         a. 덥게 *tep-key* 'warm-ly' [tʌpk̬e]
         b. 같다 *kath-ta* 'same-PLN' [katt̬a]
         c. 먹자 *mek-ca* 'eat-PROP' [mʌkt̬ɕa]
         d. 맛과 *mas+kwa* 'flavor=and' [matk̬wa]
         e. 맞다 *mac-ta* 'suit, meet-PLN' [matt̬a]

Under the geminate approach to tense consonants, it is tempting to relate post-obstruent tensification (tensing the second in a sequence of two potentially distinct obstruents) to the hypothesized underlying representation of tense consonants as a sequence of identical obstruents, but see Yu Cho (2011) for the difficulties in actually implementing this approach.

4.2.6   Sai-sios

Post-obstruent tensification plays a role in 사이시옷 *sai-sios* 'medial s' or "Bindung-s" environments, where tensification marks compound boundaries, as in (10):

(10)   사이시옷 *sai-sios* 'medial s' (tensification in compounds)
  a. 술집 *swul+cip* 'liquor+house (bar)' [sulʨip]
  b. 맥줏집 *maykcwu(-s)+cip* 'beer+house (beer parlor)' [mekʨuʨip]
  c. 강가 *kang+ka* 'river+side' [kaŋka]
  d. 이빨 *ippal* 'teeth' [ipal]
  e. 닭고기 *talk+koki* 'chicken+meat' [takkogi]
  f. 숫자 *swu(-s)+ca* 'number+letter (number)' (SK 數字) [suʨa]

The historical source of *sai-sios* is the LMK genitive particle =*s*. In LMK, words such as (10d) 이빨 *ippal* 'teeth' were written 닛발 *ni=s pal* 'tooth+foot'. In this particular word the compound structure has become opaque, but in transparent compounds where the first member ends in a vowel, like (10b) 맥줏집 *maykcwu (-s)+cip* 'beer+house (beer parlor)', current official spelling practice in the Republic of Korea mandates inserting ㅅ <s>. In compounds like (10a) and (10c), where the first member ends in a sonorant, no ㅅ <s> is written, but the compound boundary is marked in pronunciation by tensification of the initial obstruent in the second member of the compound. In cases like (10e) 닭고기 *talk +koki* 'chicken+meat' [takkogi] where the first member of the compound ends in an obstruent, the surface effect of *sai-sios* is indistinguishable from post-obstruent tensification. *Sai-sios* is traditionally considered to be a phenomenon characterizing the native lexical stratum, but as (10b) shows it applies in nativized compounds of SK origin (맥주 *maykcwu* 'beer' is SK 麥酒), and in a small number of pure SK words, such as 숫자 *swusca* 'number' (SK 數字) [suʨa] in (10f).

Traditional accounts hold that *sai-sios* in contemporary Korean still involves insertion of a "compound marking" morpheme /s/, while more abstract approaches hold that it involves insertion of /t/, or, on the yet more abstract underspecification approach, a segment specified only as [consonantal], which has the effect of [t] in coda position. On either approach, the inserted segment would trigger post-obstruent tensification of the initial consonant in the second member of the compound: thus in 술집 'bar' [sulʨip], the underlying representation would be 술=ㅅ+집 *swul=s+cip* 'liquor=s+house', and the inserted segment, /=s/ or a more abstract unspecified consonant, would trigger POT in [sulʨip]. Notice that without an inserted segment, the coda /l/ of 술 *swul* 'liquor' would not trigger POT.

To determine whether the compound marking morpheme actually has the shape /s/, it might seem useful to find compounds of the shape /CV/+/CV/. In fact only compounds formed with 위 *wi* 'upper' or its fossilized shape 우 *wu* < LMK 웋 *wuh* 'upper' show an orthographic /s/ in the /CV/+/CV/ environment, such as 웃알

wu=s+al 'upper=s+bead (upper beads on an abacus)' or 윗입술 *wi=s+ipswul* 'upper=s+lip (upper lip)'. Younger speakers pronounce these as [udal] and [widipsul] or [winnipsul]. These pronunciations therefore do not support realizing the compound marker as /s/.

Sai-sios has properties in common with two compound marking processes in Japanese, *rendaku* "sequential voicing" (11a–d), and the less well studied pattern of geminate insertion (11e–f):

(11)   Japanese rendaku (sequential voicing)
      a. *yama + kawa* 'mountain + river' > *yamagawa* 'mountain river'
      b. *yama + kawa* 'mountain + river' > *yamakawa* 'mountains and rivers'
      c. *ki + tuku* 'mind + attach' > *kiduku* 'notice'
      d. *naki + tuku* 'cry + attach' > *nakituku* 'cling to in tears'
      Japanese geminate insertion in compounds.
      e. *Edo + ko* 'Edo + child' > *Edokko* 'Edo (Tokyo) native'
      f. *oya + ko* 'parent + child' > *oyako* 'parent and child'

The most salient similarity is that all three processes apply in sub-compounds, where the first member is a modifier of the second, but not in coordinate or **dvandva compounds**, where the compound is interpreted as the union of its two members. Thus in Japanese (11a, e), 'mountain' and 'Edo' modify 'river' and 'child' (specifying the type of river or person). In both cases the compound relationship is marked, by voicing of the initial consonant of the second member in (11a), and by gemination of this consonant in (11e). But in the coordinate compounds in (11b, f), voicing and gemination cannot occur.

These processes are thus sensitive to the structure of the compound. The same is true of *sai-sios*, as we see in the compounds in (12) involving noun + 밥 *pap* 'cooked rice'.

(12)   *Sai-sios* in sub-compounds with N + 밥 *pap* 'cooked rice'
      a. 아침밥 *achim* 'morning'+ 밥 *pap* 'cooked rice' > [atɕʰimpap] 'breakfast'
      b. 점심밥 *cemsim* 'noon' + 밥 *pap* 'cooked rice' > [tɕʌmʃimpap] 'breakfast'
      c. 밤밥 *pam* 'night' + 밥 *pap* 'cooked rice' > [pampap] 'evening meal'
      d. 사발밥 *sapal* 'bowl' + 밥 *pap* 'cooked rice' > [sabalpap] 'rice in a bowl'
      e. 비빔밥 *pipim* 'mix' + 밥 *pap* 'cooked rice' > [pibimpap] 'mixed rice dish'
      No *sai-sios* in coordinate compounds with N + 밥 *pap* 'cooked rice'
      f. 밤밥 *pam* 'chestnut' + 밥 *pap* 'cooked rice' > [pambap] 'rice with chestnuts'
      g. 나물밥 *namwul* 'greens' + 밥 *pap* 'cooked rice' > [namulbap] 'rice with greens'
      h. 계란밥 *kyeylan* 'egg' + 밥 *pap* 'cooked rice' > [kjɛranbap] 'rice with egg'

In all three patterns the diachronic source is the phonological effect triggered by an original particle. In Japanese *rendaku* the source was the genitive particle =*no* in nominal sub-compounds like (11a), or the dative/locative particle =*ni* in noun–verb compounds like (11c). The particle underwent syncope (vowel loss), resulting in a prenasalized following consonant; subsequently in standard Japanese, voicing became the distinctive property of prenasalized consonants. In the geminate insertion pattern of (11e), the diachronic source is thought to have been the Old Japanese genitive particle =*tu*; again syncope resulted in a consonant cluster which came to be realized as a geminate.

However the three patterns differ in productivity: (11e) geminate insertion is quite restricted, while *sai-sios* does not apply in many compounds where we would expect it, and is subject to speaker variability. For example, sub-compounds with N + 밭 *path* 'dry field' generally do not trigger *sai-sios*:

(13)   No *sai-sios* in sub-compounds with N + 밭 *path* 'dry field'
     a. 보리밭 *poli* 'barley' + 밭 *path* 'dry field' > [poribat] 'barley field'
     b. 밤밭 *pam* 'chestnut' + 밭 *path* 'dry field' > [pambat] 'chestnut grove'
     c. 사과밭 *sakwa* 'apple' + 밭 *path* 'dry field' > [sagwabat] 'apple orchard'

An example of speaker variability is *sai-sios* in the compound 김밥 *kimpap* 'rice wrapped in dry seaweed (laver)'. Until 2016 the National Institute of Korean Language mandated the pronunciation [kimbap], without *sai-sios*, but in 2016 it recognized the prevalence of the pronunciation with *sai-sios*, [kim-pap], and declared both pronunciations acceptable.

4.2.7   Manner Assimilations

In addition to assimilations with /h/, Korean has manner assimilations triggered by nasals, the coronal fricatives ㅅ /s/ and ㅆ /ş/, and ㄹ /l/.

4.2.7.1   Nasal Assimilation of Coda Obstruents

Coda obstruents assimilate to the following nasal. This is regressive assimilation in manner of articulation because the coda obstruent acquires the manner feature [nasal] from the following nasal stop, as shown in (14):

(14)   Nasal assimilation
     a. 밥만 *pap=man* 'cooked rice=only' [pamman]
     b. 십만 *sip+man* 'ten + ten thousand (100,000)' [ʃimman]
     c. 낱말 *nath+mal* 'unit + speech (word)' [nanmal]
     d. 낮말 *nac+mal* 'daytime + speech (talk in broad daylight)' [nanmal]
     e. 낫는다 *nas-nun-ta* 'recover-PRES-PLN' [nannunda]
     f. 먹는다 *mek-nun-ta* 'eat-PRES-PLN' [mʌŋnunda]
     g. 백만 *payk+man* 'hundred + ten thousand (1,000,000)' [peŋman]

4.2.7.2   Assibilation

Coronal coda obstruents assimilate to following ㅅ /s/ and ㅆ /ş/. Although the conditions for assibilation – regressive assimilation of coda coronal obstruents – are similar to the coda coronal assimilation we saw in Section 4.2.4.1, the latter involved assimilation in place of articulation while assibilation involves assimilation in manner of articulation, as shown in (15):

(15)   Assibilation of coda coronal obstruents
          a. 뱃살 *pay=s+sal* 'belly flesh' [pesṣal]
          b. 빛살 *pich+sal* 'light + arrow (rays of light)' [pisṣal]
          c. 곧습니다 *kot-supni-ta* 'straight-DEF-PLN' [kosṣumnida]

4.2.7.3 Palatalization   Palatalization before a high front vowel /i/, /y/, or glide /j/ is often treated as assimilation, although choice of the assimilating feature is not always straightforward. Palatalization in Korean has two sub-types. Palatalization of the coronal fricatives ㅅ /s/ and ㅆ /ṣ/ to [ʃ] and [ʃ], and the coronal nasal /n/ to [ɲ] before /i/, /j/, and /y/, for older speakers who have this vowel, occurs unconditionally, regardless of morphophonemic environment. This is usually regarded as a low-level phonetic process, whose output does not feed other phonological processes. Examples are given in (16):

(16)   Palatalization of ㅅ /s/, ㅆ /ṣ/, and ㄴ /n/
          a. 맛이 *mas=i* 'taste=NOM' [maʃi]
          b. 아가씨 *akassi* 'young lady' [agaʃi]
          c. 계셨다 *kyeysi-ess-ta* 'be.HON-PAST-PLN' > contracted *kyeysy-ess-ta*
             [kjeʃjʌta]
          d. 이년 *i nyen* 'two years' [i ɲjʌn]
          e. 언니 *enni* 'self's older sister (said by a female)' [ʌɲɲi]

In contrast, palatalization of /t/, /t̯/, and /teʰ/ to [tɕ], [tɕ], and [teʰ] does not occur word-internally (17), but only across a morpheme boundary (18).

(17)   Nonpalatalization of coronal stops word-internally
          a. 어디 *eti* 'where' [ʌdi]
          b. 띠 *tti* 'girdle, long narrow strip' [t̯i]
          c. 티 *thi* 'fault' [tʰi]

(18)   Palatalization of coronal stops across morphological boundaries
          a. 밭이다 *path-i-ta* 'filter-PASS-PLN (be filtered)' [patɕʰida]
          b. 밭이다 *path-i-ta* 'field-COPULA-PLN (It is a field)' [patɕʰida]
          c. 밭이 *path=i* 'field=NOM' [patɕʰi]

In (18), palatalization of /tʰ/ to [tɕʰ] crosses derivational suffix and clitic boundaries with the copula and nominative particle. The historical background for the conditions on coronal stop palatalization is that in LMK a very general rule of palatalization eliminated all cases of word-internal /ti/, /t̯i/, and /tʰi/. Words such as 디나다 *tinata* 'pass through', *ptita* 'steam (something)', 티다 *thita* 'hit, strike', and 뎔 *tyel* 'temple' were reanalyzed as 지나다 *cinata*, 찌다*ccita*, 치다*chita*, and 절*cel* respectively. Modern instances of coronal stop + /i/ descend

from LMK coronal stop + diphthong of the shape /uy/ or /oy/, where the
diphthong has monophthongized subsequent to LMK. Examples are in (19):

(19)   Sources of Modern Korean 디 /ti/, 띠 /ti̠/, and 티 /tʰi/
      a. LMK 어듸 *etuy* > 어디 *eti* 'where' [ʌdi]
      b. LMK ㅅ듸 *stuy* > 띠 *tti* 'girdle, long narrow strip' [ti̠]
      c. LMK 틔 *thuy* > 티 *thi* 'fault' [tʰi]

The unconditioned LMK process of coronal stop palatalization was probably
identical to the modern unconditioned process of coronal fricative palatalization in (16). But since word-internal coronal stop palatalization triggered
merger with the affricates /tɕ/, /t̠ɕ/, and /tɕʰ/, the phonological domain for the
process was eliminated word-internally. By the time the new stop + /i/
sequences were generated by the monophthongizations in (19), speakers had
learned to apply coronal stop palatalization only at morpheme boundaries.
Coronal fricative palatalization, in contrast, produced the allophones [ʃ] and
[ʃ̬], not a merger. It therefore remained stable in all environments.

4.2.7.4 L-Assimilation   When /n/ and /l/ are adjacent, /n/ assimilates to /l/
whether it precedes or follows.

(20)   L-assimilation
      a. 전라 *Cenla* 'Chŏlla (province)' [tɕʌlla]
      b. 월남 *Welnam* 'Vietnam' [wʌllam]
      c. 만리 *man li* '10,000 miles' [malli]
      d. 팔년 *phal nyen* 'eight years' [pʰalljʌn]
      e. 한글날 *hankul nal* 'Hangul Day' [haŋgɯllal]
      f. 잘 났다 *cal na-ss-ta* 'well go.out-PAST-PLN (It turned out well)' [tɕallata]

Examples like (20a) and (20b) show l-assimilation applying word-internally.
Both are internal to Sino-Korean words, where Hangul spelling (and Yale
Romanization) represent the standard spellings of the individual Chinese
characters. The status of these representations in individual speaker's lexicons –
whether contemporary speakers truly store representations corresponding to
the pronunciations of individual Chinese characters – is open to question. The
examples in (20c–d) are SK number expressions, where a morphological
boundary between the initial numeral component and the following unit component is well motivated. Compounds such as (20e) and word boundary
contexts such as (20f) are hard to exemplify for the /n ... l/ sequence, due to
the paucity of l-initial words in the native, and in South Korea the SK, stratum.
The word 연록 *yenlok* 'soft green' (軟綠) is pronounced [jʌllok] due to word-
internal l-assimilation on the pattern of (20a), but the official ROK Hangul
spelling for 연녹색 *yennoksayk* 'soft green color' (軟綠色) mandates l-assimilation to /n/ [jʌnnoksek]. This is because the structure of the compound is

interpreted as (soft [green color]), where 'green color' is realized as [noksek].
In fact, speakers produce both [jʌnnoksek] and [jʌlloksek].

4.2.8   /n/-Insertion

In Section 4.2.6, we saw that younger speakers may pronounce the compound
윗입술 *wi=s+ipswul* 'upper=s+lip (upper lip)' as [winnipsul]. This shows us
that, in addition to *sai-sios*, speakers insert an /n/ at the beginning of words such
as 입술 *ipswul* 'lips' in such an environment. The *sai-sios* segment then
undergoes nasal assimilation to this /n/. The environment for /n/-insertion is
before /i/ or /j/ after a morpheme boundary.

(21)　　/n/-insertion
　　　a. 꽃잎 *kkoch+iph* 'flower+petal' [k̚onnip]
　　　b. 콩엿 *khong+yes* 'bean+jelly' [kʰoŋɲjʌt]
　　　c. 신여성 *sin+yeseng* 'new+female' [ʃinɲjʌsʌŋ]
　　　d. 색연필 *sayk+yenphil* 'color+pencil' [seŋɲjʌnpʰil]
　　　e. 한여름 *han+yelum* 'one summer' [hanɲjʌɾɯm]
　　　f. 남녀 *nam+nye* 'man+woman' [namɲjʌ]

Nasal insertion occurs in both native (21a, b, e) and Sino-Korean (21c, d, f) words.
The native word 잎 *iph* 'leaf' and the SK morpheme 여 *ye* in (21a) and (21c)
originally had initial /n/, 닢 *niph* and 녀 *nye*, but 엿 *yes* 'jelly' and 연필 *yenphil*
'pencil' did not. Around the eighteenth century, particularly in varieties from Seoul
to the south, /n/ came to be dropped in initial position before the coronal nonconso-
nantal segments /i/ and /j/. This in turn was reinterpreted as a morphophonemic
phenomenon: no /n/ before /i/ and /j/ phrase-initially, /n/ before these segments
phrase-internally. This is a classic case of **rule inversion**, similar to the phenomenon of /r/-insertion in nonrhotic (/r/ dropping) varieties of English (22):

(22)　　/r/-insertion in nonrhotic English
　　　a. *sister#* [sɪstə]　　　*sister is* [sɪstərɪz]
　　　b. *algebra#* [ældʒəbrə]　*algebra is* [ældʒəbrərɪz]

English /r/-dropping varieties omit /r/ in phrase-final position, but retain it before
another word as in (22a). Some of these varieties also "invert" this process, to insert
an /r/ after certain vowels where none existed historically, as in (22b), just like
Korean varieties that insert /n/ where none existed historically. Rule inversion seems
paradoxical, and sometimes it has been interpreted as hypercorrection,
a sociolinguistic phenomenon where speakers (perhaps of a non–/n/-deleting variety) hear a phrase such as 콩엿 *khong+yes* 'bean+jelly' pronounced as [kʰoŋjʌt],
without the inserted /n/, and compensate for what "sounds like" an instance of /n/
dropping by inserting an /n/. Whether the hypercorrection scenario is correct or not,
such cases can be understood as generalizing the marking of a morphophonemic

environment such as Korean /i/ or /j/ after a boundary internal to a phrase, or nonrhotic English /ə/ before such a boundary followed by another vowel.

4.2.9   Coda Cluster Reduction

Korean disallows consonant clusters to be realized either at the beginning or end of syllables. We saw in Chapter 2 that earlier Korean had onset (syllable-initial) consonant clusters, but these were eliminated, giving rise to initial tense consonants. There are a few fossilized remnants of onset clusters. For example, the word 좁쌀 copssal 'hulled millet' originated as a compound of 조 co 'millet' and psal 'cooked grain'. In modern Korean, initial /p/ has been resyllabified as the coda of the first syllable, and the following /s/ undergoes post-obstruent tensification.

The main reason examples like this are hard to find is that Korean does not have regular morphological processes involving prefixation. As we see in Chapter 5, suffixation is the main strategy for inflection and derivation in Korean, and many suffixes have vowel-initial allomorphs when they follow a stem ending in a consonant. The result is that speakers are exposed to alternations like the following.

(23)   Coda consonant cluster reduction

In coda position	**Resyllabified as onset**
a. 값 kaps 'price' [kap]	값을 kaps=ul 'price=ACC' [kapsɯl], [kabɯl]
b. 없다 eps-ta 'not.exist-PLN' [ʌpt̚a]	없을 eps-ul 'not.exist-FUTADN' [ʌpsɯl]
c. 앉다 anc-ta 'sit-PLN' [ant̚a]	앉아 anc-a 'sit-INF' [andʑa]
d. 많다 manh-ta 'many-PLN' [mantʰa]	많아 manh-a 'many-INF' [mana]
e. 여덟 yetelp 'eight' [jʌdʌl]	여덟은 yetelp=un 'eight=TOP' [jʌdʌlpɯn], [jʌdʌlɯn]
f. 밟다 palp-ta 'tread-PLN' [papt̚a]	밟은 palp-un 'tread-PSTADN' [palbun]
g. 삶 salm 'life' [sam]	삶이 salm=i 'life=NOM' [salmi]
h. 외곬 oykols 'single-minded' [wegol]	외곬은 oykols=un 'single-minded=TOP' [wegolsɯn]
i. 맑다 malk-ta 'clear-PLN' [makt̚a]	맑은 malk-un 'clear-ADN' [malgɯn]
j. 옳다 olh-ta 'correct-PLN' [oltʰa]	옳은 olh-un 'correct-ADN' [orɯn]
k. 읊다 ulphta 'recite-PLN' [ɯpt̚a]	읊은 ulph-un 'recite-PSTADN' [ɯlpʰun]
l. 핥다 halth-ta 'lick-PLN' [halt̚a]	핥아 halth-a 'lick-INF' [haltʰa]
m. 넋 neks 'soul' [nʌk]	넋은 neks=un 'soul=TOP' [nʌksɯn]

In all, Korean has eleven underlying coda consonant clusters (23): /ps/ (23a, b), /nc/ (23c), /nh/ (23d), /lp/ (23e, f), /lm/ (23g), /ls/ (23h), /lk/ (23i), /lh/ (23j), /lpʰ/ (23k), /ltʰ/ (23l), and /ks/ (23m). Some linguists would include a twelfth cluster, /mh/, based on the compound form of the prefix 암 *am* 'female'. This is one of the small number of nouns with final /h/ in Late Middle Korean that we commented on in 4.2.2. Others include 수 *swu* 'male' and 안 *an* 'interior'. Because they could function as independent nouns in LMK, the final /h/ surfaced when followed by a clitic, such as 암히 *amh=i* 'female=NOM' and 수흘 *swuh=ul* 'male=ACC'. In contemporary Korean, however, the /h/ is reflected only as aspiration of the initial consonant of the second member of compounds such as 암퇘지 *am+thwayci* 'sow, female pig' [amtʰwedʑi] and 수캉아지 *swu+khangaci* 'male puppy' [sukʰaŋgadʑi]. Current orthographic practice in the ROK mandates spelling the aspiration, which reflects the fact that these are lexicalized compounds rather than the result of an automatic morphophonemic alternation. Therefore we exclude /mh/ as a synchronic underlying cluster.

In terms of how they are reduced in coda position, the clusters can be grouped as in (24) in standard pronunciation.

(24)   Patterns of coda consonant cluster reduction (before a following consonant)

Group 1   **First consonant deleted**

/lm/   삶도 *salm=to* 'life=also' [samdo]

/lk/   맑다 *malk-ta* 'clear-PLN' [makṭa]

/lpʰ/   읊다 *ulph-ta* 'recite-PLN' [ɯpṭa]

               밟다 *palp-ta* 'tread-PLN' [papṭa]

Group 2   **Second consonant deleted**

/ps/   값도 *kaps=to* 'price=also' [kapṭo]

               없다 *eps-ta* 'not.exist-PLN' [ʌpṭa]

/lp/   여덟도 *yetelp=to* 'eight=also' [jʌdʌlṭo]

/ltʰ/   핥다 *halth-ta* 'lick-PLN' [halṭa]

/ls/   외곬도 *oykols=to* 'single-minded=also' [wegolṭo]

/nc/   앉다 *anc-ta* 'sit-PLN' [anṭa]

/ks/   넋도 *nek =to* 'soul=also' [nʌkṭo]

Group 3   **Coda /h/ surfaces as aspiration on following consonant**

/nh/   많다 *manh-ta* 'many-PLN' [mantʰa]

/lh/   옳다 *olh-ta* 'correct-PLN' [oltʰa]

As stated by Yu Cho (2015), the basic generalization is that the second consonant is deleted unless it is a non-coronal: the /p/, /pʰ/, /m/, and /k/ in Group 1 of (24). However this generalization fails to account for differences between the noun and verb stems: although /p/, the second, non-coronal consonant, survives in verb stems like 밟다 *palp-ta* 'tread-PLN' [papṭa], it is deleted in the noun stem 여덟도 *yetelp=to* 'eight=also' [jʌdʌlṭo]. As indicated in (23), nouns followed by a postposition like 값을 *kaps=ul* 'price=ACC' have, in addition to the prescribed standard form [kapsɯl], a common realization as [kabɯl]; likewise, some speakers accept [wegoldo] as the pronunciation of 외곬도 *oykols=to* 'single-minded=also' in Group 2 of (24). These pronunciations are what we would expect if the boundary between the noun and the postposition had the status of a word boundary, and the cluster reduced before the particle is attached. They are impossible with verb stems. In Chapter 5 we suggest that they are possible with nouns because postnominal particles have the status of clitics rather than suffixes.

4.3   Prosody and Suprasegmental Phenomena

Up until now we have focused on phonological units and processes at the segmental level. In this section, we describe larger units of sound.

4.3.1   Syllable Structure

We have seen that Korean allows at most one [consonantal] segment in onset (syllable-initial) and coda (syllable-final) position. Thus the syllable template of Korean is as in (25):

(25)   Korean syllable structure
         (C) (G) V (C)

C represents consonants, G the glides /j/ and /w/, and V a vowel, the minimal unit of the syllable; the units in parentheses are optionally present. This template mandates that clusters of more than one consonant must be resyllabified (adjusted to become part of the adjacent syllable), or eliminated, as we saw in Section 4.2. Thus the noun stem 넋 *neks* 'soul' is realized as [nʌk.], with the coda consonant cluster simplified to a single consonant, or if it is followed by a vowel-initial particle such as 넋이 *neks=i* 'soul=NOM', it is realized as [nʌk. ʃi], with coda /s/ resyllabified as the onset of the second syllable. Note that modern Hangul spelling does not represent syllable structure, although we saw in Chapter 3 that fifteenth-century spelling for the most part did. Examples of each syllable type are given in (26).

(26)   Sample syllable types
         V   이 *i* /i/ 'tooth'
         GV   위 *wi* /wi/ 'up, top'
         VC   일 *il* /il/ 'work, matter'
         CV   비 *pi* /pi/ 'rain'
         GVC   옆 *yeph* /jʌpʰ/ 'side'
         CGV   뼈 *ppye* /pjʌ/ 'bone'
         CVC   밥 *pap* /pap/ 'cooked grain'
         CGVC   별 *pyel* /pjʌl/ 'star'

Dictionaries and many linguistic descriptions make a further distinction in relation to syllable structure: they distinguish long vowels in words like 일: *il:* /i:l/ 'work, matter' and 이: *i:* /i:/ 'louse', in distinction to the short vowel in 이 *i* /i/ 'tooth'. This vowel length is the last remaining reflex in South Korea of the pitch-accent system of Late Middle Korean described in Chapter 2. The length marked on the vowels in 일: *il:* /i:l/ 'work, matter' and 이: *i:* /i:/ 'louse' is for the most part a reflex of their realization in LMK: thus LMK :일 /il/ 'work, matter' was marked with two dots to the left of the syllable, indicating a rising, and probably long tone (marked in YR by a caron or wedge above the vowel /ĭ/). However, although dictionaries mark length and it is still (to a decreasing extent) taught in schools, it has ceased to be distinctive in the speech of Seoul speakers.

We have already seen in this chapter that syllable structure governs the realization of underlying phones in Korean; for example we saw that ㄹ /l/ is pronounced as lateral [l] in coda position but as an alveolar flap [ɾ] in syllable onset position. Korean follows a common crosslinguistic tendency to maximize onsets. Thus a word such as 허리 *heli* 'waist, haunches' is syllabified as /hʌ.li/ (CV.CV) and pronounced [hʌ.ɾi], rather than being syllabified as CVC.V, which would result in the pronunciation *[hʌl.i]. Similarly, the constraint mandating that consonants be pronounced wherever possible as onsets ensures that the second consonant in coda clusters is resyllabified as the onset of a following syllable wherever possible, as we saw in (23), e.g. 앉다 *anc-ta* 'sit-PLN' [an.ṭa] but 앉아 *anc-a* 'sit-INF' [an.dʑa].

4.3.2   Prosodic Structure above the Syllable

Syllables are conventionally arranged into words, but as we see in Chapter 5, the status of the word in Korean is not straightforward. Most speakers share the intuition that an inflected verb such as 있겠다 *iss-keyss-ta* 'exist-FUT-PLN' is one word made up of three morphemes, the smallest meaningful unit of language. In Korean, this intuition is perhaps made more solid by the fact that the verb stem *iss-* cannot be pronounced by itself as a word, nor can the Future suffix *-keyss-* nor the Plain suffix *-ta*. These units must be combined to be pronounced. But what about the sequence 올 수가 *o-l swu=ka* 'come-FUTADN possibility=NOM' in (27)?

(27)   올 수가 있겠다.
       O-l   *swu=ka*   *iss-keyss-ta*
       come-FUTADN possibility=NOM exist-FUT-PLN
       'She/he will probably be able to come.'

Speakers may also have the intuition that 올 수가 *o-l swu=ka* is also some kind of unit, but it is difficult to call it a word. For one thing, the verb 오 *o-* 'come' takes the future adnominal suffix -ㄹ -*l* before *swu* 'possibility'. As its label suggests, adnominal suffixes usually precede nouns, and nouns are usually words. In Chapter 5 we clarify that *swu* belongs to the class of bound nouns in Korean, nouns that cannot stand alone but must be preceded by some element. And then what about the nominative (subject-marking) particle =*ka*? Again, postnominal particles cannot stand alone, but must follow a noun or other material bound to the noun. Some linguists take the position that postnominal particles are suffixes, just like the plain-speech suffix -*ta* in (27), but in Chapter 5 we advance the hypothesis that they are clitics, elements dependent on a host as suffixes are, but allowing freer and looser possibilities for attachment. In any case, the intuition remains that 올 수가 *o-l swu=ka* is some kind of unit.

Linguists classify units like 올 수가 *o-l swu=ka* as **phonological words**. From this standpoint, (27) is made up of two phonological words, as shown in (28):

(28)　올 수가 있겠다.

　　　[*O-l*　　　　*swu=ka*]ₒ　　　[*iss-keyss-ta*]ₒ
　　　come-FUTADN possibility=NOM exist-FUT-PLN
　　　'She/he will probably be able to come.'

Note that phonological words do not necessarily correspond to syntactic units. Korean has at least two larger units of prosodic structure. If we add the word 내일 *nayil* 'tomorrow' to the sentence in (27), we notice that we can group the phonological words in different ways (29).

(29)　a.　내일 올 수가 있겠다.
　　　　　[[*Nayil*]ₒ] [[*o-l*　　　　*swu=ka*]ₒ]　　　[[*iss-keyss-ta*]ₒ]
　　　　　tomorrow come-FUTADN possibility=NOM exist-FUT-PLN
　　　　　'She/he will probably be able to come tomorrow.'
　　　b.　내일 올 수가 있겠다.
　　　　　[[*Nayil*]ₒ [*o-l*　　　　*swu=ka*]ₒ]　　　[[*iss-keyss-ta*] ₒ]
　　　　　tomorrow come-FUTADN possibility=NOM exist-FUT-PLN
　　　　　'She/he will probably be able to come tomorrow.'
　　　c.　내일 올 수가 있겠다.
　　　　　[[*Nayil*]ₒ] [[*o-l*　　　　*swu=ka*]ₒ　　　[*iss-keyss-ta*] ₒ]
　　　　　tomorrow come-FUTADN possibility=NOM exist-FUT-PLN
　　　　　'She/he will probably be able to come tomorrow.'

The brackets outside the phonological words correspond to **phonological phrases**. Intuitively, we might say that phonological phrases are demarcated by intonation, but that means something somewhat different in Korean and in English. In Seoul Korean, phonological phrases are marked by pitch (technically, the *f*0 or funda-mental frequency of the phrase). The most basic pitch pattern in Seoul Korean is low – high ... low – high, which we will indicate as the "melody" LHLH. If we group the phonological phrases as in (29a), where each phonological word corresponds to a phonological phrase, the pitch pattern is as in (30):

(30)   내일 올 수가 있겠다.
        L H   L   H L/H   L H L
        [[*Nayil*] ω] [[*o-l*   *swu=ka*]ω]   [[*iss-keyss-ta*] ω]
        tomorrow   come-FUTADN possibility=NOM exist-FUT-PLN
        'She/he will probably be able to come tomorrow.'

In short phonological phrases like (29), the pitch after the first syllable (which will always begin low) is variable, but in longer phrases a pattern emerges. We see this in the pitch patterns for (29b) and (29c):

(31)   a.   내일 올 수가 있겠다.
              L H   H   L H   L H L
              [[*Nayil*] ω [*o-l*   *swu=ka*]ω]   [[*iss-keyss-ta*] ω]
              tomorrow come-FUTADN possibility=NOM exist-FUT-PLN
              'She/he will probably be able to come tomorrow.'
        b.   내일 올 수가 있겠다.
              L H   L   H H   H L H
              [[*Nayil*] ω] [[*o-l*   *swu=ka*]ω   [*iss-keyss-ta*] ω]
              tomorrow come-FUTADN possibility=NOM exist-FUT-PLN
              'She/he will probably be able to come tomorrow.'

In (31a), the phonological words that are grouped together in a single phonological phrase form a unit that begins low and ends with low pitch on the second or penultimate syllable before the end of the phrase.

In contemporary Seoul Korean, the LH ... LH pattern coexists with another pattern, depending on the initial consonant of the phrase. If the initial consonant is aspirated or reinforced or is a fricative, the pitch pattern is H ... HLH. We can see this in (32), where the verb has been changed to 할 *ha-l* 'do-FUTADN', beginning with the glottal fricative /h/.

(32)   내일 할 수가 있겠다.
        L H   H   H H   H L H
        [[*Nayil*] ω] [[*ha-l*   *swu=ka*]ω   [*iss-keyss-ta*] ω]
        tomorrow   do-FUTADN possibility=NOM exist-FUT-PLN
        'She/he will probably be able to do it tomorrow.'

4.4   Phonological Changes in Progress

Since the invention of Hangul in the fifteenth century, Korean has been one of the best attested languages in the world from a phonological point of view (although attestation between the sixteenth and nineteenth century is less thorough than before and after those centuries). We have seen that the sound pattern of Korean has changed remarkably during that time, losing onset consonant clusters and retaining coda clusters only at the underlying level, losing pitch accent in Seoul and other varieties, and almost entirely losing the tongue-root harmony system that was active in the language of the fifteenth century.

Many linguists have noticed that Korean continues to be a language in the midst of active phonological change. In this section, we comment briefly on some of the most salient changes in progress.

4.4.1   Tonogenesis

In Section 4.3.2, we observed that Seoul Korean has two basic pitch patterns, one for phonological phrases beginning with tense and aspirated consonants and all fricatives, and another for phrases beginning with all other segments. Phrases of the first type begin with high pitch, while phrases of the second type begin with low pitch. Recent research beginning with Silva (2006) has shown that, for younger speakers, the difference in pitch or $f0$ has become the primary cue for distinguishing plain and aspirated consonants in initial position. For such speakers, the degree of aspiration in initial position, indicated by VOT lag, has become essentially identical for plain and aspirated obstruents. They distinguish initial plain and aspirated obstruents instead by the $f0$ of the following vowel: $f0$ is lower after plain obstruents, and higher after aspirated ones. In medial position, the two are distinguished by whether voicing takes place or not: plain obstruents voice, aspirated ones do not. Pitch is not relevant for distinguishing tense consonants from the other two series: they remain distinguished by having the shortest VOT in initial position.

The term "tonogenesis" suggests that Korean is becoming a tone language. The relation between laryngeal features of consonants and pitch is well known, as in languages such as Chinese and Vietnamese where the distinction between voiced and voiceless consonants has been lost in favor of a tonal contrast; simplifying, original voiced obstruent onsets become associated with lower pitched syllables.

However a simple analogy with the kind of tonogenesis found in Southeast Asian languages and Chinese is misleading. As we saw in Section 4.3.2, Korean has the characteristics of a pitch-accent or word-tone language: words (more exactly, phonological phrases) are associated with a distinctive melody. The pitch properties of aspirated, tense, and fricative onsets have given rise to two melodies, and in minimal pairs such as LHLH 발으로도 *pal=u-lo=to* 'leg-with-also' versus HHLH 팔으로도 *pal=ulo=to* 'arm-with-also', pitch has become the cue that distinguishes the two phrases, rather than aspiration. Although the phrase is unwieldy, this change in progress might better be termed "accentogenesis."

4.4.2   Reduction of the Vowel System

We took the view in Section 4.1.2 that contemporary Seoul Korean has a seven vowel system. Research such as Silva (2006) indicates that the merger of the two non-high front vowels /e/ and /ɛ/ in Seoul Korean is essentially complete. Other varieties appear to be pursuing further reduction of the vowel system; for example, Kyŏngsang varieties typically merge /ʌ/ and /ɯ/.

4.4.3   Denasalization

One of the most remarkable changes in progress in contemporary Korean is denasalization of initial /m/ and /n/. To speakers of a language with a voicing contrast among onset consonants, words like 말 *mal* 'speech' and 나 *na* 'first person' in initial position can sound like [bal] and [da].

This change has in fact been observed for almost a century. The eminent British phonetician Daniel Jones first observed the existence of what he transcribed as [nd] and [mb] in Korean in 1924. The segmental and prosodic environments for denasalization have yet to be carefully described, but we know that it applies only to initial /m/ and /n/, not to nasals in medial or final position.

4.5   Summary

In this chapter, we have described the salient properties of the Korean phonemic inventory, focusing on issues of general linguistic interest such as the nature of the laryngeal contrasts in Korean obstruents. We also presented the main sound alternations in Korean. We described the organization of phonological units at the syllable level and above, and touched briefly on the main phonological changes in progress.

Further Readings

Choo, Miho and William O'Grady. 2003. *The Sounds of Korean*. Honolulu: University of Hawai'i Press.

Jun, Sun-Ah. 1996. *The Phonetics and Phonology of Korean Prosody: Intonational Phonology and Prosodic Structure*. New York: Garland.

Shin, Jiyoung, Jieun Kiaer, and Jaeun Cha. 2013. *The Sounds of Korean*. Cambridge: Cambridge University Press.

References

Ahn, Sang-Cheol and Gregory Iverson. 2004. Dimensions in Korean laryngeal phonology. *Journal of East Asian Linguistics* 13 (4), 345–379.

Brunelle, Marc. 2010. The role of larynx height in the Javanese tense~lax contrast. In Raphael Mercado, Eric Potsdam, and Lisa de Mena Travis (eds.), *Austronesian and Theoretical Linguistics*, 7–23. Amsterdam: John Benjamins.

Cho, Taehong, Sun-Ah Jun, and Peter Ladefoged. 2002. Acoustic and aerodynamic correlates of Korean stops and fricatives. *Journal of Phonetics* 30, 193–228.

Dryer, Matthew and Martin Haspelmath. 2013. *World Atlas of Linguistic Structures Online*.

Halle, Morris and Ken Stevens. 1971. A note on laryngeal features. Quarterly Progress Report no. 101, Research Laboratory of Electronics, Massachusetts Institute of Technology, 198–212.

Han, Jeong-Im. 1996. The phonetics and phonology of "tense" and "plain" consonants in Korean. Unpublished Ph.D. dissertation, Cornell University.

Iverson, Gregory and Kee-Ho Kim. 1987. Underspecification and hierarchical feature representation in Korean consonantal phonology. *Papers from the Annual Regional Meeting, Chicago Linguistic Society* 23(2). 182–198.

Jun, Jongho. 1994. Metrical weight consistency in Korean partial reduplication. *Phonology* 11, 69–88.

Jun, Sun-Ah. 1993. The Phonetics and Phonology of Korean Prosody. Unpublished Ph.D. dissertation, Ohio State University.

Kim, Hyunsoon. 1999. The place of articulation of Korean revisited. *Journal of East Asian Linguistics* 8, 313–347.

Kim, Hyunsoon. 2005. The representation of the three-way laryngeal contrast in Korean consonants. In M. van Oostendorp and J. van de Weijer (eds.), *The Internal Organization of Phonological Segments*, 287–315. Berlin: Mouton de Gruyter.

Kim, Hyunsoon, K. Honda, and S. Maeda. 2005. Stroboscopic-cine MRI study of the phasing between the tongue and the larynx in the Korean three-way phonation contrast. *Journal of Phonetics* 33, 1–26.

Kim, Mi-Ryoung and Duanmu San. 2004. "Tense" and "lax" stops in Korean. *Journal of East Asian Linguistics* 13 (1), 59–104.

Kim-Renaud, Young-Key. 1974. Korean consonantal phonology. Unpublished Ph.D. dissertation, University of Hawai'i.

Ladefoged, Peter and Ian Maddieson. 1996. *The Sounds of the World's Languages*. Oxford and Cambridge, MA: Blackwell.

Lombardi, Lisa. 1991. Laryngeal features and laryngeal neutralization. Unpublished Ph.D. dissertation, University of Massachusetts.

Martin, Samuel E. 1951. Korean phonemics. *Language* 27, 511–533.

Martin, Samuel E. 1954. *Korean Morphophonemics*. Baltimore: Linguistic Society of America.

Schertz, Jessamyn, Yoonjung Kang, Alexei Kochetov, Eunjong Kong, and Sungwoo Ha. 2014. Dialectal variability in place and manner of Korean affricates. In the Scottish Consortium for ICPhS 2015 (ed.), Proceedings of the 18th International Congress of Phonetic Sciences. Glasgow, UK: University of Glasgow. Retrieved from https://bit.ly/2S4NSN6.

Shin, Jiyoung. 2015. Vowels and consonants. In Lucien Brown and Jaehoon Yeon (eds.), *The Handbook of Korean Linguistics*, 3–21. Oxford: Wiley-Blackwell.

Silva, David J. 1992. The phonetics and phonology of stop lenition in Korean. Unpublished Ph.D. dissertation, Cornell University.

Silva, D. J. (2006). Acoustic evidence for the emergence of tonal contrast in contemporary Korean. *Phonology* 23 (2), 287–308.

Tak, Jin-Young and Stuart Davis. 1994. A reanalysis of Korean tense consonants. In Katharine Beals (ed.), *Papers from the 30th Regional Meeting of the Chicago Linguistic Society, 1994: The Main Session*, 405–417. Chicago: Chicago Linguistic Society.

Yu Cho, Young-mee. 2011. Laryngeal contrast in Korean. In Marc van Oostendorp, Colin Ewen, Elizabeth Hume, and Keren Rice (eds.), *The Blackwell Companion to Phonology*, 2662–2684. Malden, MA: Wiley-Blackwell.

Yu Cho, Young-mee. 2015. Syllable-based phonological processes. In Lucien Brown and Jaehoon Yoon (eds.), *The Handbook of Korean Linguistics*, 22–40. Oxford: Wiley-Blackwell.

Yu Cho, Young-mee. 2016-10-26. Korean Phonetics and Phonology. In Oxford Research Encyclopedia of Linguistics. Retrieved April 15, 2018, from https://bit.ly /2UXoWJy.

5   Morphology

Morphology is the study of word formation. It is important to understand how words are formed in heavily morphology-driven languages such as Korean. The morpheme is the minimal meaningful unit as in *boy* or *girl,* which consist of one morpheme each. Once we add the plural morpheme, the resultant word will consist of two morphemes: *boy-s, girl-s.* These examples involve two types of morphemes, bound and free. *Boy* is a free morpheme, because it can stand by itself, while *-s* is a bound morpheme, because it cannot stand alone.

Affixes are bound morphemes that are attached before a free morpheme as a prefix, after a free morpheme as a suffix or within a free/bound morpheme as an infix. In *unhappiness,* the free morpheme is *happy, un-* is a negative prefix attached before free morpheme and *-ness* is a suffix which turns adjectives into nouns. Derivational affixes such as *-ness* change the category of a word. In contrast, the past tense suffix *-ed* and the plural suffix *-s* in *Alex treat-ed girl-s* are inflectional suffixes, because they do not change the grammatical category of the word.

This chapter discusses Korean morphology, insofar as possible apart from syntax, while Chapter 6 investigates the interaction of morphology and syntax, focusing on noun phrases. Taking as our point of departure the work of Korean grammarians, we discuss morpheme classes using the so-called 구품사 *ku phumsa* 'nine parts of speech' system in this section, although no theoretical claim is intended by this and some of our generalizations depart from those made by Korean grammarians. In Section 5.2, we describe irregular predicates. In Sections 5.3 and 5.4, we discuss derivational and inflectional morphology respectively. In Section 5.5, we discuss compounding. In Sections 5.6 and 5.7, we discuss postnominal particles and provide evidence that they are clitics, contrasting them with affixes and independent words. Section 5.8 summarizes this chapter.

The examples in (1) exemplify the major part of speech classes in Korean (= marks postnominal particles, – marks verbal suffixes, and + marks compounds).

(1) a. 나는   학교에서   열심히   수학공부를
      Na=nun hakkyo=eyse yelsimhi   swuhak+kongpwu=lul
      I=TOP   school=at   diligently math study=ACC
      하고 있었어요.
      ha-ko-iss-ess-eyo.
      do-PROG-PAST-POL
      'I was diligently studying math at school.'

    b. 철수는   주말마다   강남에서   친구들하고
      Chelswu=nun cwumal mata   Kangnam=eyse chinkwu=tul=hako
      Chelswu=TOP weekend every Kangnam=at   friend=PL=with
      놀았어요.
      nol-ass-e-yo.
      play-PAST-INF-POL
      'Chelswu played at Kangnam with his friends every weekend.'

In (1), the personal pronoun *na,* the nouns *hakkyo, swuhak, cwumal,* and *chinkwu,* and the proper name *Chelswu* exemplify the class of substantives (Korean 체언 *cheyen*). The lexical verbs *ha-, nol-* and the auxiliary verb *iss-* exemplify the class of inflecting stems (Korean 용언 *yongen*). Korean traditional grammarians noticed the defining property of verbs and adjectives in Korean: although in semantic terms, they are content morphemes, with independent meanings denoting events or states, in morphological terms, they are bound forms, which cannot be pronounced alone without an inflectional suffix following the stem. This contrasts with many languages in Northeast Asia where unaffixed verb stems may surface uninflected, typically as imperatives. The topic marker *=nun,* the locative particle *=eyse,* and the object or accusative marker *=lul* exemplify the class of particles (조사 *cosa*). We mark postnominal particles with = to indicate that they are enclitic to the preceding word. Adverbs (부사 *pwusa*) are represented by *yelsimhi,* which like its English counterpart *diligent-ly* is bimorphemic, made up of an adjectival stem and the adverbial suffix *-hi.* (We mark derivational morpheme boundaries only when it is relevant to the point at hand; were we to mark the internal structure of the adverb, it would be *yelsim-hi.*) The object + verbal noun compound *swuhak+kongpwu* illustrates one kind of compounding in Korean. The verbal suffixes (어미 *emi*) - *ko, -iss, -e* and *-yo* are inflectional affixes. With these two examples, we can see how verbal inflection and postnominal particles contribute to the rich agglutinative character of Korean.

5.1   Morphological Types and Properties

5.1.1   Substantives

The basic category of substantives includes nouns, pronouns, and numerals.

(2)   Substantives (체언 *cheyen*)
        Nouns (명사 *myengsa*)
        Pronouns (대명사 *taymyengsa*)
        Numerals (수사 *swusa*)

Nouns may be quantified by numerals or quantifiers such as *motwu* 'all', and can function as main clause predicates preceding the copula *i*-. Korean lacks some of the standard distributional tests for distinguishing subclasses of nouns such as definite and indefinite articles and obligatory plural markings, but it is possible to distinguish the following subtypes, although they overlap each other:

(3)   Types of nouns   Example   Meaning
        Proper nouns: 강남 *Kangnam*   Kangnam
        Common nouns: 선생 *sensayng*   teacher
        Concrete nouns: 개   *kay*   dog
        Abstract nouns: 행복 *hayngpok*   happiness
        Count nouns: 학생 *haksayng*   student
        Mass nouns: 물   *mwul*   water
        Collective nouns: 군중 *kwuncwung*   crowd

Proper nouns are selected by name-designating suffixes, such as 강남구 *Kangnam-kwu* 'Kangnam District'. Thus while 선생 *sensayng* 'teacher' is a common noun, the same word affixed with the honorific suffix 님 *-nim*, 선생님 *sensayngnim* '(honorable) Teacher', can function as a proper noun. It is occasionally claimed that languages like Korean which lack articles and obligatory plural marking lack a count/mass distinction, or more precisely that all nouns may have a mass denotation. But predicates like 세다 *sey-ta* 'to count' select count or collective NPs as objects, while disallowing mass NPs (4).

(4)   선생님이 강남에서 학생/군중/*물을 세시었다.
        *Sensayng=nim=i   kangnam=eyse   haksayng/kwuncwung/*mwul=ul*
        teacher=HON=NOM   Kangnam=at   student/crowd/water=ACC
        sey-si-ess-ta.
        count-HON-PAST-DEC
        '(Honorable) Teacher counted students/the crowd/*water at Kangnam.'

The sociolinguistic aspects of Korean terms of address, including personal pronouns, are discussed in Chapter 9. Korean has personal, referential, demonstrative, reflexive, and reciprocal pronouns, as in (5).

(5)   Pronouns
        Personal (discourse participant) pronouns:
            나 *na* 'I' (plain), 저 *ce* 'I' (polite), 너 *ne* 'you', 자네 *caney* 'you'
        Nonindexical (third person) pronouns
            그 *ku* 'he', 그녀 *ku nye* 'she', 걔 *kyay* 'he/she', 그 애 *ku ay* 'that kid'
        Demonstrative pronouns
            이 *i* 'this', 그 *ku* 'that (near hearer; mesial)', 저 *ce* 'that (over there; distal)

Reflexive pronouns:

자기 *caki* 'oneself', 자신 *casin* 'oneself', 자기 자신 *cakicasin* 'oneself'

Reciprocal pronouns:

서로 *selo* 'each other', 피차 *phicha* 'one another'

Kin and occupational terms are commonly used in the place of personal pronouns, as described in Chapter 9. The nonindexical (third person) pronouns are all derived from the mesial demonstrative 그 *ku* 'that'. Although 그 *ku* 'he' and 그녀 *ku nye* 'she' are held to result from attempts to translate gendered third person pronouns from Western languages, the colloquial pronoun 걔 *kyay* 'he/she' < 그 애 *ku ay* 'that kid' shows that *ku* + noun is a natural source for pronouns. *Kyay* 'he/she' is an antireflexive in that it cannot be bound in its clause (6):

(6)   철수ᵢ가   그ᵢ / 자기ᵢ /*걔ᵢ 친구를   데리고 왔다.
       *Chelswuᵢ=ka   kuᵢ/cakiᵢ/*kyayᵢ   chinkwu=lul   teyli-ko   o-ass-ta.*
       Chelswu=NOM   hisᵢ/selfᵢ/hisᵢ   friend=ACC   bring-CONJ   come-PAST-DEC
       'Chelswuᵢ brought hisᵢ/selfᵢ's friend.'

There are two number systems in Korean: the native Korean system, which has the numerals 1–99 in contemporary use, and the system of Chinese (Sino-Korean) origin, which provides numerals from 0 to infinity. The native numerals have both free-standing forms (for numbers 'one' to 'four') such as *hana* 'one' and *twul* 'two', and bound or attributive forms such as *han* 'one' and *twu* 'two'. The attributive forms combine both with common nouns, e.g. *han khun chayk* 'one big book', and numeral classifiers such as SK *myeng* (classifier for persons). Examples are given in (7).

(7)   Native Korean numerals

a. 하나	*hana*	one	한명	*han myeng*	one person
b. 둘	*twul*	two	두사람	*twu salam*	two people
c. 셋	*seys*	three	세개	*sey kay*	three things
d. 넷	*neys*	four	네권	*ney kwen*	four books
e. 스물	*sumwul*	twenty	스무마리	*sumwu mali*	twenty animals

The second elements in the right-hand column in (7) are all classifiers, although some such as *salam* in (7b) can function either as a classifier or a common noun. The bound and attributive functions of numerals can be distinguished by whether a modifier can be interposed between the numeral and the following element. This is possible with numeral and common noun as in (8a), but not with numeral and classifier as in (8b). The reduced form of the numeral in the right-hand column of (7) is used in both attributive and bound functions for the numerals *ney* 'four' and below but only with classifiers for numbers higher than 'four' (8c, d).

(8)   Attributive and bound forms of native Korean numerals

a.   네 멋 있는 사람
      ney   mes iss-nun   salam
      four stylish   person
      'four stylish persons'

b.   네 (*멋 있는) 명
      *ney   (*mes iss-nun)   myeng*
      four stylish CL_{person}
      'four stylish persons'

c.   세 멋 있는 사람
      sey   mes iss-nun   salam
      three stylish   person
      'three stylish persons'

d.   스물/*스무 멋 있는 사람
      *sumwul/*sumwu mes iss-nun   salam*
      twenty   stylish   person
      'twenty stylish persons'

In possessing both bare numerals and numeral classifiers, Korean combines typological features of the two broad groups of languages around it. "Altaic" languages such as those in the Tungusic, Mongolic, and Turkic families use bare numerals, while Chinese, Japanese, and Nivkh use the numeral classifiers.

In most domains, however, the Sino-Korean numerals are dominant, reflecting the pressure of what Sohn (1999) calls SK primacy. Unlike the native numerals, the SK numerals are bound forms: they must be used in combination with a classifier, which is typically itself Sino-Korean.

(9)   Sino-Korean numerals

a.	일	*il*	one	일년	*il nyen*	one year
b.	이	*i*	two	이월	*i wel*	February
c.	삼	*sam*	three	삼분	*sam pwun*	three minutes
d.	사	*sa*	four	사층	*sa chung*	fourth floor
e.	십	*sip*	ten	십개월	*sip kaywel*	ten months
f.	이십	*i sip*	twenty	이십병	*isip pyeng*	twenty bottles
g.	삼백	*sam payk*	300			
h.	사천	*sa chen*	4000			
i	오만	*o man*	50000			
j.	백만	*payk man*	million			
k.	천만	*chen man*	10 million			
l.	억	*ek*	100 million			

5.1.2   Inflecting Stems

The second major part of speech category is made up of inflecting stems, verbs, adjectives, and the copula, all of which can appear as predicates. From a semantic standpoint, both nouns and verbs can be predicates, but in Korean, noun predicates in main clauses must be followed by the copula *i-*. Inflecting stems all select the declarative suffix *-ta* as their citation form in dictionaries (see Chapter 9 for the marking of speech style by inflectional suffixes).

(10)   Inflecting stems   (용언 *yongen*)
       Verbal stems   (동사 *tongsa*)
       Adjectival stems   (형용사 *hyengyongsa*)
       Copula   (계사 *kyeysa*)

As we pointed out above, all inflecting stems in Korean are bound stems: the bare stem does not surface unsuffixed. Verbal stems denote events while adjectival stems denote states. It is noteworthy that in Korean almost all verbs are event-denoting, unlike English, where verbs such as 'know' can denote states. The sentence in (11) shows two instances of inflecting stems, the verb 'sleep' and the adjective 'sad'.

(11)   개가 거리에서 자서 슬프다/슬퍼요.
       Kay=ka   *keli=eyse ca-se*   *sulphu-ta/sulph-eyo.*
       dog=NOM   street=at   sleep-because being sad-PLN/POL
       '(Someone) is sad, due to a dog's sleeping in the street.'

Korean has a number of devices for extending the lexical inventory of verbs. One involves combining a basic "light" verb with a variety of prefixal elements. An example is the verb *chi-* 'hit' in (12):

(12)   Prefixed "light" verbs
       치다   *chita*   to hit
       망치다   *mang-chita* to destroy
       덮치다   *teph-chita* to break into
       놓치다   *noh-chita*   to lose

Prefixal elements such as *mang-* and *teph-* extend the basic meaning of 'hit' to more specific meanings such as 'destroy' and 'break into'. This process of verb formation is largely lexicalized, and the prefixal elements are typically not free-standing words and sometimes not even etymologically identifiable. For example, *mang-* in *mangchi-* 'destroy' derives from SK *mang* 亡 'destroyed, perish', while *noh-* in *nohchi-* 'lose' probably derives from the bare verbal stem *noh-* 'place, put'. The latter reflects an earlier stage of Korean when bare verbal stems could be used as the first member of verb–verb compounds, but the loss of this process has resulted in semi-opaque forms where only the second member has an independent meaning. From a typological standpoint, the prefix plus "light" verb pattern in Korean is similar to the pattern found in certain Papuan and Australian languages, where a closed class of basic verbs with meanings such as 'hit' or 'do' occur in combination with a preceding element, often itself of verbal origin, to derive more elaborated meanings.

The second, more productive pattern involves adding another "light" verb, -ha 'do', to an uninflecting verbal noun (13):

(13)   Verbal noun plus "light" ha-
공부 kongpwu 'study'   공부하다 kongpwu-hata 'to study'
노력 nolyek   'effort'   노력하다 nolyek-hata   'to make effort'
일   il   'work'   일하다   il-hata   'to work'
말   mal   'speaking'   말하다   mal-hata   'to speak'

This process derives the verb 'to study' from the noun 'study' by adding -ha 'to do'. It is a productive way of deriving inflecting verbs from Sino-Korean words, which otherwise do not inflect. 'Study' and 'make effort' in (13) are examples of this type, but as 'work' and 'speak' show, the process can also derive verbs from native Korean nouns, as well as nouns in the loan stratum, such as *syophing* 쇼핑 'shopping', which forms the verb *syophinghata* 쇼핑하다. Formation of verbs from verbal nouns using a "light" verb 'do' is found in other languages with a large loan stratum in their lexicon, such as Turkish and Japanese.

Because both verbal stems and adjectival stems in Korean inflect, and in most patterns inflect identically, some researchers claim that verbs and adjectives are indistinct, or that adjectives form a "stative verb" subclass of verbs. The major difference between the two classes is semantic: most verbs are event-denoting, while adjectives are state-denoting. However, there are formal differences as well. Verbal stems such as 먹- *mek-* 'eat' inflect for both present tense *-(nu)n-* and progressive form, but adjectival stems such as 행복하- *hayngpokha-* 'be happy' take neither form.

(14)   Inflectional differences between verbal and adjectival stems
    a. 강남에서 피자를 먹어요.
       Kangnam=eyse   *phica=lul*   *mek-eyo.*
       Kangnam=at   pizza=ACC   eat-POL
       '(Someone) eats pizza at Kangnam.'
    b. 강남에서 피자를 먹는다.
       Kangnam=eyse   *phica=lul*   *mek-nun-ta.*
       Kangnam=at   pizza=ACC   eat-PRES-PLN
       '(Someone) eats pizza at Kangnam.'
    c. 강남에서 피자를 먹고 있어요.
       Kangnam=eyse   *phica=lul*   *mek-ko iss-eyo.*
       Kangnam=at   pizza=ACC   eat-PROG-POL
       '(Someone) is eating pizza at Kangnam.'
    d. 강남에 있으면 행복해요.
       Kangnam=ey   *iss-umyen*   *hayngpokhay-yo.*
       Kangnam=at   be-if   happy-POL
       'If in Kangnam, (I) am happy.'

e. *강남에 있으면 행복한다.
   *Kangnam=ey   iss-umyen   hayngpokha-n-ta.
   Kangnam=at   be-if   happy-PRES-PLN
   'If in Kangnam, (I) am happy.'

f. *강남에 있으면 행복하고 있다.
   *Kangnam=ey   iss-umyen   hayngpokha-ko iss-ta.
   Kangnam=at   be-if   happy-PROG-PLN
   'If in Kangnam, (I) am being happy.'

Note that 행복하- *hayngpokha-* 'be happy' shows us that adjectives too can be formed from nouns by the "light" verb *ha-* 'do', in this case from the SK noun 행복 *hayngpok* 'happiness'.

(15)   Adjectival (stative) noun plus "light" *ha-*
        부유 *pwuyu*   rich   부유하다 *pwuyu-hata*   to be rich
        귀중 *kwicwung*   precious   귀중하다 *kwicwung-hata*   to be precious
        씩씩 *ssikssik*   strong   씩씩하다 *ssikssik-hata*   to be brave
        까칠 *kkachil*   picky   까칠하다 *kkachil-hata*   to be picky
        해피 *hayphi*   happy   해피하다 *hayphi-hata*   to be happy

We see in (15) that Sino-Korean nouns such as *pwuyu* 'wealth' form inflecting adjectival stems by addition of *ha-*, just like their verbal counterparts. Other classes of noninflecting stems also participate in this process, such as mimetic stems like 씩씩 *ssikssik* 'brave' and members of the loan stratum like 해피 *hayphi* 'happy' in (15).

Adjectival stems have a number of other idiosyncrasies involving derivational morphology that distinguish them from verbs. For example, native stratum adjectives have a nominalized form in adjective stem + *-i*. Adjectives also may take the intensifying suffix *-talah-*, which emphasizes the distinctiveness of the property denoted by the base adjective. Some color adjectives have a nominal form in *-ng*, from which an additional inflecting adjectival form may be derived by substituting *-h* (probably descended from "light" *ha-*).

(16)   Derived forms of adjectives
        넓- *nelp-* 'wide'   넓이 *nelpi* 'width'   널다랗다 *nel-talah-ta* 'be wide'
        높- *noph-* 'high'   높이 *nophi* 'height'   높다랗다 *noph-talah-ta* 'be high'
        희- *huy-* 'white'   하양 *hayang* 'white'   하얗다 *haya-h-ta* 'be white'

These properties help us distinguish certain borderline cases of stative verbs from true adjectives. For example, the existential verbs 있- *iss-* 'be, exist' and 없- *eps-* 'not exist' pattern like adjectives in that they do not allow the progressive. But unlike adjectives, they allow present tense (있는다 *iss-nun-ta* 'exists', 없는다 *epsnun-ta* 'does not exist'), and they disallow the intensifying suffix *-talah-* in (16). We are therefore justified in classifying these stems as true stative verbs, distinct from adjectives. The same criteria allow us to distinguish the copula 이- *i-*. The copula disallows present tense, like adjectives, but it also disallows the adjectival derivational processes in (16). Also unlike verbs and adjectives, it is a phonologically dependent form: it can only appear immediately following a predicate nominal. We return to this issue at the end of the chapter, where we suggest that copula *i-* belongs to the class of clitics in Korean.

5.1.3 *Modifiers*

The third morphological category distinguished by traditional Korean linguists is modifiers (수식언 *swusiken*). This category is made up of morphemes which are not affixal but which also cannot serve as predicates, unlike nouns, verbs, and adjectives. It includes determiners, adnominals, and adverbs.

(17)   Modifiers
       Determiners (지시사 *cisisa*)
       Adnominals (관형사 *kwanhyengsa*)
       Adverbs (부사 *pwusa*)

The class of determiners includes the three demonstratives, as in 이 책 *i chayk* 'this book' (proximal), 그 책 *ku chayk* 'that book' (mesial), and 저 책 *ce chayk* 'that book over there' (distal); as well as the interrogative determiners 어느 *enu* 'which' and 무슨 *musun* 'what'. The small class of adnominals have adjectival semantics but do not inflect, and cannot serve as clausal predicates, such as 새 *say* 'new' in 새 차 *say cha* 'new car'.

The class of adverbs modifies verb phrase elements, verbs, adjectives, nominal predicates formed with the copula, or the entire clause in the case of higher adverbs. As in other languages, adverbs can be productively derived from adjectival stems, but corresponding to the multiple lexical strata of Korean, Korean has four major adverbializing affixes in the role of English *-ly*: -이 *-i*, -히 *-hi*, -리 *-li*, -게 *-key*.

(18)   Korean derived adverbs
    a. 많이   *manh-i*   much, a lot
          적잖이   *cekcanh-i*   few
    b. 열심히   *yelsim-hi*   diligently
          조용히   *coyong-hi*   quiet
    c. 빨리   *ppal-li*   quickly
          멀리   *mell-i*   distantly
    d. 행복하게 *hayngpokha-key* happily
          느리게   *nuli-key*   slowly

Native Korean adjectival stems derive adverbs in *-i* (*l*-irregular stems in *-li*). SK adjectives derived with "light" *ha-* have corresponding adverbs in *-hi-*. The adverbial suffix *-key* tends to derive higher adverbs, such as the subject-oriented adverb *hayngpokha-key* 'happily'.

Korean links conjoined clauses with conjunctive adverbs, which are etymologically derived from contractions of *kuli ha-* 'do thus'.

(19)   Korean conjunctive adverbs
         a. 그리고   *kuliko*   and (then)
         b. 그러나   *kulena*   but, however
         c. 그래서   *kulayse*   so
         d. 그런데   *kulentey*   by the way
         e. 그러니까   *kulenikka*   because (of that)
         f. 그러므로   *kulemulo*   therefore

5.1.4   Particles

Particles (관계언 *kwankyeyen*/조사 *cosa*) combine with substantives and nonfinite inflecting stems. (Syntactically speaking, they combine with phrases headed by these elements, as we see in Chapter 6.) Case particles and some postpositions are identified with grammatical functions in (20).

(20)   Case particles and postpositions (partial list)
         a. Case particle
             이/가   *=i/=ka*   Nominative
             을/를   *=ul/=lul*   Accusative
             의   *=uy*   Genitive
         b. Postpositions
             에   *=ey*   Locative/Allative
             에게   *=eykey*   Dative
             에서   *=eyse*   (Dynamic) locative
             에게서   *=eykeyse*   Ablative

Case particles have traditionally been labeled nominative, accusative, and genitive. These labels are useful because they underline that the particles largely but not completely mark familiar grammatical relations such as subject and object, as we see in Chapter 6. The nominative and accusative particles have two allophones each, preserving CVCV(C) syllable structure, e.g. 존이/존을 *John-i/John-ul* versus 싸이가/싸이를 *Psy-ka/Psy-lul*. Some linguists distinguish nominative, accusative, and genitive as structural case particles. We will call them case particles, and call the larger class of postnominal particles marking grammatical function postpositions. We return to this issue in Section 5.5.

In contrast to case particles, delimiters are defined by their semantic function. This is either information structural, as in the case of the topic marker *=un/=nun*, or the type of meaning termed "association with focus," comparable to 'even' and 'only' in English. The postpositions 부터 *=pwuthe* 'from' and 까지 *=kkaci* 'until' can serve as delimiters based on their meanings denoting the starting point or end point on a scale.

(21)   Delimiters
     은/는   =*un*/=*nun*   TOPIC
     만   =*man*   only
     조차   =*cocha*   even
     부터   =*pwuthe*   from, starting with
     까지   =*kkaci*   until, up to

Note that in contrast to case particles, which in general may only follow substantives, delimiters may follow nonfinite forms of verbs and adjectives, as well as complement clauses:

(22)   먹고는/만 있습니다.
     Mek-ko=*nun*/=*man*   *iss-supni-ta.*
     eat-ing=TOP/=only   be-DEF-DEC
     'Eating, (someone) is/(Someone) is only eating.'

Conjunctive particles combine phrases headed by substantives, that is, noun phrases.

(23)   Conjunctive particles
     와/과   =*wa*/=*kwa* and, with
     하고   =*hako*   and, with
     (이)랑 =*(i)lang*   and, with

Conjunctive particles in Korean have a number of properties in common with other head-final languages of Northeast Asia. First, they only combine noun phrase and noun phrase; they may not combine inflecting stems or clauses. Second, as in many other head-final languages, conjunctive particles may be doubled after the whole conjoined phrase, e.g. *Chelswu*=*hako Mica*=*hako* 'Chelswu and Mica and'. This contrasts with head-initial languages like French, where the conjunction is doubled before the whole conjoined phrase, e.g. *et moi et toi* 'and me and you'. Finally, all of the conjunctive particles may function as comitative particles or postpositions meaning 'with', like *chinkwu-tul*=*hako* 'with friends' in example (1b).

5.1.5   Dependent Morphemes

Dependent morphemes must attach to stems, either noninflecting stems such as nouns or inflecting stems such as verbs and adjectives. Four types of dependent morphemes can be distinguished in Korean, depending on the type of stem they attach to and how they attach.

(24)   Types of dependent morphemes

     a. Verbal/adjectival suffixes
         먹어요   *mek-eyo*   eat-POL   eats
         행복해요 *hayngpokha-yyo* happy-POL is happy

     b. Postnominal particles
         현순이   *Hyenswun=i*   Hyenswun=NOM Hyunsoon
         현순만   *Hyenswun=man*   Hyenswun=only only Hyunsoon
         현순하고 *Hyenswun=hako* Hyenswun=and   and Hyunsoon

     c. Dependent nouns
         개구쟁이 *kaykwu-cayngi* troublemaker
         톱질   *thop-cil*   sawing

     d. Prefixes
         풋사과 *phwus-sakwa* young-apple
         진 키스 *cin-khisu*   a real kiss

The inflected forms in (24a) consist of the stems of the verbal stem *mek-* 'eat' and the adjectival stem *hayngpok-ha-* 'happy', the latter derived from an SK verbal noun and "light" *ha-*, combined with the polite (POL) suffix *-(a/e)yo*. Korean raises many interesting problems of morphological analysis; for example, *mek-eyo* eat-POL 'eats' could be analyzed as verb stem *mek-* plus infinitive *-e-* plus polite suffix *-yo*. Etymologically this is the right analysis, but the same could be said of the past-tense suffix *-(a/e)ss-*, which derives from infinitive *-a/e-* plus *-ss-* (derived from *-is(s)* 'exist'). In general, we avoid complex analyses and thus treat the polite suffix as monomorphemic *-(a/e)yo*.

The noun phrases in (24b) consist of a proper noun, *Hyenswun*, combined with the nominative case particle *=i*, the delimiter *=man* 'only', and the conjunctive particle *=hako*. The dependent nouns *cil* 'work, activity' (combining with the type of tool used for that work) and *cayngi* '-er, person' (combining with a word expressing the kind of person) resemble the second members of compounds, but they are dependent in the sense that they cannot stand alone as nouns. Korean has a small number of prefixes, as in (24d), which resemble dependent nouns in that they cannot stand alone. In Sections 5.3–5.5, we discuss the morphological processes involved in the attachment of these dependent morphemes.

5.2   Irregular Stems

Inflecting stems in a clause are made up of a stem and its endings. When the stem does not change its form, we call it a "regular stem," but there are seven irregular inflecting stems in which the stem form changes, phonologically conditioned by the following sound.

(25)   Irregular stems

    a. *T*-irregular

듣다	*tutta*	listen	걷다	*ketta*	walk
일컫다	*ilkhetta*	claim	묻다	*mwutta*	ask
깨닫다	*kkaytatta*	realize	싣다	*sitta*	load

    T becomes *l* before a vowel.

    b. *L*-irregular

멀다	*melta*	far away	길다	*kilta*	long
열다	*yelta*	open	팔다	*phalta*	sell
놀다	*nolta*	play	알다	*alta*	know

    L is deleted before /n/.

    c. *P*-irregular

즐겁다	*culkepta*	joyful	돕다	*topta*	help
어렵다	*elyepta*	difficult	쉽다	*swipta*	easy
반갑다	*pankapta*	glad	춥다	*chwupta*	cold

    P is deleted before a vowel.

    d. *S*-irregular

짓다	*cista*	make	잇다	*ista*	link
젓다	*cesta*	swirl	붓다	*pwusta*	pour

    S is deleted before a vowel.

    e. *H*-irregular

그렇다	*kulehta*	like that	이렇다	*ilehta*	like this
빨갛다	*ppalkahta*	red	노랗다	*nolahta*	yellow

    H is deleted before a consonant.

    f. *U*-irregular

크다	*khuta*	big	쓰다	*ssuta*	write
바쁘다	*papputa*	busy			

    U is deleted before a vowel.

    g. *Lu*-irregular

다르다	*taluta*	different	빠르다	*ppaluta*	fast
부르다	*pwuluta*	call	고르다	*koluta*	select
모르다	*moluta*	not know	흐르다	*huluta*	flow

    L is added before a vowel.

With *L*-irregular stems *l* is deleted before /n/. *L* in *mel-* 'far away' and *al-* 'know' are deleted before *n* in (26b) and (26d), but the *l* does not delete before a vowel in (26a) and (26c).

(26)   *L*-stems

    a. 학교에서 집까지 멀어요.
       Hakkyo=eyse cip=kkaci mel-eyo.
       school=from   home=to   far away-POL
       'It is far from school to home.'

    b. 여기에서 학교까지 머니?
       Yeki=eyse hakkyo=kkaci me-ni?
       here=from   school=to   far away-Q
       'Is it far from here to school?'

c. 나는 언어학을 잘 알아요.
   Na=nun enehak=ul cal al-ayo.
   I=TOP linguistics=ACC well know-POL
   'I know linguistics well.'

d. 언어학을 잘 아니?
   Enehak=ul cal a-ni?
   linguistics=ACC well know-Q
   'Do you know linguistics well?'

With *H*-irregular stems *h* is deleted before *n*. The *h* in the stems *ppalkah-* 'red' and *kuleh-* 'like that' is deleted before *n* in (27b), (27c), and (27d), but not in (27a).

(27) *H*-stems

a. 이 옷이 빨갛다.
   I os=i ppalkah-ta.
   these clothes=NOM red-PLN
   'These clothes are red.'

b. 나는 빨간색을 좋아해요.
   Na=nun ppalka-n-sayk=ul cohahay-yo.
   I=TOP red-ADN-color=ACC like-POL
   'I like the color red.'

c. 이 학교가 그렇게 좋아?
   I hakkyo=ka kuleh-key coh-a?
   this school=NOM like that-ADV like-Q
   'Do you like this school like that?'

d. 나는 그런 사람이다.
   Na=nun kule-n salam-ita.
   I=TOP like that-ADN person-PRED
   'I am a person like that.'

P-stems have both a regular and an irregular conjugation. For the *p*-irregular conjugation, *p* is deleted before a vowel, in (28b), while it does not change its form in regular predicates such as 뽑다 *ppopta* 'pick out', 씹다 *ssipta* 'chew', 입다 *ipta* 'put on', 잡다 *capta* 'catch', 접다 *cepta* 'fold', 굽다 *kwupta* 'bake', and 좁다 *copta* 'narrow'.

(28) *P*-stems (including regular)

a. 이 문제는 아주 쉽다.
   I mwuncey=nun acwu swip-ta.
   this question=TOP very easy-PLN
   'This question is very easy.'

b. 이번 시험에는 쉬운 문제가 많다.
   Ipen sihem=ey=nun swiwu-n mwuncey=ka manh-ta.
   this exam=LOC=TOP easy-ADJ question=NOM a lot-PLN
   'There are a lot of easy questions in this exam.'

c. 오늘은 이 옷을 입어.
Onul=un   i   os=ul   ip-e.
today=TOP these clothes=ACC put on-COM
'Put on these clothes today.'

d. 오늘은 무슨 옷을 입니?
Onul=un   mwusun os=ul   ip-ni?
today=TOP what   clothes=ACC put on-Q
'What clothes will you put on today?'

S-stems also have a regular and an irregular conjugation. *S*-irregular stems are deleted before a vowel as in (29b), but they do not delete in other phonological conditions or in regular predicates such as벗다 *pesta* 'take off', 빗다 *pista* 'comb', 빼앗다 *ppayasta* 'take out', 씻다 *ssista* 'clean', and 솟다 *sosta* 'rise'.

(29)   *S*-stems (including regular)
a. 나는 밥을 짓는다.
Na=nun   pap=ul   cis-nun-ta.
I=TOP   cooked rice=ACC make-PRES-PLN
'I make cooked rice.'

b. 어머니가 밥을 지어요.
Emeni=ka   pap=ul   ci-eyo.
mother=NOM cooked rice=ACC make-POL
'Mother makes cooked rice.'

c. 더우니까 이 옷을 벗어라.
Tewu-nikka i   os=ul   pes-ela.
hot-due to this clothes=ACC take off-COM
'Please take off your clothes, due to the heat.'

d. 언제 옷을 벗니?
Encey   os=ul   pes-ni?
when   clothes=ACC take off-Q
'When do you take off your clothes?'

U-stems have an irregular conjugation in which *u* is deleted before a vowel, shown in (30b). *U* does not delete in other environments, as in (30a), (30c) and (30d).

(30)   *U*-stems
a. 이 옷이 너무 크니?
I   os=i   nemwu khu-ni?
these clothes=NOM too   big-Q
'Are these clothes too big?'

b. 이 옷은 아주 커요.
I   os=un   acwu kh-eyo.
these clothes=NOM very   big-POL
'These clothes are very big.'

c. 철수는 아주 바빠요.
Chelswu=nun   acwu papp-ayo.
Chelswu=TOP   very busy-POL
'Chelswu is very busy.'

d. 나는 요즘 많이 바빠요.
Na=nun   yocum   manhi papp-ayo.
I=TOP   nowadays a lot   busy-POL
'I am very busy nowadays.'

T-stems have both irregular and regular conjugations. In *T*-irregular stems, *t* becomes *l* before a vowel, as in (31b). The stem does not change in regular predicates such as 닫다 *tatta* 'close', 돋다 *totta* 'sprout', 믿다 *mitta* 'believe', 쏟다 *ssotta* 'pour into', 얻다 *etta* 'gain', and 묻다 *mwutta* 'ask'.

(31)   *T*-stems (including regular)
a. 나는 친구한테 길을 묻는다.
Na=nun   chinkwu=hanthey kil=ul   mwut-nun-ta.
I=TOP   friend=DAT   road=ACC ask-PRES-PLN
'I ask a friend for directions (road).'

b. 나는 친구한테 길을 물어요.
Na=nun   chinkwu=hanthey kil=ul   mwul-eyo.
I=TOP   friend=DAT   road=ACC ask-POL
'I ask a friend for directions (road).'

c. 철수는 친구를 믿는다.
Chelswu=nun   chinkwu=lul mit-nun-ta.
Chelswu=TOP   friend=ACC believe-PRES-PLN
'Chelswu believes in his friend.'

d. 철수는 친구를 믿어요.
Chelswu=nun   chinkwu=lul mit-eyo.
Chelswu=TOP   friend=ACC believe-POL
'Chelswu believes in his friend.'

Lu-stems have an irregular conjugation where *l* is added before a vowel, as in (32b) and (32d).

(32)   *Lu*-stems
a. 한국은 미국과 많이 다르다.
Hankwuk=un mikwuk=kwa manhi talu-ta.
Korea=TOP   America=and a lot   different-PLN
'Korea is very different from America.'

b. 한국은 미국과 많이 달라요.
Hankwuk=un mikwuk=kwa manhi tal-layo.
Korea=TOP   America=and a lot   different-POL
'Korea is very different from America.'

c. 비행기가 기차보다 빠르다.
Pihayngki=ka kicha=pota ppalu-ta.
airplane=NOM train=than   fast-PLN
'An airplane is faster than a train.'

d. 비행기가 기차보다 빨라요.
   Pihayngki=ka   kicha=pota ppal-layo.
   airplane=NOM   train=than   fast-POL
   'An airplane is faster than a train.'

5.3   Types of Word Formation

Korean has three major types of word formation. To the word formation processes in (33a–c) we add cliticization in (33d).

(33)   Rules for attaching dependent morphemes
         a. Derivation
         b. Inflection
         c. Compounding
         d. Cliticization

Derivational processes change the meaning or grammatical category of a stem.

(34)   Derivation
         a. Hyunsoon quiet-ly studies psychology at the library.
         b. 현순은 도서관에서 조용하게 심리학을 공부한다.
            Hyenswun=un   tosekwan=eyse coyong-ha-key   simlihak=ul
            Hyenswun=TOP   library=LOC   quiet-do-ADV   psychology=ACC
            kongpwu-ha-n-ta.
            study-do-PRES-DEC
            'Hyunsoon quietly studies psychology at the library.'

In English (34a), the derivational suffix *-ly* derives adverbs from adjectival stems, while *-key* in *coyong-ha-key* 'quietly' does the same in Korean (34b).

(35)   Inflection
         a. Psy sing-s many song-s about gentlemen.
         b. 싸이가 신사에 관한 많은 노래를 한다.
            Ssai=ka   sinsa=ey kwanhan manhun nolay-lul ha-n-ta.
            Psy=NOM   gentleman=about   a lot   song-ACC do-PRES-DEC
            'Psy sings a lot of songs about gentlemen.'

In (35), English *-s* in *sing-s* is the third person singular present tense suffix. It shows agreement with the third person singular subject *Psy*. The suffix *-s* in *song-s* shows that English nouns inflect for number. The suffixes *-n* and *-ta* in *ha-n-ta* show that Korean verbs inflect for tense, like English, but also for sentence type, a kind of inflection not found in English. Korean and English are alike in having inflectional suffixes, but they differ in other respects. Korean does not have obligatory inflection for number; *sinsa* 'gentleman' can be understood as singular or plural in context. On the other hand, Korean nouns combine with postpositional particles. Some of these, like =*ey kwanhan* 'about' in (35), appear to correspond to English prepositions, but as we show below they combine more tightly with their host.

5.3.1   Derivational Morphology

A noun can be derived from another noun, verb, or adjective by compounding and a variety of derivational processes. Although we will occasionally comment on whether nouns and other morphemes are native or Sino-Korean, we will not systematically distinguish these lexical strata in this book, as the distinction is difficult for nonnative learners and not always clear to native speakers either. If the basic stem is a noun, we call the derivational process denominal; if it is a verb or adjective, we call it a deverbal/deadjectival derivation.

(36)   Nominal derivation
    a. Noun from noun

술꾼	*swul-kkwun*	liquor-Master	'drunkard'
바느질	*panu-cil*	needle-work	'sewing'
대장장이	*taycang-cangi*	hammer-person	'blacksmith'
욕심쟁이	*yoksim-cayngi*	greed-person	'greedy person'
한글화	*hankul-hwa*	hangul-ization	'hangulization'

    b. Noun from verb

읽기	*ilk-ki*	read-NOMNL	'reading (action)'
보기	*po-ki*	see-NOMNL	'seeing (action)'
걸음	*kel-um*	walk-NOMNL	'walking, steps'

    c. Noun from adjective

슬픔	*sulphu-m*	sad-NOMNL	'sadness'
키	*kh-i*	big-NOMNL	'height'

The first three examples in (36a) show a noun derived from another noun by adding one of the dependent nouns introduced in (32c). These forms undergo some of the phonological processes seen in compounding. For example, the initial consonant in -*kkwun* (probably from the SK title *kwun* 'Master') undergoes tensification. However they are distinct from noun–noun compounds, because the second element cannot stand by itself. The dependent noun *cangi* and its umlauted form *cayngi* combine with *taycang* 'hammer' and *yoksim* 'greed' to yield 'blacksmith' and 'greedy person'. The SK morpheme -*hwa* 'change' attaches to SK nouns quite productively to derive nouns meaning '-ization'; the example noun *hankul-hwa* 'hangulization' shows that it can attach to nouns that are not Sino-Korean.

The examples in (36b) show nouns derived from verbs by the nominalizing suffixes (marked in the examples with the abbreviation NOMNL) -*i, -ki* and -*(u) m*. Like English -*ing*, these deverbal nominalizing suffixes can derive concrete nouns as in *hanca ilk-i* 'a Chinese character reading', action nominalizations as in *hanca=uy ilk-ki* 'the reading of Chinese characters', and even clausal nominalizations as in *hanca=lul ilk-ki (sicakhanta)* '(begin) reading Chinese characters=ACC'. (Chapter 6 explains clausal nominalization in detail.) As we see in (36c), deadjectival and deverbal nominalizing suffixes are largely identical. In both cases, *-i* is the most lexicalized and least productive. It derives concrete nouns and is subject to semantic and phonological irregularities.

(37)   Verbal derivation
    a. Verb from noun
       위반하다   *wipan-hata*   violation-do   'violate'
       위반되다   *wipan-toyta*   violation-become 'be violated'
       값지다   *kaps-cita*   price-become   'expensive'
    b. Verb from verb
       넘치다   *nem-chita*   exceed-hit   'overflow'
       그려지다   *kuly-e-cita*   draw-INF-become 'be drawn'
    c. Verb from bound adverb and verb
       덧붙이다   *tes-pwuthita*   more-attach 'add'
       덧신다   *tes-sinta*   more-put in 'layer'
    d. Verb from adjective
       더워지다   *tew-e-ci-ta*   hot-INF-become-DEC 'become hot'

The first two examples in (37a) show inflecting verbs derived from verbal nouns with "light" *ha-* and its intransitive counterpart *toy-* 'become'. As in this case, *toy-* often derives a passive counterpart of a transitive verb in *ha-*. The third example shows a verb derived from the noun *kaps* 'price' plus the verb *ci-* 'become, have the characteristic of, passive'. The first example in (37b) is a verb derived from a deverbal prefix plus "light" *chi-* 'hit'. The second, *kuly-e-ci-* 'be drawn', also involves the verb *ci-* 'become', this time deriving a passive from the infinitive form of a transitive verb. Combining the infinitive form of the verb with other verbs is the most productive way of extending verb stems in Korean, but in most cases, we treat such patterns as syntactically derived. The reason for analyzing the passive in infinitive plus *ci-* as morphologically derived is that the sequence cannot be broken up; thus **kuly-e=to ci-ess-ta* 'write-INF=even become-PAST-DEC' is ungrammatical. The examples in (37c) indicate a verbal derivation from the bound adverb *tes-* prefixed to the verb. In (37d) a deadjectival verb is again derived by inchoative *ci-* 'become' plus the infinitive.

(38)   Adjectival derivation
    a. Adjective from noun
       존경스럽다   *conkyeng-sulepta* respect-ADJM 'respectable'
       남자답다   *namca-tapta*   man-like   'manly'
    b. Adjective from verb
       바쁘다   *papputa*   rush-ADJM 'busy'
       쉽다   *swipta*   rest-ADJM 'easy'

c. Adjective from prefix or bound adverb and adjective

샛노랗다	*says-nolahta*	vivid-yellow	'bright yellow'
짙푸르다	*cith-phwuluta*	deep-blue	'deep blue'
무덥다	*mwu-tepta*	too much-hot	'be sultry'

Denominal adjectives derived from nouns by adjectivalizing *-sulep-* and *-tap-* (38a) are very productive, but deverbalizing *-p(u)-* in (38b) is completely lexicalized and no longer productive. Other than sychronically still relatively transparent cases like 쉽- *swip-* 'easy' from 쉬- *swi-* 'rest', most of the derivations involving *-p(u)-* are now opaque to all but historical linguists, but diachronically this suffix accounts for the many adjective stems ending in /pwu/, /phwu/, and /p/. The examples in (38c) show adjectives derived from an adjectival stem plus intensifying prefix. *Cith-* comes from the adjectival stem *cith-* 'be thick, deep', but the other two forms exist only in their prefixal or bound adverb function.

(39)   Adverbial derivation

      a. Adverb from noun

| 깨끗이 | *kkaykkus-i* | clean-ADV | 'cleanly' |
| 조용히 | *coyong-hi* | quiet-ADV | 'quietly' |

      b. Adverb from verb

| 없이 | *eps-i* | not/exist-ADV | 'lacking, without' |
| 결단코 | *kyeltan-kho* | decide-ADV | 'decisively' |

      c. Adverb from adjective

기쁘게	*kippu-key*	glad-ADV	'gladly'
빨리	*ppal-li*	fast-ADV	'fast'
같이	*kath-i*	same-ADV	'same'

      d. Adverb from adjective

| 가득히 | *katuk-hi* | full-ADV | 'fully' |

The basic adverbializers in (39) are *-key, -i, -ko* and their allomorphs, all equivalent to *-ly* in English. The adverbs in (39a) can also be regarded as adverbializations of "light" *ha-* from the adjectives *kkaykkusha-* 'clean' and *coyongha-* 'quiet'. The example in (39d) can be analyzed in the same way, as an adverbialization of the adjective *katukha-* 'full'.

5.4   Inflection

Korean is well known as an agglutinative language, with a complex system of inflectional suffixes attached to various stem types. Much research has been done to explain what those suffix orderings are, although not all approaches agree (cf. Martin 1954, Yang 1972, Cho and Sells 1995). We adopt the distinction between inflecting stems (verbs and adjectives) and noninflecting stems (substantives) made by Martin and traditional Korean grammarians. This section discusses the suffixal morphology of inflecting stems.

Suffix order with inflecting stems is intricate. We follow the template in (40) from Cho and Sells (1995), which shows a strict order among morphemes following the stem. Since a verb root is a bound morpheme, it must be suffixed with at least one item in the V3 (MOOD) category. The linear order of morphemes in (40) is Verb stem, V1 (Honorific, HON), V2 (Tense, Aspect and Modality, TAM), V3 (MOOD, expressing sentence type and speech style), and V4 (Discourse, DIS).

(40)   Linear order of inflecting stems
         Verb – V1 (HON) – V2 (TAM) – **V3 (MOOD)** – V4 (DIS)

Honorific *-(u)si-*, representing a distinctive linguistic subsystem in Korean, occupies the first slot. It is a referent honorific, reflecting the age and social status of an individual denoted by an NP in the sentence, normally the subject.

(41)   V1 (Honorific)
         (으)시 *-(u)si-*

The following examples show that *-(u)si-* is added directly to the stem when the subject is the target of honorification. If the stem ends in a vowel, *-si-* is selected (42b), otherwise *-usi-* (42d).

(42)   Honorific *-(u)si-*
         a. 철수가 학교에 간다.
            Chelswu=ka   hakkyo=ey   ka-n-ta.
            Chelswu=NOM school=DIR go-PRES-PLN
            'Chelswu goes to school.'
         b. 선생님이 학교에 가신다.
            Sensayngnim=i hakkyo=ey ka-si-n-ta.
            teacher=NOM   school=DIR go-HON-PRES-PLN
            'A teacher goes to school.'
         c. 철수가 식당에서 밥을 먹는다.
            Chelswu=ka   siktang=eyse   pap=ul   mek-nun-ta.
            Chelswu=NOM restaurant=LOC cooked rice=ACC eat-PRES-PLN
            'Chelswu eats (rice = a meal) at a restaurant.'
         d. 선생님이 식당에서 밥을 먹으신다.
            Sensayngnim=i siktang=eyse   pap=ul   mek-usi-n-ta.
            teacher=NOM   restaurant=LOC cooked rice=ACC eat-HON-PRES-PLN
            'The teacher eats (rice) at the restaurant.'

The V2 slot is occupied by suffixes expressing tense, aspect, or modality. Tense locates the event or state expressed by the predicate in time. Aspect expresses the internal nature of the time period of the event, for example whether the event is viewed as complete. Modality expresses the clause type and the speaker's degree of commitment to the proposition expressed by the clause. Modality (M) is grouped with tense (T) and aspect (A) in the cover label TAM because tense, aspect, and modality all interact to express a speaker's viewpoint about the event or situation the utterance refers to. Korean, like English, distinguishes present, past, and future; here we classify the future as a tense when it occurs alone, but as a modal when it co-occurs with past tense. Likewise we classify "past" -e/ass- as an aspect, past perfect, when it is doubled, and retrospective -te- as a modal, due to its ability to co-occur with tense. Korean distinguishes the same three tenses in its adnominal suffixes, which also occur in the V2 slot.

(43)   V2 (Tense/Aspect/Modality)

Tense	Present	ㄴ/는	*-(nu)n-*
	Past	ㅆ/었	*-(a/e)ss-*
	Future	겠	*-keyss-*
Prenominal	Present	는	*-nun-*
	Past	ㄴ/은	*-(u)n-*
	Future	ㄹ/을	*-(u)l-*
Aspect	Past perfect	ㅆ었/었었	*-(a/e)ss-/-ess ess-*
Modality	Prospective	ㅆ겠	*-(a/e)ss-keyss-*
	Retrospective	더	*-te-*

The following sentences show present tense *-(nu)n-*, past tense *-(a/e)ss-*, and future *–keyss-*.

(44)   Tense
   a.   나는 학교에 간다.
        Na=nun   hakkyo=ey   ka-n-ta.
        I=TOP   school=DIR   go-PRES-PLN
        'I go to school.'
   b.   나는 스웨터를 입는다.
        Na=nun   suweythe=lul   ip-nun-ta.
        I=TOP   sweater=ACC   wear-PRES-PLN
        'I wear a sweater.'
   c.   나는 학교에서 공부한다.
        Na=nun   hakkyo=eyse   kongpwuha-n-ta.
        I=TOP   school=LOC   study-PRES-PLN
        'I study at school.'
   d.   나는 학교에 갔다.
        Na=nun   hakkyo=ey   ka-ss-ta.
        I=TOP   school=LOC   go-PAST-PLN
        'I went to school.' or 'I have gone to school.'
   e.   나는 스웨터를 입었다.
        Na=nun   suweythe=lul   ip-ess-ta.
        I=NOM   sweater=ACC   wear-PAST-PLN
        'I wore a sweater' or 'I have put on a sweater.'

   f. 나는 학교에서 공부했다.
     Na=nun   hakkyo=eyse   kongpwuhay-ss-ta.
     I=NOM   school=LOC   study-PAST-PLN
     'I studied at school' or 'I have studied at school.'

   g. 나는 학교에서 공부하겠다.
     Na=nun   hakkyo=eyse kongpwuha-keyss-ta.
     I=NOM   school=LOC   study-FUT-PLN
     'I will study at school.'

Past, present, and future generally correspond to their English counterparts, but past *-(a/e)ss-* can also convey meanings usually expressed by the English present perfect. This is especially clear in (44e). When *ip-* 'wear, put on (clothes)' receives its telic interpretation 'put on', this sentence can denote a situation where the speaker has put on a sweater and is still wearing it.

    The next examples show the adnominal tense suffixes, present *-nun-*, past *-(u)n-*, and future *-(u)l-*.

(45)   Prenominal Modifier
    a. 학교에 가는 사람
      Hakkyo=ey ka-nun   salam
      school=DIR   go-PRESADN   person
      'A person who goes to school'

    b. 스웨터를 입는 사람
      Suweythe=lul   ip-nun   salam
      sweater=ACC   wear-PRESADN   person
      'A person who wears a sweater'

    c. 학교에서 공부하는 사람
      Hakkyo=eyse   kongpwuha-nun   salam
      school=LOC   study-PRESADN   person
      'A person who studies at school'

    d. 학교에 간 사람
      Hakkyo=ey   ka-n   salam
      school=DIR   go-PSTADN   person
      'A person who went to school'

    e. 스웨터를 입은 사람
      Suweythe=lul   ip-un   salam
      sweater=ACC   wear-PSTADN person
      'A person who wore/put on a sweater'

    f. 학교에서 공부한 사람
      Hakkyo=eyse   kongpwuha-n   salam
      school=LOC   study-PSTADN   person
      'A person who studied at school'

    g. 학교에 갈 사람
      Hakkyo=ey   ka-l   salam
      school=DIR   go-FUTADN   person
      'A person who will go to school'

h. 스웨터를 입을 사람
   Suweythe=lul   *ip-ul*   *salam*
   sweater=ACC   wear-FUTADN   person
   'A person who will wear/put on a sweater'

i. 학교에서 공부할 사람
   Hakkyo=eyse   *kongpwuha-l*   *salam*
   school=LOC   study-FUTADN   person
   'A person who will study at school'

The aspectual and modal features of the V2 suffixes emerge when they are combined with another tense suffix. "Doubled" past, *-ss-ess* expresses the past perfect, denoting an event that was completed before the reference time. Past plus future *-ss-keyss-* expresses a conjectural past, denoting a past event that the speaker is to varying degrees uncertain about. We classify the retrospective suffix *-te-* as a modal because it can combine with a past tense suffix, as in (46g, h).

(46)   Aspect/Modality (A/M)
   a. 나는 학교에 갔었다.
      Na=nun   *hakkyo=ey*   *ka-ss-ess-ta.*
      I=TOP   school=DIR   go-A/M-PLN
      'I had gone to school.'
   b. 나는 스웨터를 입었었다.
      Na=nun   *suweythe=lul ip-ess-ess-ta.*
      I=TOP   sweater=ACC   wear-A/M-PLN
      'I had worn/put on a sweater.'
   c. 나는 학교에서 공부했었다.
      Na=nun   *hakkyo=eyse kongpwuhay-ss-ess-ta.*
      I=TOP   school=LOC   study-A/M-PLN
      'I had studied at school.'
   d. 나는 학교에 갔겠다.
      Na=nun   *hakkyo=ey*   *ka-ss-keyss-ta.*
      I=TOP   school=LOC   go-A/M-PLN
      'I would have been at school.'
   e. 나는 스웨터를 입었겠다.
      Na=nun   *suweythe=lul ip-ess-keyss-ta.*
      I=TOP   sweater=ACC   eat-A/M-PLN
      'I would have worn/put on a sweater.'
   f. 나는 학교에서 공부했겠다.
      Na=nun   *hakkyo=eyse kongpwuhay-ss-keyss-ta.*
      I=TOP   school=LOC   study-A/M-PLN
      'I would have studied at school.'
   g. 철수는 한국어를 잘 했더라.
      Chelswu=nun   *hankwuke=lul cal*   *hay-ss-te-la.*
      Chelswu=TOP   Korean=ACC   well   do-PAST-RET-PLN
      '(I noticed that) Chelwsu spoke Korean well.'

h. 여름에 자주 입던 옷
   Yelum=ey   cacwu ip-te-n   os
   summer=LOC   often   wear-RET-PSTADN   clothes
   'Clothes that (I) often wore in summer'

Linguists have sometimes argued about whether specific V2 suffixes are inherently Tense, Aspect, or Modal. We take the view that *-ss-* can express (past) tense or (perfect) aspect, and *-keyss-* either (future) tense or conjectural modality. When these suffixes appear in combination with another V2 suffix, only one can provide the tense interpretation. Retrospective *-te-* too has both a tense and a modal meaning: it picks out a past event (tense) of which the speaker has direct experience (modal).

In general the internal order of suffixes in the V2 slot follows the order aspect – tense – modal. Crosslinguistically, aspect tends to be closer to the verb than tense, and tense closer than modals; Korean conforms to this pattern. Thus in the combinations *-ss-keyss-* and *-ss-te-,* the first suffix expresses tense and the second modality. However in the combination of retrospective *-te-* and adnominal past *-n-*, the adnominal suffix follows; this is because the adnominal suffixes also have the function of marking clause type, and as we see below, clause type is marked in the slot after V2.

The V2 slot is occupied by prefinal or adnominal suffixes, neither of which can form a complete utterance by themselves. The next slot, V3, is occupied by final suffixes, which can close off an utterance; in terms of function, they mark clause type. V3 suffixes are conventionally referred to as mood suffixes. They mark certain types of subordinate clauses as well as the type of the matrix clause.

(47)   V3 (Mood) subordinate clause type markers
         Sentence type and speech style
         Conjunctive   고   *-ko*   and, -ing
         Disjunctive   지만   *-ciman*   but
         Conditional   면   *-myen*   if, when

The following sentences show V3 subordinate clause markers.

(48)   V3 Subordinate clause markers
         a. 나는 학교에 가고 공부한다.
            Na=nun   hakkyo=ey ka-ko   kongpwuha-n-ta.
            I=NOM   school=DIR go-M (and) study-PRES-PLN
            'I go to school and study.'
         b. 나는 학교에 가지만 공부 안 한다.
            Na=nun   hakkyo=ey ka-ciman   kongpwu an ha-n-ta.
            I=NOM   school=DIR go-M (but) study   NEG do-PRES-PLN
            'I go to school, but I do not study.'
         c. 나는 학교에 가면 공부한다.
            Na=nun   hakkyo=ey ka-myen   kongpwuha-n-ta.
            I=NOM   school=DIR go-M (if)   study-PRES-PLN
            'If/when I go to school, I study.'

When people form sentences, they perform speech acts, which include state-
ments or declarations, questions, proposals, suppositions, and commands.
Declarative sentences are formed with tense -*ta* in plain speech style. The
dominant pattern for questions (interrogative sentences) in plain speech style
forms them with tense -*ni*. Propositive sentences, embodying a proposition or
request, are formed with -*ca* in a plain speech style. Commands (imperative
sentences) are formed with -*la/-ela* in plain speech style. Suspective sentences
express a hedged or weak assertion, such as a supposition or statement the
speaker considers probable but not certain. This weak assertive function is
extended to use the suspective to ask for confirmation, as in (50d) below, or
with non-tensed verb plus -*ci*, to issue a non-coercive invitation, as in (56) below.

(49)   V3 Matrix clause type markers (based on Plain speech style)
        a.   Declarative   Tense-다   Tense-*ta*
        b.   Interrogative   Tense-니   Tense-*ni*
        c.   Propositive   자   -*ca*
        d.   Suspective   Tense-지   Tense-*ci*
        e.   Imperative   라/어라   -*la/-ela*

(50)   Main clause types marked by V3 suffixes
        a. 나는 학교에서 공부한다.
           Na=nun   hakkyo=eyse   kongpwuha-n-ta.
           I=TOP   school=LOC   study-PRES-M (PLN DEC)
           'I study at school.'
        b. 너는 어디에서 공부하니?
           Ne=nun   eti=eyse   kongpwuha-ni?
           you=TOP   where=LOC   study-M (PLN INTERROGATIVE)
           'Where do you study?'
        c. 이제 공부하자.
           Icey   kongpwuha-ca.
           now   study- M (PROP + PLN)
           'Let us study now.'
        d. 너는 학교에서 공부하지?
           Ne=nun   hakkyo=eyse   kongpwuha-ci?
           you=TOP   school=LOC   study-PRES-M (PLN SUSP)
           'You study at school, don't you?'
        e. 이제 공부해라.
           Icey   kongpwuhay-la.
           now   study-M (PLN IMP)
           'Study now.'

The category of speech styles in Korean is based on the notion of addressee
politeness; that is, how much deference the speaker pays to the hearer. The
more deference, the more polite the speech style is. Researchers differentiate
between four and seven speech styles in contemporary Korean. We distinguish
the following four here:

(51)   Speech style
  a. Deferential
  b. Polite
  c. Intimate
  d. Plain

The pragmatic and sociolinguistic aspects of speech style are discussed in Chapter 9. We can generate twenty combinations from the five sentence types and four speech styles in (52), as in (53)–(57).

(52)   20 combinations of sentence type and speech style

	Declarative	Interrogative	Propositive	Suspective	Imperative
Plain	ㄴ/는다	니	자	지	라/어라
	Tense-*ta*	Tense-*ni*	-*ca*	-*ci*	-*la*/-*ela*
Intimate	아/어/해	아/어/해	아/어/해	지	아/어/해
	-*a/e/hay*	-*a/e/hay*	-*a/e/hay*	-*ci*	-*a/e/hay*
Polite	아/어/해요	아/어/해요	아/어/해요	지요	아/어/해요
	-*a/e/hay-yo*	-*a/e/hay-yo*	-*a/e/hay-yo*	-*ci-yo*	-*a/e/hay-yo*
Deferential	ㅂ/습니다	ㅂ/습니까	ㅂ/읍시다	시지요	ㅂ/으십시오
	-*(su)pnita*	-*(su)pnikka*	(-*u*)*p-sita*	-(*u*)*siciyo*	-*p/usipsio*

(53)   Declaratives
  a. 나는 학교에 간다.
   Na=nun   hakkyo=ey   ka-n-ta.
   I=TOP   school=DIR   go-PRES-M (Plain Declarative)
   'I go to school.'
  b. 나는 식당에서 밥을 먹는다.
   Na=nun siktang=eyse   pap=ul   mek-nun-ta.
   I=TOP   restaurant=LOC cooked rice=ACC   eat-PRES-M (Plain)
   'I eat (rice) at a restaurant.'
  c. 나는 학교에 가.
   Na=nun   hakkyo=ey   ka.
   I=TOP   school=DIR   go-M (Intimate)
   'I go to school.'
  d. 나는 식당에서 밥을 먹어.
   Na=nun   siktang=eyse   pap=ul   mek-e.
   I=TOP   restaurant=LOC cooked rice=ACC eat-M (Intimate)
   'I eat (rice) at a restaurant.'
  e. 나는 학교에 가요.
   Na=nun   hakkyo=ey   ka-yo.
   I=TOP   school=DIR   go-M (Polite)
   'I go to school.'
  f. 나는 식당에서 밥을 먹어요.
   Na=nun siktang=eyse   pap=ul   mek-eyo.
   I=TOP   restaurant=LOC cooked rice=ACC   eat-M (Polite)
   'I eat (rice) at a restaurant.'

g. 나는 학교에 갑니다.
   Na=nun   hakkyo=ey   ka-pnita.
   I=TOP   school=DIR   go-M (Deferential)
   'I go to school.'

h. 나는 식당에서 밥을 먹습니다.
   Na=nun siktang=eyse pap=ul   mek-supnita.
   I=TOP   restaurant=LOC cooked rice=ACC eat-M (Deferential
                                            Declarative)
   'I eat (rice) at a restaurant.'

(54) Interrogatives

a. 너는 학교에 가니?
   Ne=nun hakkyo=ey   ka-ni?
   you=TOP school=DIR   go-M (Plain Interrogative)
   'Do you go to school?'

b. 너는 식당에서 밥을 먹니?
   Ne=nun siktang=eyse   pap=ul   mek-ni?
   you=TOP restaurant=LOC cooked rice=ACC eat-M (Plain Interrogative)
   'Do you eat (rice) at a restaurant?'

c. (너는) 학교에 가?
   Ne=nun   hakkyo=ey ka?
   you=TOP   school=DIR go-M (Intimate)
   'Do you go to school?'

d. (너는) 식당에서 밥을 먹어?
   Ne=nun siktang=eyse   pap=ul   mek-e?
   you=TOP restaurant=LOC cooked rice=ACC eat-M (Intimate)
   'Do you eat (rice) at a restaurant?'

e. (너는) 학교에 가요?
   Ne=nun hakkyo=ey   ka-yo?
   you=TOP school=DIR   go-M (Polite)
   'Do you go to school?'

f. (너는) 식당에서 밥을 먹어요?
   Ne=nun siktang=eyse   pap=ul   mek-e-yo?
   you=TOP restaurant=LOC cooked rice=ACC eat-M (Polite)
   'Do you eat (rice) at a restaurant?'

g. (너는) 학교에 갑니까?
   Ne=nun hakkyo=ey   ka-pnikka?
   you=TOP school=DIR   go-M (Deferential Interrogative)
   'Do you go to school?'

h. (너는) 식당에서 밥을 먹습니까?
   Ne=nun siktang=eyse   pap=ul   mek-supnikka?
   you=TOP restaurant=LOC cooked rice=ACC eat-M (Deferential
                                            Interrogative)
   'Do you eat (rice) at a restaurant?'

(55)   Propositives
    a. 학교에 가자.
       Hakkyo=ey   ka-ca.
       school=DIR   go-M (Plain Propositive)
       'Let's go to school.'
    b. 식당에서 밥을 먹자.
       Siktang=eyse   pap=ul   mek-ca.
       restaurant=LOC   cooked rice=ACC   eat-M (Plain Propositive)
       'Let's eat (rice) at a restaurant.'
    c. 학교에 가.
       Hakkyo=ey   ka.
       school=DIR   go-M (Intimate)
       'Let's go to school.'
    d. 식당에서 밥을 먹어.
       Siktang=eyse   pap=ul   mek-e.
       restaurant=LOC   cooked rice=ACC   eat-M (Intimate)
       'Let's eat (rice) at a restaurant.'
    e. 학교에 가요.
       Hakkyo=ey   ka-yo.
       school=DIR   go-M (Polite)
       'Let's go to school.'
    f. 식당에서 밥을 먹어요.
       Siktang=eyse   pap=ul   mek-eyo.
       restaurant=LOC   cooked rice=ACC   eat-M (Polite)
       'Let's eat (rice) at a restaurant.'
    g. 학교에 갑시다.
       Hakkyo=ey   ka-psita.
       school=DIR   go-M (Deferential Propositive)
       'Let's go to school.'
    h. 식당에서 밥을 먹읍시다.
       Siktang=eyse   pap=ul   mek-up sita.
       restaurant=LOC   cooked   eat-M (Deferential
                      rice=ACC   Propositive)
       'Let's eat (rice) at a restaurant.'

(56)   Suspective
    a. 학교에 가지.
       Hakkyo=ey   ka-ci.
       school=DIR   go-M (Plain/Intimate Suspective)
       'Let's go to school.'
    b. 식당에서 밥을 먹지.
       Siktang=eyse   pap=ul   mek-ci.
       restaurant=LOC   cooked rice=ACC   eat-M (Plain/Intimate Suspective)
       'Let's eat (rice) at a restaurant.'
    c. 학교에 가지요.
       Hakkyo=ey   ka-ciyo.
       school=DIR   go-M (Polite)
       'Let's go to school.'

d. 식당에서 밥을 먹지요.
  Siktang=eyse   pap=ul   mek-ciyo.
  restaurant=LOC cooked rice=ACC   eat-M (Polite)
  'Let's eat (rice) at a restaurant.'

e. 학교에 가시지요.
  Hakkyo=ey   ka-siciyo.
  school=DIR   go-M (Deferential Suspective)
  'Let's go to school.'

f. 식당에서 밥을 먹으시지요.
  Siktang=eyse   pap=ul   mek-usiciyo.
  restaurant=LOC cooked rice=ACC eat-M (Deferential Suspective)
  'Let's eat (rice) at a restaurant.'

(57)   Imperatives

a. 학교에 가라.
  Hakkyo=ey   ka-la.
  school=DIR   go-M (Plain Imperative)
  'Go to school.'

b. 식당에서 밥을 먹어라.
  Siktang=eyse   pap=ul   mek-ela.
  restaurant=LOC   cooked rice=ACC   eat-M (Plain Imperative)
  'Eat (rice) at a restaurant.'

c. 학교에 가.
  Hakkyo=ey   ka.
  school=DIR   go-M (Intimate)
  'Go to school.'

d. 식당에서 밥을 먹어.
  Siktang=eyse   pap=ul   mek-e.
  restaurant=LOC   cooked rice=ACC   eat-M (Intimate)
  'Eat (rice) at a restaurant.'

e. 학교에 가요.
  Hakkyo=ey   ka-yo.
  school=DIR   go-M (Polite)
  'Go to school.'

f. 식당에서 밥을 먹어요.
  Siktang=eyse   pap=ul   mek-e-yo.
  restaurant=LOC   cooked rice=ACC   eat-M (Polite)
  'Eat (rice) at a restaurant.'

g. 학교에 가십시오.
  Hakkyo=ey   ka-sipsio.
  school=DIR   go-M (Deferential)
  'Go to school.'

h. 식당에서 밥을 먹으십시오.
  Siktang=eyse   pap=ul   mek-usipsio.
  restaurant=LOC   cooked rice=ACC   eat-M (Deferential)
  'Eat (rice) at a restaurant.'

The final suffixal slot following inflecting stems is V4 (discourse) (Cho and Sells 1995). The polite suffix -yo in this slot follows V3 suffixes. It does not change clause type, but has the effect of softening the speech level. As shown in (58a, b), the polite forms in (57e, f) could be analyzed as adding -yo in slot V4 to the plain (infinitive) or suspective ending in slot V3. These raise the level of addressee politeness, but -yo added to the deferential declarative in V3 is less formal than the deferential alone; in both cases the effect is softening.

(58)   V4 (Discourse)
        a. 나는 학교에 가요.
           Na=nun   hakkyo=ey   ka-yo.
           I=TOP   school=DIR go-POL
           'I go to school.'
        b. 너는 학교에 가지요.
           Ne=nun   hakkyo=ey   ka-ciyo.
           you=TOP   school=DIR go-SUSP-POL
           'You probably go to school.'
        c. 학교에 갔습니다요.
           Hakkyo=ey   ka-ss-supnita-yo.
           school=DIR   go-PAST-DEF-DIS
           '(I) went to school.'

To recapitulate the suffix ordering after inflecting stems, seven different orderings are possible given that the verb stem is a bound morpheme and minimally V3 (Mood) is obligatory:

(59)   Suffix slot combinations
        a. Verb – V3
        b. Verb – V1 – V3
        c. Verb – V2 – V3
        d. Verb – V3 – V4
        e. Verb – V1 – V2 – V3
        f. Verb – V1 – V3 – V4
        g. Verb – V1 – V2 – V3 – V4

(60)   Examples of suffix slots for inflecting stems.
        a. 갑니다
           ka-pnita   V – V3
           go-DEFDEC
        b. 가십니다
           ka-si-pnita   V – V1 – V3
           go-HON-DEFDEC
        c. 갔습니다
           ka-ss-supnita   V – V2 – V3
           go-PAST-DEFDEC
        d. 갔습니다요
           ka-ss-supnita-yo   V – V3 – V4
           go-PAST-DEFDEC-POL

e. 가시었습니다
   ka-si-ess-supnita   V – V1 – V2 – V3
   go-HON-DEFDEC
f. 가십니다요
   ka-si-pnita-yo   V – V1 – V3 – V4
   go-HON-DEFDEC-POL
g. 가시었습니다요
   ka-si-ess-supnita-yo   V – V1 – V2 – V3 – V4
   go-HON-PAST-DEFDEC-POL

Both subordinate clause V3 morphemes and V4 -*yo* can be followed by postnominal particles, specifically delimiters:

(61)   Verb with nominal inflection
   a. V – V1 ~ V3 (subordinate) = Delimiter
   b. V – V1 ~ V4   =   Delimiter

(62)   Sentences with Verbal and Nominal Inflection
   a. 가시었지만
      ka-si-ess-ci-man
      go-V1(HON)-V2 (TAM)-V3 (Mood)=Delimiter
      '(Someone) went (somewhere), but –'
   b. 가시었습니다요만
      ka-si-ess-supnita-yo-man
      go-V1(HON)-V2(TAM)-V3(Mood)-V4(DIS)=Delimiter
      '(Someone) only went to (somewhere). But –'

5.5 Compounding

Compounding is a word formation process in which two or more free morphemes combine to form a single word. We distinguish two types relevant for Korean, co-compounding and sub-compounding. In this section we introduce patterns of co-compounding and sub-compounding for nouns, verbs, adjectives, and adverbs. Phonological processes involved in compounding are discussed only in relation to Chapter 4. We discuss compounding in relation to all lexical strata, including native and Sino-Korean lexical items.

5.5.1 Co-compounding

In co-compounding, the members of the compound are of equivalent status. The meaning of the compound is the union of its members; therefore co-compounds are sometimes called coordinate compounds. Examples can be found with both substantives (nouns) and inflecting stems. We indicate compounds of all types with a plus (+) sign.

(63)   NN Co-compounds
논밭   *non+path*   rice paddies-dry fields
남녀   *nam+nye*   man-woman
밤낮   *pam+nac*   night-day
손발   *son+pal*   hand-foot

(64)   VV Co-compounds
오가다   *o+kata*   come-go
여닫다   *ye+tatta*   open-close
우짖다   *wu+cicta*   cry-bark
오르내리다 *olu+naylita* go up-go down

The VV co-compounds in (64) result from the same process of unaffixed
verb stem compounding that we saw with *noh-chita* 'put-break' = 'lose'
and *nem-chita* 'exceed-hit' = 'overflow'. The difference is that while both
verb stems contribute equally to the meaning of the compound in the co-
compounds, in *noh-chita* and *nem-chita* the semantic contribution of the
two components is more opaque, with *chi-* 'hit' contributing an intensifying sense, and the first component contributing much of the lexical meaning. Bare stem VV compounds of both types are not productive in
Contemporary Korean.

5.5.2   Sub-compounding

In Korean sub-compounds, the second member is the head of the compound,
while the first member functions as a modifier or argument of the head. There
are nominal, verbal, adjectival, and adverbial sub-compounds. Nominal sub-
compounds include four patterns: NN (65), VN (66), AN (67), and
AdvN (68).

(65)   NN
돌다리   *tol-tali*   stone bridge
꽃밭   *kkoch-path*   flower field
사과나무 *sakwa-namwu* apple tree
집비둘기 *cip-pitwulki*   house pigeon

(66)   VN
비빔밥 *pipim-pap*   mix-cooked rice
갈림길 *kallim-kil*   crossroad
디딤돌 *titim-tol*   stepping stone
날짐승 *nal-cimsung* flying beast

Although the initial elements in the VN sub-compounds in (66) all involve
verbal stems, formally the first three examples are nouns, involving nominalizations in *-(u)m*.

(67)   AN

오른손	*olun-son*	right hand
늦더위	*nuc-tewi*	late heat
작은형	*cakun-hyeng*	younger brother
된서리	*toyn-seli*	hard frost
빈주먹	*pin-cwumek*	empty hand

The last three examples in (67) involve the regular adnominal form of the adjective in *-(u)n*, but they are identifiable as compounds because of their lexicalized meanings.

(68)   AdvN

부슬비	*pwusul-pi*	thin-rain
혼잣말	*honcas-mal*	alone-language

There are four major patterns of verbal sub-compounding in VV (69), NV (70), AV (71) and AdvV (72).

(69)   VV

돌아가다	*tol-a-kata*	return-go	'go back'
타고가다	*tha-ko-ka-ta*	ride-go	'go by (riding a) vehicle'
내려다보다	*nayly-e-ta-po-ta*	descend-see	'look down'

Examples such as *tola-ka-* 'go back' have traditionally been treated as serial verb constructions, but in its idiomatic meaning 'pass away, die' *tola-ka-* is arguably a lexicalized compound. Similarly, the first members of *tha-ko-ka-* 'go by vehicle' and *nayly-e-ta-po-* 'look down' are suffixed by the gerundive suffix *-ko* and the sequential suffix *-ta* and thus are better regarded as VP adjuncts rather than true compounds.

(70)   NV

힘들다	*him-tulta*	effort-enter	'difficult, trying'
본받다	*pon-patta*	example-receive	'imitate'
손익다	*son-ikta*	hand-be skillful	'thrilled'
목마르다	*mok-maluta*	neck-dry up	'thirsty'
손잡다	*son-capta*	hand-grab	'handy'

Korean has a fairly productive process of object–verb compounding exemplified by *son-capi* 'handle, knob'. This process has sometimes been analyzed as noun incorporation. Object–verb compounds with non-nominalized verbs such as *him-tulta* 'difficult, trying' and *pon-patta* 'imitate' are less productive.

(71)   AV

게을러빠지다	*keyulle-ppacita*	lazy-fall into	'become very lazy'

(72)   AdvV

가로막다	*kalo-makta*	cross-block	'block, obstruct'
가만두다	*kaman-twuta*	quietly-put	'leave as is'
마주서다	*macwu-seta*	facing-stand	'stand face-to-face'

In adjectival sub-compounding, there are two major patterns; NA (73) and AA (74).

(73)   NA
         낯설다 *nach-selta* face-unused to 'unfamiliar'

(74)   AA
         굳세다   *kwut-seyta*   firm-strong   'very strong'
         남사스럽다 *namsa-sulepta* other's laugh-like 'ridiculous'

An interesting generalization about compounding in Korean is that patterns where both members of the compound match in syntactic category seem to be the most productive. Even with sub-compounds, for example in VN compounds such as *pipim-pap* in (64), the pattern which nominalizes the verb member of the compound is most productive; likewise with NV compounds (70), the productive pattern involves nominalizing the verbal member of the compound.

5.6   Postnominal Particles

As described in Section 5.1.4, Korean particles can be classified into postpositions, delimiters, and case markers. A major issue in Korean morphology is whether particles are to be treated as a kind of inflection, comparable to verbal inflection. In Section 5.6, we defend a position closer to the view in traditional Korean linguistics, that is, postnominal particles are distinct from the suffixes found in verbal inflection. Here we focus on the basic distribution of particles.

The linear ordering of nominal inflection is quite strict, as shown in (75) and (76):

(75)   Linear order of nominal inflection
         Noun   – Postposition – Delimiter – Case
         시장   에   만   이
         sicang – *ey*   – *man*   – *i*
         market – LOC   – only   – NOM
         '(It is) only in the market (that)'

(76)   Postpositions
         a. 에   *ey*   'in, at, to'   Locative
         b. 에게/한테   *eykey/hanthey*   'to'   Dative
         c. 에서   *eyse*   'at/to'   Dynamic
                                                                          locative
         d. (으)로   *(u)lo*   'with, to'   Directional,
                                                                          Instrumental
         e. 부터   *pwuthe*   'from'   Ablative
         f. 에서/에게서/한테서   *eyse/eykeyse/*   'from'   Ablative
                                  hantheyse
         g. 까지   *kkaci*   'until'   Goal

h.	처럼	*chelem*	'like'	Simulative
i.	보다	*pota*	'than'	Comparative
j.	하고/과/와	*hako/kwa/wa*	'with, and'	Comitative, Conjunctive
k.	(이)나	*(i)na*	'or'	Disjunctive
l.	께서	*kkeyse*		Subject honorific
m.	께	*kkey*		Indirect object honorific

The location and goal marking postpositions are distinguished by animacy and the dynamic properties of the predicate. *Ey* marks static location in a place or motion toward an inanimate goal. Dative *eykey* and *hanthey* mark animate goals. Addition of *se* derives ablative (source) postposition 'from', with the animacy contrasts retained as in the following examples.

(77)   Source and goal marking postpositions
  a. 나는 철수에게/한테 책을 줘요.
Na=nun   *Chelswu=eykey/hanthey chayk=ul   cwu-eyo.*
I=TOP   Chelswu=DAT   book=ACC   give-POL
'I give a book to Chelswu.'
  b. 나는 철수에게서/한테서 책을 받아요.
Na=nun   *Chelswu=eykeyse/hantheyse chayk=ul   pat-ayo.*
I=TOP   Chelswu=from   book=ACC   receive-POL
'I receive a book from Chelswu.'
  c. 나는 학교에 가요.
Na=nun   *hakkyo=ey   ka-yo.*
I=TOP   school=to   go-POL
'I go to school.'
  d. 나는 도서관에서 와요.
Na=nun   *tosekwan=eyse   wa-yo.*
I=TOP   library=from   come-POL
'I come from the library.'

The difference between *eykey* and *hanthey* lies in the degree of formality: the former is more formal than the latter. Locative *ey* marks an inanimate goal as in (77c) with a verb of motion, and a location with an existential verb as in (78a). The postposition *(u)lo* marks direction toward (78b) and instruments (78d). The link between these two functions is the perlative 'motion through' meaning shown in (78c).

(78)   Locative and Directional Postpositions
  a. 나는 집에 있어요.
Na=nun cip=ey   iss-eyo.
I=TOP   home=at   be-PRES-POL
'I am at home.'

b. 나는 학교로 가요.
   Na=nun   hakkyo=lo   ka-yo.
   I=TOP   school=to   go-POL
   'I go to school.'

c. 나는 정문으로 가요.
   Na=nun   cengmwun=ulo   ka-yo.
   I=TOP   main.gate=through go-POL
   'I go through the main gate.'

d. 나는 연필로 이름을 썼다.
   Na=nun   yenphil=lo   ilum=ul   ss-ess-ta.
   I=TOP   pencil=with name=ACC write-PAST-DEC
   'I wrote my name with a pencil.'

As these examples show, many Korean particles are polysemous, with their meaning determined by context. Therefore, where necessary, we gloss postpositions with the English preposition whose meaning is most appropriate in the context given.

The nominative and accusative particles are discussed in 6.1. Nominative has a corresponding subject–honorific counterpart, as do the postpositions marking the indirect object. The honorific particles are postpositions, not case particles, as shown by their ability to be followed by delimiters such as the topic marker *(n)un* or *to* 'also' in (79b). In contrast, case particles such as nominative *i/ka* cannot be followed by delimiters in (79a).

(79)   Subject and Indirect Object honorific postpositions

a. 선생님이(*=는/=도) 학교에 가요.
   Sensayngnim=i(=nun/=to) hakkyo=ey ka-yo.*
   teacher=NOM(=TOP/=also)   school=to go-POL
   'The teacher goes to school.'

b. 선생님께서(는/도) 학교에 가세요.
   Sensayngnim=kkeyse(=nun/=to) hakkyo=ey ka-sey-yo.
   teacher=NOM(HON)(=TOP/=also)   school=to go-HON-POL
   'The teacher goes to school.'

c. 나는 선생님에게(는/도) 책을 드려요.
   Na=nun sensayngnim=eykey(=nun/=to) chayk=ul tulye-yo.
   I=TOP   teacher=DAT(=TOP/=also)   book=ACC give-POL
   'I give a book to the teacher.'

d. 나는 선생님께(는/도) 책을 드려요.
   Na=nun sensayngnim=kkey(=nun/=to) chayk=ul tulye-yo.
   I=TOP   teacher=DAT(HON)(=TOP/=also)   book=ACC give-POL
   'I give a book to the teacher.'

In examples (79b) and (79d), the honorific particles *kkeyse* and *kkey* express the speaker's deference toward the subject and indirect object respectively.

The postpositions *kkaci* 'until, as far as' and *pwuthe* 'from' are used with both location and time expressions (80). They can also express the first in a sequence or the endpoint in a scale as in (80). In this last, scalar meaning *kkaci* functions as a delimiter.

(80)   *Kkaci* 'until, as far as' and *pwuthe* 'from'
    a. 나는 5시까지 학교에 가요.
       Na=nun   *tasessi=kkaci*   *hakkyo=ey* *ka-yo.*
       I=TOP   5 o'clock=until   school=to go-POL
       'I go to school until 5 o'clock.'
    b. 나는 5시부터 공부해요.
       Na=nun   *tasessi=pwuthe kongpwuhay-yo.*
       I=TOP   5 o'clock=from study-POL
       'I study from 5 o'clock.'
    c. 나는 뉴욕까지 가요.
       Na=nun   *nyuyok=kkaci*   *ka-yo.*
       I=TOP   New York=until go-POL
       'I go as far as New York.'
    d. 나는 마이애미부터 여행해요.
       Na=nun   *maiaymi=pwuthe yehaynghay-yo.*
       I=TOP   Miami=from   travel-POL
       'I travel from Miami.'
    e. 나는 마이애미부터 뉴욕까지 여행해요.
       Na=nun   *maiaymi=pwuthe nyuyok=kkaci*   *yehaynghay-yo.*
       I=TOP   Miami=from   New York=until travel-POL
       'I travel from Miami to New York.'
    f. 철수부터 말하기 시작했어요.
       Chelswu=pwuthe malha-ki   *sicakhay-ss-eyo.*
       Chelswu=from   speak-COMP   begin-PAST-POL
       '(They) began speaking starting from Chelswu.'
    g. 철수까지 말했어요.
       Chelswu=kkaci   *malhay-ss-eyo.*
       Chelswu=until   speak-PAST-POL
       'Even Chelswu spoke.'

The conjunctive postpositions ('and') in Korean also function as comitative 'with' (81d). Among them the allomorphy of *wa/kwa* is conditioned by whether the preceding noun ends in a vowel or consonant, while *hako* is invariant. Disjunction is expressed by *(i)-na* 'or' which is derived from the copula stem *i-* plus the alternative ending *(i)-na*. Conjunctive and disjunctive postpositions share the property pointed out in Section 5.1.4 that they link only NP and NP; they cannot link VPs or clauses. Both may be doubled after the second member of the conjunct, as shown in (81c) for *hako* and (81e–f) for alternative *(i)-na*.

(81)   Conjunctive postpositions
    a. 나는 사과와 포도를 먹어요.

Na=nun	*sakwa=wa*	*photo=lul*	*mek-eyo.*
I=TOP	apple=and/or	grape=ACC	eat-POL

       'I eat apples and grapes.'
    b. 나는 도서관과 극장을 가요.

Na=nun	*tosekwan=kwa*	*kukcang=ul*	*ka-yo.*
I=TOP	library=and	theater=ACC	go-POL

       'I go to the library and theater.'
    c. 나는 사과하고 포도를 먹어요.

Na=nun	*sakwa=hako*	*photo(=hako)=lul*	*mek-eyo.*
I=TOP	apple=and	grape=ACC	eat-POL

       'I eat apples and grapes.'
    d. 나는 수원과/하고 극장에 가요.

Na=nun	*Swuwen=kwa/hako*	*kukcang=ey*	*ka-yo.*
I=TOP	Suwon=with	theater=ACC	go-POL

       'I go to the theater with Suwon.'
    e. 사과나 배나 다 좋다.

Sakwa=na	*pay=na*	*ta*	*coh-ta.*
apple=or	pear=or	all	like-PLN

       'I like both apples and pears.'
    f. 한국이나 미국이나 다 좋다.

Hankwuk=ina	*mikwuk=i-na*	*ta*	*coh-ta.*
Korea=or	America=or	all	like-PLN

       'I like both Korea and America.'

Postpositions expressing comparison include *chelem* 'like' and *pota* 'than'.

(82)   Postpositions of comparison
    a. 나는 철수처럼 일하고 싶다.

Na=nun	*Chelswu=chelem*	*ilha-ko siph-ta.*
I=TOP	Chelswu=like	work-would like-PLN

       'I would like to work like Chelswu.'
    b. 미국이 한국보다 더 크다.

Mikwuk=i	*hankwuk=pota*	*te*	*khu-ta.*
America=NOM	Korea=than	more	big-PLN

       'America is bigger than Korea.'

Two or more postpositions can be combined, as in (83):

(83)   Stacked postpositions
    a. *Eykey=lo=pwuthe*
       친구에게로부터 그 책을 받았어요.

Chinkwu=eykey=lo=pwuthe	*ku*	*chayk=ul*	*pat-ass-eyo.*
friend=DAT=DIR=from	that	book=ACC	receive-PAST-POL

       '(Someone) received that book from a friend.'

b. *Kkey=lo*
아버님께로 보냅니다.
Apenim=kkey=lo   ponay-pnita.
father=DAT(HON)=DIR send-DEF
'(Someone) sends (something) to his father.'

c. *Eyse=kkaci*
학교에서까지 해라.
Hakkyo=eyse=kkaci   hayla.
school=LOC=GOAL   do-IMP
'Do it at school.'

These combinations fit with the crosslinguistic generalization that when adpositions combine, the pre- or postposition expressing 'place' is most deeply embedded, while the adposition expressing 'path' is higher in the structure. This can be seen in languages which have so-called "circumpositions," like German *unter der Brücke durch* 'through under the bridge' or Chinese *cóng zhuōzi shàng* 'from on the table'. In these PPs, the path expression ('through', 'from') dominates the adposition expressing location. The structure is shown in (84) and compared with Korean. The only difference is that while Chinese and German have both prepositions and postpositions, in Korean place and path are both expressed by postpositions.

(84)   Complex postpositional phrases in Korean and other languages
a.   [$_{\text{PATH}}$ *cóng* [$_{\text{PLACE}}$ [$_{\text{NP}}$ *zhuōzi*] *shàng*]]   Chinese
          from   table   on
'From on the table'
b.   [$_{\text{PATH}}$ [$_{\text{PLACE}}$ [$_{\text{NP}}$ *hakkyo ey*] *kkaci*]   Korean
          school   to   as far as
'As far as to school'

The second slot for postnominal particles after postpositions is for delimiters (Yang's [1972] term). Delimiters specify the semantic or information structural status of the NP they follow, rather than its grammatical relation in the clause or location in time or space. Below is a list of delimiters.

(85)   Delimiters
a. 만   *man*   only
b. 밖에   *pakkey*   only (exceptive negative polarity item or NPI)
c. 도   *to*   also
d. 까지   *kkaci*   even
e. 마저   *mace*   even
f. 조차   *cocha*   even (NPI)
g. (이)라도   *(i)lato*   even
h. 도   *to*   also, too, even

Korean provides two ways of saying 'only', but the exceptive delimiter *pakkey* is a negative polarity item comparable to English 'anything but'; it requires that the clause it occurs in be negated.

(86)   'Only'
a. 나는 돈만 있어요.
   Na=nun   ton=man   iss-eyo.
   I=TOP   money=only   have-POL
   'I have only money.'
b. 나는 돈밖에 없어요.
   Na=nun   ton=pakkey   eps-eyo.
   I=TOP   money=nothing but   not have-POL
   'I don't have anything but money.'
c. 나는 학교에서만 공부해요.
   Na=nun   hakkyo=eyse=man   kongpwuhay-yo.
   I=TOP   school=at=only   study-POL
   'I study only at school.'
d. 나는 학교에서밖에 공부 안해요.
   Na=nun   hakkyo=eyse=pakkey   kongpwu   an-hay-yo.
   I=TOP   school=at=nothing but   study   not-do-POL
   'I don't study anywhere but at school (I study only at school).'

Numerous delimiters have the basic meaning 'even': *kkaci, cocha, mace,* and *(i)lato*. These delimiters have diverse sources; as we have seen, the delimiter function of *kkaci* derives from its meaning indicating the endpoint of a scale, while *(i)-la-to* derives from the alternative form of the copula *i-* plus the delimiter *to* 'also, even'. *Cocha* 'even' is another NPI delimiter.

(87)   'Even'
a. 나는 학교까지 가요.
   Na=nun   hakkyo=kkaci   ka-yo.
   I=TOP   school=even/until go-POL
   'I go even to school.' (Delimiter meaning)
   'I go as far as school.' (Postposition meaning)
b. 너마저 나를 배반했어.
   Ne=mace   na=lul   paypanhay-ss-e.
   you=even   I=ACC   betray-PAST-INT
   'Even you betrayed me.'
c. 너조차 숙제를 안 했어?
   Ne=cocha   swukcey=lul   an   hay-ss-e.
   you=even   homework=ACC   NEG   do-PAST-Q
   'Even you didn't do your homework?'
d. 너라도 가야지.
   Ne=lato   ka-yaci.
   you=even/at least   go-should
   'You, at least, should go.'

Items like 'even' are classified by semanticists as association-with-focus markers, because in languages like English the focus expressed by 'even' can be associated with a constituent at some distance from it by intonational prominence:

(88)   Suwon even read the BOOK = Suwon read even the book.

This kind of possibility is more limited in Korean, but in Korean as well, delimiters can mark association with focus on a constituent contained inside the phrase they are attached to:

(89)   a. 너는 수학 숙제조차 안 했어?
             Ne=nun   *SWUHAK*   *swukcey=cocha*   *an*   *hay-ss-e?*
             you=TOP   math   homework=even   NEG   do-PAST-Q
             'You didn't even do your MATH homework?'
         b. 너는 수학의 숙제조차 안 했어?
             Ne=nun   *swuhak=uy*   *SWUKCEY=cocha*   *an*   *hay-ss-e?*
             you=TOP   math=GEN   homework=even   NEG   do-PAST-Q
             'You didn't even do your math HOMEWORK?'

Association-with-focus particles like 'even' have a function in common with intensifiers, in that they specify the extreme degree of an expression interpreted as picking out a scale. Some of the delimiters with scalar meanings like this are combined with one another to further emphasize the extreme point of a scale, but others, such as *kkaci*, do not allow this possibility:

(90)   'Even' iterated
         a. 너마저조차 나를 싫어해.
             Ne=mace=cocha   *na=lul*   *silhe-hay.*
             you=even=even   me=ACC   dislike-INT
             'Even you dislike me.'
         b. 너조차마저 나를 싫어해.
             Ne=cocha=mace   *na=lul*   *silhe-hay.*
             you=even=even   me=ACC   dislike-INT
             'Even you dislike me.'
         c. *너까지마저/라도 나를 싫어해.
             Ne=kkaci=mace/=lato   *na=lul*   *silhe-hay.*
             you=even=even   me=ACC   dislike-INT
             'Even you dislike me.'
         d. *너까지라도 나를 싫어해.
             Ne=kkaci=lato   *na=lul*   *silhe-hay.*
             you=even=even   me=ACC   dislike-INT
             'Even you dislike me.'

Two of the most important delimiters are the topic marker *(n)un* and the association-with-focus particle *to* 'also, too, even'. From the standpoint of English, the meanings of 'also' and 'even' may seem quite distinct, but both mark association with focus and both indicate a point on a scale. Consider the following two Korean examples.

(91)   The delimiter *to* 'also' and 'even'
    a. 너도 나를 싫어해.
       Ne=to   na=lul   silhe-hay.
       you=also   me=ACC dislike-INT
       'You too dislike me.'
    b. 그것은 어린애도 알아요.
       Ku kes=un   elin   ay=to   al-ayo.
       that thing=TOP   young child=even know-POL
       'That, even a little child knows.'

An English translation of (91b) as 'That, also a little child knows' would be somewhat odd, because the force of the sentence is to express a limit (in this case, the lower limit) on a scale. In the interpretation of *to*, the scalar interpretation is determined by context.

While the function of the other delimiters is to express association with focus, the delimiter *(n)un* marks topic, a different kind of information structural status. The syntax and semantics of topic and focus are discussed in Chapter 8. Here we simply show on distributional grounds that *(n)un* is a delimiter: it follows postpositions and is in complementary distribution with case particles:

(92)   a. 철수가*=는/*도 학교에서 공부해요.
       Chelswu=ka*=nun/*=to   hakkyo=eyse kongpwuhay-yo.
       Chelswu=NOM*=TOP/*=also   school=at   study-POL
       'Chelswu studies at school.'
    b. 학교에서는/도 공부해요.
       Hakkyo=eyse=nun/=to   kongpwuhay-yo.
       school=at=TOP/=also   study-POL
       'At school, (someone) studies.'
       'At school too, someone studies.'

Because, as we have seen, delimiters may co-occur with one another, the topic marker may co-occur with other delimiters, but it must follow them, and it does not co-occur with *to* 'also':

(93)   수원에게만은 책을 주었다.
       Swuwen=eykey=man=un chayk=ul cwu-ess-ta.
       Suwon=DAT=only=TOP   book=ACC give-PAST-DEC
       'Only to Suwon did (someone) give a book.'

We pointed out in Section 5.1.4 that delimiters can follow nonfinite forms of verbs and adjectives, as well as embedded clauses and adverbs. We illustrate this in (94) with adverbs.

(94) a. 행복하게만 사세요.
     Hayngpokhakey-man   sa-seyyo.
     happily-DELIMITER (only) live-POL
     'Please live happily.'
    b. 행복하게는 살아요?
     Hayngpokhakey-nun   sal-ayo?
     happily-CASE   live-Q
     'Do (they) live happily?'
    c. 행복하게만은 안 돼요.
     Hayngpokhakey-man-un   an   tway-yo.
     happily-DELIMITER-CASE   NEG become-POL
     'It is not the case that (they) live happily.'

The third or outermost slot for postnominal particles is occupied by case markers, specifically nominative, genitive, and accusative as in (95) with examples in (96). As the examples show, the nominative and accusative particles fall into the group of particles whose shape alternates depending upon whether the preceding word ends in a vowel or consonant.

(95)   Case markers
    a. 이/가   *i/ka*   'nominative'
    b. 의   *uy*   'genitive'
    c. ㄹ/을/를 *l/ul/lul* 'accusative'

(96)   Case markers in context
    a. 수원이/철수가 학교에 가요.
     Swuwen=i/Chelswu=ka   hakkyo=ey   ka-yo.
     Swuwen=NOM/Chelswu=NOM school=to   go-POL
     'Suwon/Chelswu goes to school.'
    b. 철수의 집에서 공부해요.
     Chelswu=uy   cip=eyse   kongpwuhay-yo.
     Chelswu=GEN   home=LOC   study-POL
     '(Someone) studies at Chelswu's house.'
    c. 나는 선생님을/친구를 만나요.
     Na=nun   sensayngnim=ul/chinkwu=lul manna-yo.
     I=TOP   teacher=ACC/friend=ACC   meet-POL
     'I meet a teacher/friend.'

Within the template, postposition – delimiter – case marker, all slots can be filled:

(97)   Combinations of postposition, delimiter, and case marker
    a. 이제부터   Noun=Postposition
     I cey=pwuthe
     now=from
     'from now'
    b. 이제만   Noun=Delimiter
     I cey=man
     now=only
     'only now'

c. 이제가 (시작이다)   Noun=Case
  I cey=ka   *(sicak=i-ta)*
  now=NOM   start=be-DEC
  'Now is the start.'

d. 이제부터만   Noun=Postposition=Delimiter
  I cey=pwuthe=man
  now=from=only
  'only from now'

e. 이제부터가 (시작이다)   Noun=Postposition=Case
  I cey=pwuthe=ka   *(sicak=i-ta).*
  now=from=NOM   start=be-DEC
  'From now is the start.'

f. 이제부터만이 (있을 뿐   Noun=Postposition=Delimiter=Case
  이다)
  I cey=pwuthe=man=i   *(iss-ul*   *ppwun=i-ta).*
  now=from=only=NOM   (exist-FUTADN   just=be-DEC)
  'It is just only from now that it could be.'

5.7   The Clitic Status of Postnominal Particles

Up until now we have avoided taking a position on the status of postnominal particles, although we have represented them in examples as connected to the preceding word with an equal sign (=). This is the conventional way of representing clitics, elements that are phonologically dependent on the following word (proclitics) or the preceding word (enclitics), but not as tightly bound as affixes. An outstanding issue in Korean linguistics is whether particles should be considered affixes, clitics, or even a type of word. In this section, we explore that issue. As we mentioned in Section 5.1, traditional Korean grammarians treat verbal suffixes (어미 *emi*) and postnominal particles (조사 *cosa*) as quite different categories, but contemporary Korean linguists writing in English have tended to be less careful about the distinction. Kuh (1988), Chae and No (1998), Chae (2007), and Chae and Roh (2010) are among those who have looked at the issue in detail; they conclude that postnominal particles are clitics, not suffixes. See Vance (1993) for a similar conclusion regarding Japanese postnominal particles. In this section we apply the criteria of Zwicky and Pullum (1983) to investigate this issue.

English has a variety of clitics such as possessive *'s* and reduced auxiliaries like the future auxiliary in *she'll* (Zwicky 1977, Zwicky and Pullum 1983). Zwicky and Pullum (1983) and Zwicky (1987) list the following criteria for distinguishing affixes and clitics:

(98)   Differences between affixes and clitics

	Affixes	Clitics
Selectivity	High degree	Low degree
Morphological idiosyncrasy	Yes	No
Ordering	*Clitic + affix	Clitic + clitic

First, Zwicky and Pullum (1983: 503) say that clitics exhibit a low degree of selectivity with respect to their hosts, while affixes exhibit a high degree. For example, the English past tense suffix *-ed* is added only to verb stems, but the clitic *'s* (the contraction of *is*) can be added to a host of almost any category. The selectivity test supports the classification of English *'s* as a clitic. What about Korean particles? We have seen that delimiters in particular show a very low degree of selectivity: they occur following virtually every category including nonfinite forms of verbs, adjectives, and adverbs, as well as postpositions and other delimiters. Postpositions occur after nouns and other postpositions. Case markers occur after nouns, postpositions, and delimiters. This lack of selectivity contrasts with verbal suffixes in Korean, which generally follow only a small set of possible hosts. For example, subject-honorific *-(u)si-* follows only the bare verb or auxiliary stem.

A second kind of selectivity has to do with the specific form of the host selected by the clitic or affix. As we saw in Chapter 4, Korean consonant clusters are invariably reduced, either by deletion leaving a single consonant in coda position, or by resyllabification of the second member of the cluster as the onset of the following syllable. Vowel-initial verbal suffixes select only the second option, as shown in (99a). But vowel-initial postnominal particles permit two options. They may trigger resyllabification of the final consonant, or they may treat the boundary before the particle as equivalent to word-final position (99b). In the latter case, the cluster is simplified, just as it would be at a word boundary.

(99)   a. /eps-ul/   →   [əpsɨl] (*[əbɨl])
           not.exist-FUTADN
        b. /kaps=ul/   →   [kapsɨl], [kabɨl]
           price=ACC

This variable behavior on the part of postnominal particles is very hard to explain on the view that particles are suffixes. No verbal suffix shows behavior of this type. On the standard view that clitics are closer to independent words than affixes, it makes sense that a clitic boundary can behave like a word boundary.

Second, Zwicky and Pullum (1983: 504) say that morphological idiosyncrasies are more characteristic of affixed words than clitic groups. Korean common-noun + particle combinations show essentially no idiosyncrasies, except for a few examples involving dependent nouns and pronouns plus case markers, pointed out by Cho and Sells (1995).

(100)   Morphological idiosyncrasies with dependent noun/pronoun + particle
        a.   이것이   becomes   이게
                 i-kes-i   *i-key*
                 this-thing-NOM   this-NOM

b.	무엇을	becomes	뭘
	mwues-ul		*mwel*
	what-ACC		what-ACC
c.	나는	becomes	난
	na-nun		*nan*
	I-TOP		I-TOP
d.	너를	becomes	널
	ne-lul		*nel*
	you-ACC		you-ACC

Pronouns and dependent nouns such as *kes* 'thing, one' plus particles are high-frequency combinations which are subject to the kind of reductions found in fast speech. The same is true of English *I am* → *I'm*, but no linguist would call *-m* in this contraction a suffix. To sharpen Zwicky and Pullum's criteria, we must distinguish contraction phenomena associated with high-frequency items in fast speech from idiosyncrasies that show no relation to the phonetic input. Examples of such idiosyncrasies are easy to find in Korean verbal inflection: they include the contrast between the infinitive of *t*-irregular verbs such as *ket-* 'walk', infinitive *kel-e*, and regular *t*-stems such as *pat-* 'receive', infinitive *pat-a*; or *p*-irregular verbs such as *top-* 'help', infinitive *tow-a*, versus regular *p*-stems such as *cap-* 'grab', infinitive *cap-a*. None of these idiosyncrasies are predictable from the segmental input alone. No comparable idiosyncrasies are to be found among postnominal particles.

Third, Zwicky and Pullum (1983: 504) say that clitics can attach to material already containing clitics, but affixes cannot. This argument requires that we first show that certain particles are clitics; then it follows by Zwicky and Pullum's argument that particles that can follow them are also clitics. We have seen that delimiters have the strongest claim to be clitics, since they can follow almost any grammatical category. Since, as we saw in (97f), repeated as (101) below, case markers can follow delimiters, it follows that they too are clitics.

(101)　이제부터만이 (있을 뿐이다) (=97 f)
　　　I cey=pwuthe=man=i (iss-ul　　ppwun=i-ta)
　　　now=from=only=NOM (exist-FUTADN just=be-DEC)
　　　'It is just only from now that it could be.'

In sum, Pullum and Zwicky's tests to distinguish affixes and clitics indicate that Korean particles are clitics, not affixes. Let us take a look at the tests distinguishing clitics and words, given in Zwicky (1987). All of these tests are based on the idea that a clitic is dependent on an adjacent word (102).

(102)   Differences between clitics and independent words

	Clitics	Independent words
Sandhi	Internal	External
Prosodic phonology	Word domain	Phrase domain
Binding	Bound	Free
Distribution	Simple	Complex
Deletion	No	Yes
Replacement	No	Yes
Movement	No	Yes

Among the phonological processes we saw in Chapter 4, most apply within the domain of the accentual phrase, such as post-obstruent tensing, or a larger domain, such as intersonorant voicing. Since these include some word boundaries, they qualify as what Zwicky (1987: 286) calls external sandhi. Exceptions to this are the rules governing vowel–vowel hiatus. As we have seen, these apply to the allomorphs of some nonfinal verbal suffixes, such as subject-honorific *-(u)si-*, past *-(a/e)ss-*, some final suffixes like conditional *-(u) myen* and interrogative *-(u)ni*, and also to some postnominal particles, including some case particles, (nominative = *i/=ka*, accusative = *(l)ul*), some delimiters (topic marker = *(n)un*), and some postpositions (directional = *(u)lo*). This is a clear boundary phenomenon that applies to some affixes and particles, but not to words, even in compound environments.

Second, according to Zwicky (1987: 286), "If an element counts as belonging to a phonological word for the purposes of accent, tone, or length assignment, then it should be a clitic. If an element counts as belonging to a phonological phrase for these purposes, then it should be an independent word." In varieties of Korean with lexical tone, postnominal particles invariably pattern as part of the domain for realizing lexical tone (Ramsey 1978). For example, monosyllabic nouns of the rising class in South Kyŏngsang Korean are realized with rising pitch when pronounced in isolation. But the same contour is extended over the noun and particle when a particle is added, to give a low–high contour:

(103)   a. *nŭn* 'snow' (rising)
          b. *nùn=i* 'snow=NOM' (low–high)

This pattern of extension of the rising contour does not occur across word boundaries.

Third, Zwicky (1987: 287) states: "If an element is bound, and especially if it cannot occur in complete isolation, it should be a clitic; if free, and especially if it occurs in complete isolation, it should be an independent word." Korean particles obey this test more strictly than postnominal particles in Japanese. For example, in Japanese a speaker may break in and continue another speaker's utterance, beginning with a particle. This is less felicitous in Korean:

(104)   Korean   Japanese
        Speaker A: 파리 ...
                    Phali   *Pari*
                    Paris   Paris
                    'Paris ...'   'Paris ...'
        Speaker B: %에는 못갔어요.
                    %=*ey*=*nun mos-ka-ss-eyo.*   =*ni*=*wa ik-ana-katta.*
                    =to=TOP   cannot-go-PAST-POL =to-TOP go-PAST
                    '(I) didn't go to.'   'I didn't go to.'

Zwicky's fourth criterion (1987: 288) states: "An element with a simple distribution is a clitic and an element with a complex distribution is almost surely
an independent word." We have seen that postpositions in particular have
a simple distribution: they are restricted to the position following an overt
NP. This contrasts with prepositions in English, which may be stranded, for
example in relative clauses (105a). The corresponding example in Korean
(105b) shows that postposition stranding is not possible.

(105)   a. [The village that I returned to Ø]
         b. *[Nay=ka (*Ø=ey) tol-a ka-n   maul]*
             I=NOM   =to   return-INF go-PSTADN village
             'The village that I returned (to)'

Few if any linguists would argue that Korean postnominal particles are words,
and Zwicky's tests confirm this. Of more significance is the demonstration that
tests in the same tradition show that these particles are also distinct from
affixes. They belong to the morphological class of clitics.

5.8   Summary

In this chapter, we have described morphological categories, their properties,
and major morphological processes. In Section 5.1, we distinguished five major
morpheme classes, following the traditional Korean *kwu phwumsa* (nine category) classification. In Section 5.2, we described irregular predicates.

In Section 5.3, we discussed derivational processes for all three major word
types: nouns, verbs, and adjectives. In Section 5.4 we showed how inflection
applies to the three types of inflecting stems, verbs, adjectives, and the copula.
Inflecting stems, which are bound, are followed by V1 (Honorifics), V2 (Tense,
Aspect, Modality), V3 (Mood), and V4 (Discourse), where V3 is the only
obligatory member, since V3 decides the sentence type and speech style. We
showed that non-finite inflecting stems as well as substantives and adverbs can
be followed by postnominal particles, in particular delimiters.

In Section 5.5, we described two compounding processes, co-compounding
and sub-compounding. Both NN and VV co-compounding exist in Korean and

three patterns of sub-compounding are prevalent; nominal sub-compounding (NN, VN, AN, AdvN), verbal sub-compounding (NV, VV, AV, AdvV), and adjectival sub-compounding (NA, AA).

In Section 5.6 we described the behavior of postnominal particles and their subtypes: postpositions, delimiters, and case markers. Finally, in Section 5.7 we applied the influential tests of Zwicky and Pullum to show that contrary to the assumption found in much current work on Korean – but conforming to the view of earlier Korean grammarians – Korean postnominal particles form a distinct class from postverbal affixes, the class of clitics.

References

Chae, Hee-Rak. 2007. Clitics and a classification of parts of speech in Korean. *Korean Journal of Linguistics* 32 (4).

Chae, Hee-Rak and Chang-Hwa Roh. 2010. Clitics and related phenomena in Korean and English. In Susumo Kuno et al. (eds.), *Harvard Studies in Korean Linguistics* Vol. XIII, 395–403. Harvard University.

Chae, Hee-Rak and Yongkyoon No. 1998. A survey of morphological issues in Korean: Focusing on syntactically relevant phenomena. *Korean Linguistics* 9.

Cho, Young-Mee Yu and Peter Sells. 1995. A lexical account of inflectional suffixes in Korean. *Journal of East Asian Linguistics* 4.

Kuh, Hakan. 1988. The morphological status of Korean case markers. Papers from the Sixth International Conference on Korean Linguistics, 324–338.

Martin, Samuel E. 1954. *Korean Morphophonemics*. Baltimore: Linguistic Society of America.

Ramsey, Samuel R. 1978. Accent and morphology in Korean dialects. Unpublished Ph. D. dissertation, Yale University.

Sohn, Ho-min. 1999. *The Korean Language*. Cambridge University Press.

Vance, Timothy. 1993. Are Japanese particles clitics? *Journal of the Association of Teachers of Japanese* 27 (1), 3–33.

Yang, In-Seok. 1972. Korean syntax: Case markers, delimiters, complementation, and relativization. Unpublished Ph.D. thesis, University of Hawai'i, Honolulu.

Zwicky, Arnold M. 1977. *On Clitics*. Bloomington, IN: Indiana University Linguistics Club.

Zwicky, Arnold M. 1987. Clitics and particles. *Language* 61 (2), 283–305.

Zwicky, Arnold M. and Geoffrey K. Pullum. 1983. Cliticization vs inflection: English *n't*. *Language* 59 (3), 502–513.

6 Morphosyntax: Case, Grammatical Relations, and Nominalization

In this chapter, we describe the interaction of morphology and syntax with a focus on noun phrases and their role in the sentence. We investigate the syntactic roles of postnominal particles, case markers, postpositions and delimiters. We show how NPs are formed from VPs and clauses, a process called nominalization. We conclude the chapter with an investigation of the morphosyntax of number in Korean and three contentious issues relating to types of double case marking, subjecthood and objecthood.

6.1   Case

From a functional standpoint, case morphology is added to NPs to show the relationship between the constituents of the sentence, in particular, between the verb and its NP arguments and adjuncts. In traditional generative theory, nouns are seen as requiring Case, often written with a capital C to indicate that the relevant notion of "case" is more abstract than morphological case. In a language like Russian, where nouns inflect for case, the relationship between morphological case and abstract case is relatively clear, as shown in (1b). In a language like English, where case inflection is limited to pronouns, and limited to the contrast between subject case and non-subject case for first and third persons (*I* versus *me; she/he* versus *him/her; they* versus *them*), the relation between morphological and abstract case is less obvious. Superficially, Korean looks more like Russian than English, in that there are distinct case markers for each of the NP arguments in a sentence like (1c).

(1)   Case marking
    a. I gave a book to John's friend.
    b. *Ja   dal   knig-u   drug-u   Ivan-a.*
        I.NOM give.MASCSG book-ACC friend-DAT Ivan-GEN
        'I gave a book to Ivan's friend.'
    c. 내가 철수의 친구한테 책을 주었다.
        Nay=ka Chelswu=uy   chinkwu=hanthey chayk=ul cwu-ess-ta.
        I=NOM   Chelswu=GEN friend=DAT   book=ACC give-PAST-PLN
        'I gave a book to Chelswu's friend.'

In Russian (1b), there is a distinct case form for the subject (*ja*, the nominative form of the first-person singular pronoun), the direct object (feminine singular accusative *-u*), the indirect object (masculine singular dative *-u*), and the possessor (masculine singular genitive *-a*). In English (1a), the only visible case inflection is the form of the first-person singular subject *I*. In Korean (1c), there is a distinct case marker corresponding to each of the case forms in Russian: nominative, accusative, dative, and genitive. So superficially, Korean looks like a rich case-marking language, similar to Russian where the noun root is bound.

In fact, this superficial similarity overlies a basic difference. In Russian, case morphology involves inflection on the noun. To be more precise, the head noun in each NP is inflected for the case associated with the whole NP. For example, in (1b) the indirect object is not *drug-u* 'friend-DAT', but [*drug-u Ivan-a*] 'friend-DAT Ivan-GEN'. *Drug-* 'friend' is inflected for dative case because it is the head of the NP. But as we saw in Chapter 5, Korean case markers are not inflectional affixes, but clitics. It may seem strange that case could be marked by clitics. But consider English possessive or genitive *'s* in (1a). Like Korean case markers, *'s* is a clitic. Examples like (2) show that *'s* is not a suffix attached to the head noun of the possessive NP:

(2)   I gave a book to [the person I live next door to]'s sister.

We saw in Chapter 5 that a property of clitics is that they are less selective than affixes. This property holds for *'s*: it attaches to the last item in the NP it is associated with, not necessarily the head of the NP. The Korean genitive postposition *=uy* behaves in a similar way, as we would expect of a clitic. For example, just as English *'s* follows a preposition in (2), *=uy* can follow a postposition in examples like (3):

(3)   서울에서의 회의참석
        Sewul=eyse=uy hoyuy chamsek
        Seoul=LOC=GEN   meeting attendance
        'Attendance at a meeting in Seoul'

So we see that Case information can be realized in a variety of ways. When we write Case with a capital C, we are abstracting away from this exact realization of case. In this sense, we can say that the first-person singular subjects in English, Russian, and Korean in (1) all receive nominative Case, even though the realizations are very different.

There is another, even more important issue. That is how Case patterns relate to grammatical relations: notions such as subject, object, and indirect object. One of the very important findings of modern linguistics is that there is not a one-to-one relationship between case and grammatical relations: nominative case may not be related exclusively to subjects, accusative to direct objects, and so on. We will investigate this kind of relationship in Korean. In generative grammar, it is widely assumed that nominative case is assigned by the head of the clause, which is often assumed to be the morpheme expressing Tense. We will look at this more abstract approach to explaining Case as well. In the following subsections, we will describe the morphological and syntactic properties of different case markers.

6.1.1   Nominative

There are several forms of nominative cases in Korean, as we saw in Chapter 5. Aside from the phonologically conditioned alternation between $=i$ and $=ka$, recall that honorific $=kkeyse$ behaves like a postposition rather than a case marker. Examples are in (4).

(4)   Forms of nominative Case (*i/ka/kkeyse*)
     a. 철수가 학교에 간다.
        Chelswu=ka   hakkyo=ey ka-n-ta.
        Chelswu=NOM   school=DIR   go-PRES-PLN
        'Chelswu goes to school.'
     b. 현이 도서관에 간다.
        Hyen=i   tosekwan=ey ka-n-ta.
        Hyen=NOM   library=DIR   go-PRES-PLN
        'Hyen goes to the library.'
     c. 선생님이 학교에 간다.
        Sensayngnim=i   hakkyo=ey ka-n-ta.
        teacher=NOM   school=DIR go-PRES-PLN
        'A teacher goes to school.'
     d. 선생님께서 학교에 가신다.
        Sensayngnim=kkeyse   hakkyo=ey ka-si-n-ta.
        teacher=NOM (HON)   school=DIR go-HON-PRES-PLN
        'A teacher goes to school.'

The nominative case marker $=i/ka$, together with accusative $=(l)ul$ and genitive $=uy$, share the property that they are in complementary distribution with the delimiters $=(n)un$ (topic marker) and $=to$ ('also').

(5)   Case markers in complementary distribution with delimiters $=(n)un$ and $=to$

a.	철수가(*는/*도) 학교에 간다.		
	Chelswu=ka (=nun/*=to)*	*hakkyo=ey*	*ka-n-ta.*
	Chelswu=NOM (*=TOP/*=also)	school=DIR	go-PRES-PLN
	'Chelswu goes to school.'		
b.	학교에(는/도) 철수가 간다.		
	Hakkyo=ey (=nun/=to)	*Chelswu=ka*	*ka-n-ta.*
	school=DIR (=TOP/=also)	Chelswu=NOM	go-PRES-PLN
	'Chelswu goes to school.'		

c. *철수가은 학교에 간다.
    *Chelswu=ka=un   hakkyo=ey   ka-n-ta.
    Chelswu=NOM=TOP   school=DIR   go-PRES-PLN
    'Chelswu goes to school.'
d. *존이은 도서관에 간다.
    *Con=i=un   tosekwan=ey   ka-n-ta.
    John=NOM=TOP   school=DIR   go-PRES-PLN
    'John goes to school.'

However, honorific =kkeyse co-occurs with =(n)un and =to, as expected of a postposition.

(6)   =Kkeyse/eyse co-occurring with =(n)un and =to
        a. 우리 선생님께서는/도 일등을 하셨어요.
            Wuli sensayngnim=kkeyse=nun/=to iltung=ul   ha-si-ess-eyo.
            our teacher=NOM(HON)=TOP/=also first place=ACC do-HON-PAST-POL
            'Our teacher took first place.'
        b. 우리 어머님께서는/도 행사에 가셨어요.
            Wuli emenim=kkeyse=nun/=to   hayngsa-ey   ka-si-ess-eyo.
            our mother=NOM(HON)=TOP/=also   event=DIR   go-HON-PAST-POL
            'Our mother went to the event.'

In part because it is in complementary distribution with the topic marker =(n) un, nominative =i/=ka plays a role in the marking of information structure in Korean. We discuss this function in detail in Chapter 8, but we introduce the information structural status of =i/=ka briefly here. The functions of =i/=ka are often compared to those of nominative =ga in Japanese, but as a number of researchers have pointed out, the Korean nominative marker has a broader range of functions. In (7) below we classify these as broad focus (7a), narrow focus (7b), new (or resumed) topic (7c), and default (7d).

(7)   Functions of nominative =i/=ka
        a. Broad focus
            비가 왔다.
            Pi=ka   o-ass-ta.
            rain=NOM   come-PAST-PLN
            'It was raining.'
        b. Narrow focus
            누가 왔어? 철수가 왔어.
            Nwu=ka o-ass-e?   Chelswu=ka   o-ass-e.
            who=NOM come-PAST-Q   Chelswu=NOM come-PAST-INT
            'Who came? Chelswu came.'
        c. New (or resumed) topic
            피자가 맛있어?
            Phica=ka   masiss-e?
            pizza=NOM tasty-Q
            'Is the pizza tasty?'

    d. Default
      나는 그 사람이 좋다.
      Na=nun ku   salam=i   coh-ta.
      I=TOP   that person=NOM fond.of-PLN
      'I'm fond of that person.'

In a broad focus such as (7a), the entire sentence is presented as new informa-tion. In a narrow focus such as the question in (7b) and its answer, a single item is focused, and the remainder of the sentence is presupposed. Both the question and the answer in (7b) presuppose that someone came; the focus, the new information demanded, is who that comer is. The topic marker *=(n)un* is incompatible with narrow focus, and therefore cannot be used to mark inter-rogative pronouns in *wh*-questions:

(8)   누(구)가/*는 가니?
        *Nwu(kwu)=ka/*nun ka-ni?*
        who=NOM/*TOP   go-Q
        'Who is going?'

The broad- and narrow-focus functions of nominative *=i/=ga* in (7a–b) are similar to functions of the nominative marker in Japanese and other SOV languages with postnominal subject markers. For example, the Burmese sub-ject marker *ká* (only accidentally homophonous with its Korean counterpart!) must be used in the corrective focus context of (9):

(9)   Nominative marking for corrective focus
      a. Burmese corrective focus
          Speaker A: *Maun.maun.   Win.wìn   tcai? tɛ.*
                  Maung Maung Win Win like   NONFUTURE
                  'Maung Maung likes Win Win.'(Jenny and Hnin Tun
                  2013: 697)
          Speaker B: *Mə ho? phù, Ne.?aun ká/*Ø/*tɔ Wìn.wìn tcai?*
                  not be.so NEG Nay Aung Subj/TOP Win Win like
                  tɛ.
                  NONFUTURE
                  'No, Nay Aung likes Win Win.'
      b. Korean corrective focus
          Speaker A: 유리가 철수를 좋아해.
                  Yuli=ka   Chelswu=lul cohaha-y.
                  Yuli=NOM Chelswu=ACC like-INT
                  'Yuli likes Chelswu.'
          Speaker B: 아니, 순위가/*Ø/*는 철수를 좋아해.
                  *Ani, Swunwi=ka/*Ø/=*nun Chelswu=lul cohaha-y.*
                  no, Suni=NOM/*Ø/=*TOP   Chelswu=ACC like-INT
                  'No, Suni likes Chelswu.'

Corrective focus is a subtype of exhaustive focus: Speaker B uses the nominative or subject marker to specify the unique individual under consideration who likes Win Win or Chelswu, correcting Speaker A's mistaken assertion that it is someone else. Although both Korean and Burmese allow dropping of nominative or subject marking in certain environments, in the strongly focused context of (9), it is obligatory, and the same would be true for Japanese.

In other respects, however, the discourse function of nominative marking in Korean differs from Japanese and other languages with superficially similar particles such as Burmese. In (7c), the nominative marking of the subject 'pizza' is natural if, for example, the speaker approaches the hearer in the context of a party and casually asks if the pizza is tasty. In this context, 'pizza' is not the established topic of their conversation, and the speaker is not asking about pizza in general. If that were the case, she would be more likely to use the topic marker $=(n)un$. In (7c), the speaker is making pizza the new topic of conversation. In such a context in Japanese, the speaker would be more likely to use zero marking on 'pizza', or possibly the topic maker $=wa$. Lee and Shimojo (2016) show that while Japanese uses topic marking both for topics continuing from prior discourse and renewed topics – information that once had topic status but has ceased to be the current topic of discourse – Korean uses nominative $=i/=ka$ for the latter function. The consequence of this is that the relative proportion of nominative to topic marking is higher in Korean than in Japanese. The focus in a question like (7c) is on 'delicious': the speaker wants to know if the pizza is delicious or not; thus the other material in the sentence, 'pizza', must be given non-focus, that is, topic or background status. Korean can do this with nominative marking in a main clause, but Japanese cannot.

The broader range of nominative marking in Korean is consistent with its fourth function in (7): the "default" function in (7d). Nominative $=i/=ka$ is assigned in contexts where no other case is available. In Korean, as in many other languages, adjectives cannot assign accusative case, even when they are transitive, as in the case of *coh-* 'good, like' in (7d). When *coh-* takes an object in the meaning of 'like', the object can only be marked nominative. Korean transitive psychological adjectives have the restriction that they can only be used to express the psychological state of the speaker, or to inquire about the psychological state of the hearer. When a third person's psychological state is referenced, the derived verbal form of the adjectival stem must be used. When the verbal form is used, the object must be marked accusative:

(10)   a. 나는 그 사람이/*을 좋다.

        Na=nun   *ku*   *salam=i/*ul*   *coh-ta.*
        I=TOP   that   person=NOM/*=ACC fond.of-PLN
        'I'm fond of that person.'

b. 순이는 그 사람*이/을 좋아한다.

*Swuni=nun   ku   salam=*i/=ul   cohaha-n-ta.*
Swuni=TOP   that   person=*NOM/=ACC   like-PRES-PLN
'Swuni likes that person.'

Another context where default nominative surfaces is with predicate nominals. As we saw in Chapter 5, the affirmative copula =*i-* is a clitic which attaches directly to the predicate nominal, leaving no place for a case marker. But the negative copula *ani-* does not cliticize. In negated nominal predicate sentences, nominative case appears on the predicate nominal:

(11)   순이는 바보가 아니다.

Swuni=nun   papo=ka   ani-ta.
Swuni=TOP   fool=NOM   not.be-PLN
'Swuni is not a fool.'

Here we can say that the copula assigns nominative case, but overt nominative surfaces only when the copula does not cliticize, or alternatively, that (11) is part of the default nominative pattern also found in (10): nominative is assigned where no other case is available.

Then, what about the relationship between nominative case marking and the grammatical relation of subject? Aside from the default function in (7d), it is generally assumed that a noun with a nominative case-marking functions as the subject of the sentence. The subject is, according to traditional grammar, one of the two immediate constituents of a clause, the other constituent being the predicate. There are two widely cited tests for subjecthood in Korean: subject honorification, and reflexivization. The examples in (12) show us that subject-honorific -*(u)si-* is added into the verb when the subject is a pragmatically acceptable target of deference.

(12)   Subjecthood test 1: subject honorification

a. 철수가 학교에 간다.

Chelswu=ka   hakkyo=ey   ka-n-ta.
Chelswu=NOM   school=LOC   go-PRES-PLN
'Chelswu goes to school.'

b. 선생님이 학교에 가신다.

Sensayngnim=i   hakkyo=ey   ka-si-n-ta.
teacher=NOM   school=DIR   go-HON-PRES-PLN
'The teacher goes to school.'

c. 철수가 피자를 먹는다.

Chelswu=ka   phica=lul   mek-nun-ta.
Chelswu=NOM   pizza=ACC   eat-PRES-PLN
'Chelswu eats pizza.'

d. 교수님이 피자를 드신다.

Kyoswunim=i   phica=lul   tu-si-n-ta.
professor=NOM   pizza=ACC   eat-HON-PRES-PLN
'The professor eats pizza.'

The choice of whether to express deference or not is pragmatic, not syntactic; thus the speaker may use subject-honorific -*(u)si*- or not in (12a). Note also that the expression of subject honorification involves not only the regular suffix -*(u)si*- but also lexical honorific forms such as the verb *tu-si*- 'eat (honorific)', the honorific form of the verb *tul*- 'raise'. The syntactic component of subject honorification is that it cannot be triggered by non-subjects, as shown in (13):

(13)   #철수가 선생님을 만나셨다.
   #*Chelswu=ka   sensayngnim=ul manna-si-ess-ta.*
   Chelswu=NOM   teacher=ACC   meet-HON-PAST-PLN
   'Chelswu met the teacher.'

The example in (13) can only be interpreted as expressing deference to *Chelswu*, not the accusative-marked object 'teacher'. In Section 6 we return to certain complications of the subject-honorification test.

The examples in (14) show that the reflexive pronoun *caki* is anteceded by a subject.

(14)   Subjecthood test 2: reflexivization
   a. 철수가 자기를 칭찬한다.
      Chelswu$_i$=ka   caki$_i$=lul chingchanha-n-ta.
      Chelswu=NOM   self=ACC compliment-PRES-PLN
      'Chelswu compliments himself.'
   b. 철수가 미자한테 자기 친구를 소개했다.
      Chelswu$_i$=ka   Mica$_j$=hanthey caki$_{i,*j}$ chinkwu=lul
      Chelswu=NOM   Mica=to   self   friend=ACC
      sokayhay-ss-ta.
      introduce-PAST-PLN
      'Chelswu$_i$ introduced self$_{i,*j}$'s friend to Mica$_j$.'

The reflexive pronoun *caki* may be anteceded only by the subject *Chelswu* in (14a–b). It cannot be anteceded by the object *Mica* in (14b).

An important syntactic property of Korean is the ability to permit more than one nominative-marked NP in a sentence. The default nominative pattern in (7d), (10), and (11) is one context for multiple nominatives: in addition to nominative case on the subject NP, nominative occurs on a second NP in the default position as in (15).

(15)   Double nominative: subject nominative + default nominative
   a. 내가 그 남자가 좋다.
      Nay=ka   ku   namca=ka coh-ta.
      I=NOM   that   man=NOM like-PLN
      'I like that man.'
   b. 그 도시가 파괴가 되었다.
      Ku   tosi=ka   phakoy=ka   toy-ess-ta.
      that city=NOM   destruction=NOM become-PAST-PLN
      'That city was destroyed.'

c. 철수가 교수가 되었다.
   Chelswu=ka　　　kyoswu=ka　　　toy-ess-ta.
   Chelswu=NOM　　professor=NOM　become-PAST-PLN
   'Chelswu became a professor.'

d. 이것은 책이 아니다.
   I kes=un　　　　chayk=i　　an-i-ta.
   this-thing=NOM　book=NOM　NEG-be-PLN
   'This is not a book.'

The examples in (15) show that Korean does not restrict nominative case to
a single position; (15a) involves the object of an adjective, (15b) the passive of
a Sino-Korean verbal noun, formed with *toy-* 'become', (15c) a predicate
nominal with *toy-*, and (15d) a predicate nominal with the negative copula
ani-. A more interesting class of multiple nominative constructions involves
what are known as major subject constructions. In (16) examples are classified
by the alternative case marking available for the leftmost NP.

(16)　　Double nominative: major subject constructions

　　a. Genitive
　　　철수가/의 키가 크다.
　　　Chelswu=ka/=uy　　khi=ka　　　khu-ta.
　　　Chelswu=NOM/=GEN　height=NOM　tall-PLN
　　　'Chelswu is tall.'

　　b. 내가/의 아버지가 아프시다.
　　　Nay=ka/=uy　　apeci=ka　　　aphu-si-ta.
　　　I=NOM/=GEN　　father=NOM　　sick-HON-PLN
　　　'My father is sick.'

　　c. Locative
　　　서울이/에 사람이 많다.
　　　Sewul=i/=ey　　　salam=i　　　manh-ta.
　　　Seoul=NOM/=LOC　people=NOM　a lot-PLN
　　　'There are a lot of people in Seoul.'

　　d. Class–member
　　　꽃이 장미가 아름답다.
　　　Kkoch=i　　　cangmi=ka　　　　alumtap-ta.
　　　flower=NOM　rose=NOM　　　　beautiful-PLN
　　　'As for flowers, the rose is beautiful.'

The leftmost nominative NP in (16a–d) is commonly called the major subject.
In (16a–c) the major subject is at least marginally acceptable with another case-
marking pattern, such as genitive or locative. The class–member pattern (16d),
however, has no alternative case-marking pattern, although it is in fact more
natural with the topic marker =(n)un on the first NP.

　　In contrast to default nominatives, major subjects pass subjecthood tests in at
least some contexts, as shown in (17).

(17)   a. 김 선생님이 키가 크시다.
        Kim sensayngnim=i   *khi=ka*   *khu-si-ta.*
        Kim teacher=NOM/   height=NOM   tall-HON-PLN
        'Teacher Kim is tall.'
       b. 철수가 자기 아들보다 키가 크다.
        Chelswu=ka   *caki atul=pota khi=ka*   *khu-ta.*
        Chelswu=NOM   self son=than   height=NOM   tall-PLN
        'Chelswuᵢ is taller than self ᵢ's son.'

In (17a) the major subject triggers subject honorification, while in (17b) it
antecedes reflexive *caki*. Note though that (16b) shows us that the second or
minor subject *apeci* 'father' also passes the honorification test. These facts
indicate that in addition to multiple nominative case, Korean gives evidence for
the availability of more than one subject position.

A final context for multiple nominatives is quantifier-float contexts like (18).

(18)   학생이 셋이 왔다.
       Haksayng=i   *seys=i*   *wa-ss-ta.*
       student=NOM   three=NOM   come-PAST-PLN
       'Three students came.'

As we see in the next section, (18) is part of a general pattern of case spreading
with quantifiers.

6.1.2   Accusative

As we saw in Chapter 5, the accusative case marker in Korean belongs to the set
of postnominal particles whose shape is phonologically conditioned: *=lul* if
preceded by a vowel, *=ul* if by a consonant. Traditional theories of grammar
analyze accusative as the case assigned to the direct object. However, Korean
has many sentence patterns in which the accusative-marked noun is not analyz-
able as the direct object of the sentence. We classify these as double accusatives
(19), adjuncts/quasi-arguments (21), and case spreading (23).

(19)   Double accusatives
       a. Transitive verbal noun + "light" *ha-* 'do'
          철수가 한국어를 공부(를) 한다.
          Chelswu=ka   *hankwuke=lul kongpwu(=lul)*   *ha-n-ta.*
          Chelswu=NOM   Korean=ACC   study(=ACC)   do-PRES-PLN
          'Chelswu studies Korean.'
       b. Ditransitives
          철수가 영희에게/를 책을 주었다.
          Chelswu=ka   Yenghuy=eykey/=lul   *chayk=ul*   *cwu-ess-ta.*
          Chelswu=NOM Yenghuy=DAT/=ACC   book=ACC   give-PAST-PLN
          'Chelswu gave a book to Yenghuy.'

One possible test for object status is passivizability, although as we see in Chapter 8, this test must be treated with caution in Korean. As it turns out, both arguments in ditransitive (20b) can be passivized, but only the object of the verbal noun can be passivized in (20a):

(20)   a. 한국어가 잘 공부된다.[1]
            Hankwuke=ka   cal   kongpwu toy-n-ta.
            Korean=NOM   well   study   become-PRES-PLN
            'Korean is well (widely) studied.'
        b. *한국어가 공부(가) 되었다.
            **Hankwuke=ka   kongpwu=ka   toy-ess-ta.*
            Korean=NOM   study(=NOM)   become-PAST-PLN
            'Korean was studied.'
        c. *영희가 주어졌던 책
            **Yenghuy=ka   cwu-e-ci-ess-te-n   chayk*
            Yenghuy=NOM   give-INF-become-PAST-RET-PASTADN book
            'the book that Yenghuy was given'
        d. 그 책이 주어졌던 영희
            ku   chayk=i   cwu-e-ci-ess-te-n   Yenghuy
            that book=NOM   give-INF-become-PAST-RET-PASTADN Yenghuy
            'Yenghuy, who was given that book'

The second type of noncanonical accusatives involves adjuncts or quasi-arguments of intransitive verbs. With deictic directional (path) verbs such as *ka-* 'go' and *o-* 'come', accusative marks the goal. With nondeictic path verbs such as *tul-* 'enter' and *naka-* 'go out', accusative marks goal and source respectively. With manner of motion verbs such as *ttwi-* 'run', accusative marks the relation sometimes described as perlative, meaning 'cover the whole area'.

(21)   Intransitives with locational quasi-arguments
        a. 철수가 학교에/를 갔다/왔다.
            Chelswu=ka   hakkyo=ey/=lul   ka-ss-ta/o-ass-ta.
            Chelswu=NOM   school=LOC/=ACC   go-PAST-PLN/come-PAST-PLN
            'Chelswu went/came to school.'
        b. 철수가 학교에/를 들어갔다.
            Chelswu=ka   hakkyo=ey/=lul   tule-ka-ss-ta.
            Chelswu=NOM   school=DIR/=ACC   enter-PAST-PLN
            'Chelswu entered school.'
        c. 철수가 학교에서/를 나갔다.
            Chelswu=ka   hakkyo=eyse/=lul naka-ss-ta.
            Chelswu=NOM   school=from/=ACC go.out-PAST-PLN
            'Chelswu went out from the school.'

---

[1] These examples reflect some of the issues with Korean passives that are described in more detail in Chapter 8. Passives of verbal nouns in "light" *ha-* are formed with *toy-* 'become' replacing *ha-*, as in (20a, b). The verb *cwu-* 'give' allows only *ci-* passives, which are unable to assign accusative case. To get around this problem we use relative clauses in (20c, d).

    d. 철수가 공원에서/을 뛰었다.
       Chelswu=ka   *kongwen=eyse/=ul ttwi-ess-ta.*
       Chelswu=NOM   park=in/=ACC   run-PAST-PLN
       'Chelswu ran in the park/ran the park.'

Unlike the indirect object in (20c), the accusative-marked NPs in (21) give no evidence of having object status; for example, they cannot be passivized:

(22)   *공원이 뛰어졌다.
       **Kongwen=i*   *ttwi-e-ci-ess-ta.*
       park=NOM   run-INF-become-PAST-PLN
       'The park was run.'

In general, the location expression that appears with accusative case has unmarked status with respect to the predicate involved; for example, with *naka-* 'go out', only the source location, not the goal location, can be marked accusative, while with *tul-* 'enter' it is the reverse. In most cases the accusative-marked expression is semantically equivalent to its counterpart with a lexical postposition, but in (21d) accusative implies that Chelswu ran around the whole park, like its English equivalent.

    The third pattern where the accusative case does not mark a direct object involves floated quantifiers, adverbs of duration, and other adverbs. Adverbs such as *manhi* 'a lot' or *ppalli* 'quickly' bear accusative case in (23b–c).

(23)   a. Floated quantifier
       철수가 고기를 열 마리(를) 먹었다.
       Chelswu=ka   *koki=lul*   *yel mali(=lul)*   *mek-ess-ta.*
       Chelswu=NOM   fish=ACC   ten CLSF(=ACC)   eat-PAST-PLN
       'Chelswu ate ten fish.'
     b. Adverb of quantification
       철수가 피자를 많이(를) 먹는다.
       Chelswu=ka   *phica=lul*   *manhi(=lul)*   *mek-nun-ta.*
       Chelswu=NOM   pizza=ACC   a lot(=ACC)   eat-PRES-PLN
       'Chelswu eats a lot of pizza.'
     c. Durational adverb
       철수가 공부를 세 시간(을) 한다.
       Chelswu=ka   *kongpwu=lul sey sikan(=ul)*   *ha-n-ta.*
       Chelswu=NOM   study=ACC   three hours(=ACC)   do-PRES-PLN
       'Chelswu studies for three hours.'
     d. Manner adverb
       철수가 학교에/를 빨리(를) 갔다.
       Chelswu=ka   *hakkyo=ey/=lul ppalli(=lul)*   *ka-ss-ta.*
       Chelswu=NOM   school=DIR/=ACC quickly(=ACC)   go-PAST-PLN
       'Chelswu quickly went to school.'

Although the first examples, including the durational adverb (23c), are quantificational, the manner adverb example in (23d) is not. The example in (23d) also shows us that these accusatives cannot simply be a matter of copying the case on the direct object, since (23d) is acceptable with directional =*ey* on *hakkyo* 'school'. The accusative-marked quantifiers and adverbs are not true objects, as they cannot be passivized. They are also possible with some intransitives, as in (24).

(24)   a. 철수가 삼일 동안(을) 여행했다.
           Chelswu=ka   *samil tongan(=ul)*   *yehaynghay-ss-ta.*
           Chelswu=NOM   three days duration(=ACC) travel-PAST-PLN
           'Chelswu traveled for three days.'
     b. 철수가 세 시간(을) 뛰었다.
           Chelswu=ka   *sey sikan(=ul)*   *ttwi-ess-ta.*
           Chelswu=NOM   three hours(=ACC) run-PAST-PLN
           'Chelswu ran for three hours.'
     c. 철수가 빨리(를) 뛰었다.
           Chelswu=ka   *ppalli(=lul)*   *ttwi-ess-ta.*
           Chelswu=NOM   quickly(=ACC) run-PAST-PLN
           'Chelswu ran quickly.'
     d. 철수가 빨리(*를) 죽었다.
           Chelswu=ka   *ppalli(*=lul)*   *cwuk-ess-ta.*
           Chelswu=NOM   quickly(*=ACC) die-PAST-PLN
           'Chelswu died quickly.'

Instead, it seems that the aktionsart or verbal aspect of the verb is related to its accusative-assigning ability. Verbs like *ttwi-* 'run' have an activity or an accomplishment interpretation. They may assign accusative to a location argument as in (21d) or a durational adverb as in (24b) even when no direct object is present. In contrast, achievements such as *cwuk-* 'die' (24d) do not allow this possibility. The contrast is also related to the deep transitivity of the verb: verbs like *ttwi-* 'run' are classified as unergatives, while *cwuk-* 'die' is an unaccusative. Across languages it has been observed that unergatives often show transitive-like properties, such as the ability to form an impersonal passive, while unaccusatives do not.

Accusative is also assigned in a context parallel to the environment for default nominative we saw, before negative 않- *anh-*. Again, this possibility is conditioned by the basic accusative-assigning potential of the verb.

(25)   a. 영희는 밥을 먹지(를) 않아요.
           Yenghuy=nun   *pap=ul*   *mek-ci(=lul)*   *anh-ayo.*
           Yenghuy=TOP   rice=ACC   eat-SUSP(=ACC) NEG-POL
           'Yenghuy does not eat rice.'

b. 영희는 뛰지(=를/*=가) 않아요.
   Yenghuy=nun   *ttwi-ci(=lul/*=ka)* *anh-ayo.*
   Yenghuy=TOP   run-SUSP(=ACC/*=ka) NEG-POL
   'Yenghuy does not run.'

c. 영희는 죽지(=를/*=가) 않아요.
   Yenghuy=nun   *cwuk-ci(=lul/*=ka)* *anh-ayo.*
   Yenghuy=TOP   run-SUSP(=ACC/*=ka) NEG-POL
   'Yenghuy does not die.'

Nominative and accusative are interchangeable in negatives like this when the predicate is stative or passive:

(26) a. 영희는 예쁘지가/를 않다.
   Yenghuy=nun   *yeyppu-ci=ka/=lul* *anh-ta.*
   Yenghuy=TOP   pretty-SUSP=NOM=ACC NEG-PLN
   'Yenghuy is not pretty.'

  b. 밥이 먹히지가/를 않아요.
   Pap=i   *mek-hi-ci=ka/=lul*   *anh-ayo.*
   rice=NOM eat-PASS-SUSP=NOM/=ACC   NEG-PLN
   'Rice is not eaten.'

  c. 나는 영화가/를 보고 싶다.
   Na=nun   *yenghwa=ka/=lul* *po-ko* *siph-ta.*
   I=NOM   movie=NOM/=ACC watch-COMP like-PLN
   'I would like to watch a movie.'

6.1.3 *Genitive*

Genitive case can appear on most non-inflecting modifiers and arguments of nouns, including possessors.

(27) Genitive case
  a. 그의 집은 서울이다.
   Ku=uy   *cip=un*   *Sewul=i-ta.*
   he/her=GEN home=TOP Seoul=be-PLN
   'His/her home is in Seoul.'

  b. 영희는 철수의 학교에서 공부했다.
   Yenghuy=nun   *Chelswu=uy* *hakkyo=eyse* *kongpwuhay-ss-ta.*
   Yenghuy=NOM   Chelswu=GEN school=LOC study-PAST-PLN
   'Yenghuy studied at Chelswu's school.'

First- and second-person personal pronouns have the inflected genitive forms 내 *nay* 'my', 네 *ney* 'your', etc., historically derived from the contraction of the pronoun and the genitive particle. These may alternate with the uninflected pronoun and particle:

(28)   나의/내 집은 서울이다.
         Na=uy/nay cip=un   Sewul=i-ta.
         I=GEN/my   home=TOP Seoul=be-PLN
         'My home is in Seoul.'

Certain other quasi-pronominal forms such as 우리 *wuli* 'our' occur without the genitive:

(29)   우리 집은 서울이다.
         Wuli cip=un   Sewul=i-ta.
         we   home=TOP   Seoul=be-PLN
         'Our home is in Seoul.'

Kinship terms commonly occur without genitive on the preceding possessor:

(30)   영희 오빠는 철수의 학교에서 공부했다.
         Yenghuy oppa=nun   Chelswu=uy   hakkyo=eyse
         Yenghuy older brother=TOP   Chelswu=GEN school=LOC
         kongpwuhay-ss-ta.
         study-PAST-PLN
         'Yenghuy's older brother studied at Chelswu's school.'

One pattern shows that the function of the genitive cannot be solely linked to a requirement that NPs receive case. Genitive is also assigned to PP modifiers of NP:

(31)   영희는 서울에서의 학회에 참석했다.
         Yenghuy=nun   Sewul=eyse=uy hakhoy=ey   chamsekhay-ss-ta.
         Yenghuy=TOP   Seoul=LOC=GEN conference=DIR take.part-PAST-PLN
         'Yenghuy took part in a conference (which was) in Seoul.'

Nominative, accusative, and genitive are generally said to be the structural cases in Korean. However, (31) shows that genitive has a different status from the other two. In Section 6.6 we will see that nominative and accusative may also be assigned to PPs in certain contexts, but such examples of "case stacking" are never obligatory. In contrast, genitive =*uy* is obligatory in order for the PP to be interpreted as a modifier of 학회 *hakhoy* 'conference' in (31).

6.2   Postpositions

Postpositions are functionally comparable to English prepositions. As their name indicates, they occur after an NP. Like English prepositions and unlike the nominative, accusative, and genitive structural case markers, postpositions generally make their own semantic contribution. Postpositions can be distinguished from structural case markers by a number of criteria. Structural case markers may not occur before delimiters, while postpositions do. When structural case markers and postpositions co-occur, the order is always NP=postposition=structural case marker.

6.2.1   Dative

The Korean dative postpositions indicate goal arguments, like 'to' in 'Chelswu gave a book to Yenghuy'.

(32)   Dative
철수가 영희에게 책을 주었다.
Chelswu=ka   Yenghuy=eykey chayk=ul   cwu-ess-ta.
Chelswu=NOM   Yenghuy=DAT   book=ACC give-PAST-PLN
'Chelswu gave a book to Yenghuy.'

Korean has a number of dative postpositions, depending on the animacy of the goal NP, the formality of the sentence, and whether or not honorific speech style is used. In (33), animate *koyangi* 'cat' takes dative *=eykey* while inanimate *yenmos* 'pond' takes *=ey*.

(33)   Korean dative: *eykey/ey*
a. Animate NP
개가 고양이에게 먹이를 준다.
Kay=ka   koyangi=eykey   meki=lul cwu-n-ta.
dog=NOM   cat=DAT   food=ACC give-PRES-PLN
'The dog gives food to the cat.'
b. Inanimate NP
철수가 연못에 먹이를 준다.
Chelswu=ka   yenmos=ey meki=lul cwu-n-ta.
Chelswu=NOM   pond=DAT feed=ACC give-PRES-PLN
'Chelswu gives feed to the pond.'

The animate datives *=eykey/=hanthey* are distinguished by formality or register: *=eykey* for formal/written style and *=hanthey* for informal/spoken style:

(34)   *=eykey/=hanthey*
a. Formal/Written
철수가 선생님에게 질문을 한다.
Chelswu=ka   sensayngnim=eykey   cilmwun=ul   ha-n-ta.
Chelswu=NOM   teacher=DAT   question=ACC do-PRES-PLN
'Chelswu asks a question to the teacher.'
b. Informal/Spoken
철수가 선생님한테 질문을 한다.
Chelswu=ka   sensayngnim=hanthey cilmwun=ul   ha-n-ta.
Chelswu=NOM   teacher=DAT   question=ACC do-PRES-PLN
'Chelswu asks a question to a teacher.'

There are also the two colloquial dative forms, as shown in (35):

(35)   Colloquial datives *tele/poko*
    a. Unmarked (written or colloquial)
    철수가 친구에게 학교에 가라 한다.
    Chelswu=ka   chinkwu=eykey   hakkyo=ey   ka-la   ha-n-ta.
    Chelswu=NOM   friend=DAT   school=DIR   go-COM   do-PRES-PLN
    'Chelswu commands to his friend that he should go to school.'
    b. Colloquial
    철수가 친구더러/보고 학교에 가라 한다.
    Chelswu=ka   chinkwu=tele/=poko   hakkyo=ey   ka-la
    Chelswu=NOM   friend=DAT   school=DIR   go-COM
    ha-n-ta.
    do-PRES-PLN
    'Chelswu commands to his friend that he should go to school.'

All the dative particles pass the test for postpositions in that they appear before delimiters, while structural case markers do not:

(36)   철수가 친구에게/한테/보고/*을만 돈을 준다.
    Chelswu=ka   chinkwu=eykey/=hanthey/=poko/*=ul=man
    Chelswu=NOM   friend=DAT/=DAT/=DAT/*=ACC=only
    ton=ul   cwu-n-ta.
    money=ACC   give-PRES-PLN
    'Chelswu gives money only to his friend.'

6.2.2   Locative

The locative postpositions =*ey* and =*eyse* are translated as 'at', 'on', or 'in', depending on the kinds of predicates with which they co-occur. If the predicate is stative or represents static activity, the locative postposition is =*ey*, which also serves as a directional postposition. If the predicate is active and non-static, the locative postposition is =*eyse*.

(37)   Locative =*ey*
    a. 철수가 학교에 있어요.
    Chelswu=ka   hakkyo=ey   iss-eyo.
    Chelswu=NOM   school=LOC   be-POL
    'Chelswu is at school.'
    b. 철수가 의자에 앉아 있어요.
    Chelswu=ka   uyca=ey   anc-a   iss-eyo.
    Chelswu=NOM   chair=LOC   sit-INF   be-POL
    'Chelswu is sitting in a chair.'

(38)   Locative =*eyse*
    철수가 학교에서 공부해요.
    Chelswu=ka   hakkyo=eyse   kongpwuhay-yo.
    Chelswu=NOM   school=LOC   study-POL
    'Chelswu studies at school.'

6.2.3   Directional and Instrumental

There are four directional postpositions, two derived from combinations of
animate dative plus directional = *(u)lo* to mark direction toward an animate NP.

(39)   Directional =*ey*
      철수가 학교에 간다.
      Chelswu=ka   hakkyo=ey   ka-n-ta.
      Chelswu=NOM school=DIR go-PRES-PLN
      'Chelswu goes to school.'

(40)   Directional =*(u)lo*
      a. 철수가 학교로 간다.
          Chelswu=ka   hakkyo-lo   ka-n-ta.
          Chelswu=NOM   school=DIR   go-PRES-PLN
          'Chelswu goes to school.'
      b. 철수가 도서관으로 간다.
          Chelswu=ka   tosekwan=ulo ka-n-ta.
          Chelswu=NOM   library=DIR   go-PRES-PLN
          'Chelswu goes to the library.'

(41)   Animate directional =*eykeylo/=hantheylo*
      a. 철수가 영희에게로 간다.
          Chelswu=ka   Yenghuy=eykeylo   ka-n-ta.
          Chelswu=NOM   Yenghuy=DIR   go-PRES-PLN
          'Chelswu goes to Yenghuy.'
      b. 철수가 영희한테로 간다.
          Chelswu=ka   Yenghuy=hantheylo ka-n-ta.
          Chelswu=NOM   Yenghuy=DIR   go-PRES-PLN
          'Chelswu goes to Yenghuy.'

The postposition = *(u)lo* also serves as an instrumental:

(42)   철수가 연필로 글자를 쓴다.
      Chelswu=ka   yenphil=lo   kulca=lul   ssu-n-ta.
      Chelswu=NOM pencil=INST character=ACC write-PRES-PLN
      'Chelswu writes characters with a pencil.'

6.2.4   Goal

= *Kkaci* 'as far as' marks the goal or target of motion predicates.

(43)   Goal =*kkaci*
      철수가 학교까지 간다.
      Chelswu=ka   hakkyo=kkaci ka-n-ta.
      Chelswu=NOM   school=GOAL   go-PRES-PLN
      'Chelswu goes to school.'

6.2.5   Source

The five source postpositions indicate the origin of an action:

(44)   Source
         부터   =*pwuthe*
         (으)로부터   =*(u)lopwuthe*
         에게서   =*eykeyse*
         한테서   =*hantheyse*

The unmarked source postposition is =*pwuthe* in (45a). The complex postposition =*(u)lopwuthe* is derived from directional/instrumental =*(u)lo* plus =*pwuthe*.

(45)   Source =*pwuthe* and =*(u)lopwuthe*
         a. 철수가 책부터 읽었다.
            Chelswu=ka   chayk=pwuthe ilk-ess-ta.
            Chelswu=NOM   book=SOURCE   read-PAST-PLN
            'Chelswu read (starting from) a book.'
         b. 철수가 학교로부터 왔다.
            Chelswu=ka   hakkyo=lopwuthe o-ass-ta.
            Chelswu=NOM   school= SOURCE   come-PAST-PLN
            'Chelswu came from school.'
         c. 나는 도서관에서 와요.
            Na=nun   tosekwan=eyse o-ayo.
            I=TOP   library=from   come-POL
            'I come from library.'

Animate sources are marked by dative plus =*eyse*, with formality again distinguishing between the two datives:

(46)   Animate source =*eykeyse*/=*hantheyse*
         a. 철수가 영희에게서 책을 받았다.
            Chelswu=ka   Yenghuy=eykeyse chayk=ul pat-ass-ta.
            Chelswu=NOM Yenghuy=SOURCE book=ACC receive-PAST-PLN
            'Chelswu received a book from Yenghuy.'
         b. 철수가 영희한테서 책을 받았다.
            Chelswu=ka   Yenghuy=hantheyse chayk=ul   pat-ass-ta.
            Chelswu=NOM   Yenghuy=SOURCE   book=ACC   receive-PAST-PLN
            'Chelswu received a book from Yenghuy.'

6.2.6   Conjunctive

As noted in Section 5.5, the conjunctive postpositions also function as comitatives.

(47)   Conjunctive/comitative
         과   =*(k)wa*
         하고   =*hako*
         이며   =*imye*
         에다   =*eyta*
         이랑   =*ilang*

The most unmarked conjunctive =*kwa/wa* has a different pattern of allomorphy than postnominal particles such as directional/instrumental =*(u)lo*: the stop-initial form =*kwa* appears when the preceding noun ends in a consonant, the glide-initial form =*wa* when the preceding noun ends in a vowel:

(48)   Conjunctive =*(k)wa*
        철수가 톰과 메리에게 책을 주었다.
        Chelswu=ka   Thom=kwa Meyli=eykey chayk=ul cwu-ess-ta.
        Chelswu=NOM   Tom=CONJ Mary=DAT   book=ACC give-PAST-PLN
        'Chelswu gave a book to Tom and Mary.'

Another common conjunctive postposition is =*hako*, which derives diachronically from *ha-* 'do' plus the gerundive suffix.

(49)   Conjunctive =*(ha)ko*
        철수가 메리하고 톰에게 책을 주었다.
        Chelswu=ka   Meyli=hako Thom=eykey chayk=ul cwu-ess-ta.
        Chelswu=TOP   Mary=CONJ Tom=DAT   book=ACC give-PAST-PLN
        'Chelswu gave a book to Mary and Tom.'

Other conjunctive postpositions are =*imye,* =*eyta*, and =*ilang*:

(50)   Conjunctive =*imye,* =*eyta,* =*ilang*
        철수가 책이며/에다/이랑 노트를 샀다.
        Chelswu=ka   chayk=imye/=eyta/=ilang nothu=lul   sa-ss-ta.
        Chelswu=NOM   book=CONJ   notebook=ACC buy-PAST-PLN
        'Chelswu bought a book and a notebook.'

6.2.7   Disjunctive

The disjunctive postposition is =*(i)-na*. Like the conjunctive postpositions, it can be optionally doubled after the second disjunct:

(51)   Disjunctive =*(i)-na*
        철수가 밥이나 피자나 먹는다.
        Chelswu=ka   pap=i-na   phica=na mek-nun-ta.
        Chelswu=NOM   rice=DISJ   pizza=DISJ eat-PRES-PLN
        'Chelswu eats rice or pizza.'

6.3   Delimiters

As we saw in Section 5.5, the function of delimiters is to limit the meaning of the phrase, and they appear between the postposition and case. 'Only', 'too', and 'even' are English counterparts of Korean delimiters. Delimiters function to mark association with focus, like their English counterparts. They may appear after virtually any constituent in the clause except the tensed verb.

6.3.1   *Delimiters:* =man *and* =pakkey

=*Man* 'only' and =*pakkey* 'except (. . . not)' appear after an NP in (52a), a verbal in (52b), an adverbial in (52c), and multiple categories in (52d). Since =*man* may not, like other delimiters, follow the tensed verb, the dummy verb *ha-* 'do' must bear tense when the lexical verb is followed by =*man*, as in (52b).

(52)   Delimiter: =*man*

a. 나는 철수만을 좋아해.
   Na=nun   Chelswu=man=ul   cohaha-y.
   I=NOM   Chelswu=only=ACC   like-INT
   'I like only Chelswu.'

b. 나는 학교에 가기만 한다.
   Na=nun   hakkyo=ey   ka-ki=man   ha-n-ta.
   I=NOM   school=DIR   go-NOMNL=only   do-PRES-PLN
   'The only thing that I do is go to school.'

c. 나는 빨리만 간다.
   Na=nun   ppalli=man   ka-n-ta.
   I=NOM   quickly=only   go-PRES-PLN
   'I only go quickly.'

d. 나만 학교에만 빨리만 간다.
   Na=man   hakkyo=ey=man ppalli=man   ka-n-ta.
   I=only   school=DIR=only quickly=only go-PRES-PLN
   'Only I go to only school and only quickly.'

The major difference between =*man* and =*pakkey* is that the latter is an exceptive: it co-occurs in the same clause under the scope of negation, giving it the meaning 'not . . . except XP', which is generally equivalent to 'only XP'. Like =*man*, =*pakkey* may follow all categories except the tensed verb.

(53)   Delimiter: =*pakkey*

a. 나는 철수밖에 안 좋아해.
   Na=nun   Chelswu=pakkey   an   cohaha-y.
   I=TOP   Chelswu=only   NEG   like-INT
   'I like no one but Chelswu.'

b. 나는 학교에 가기밖에 안 한다.
   Na=nun   hakkyo=ey   ka-ki=pakkey   an   ha-n-ta.
   I=TOP   school=DIR   go-NOMNL=only   NEG   do-PRES-PLN
   'I don't do anything but go to school.'

c. 나는 빨리밖에 안 간다.
   Na=nun   ppalli=pakkey   an   ka-n-ta.
   I=TOP   quickly=only   NEG   go-PRES-PLN
   'I don't go unless I go quickly.'

d. 나밖에 학교에밖에 빨리밖에 안 간다.
   Na=pakkey hakkyo=ey=pakkey ppalli=pakkey an   ka-n-ta.
   I=only   school=DIR=only   quickly=only   NEG   go-PRES-PLN
   'Only I go to only school and only quickly.'

The examples in (52–53c) illustrate a major difference between Korean and English touched on in Chapter 5. In English, association-with-focus particles such as 'only', 'even' and 'also' may be quite freely associated with the target of focus by intonation. Thus in the English translations of (52–53c) 'only' appears before the VP, separated from the adverb 'quickly'. Because VP-final adverbs naturally receive focus intonation, 'I only go QUICKLY', where 'quickly' is focused, is a natural interpretation of the sentence. In Korean, however, the delimiter immediately follows the focused constituent.

6.3.2   Delimiter =to

The delimiter =to 'too, also' has the same distribution as other delimiters, appearing after all constituents but the tensed verb. It may also appear multiply in a sentence.

(54)   Delimiter: =to
    a. 나는 철수도 좋아해.
        Na=nun   Chelswu=to   cohaha-y.
        I=TOP   Chelswu=too   like-INT
        'I like Chelswu too.'
    b. 나는 학교에 가기도 한다.
        Na=nun   hakkyo=ey   ka-ki=to   ha-n-ta.
        I=TOP   school=DIR   go-NOMNL=too   do-PRES-PLN
        'I go to school too.'
    c. 나는 빨리도 간다.
        Na=nun   ppalli=to   ka-n-ta.
        I=TOP   quickly=too   go-PRES-PLN
        'I go to school quickly too.'
    d. 나도 학교에도 빨리도 간다.
        Na=to   hakkyo=ey=to   ppalli=to   ka-n-ta.
        I=too   school=DIR=too   quickly=too   go-PRES-PLN
        'I too go to school too in a quick manner too.'

6.3.3   Delimiters =kkaci/=mace/=cocha/=ilato

There are four delimiter counterparts of 'even'. =*Kkaci* and =*mace* in (55) appear in both positive and negative sentences. =*Cocha* in (56) appears only in negative sentences, while =*ilato* in (57) appears only in commands.

(55)   Delimiter: =*kkaci/=mace*
    a. 철수는 공부까지/마저 안한다.
        Chelswu=nun   kongpwu=kkaci/=mace   an   ha-n-ta.
        Chelswu=TOP   study=even   NEG   do-PRES-PLN
        'Chelswu does not even study.'

b. 추운데 바람까지/마저 분다.

  Chwuwun-tey   *palam=kkaci/=mace*   *pwu-n-ta.*
  cold-and   wind=even   blow-PRES-PLN
  'It is cold and even the wind blows.'

c. 힘든데 개까지/마저 쫓아온다.

  Himtun-tey   *kay=kkaci/=mace* *ccochao-n-ta.*
  difficult-and   dog=even   chase-PRES-PLN
  'It's tough; a dog even chased me.'

(56)   Delimiter: *=cocha*

a. 철수는 공부조차 안한다.

  Chelswu=nun   *kongpwu=cocha* *an*   *ha-n-ta.*
  Chelswu=TOP   study=even   NEG do-PRES-PLN
  'Chelswu does not even study.'

b. *추운데 바람조차 분다.

  **Chwuwun-tey*   *palam=cocha*   *pwu-n-ta.*
  cold-and   wind=even   blow-PRES-PLN

c. *힘든데 개조차 쫓아온다.

  **Himtun-tey*   *kay=cocha*   *ccochao-n-ta.*
  difficult-and   dog=even   chase-PRES-PLN

Finally, *=(i)lato* appears only in imperatives, both affirmative and negative:

(57)   Delimiter: *=(i)lato*

a. 공부라도 잘 해라.

  Kongpwu=lato   *cal*   *hay-la.*
  study=even   well   do-COM
  'Please even study well.'

b. 잠자기라도 못 해라.

  Camca-ki=lato   *mos*   *hay-la.*
  sleep-NOMNL=even cannot do-COM
  'Please do not even sleep.'

c. 빨리라도 가라.

  Ppalli=lato   *ka-la.*
  quickly=even   go-COM
  'Please even go quickly.'

6.4   Nominalization

Nominalization is the process of changing a verb or adjective into a noun. Contemporary Korean has a wide variety of forms, perhaps as many as twenty, that have been described as nominalizers. In an agglutinative language, morphological derivation plays an important role in nominalization, but functionally the process of nominalization overlaps with clausal complementation; that is, ways of making clauses arguments of higher predicates. We will focus on two affixal nominalizers, *-(u)m* and *-ki,* and the complementizer or bound noun *kes.*

6.4.1   Nominalizers -(u)m and -ki

Both *-(u)m* and *-ki* are productive nominalizers deriving nominalized forms of verbs in (58) and adjectives in (59). The nominalization may function as arguments of the main clause predicate, and be case marked accordingly.

(58)   Deverbal nominalizations
    a. 철수가 피자를 먹는다.
       Chelswu=ka   *phica=lul mek-nun-ta.*
       Chelswu=NOM   pizza=ACC eat-PRES-PLN
       'Chelswu eats pizza.'
    b. 철수가 피자를 먹기가 어렵다.
       Chelswu=ka   *phica=lul mek-ki=ka*   *elyep-ta.*
       Chelswu=NOM   pizza=ACC eat-NOMNL=NOM   difficult-PLN
       'It is difficult for Chelswu to eat pizza.'
    c. 철수가 학교에 간다.
       Chelswu=ka   *hakkyo=ey ka-n-ta.*
       Chelswu=NOM   school=DIR go-PRES-PLN
       'Chelswu goes to school.'
    d. 철수가/의 학교에 갔음을 알렸다.
       Chelswu=ka/=uy   *hakkyo=ey ka-ss-um=ul*
       Chelswu=NOM/=GEN school=DIR go-PAST-NOMNL=ACC
       ally-ess-ta.
       know-PAST-PLN
       'It was announced that Chelswu went to school.'

(59)   Deadjectival nominalizations
    a. 철수가 기뻐한다.
       Chelswu=ka   *kippeha-n-ta.*
       Chelswu=NOM   glad-PRES-PLN
       'Chelswu is glad.'
    b. 철수가 기뻐하기가 쉽지 않다.
       Chelswu=ka   *kippeha-ki=ka* *swipci-anh-ta.*
       Chelswu=NOM glad-NOMNL=NOM easy-not-PLN
       'It is not easy for Chelswu to be glad.'
    c. 철수가 행복하다.
       Chelswu=ka   *hayngpokha-ta.*
       Chelswu=NOM   happy-PLN
       'Chelswu is happy.'
    d. 철수가/의 행복함을 아무도 모른다.
       Chelswu=ka/=uy   *hayngpokha-m=ul*   *amwuto molu-n-ta.*
       Chelswu=NOM/=GEN happy-NOMNL=ACC nobody not know-PRES-PLN
       'No one knows Chelswu is happy.'

The nominalizing suffixes *-(u)m* and *-ki* show important differences. *-(U)m* permits nominative or genitive case on the subject of the nominalized clause, as shown in (59d). Nominalizations in *-ki* do not assign genitive, and typically serve as the arguments of raising or control predicates. The latter property is shown in (60):

(60)   a. 남 교수님ᵢ이 [PROᵢ 술을 마시기]]를 싫어하세요.
        Nam kyoswunimᵢ=i   [PROᵢ swul=ul masi-ki]=lul   silheha-sey-yo.
        Nam professor=NOM   alcohol=ACC drink-NOMNL=ACC   dislike-HON-POL
        'Professor Nam dislikes drinking alcohol.'
      b. 철수가 귀ᵢ가 [tᵢ가렵기] 시작했다.
        Chelswu=ka   kwiᵢ=ka   [tᵢ kalyep-ki]   sicakhay-ss-ta.
        Chelswu=NOM   ear=NOM itch-NOMNL   begin-PAST-PLN
        'Chelswu's ears began to itch.' (literal meaning)
        'Chelswu began to feel he was being talked about.' (idiomatic meaning)

In (60a), both the main predicate 싫어하- *silheha-* 'dislike' and the nominalized predicate 마시- *masi-* 'drink' require a subject. The usual analysis of "control" constructions like this is that the main clause predicate is generated with a subject, in this case *Nam kyoswu* 'Professor Nam', which is then coindexed with the unpronounced subject of *masi-* 'drink', shown as *PRO* in (60a). In (60b), in contrast, Chelswu's ears don't begin doing anything, especially in the idiomatic interpretation of *kwi=ka kalyep-ki* '(feel that one is) being talked about'. Instead what begins is the event of being talked about. Such patterns are usually analyzed as "raising" constructions, where the subject of the nominalization, here *kwi* 'ears', begins inside the nominalization and is then displaced to the main clause subject position. What is notable for our discussion here is that *-ki* complements show this kind of raising and control behavior, while *-(u)m* nominalizations do not.

This difference is related to the fact that nominalizations with *-(u)m* as main clause complements allow tense, but nominalizations with *-ki* as main clause complements do not. Crosslinguistically, tenseless clausal complements are likelier to undergo control or raising. These differences are summarized in (61).

(61)   Differences between *-(u)m* and *-ki* as main clause complements
        -(u)m   *-ki*
        Genitive subjects   No genitive subjects
        + tense   - tense
        No control or raising   Control or raising possible

Differences with respect to case marking and control are shown in (62).

(62)   a. 철수는 [영희가/의 늦게 감]이 싫다.
        Chelswu=nun   [Yenghuy=ka/=uy   nuckey   ka-m]=i
        Chelswu=TOP   Yenghuy=NOM/=GEN late   go-NOMNL=NOM
        silh-ta.
        dislike-PLN
        'Chelswu dislikes that Yenghuy goes late.'

b. *철수는 영희에게 늦게 감이 싫다.

*Chelswu=nun   Yenghuy=eykey   nuckey   ka-m=i   silh-ta.
Chelswu=TOP   Yenghuy=DAT   late   go-NOMNL=NOM   dislike-PLN
'Chelswu dislikes that Yenghuy goes late.'

c. 철수는 [영희가/*의 빨리 돌아오기]를 원한다.

Chelswu=nun   [Yenghuy=ka/*=uy ppalli   tolao-ki]=lul
Chelswu=TOP   Yenghuy=NOM/*=GEN quickly   return-NOMNL=ACC
wenha-n-ta.
want-PRES-PLN
'Chelswu wants Yenghuy to return quickly.'

d. 철수는 영희ᵢ에게 [proᵢ빨리 돌아오기]를 원한다.

Chelswu=nun   [Yenghuyᵢ=eykey   [proᵢ ppalli tolao-ki=lul
Chelswu=TOP   Yenghuy=DAT quickly   return-NOMNL=ACC
wenha-n-ta.
want-PRES-PLN
'Chelswu wants Yenghuy to return quickly.'

We analyze (62d) as a control structure, while (62b) shows that the corresponding pattern is impossible with -(u)m. The contrast between (62c) and (62d) shows that -ki clauses can license a nominative subject. We can show that the nominative subject is inside the -ki clause, while the dative-marked subject is not, by scrambling the complement clause:

(63)   철수는 [빨리 돌아오기]를 영희에게/*가 원한다.

Chelswu=nun [ppalli tolao-ki]=lul   Yenghuy=eykey/*=ka
Chelswu=TOP quickly return-NOMNL=ACC   Yenghuy=DAT/*=NOM
wenha-n-ta.
want-PRES-PLN
'Chelswu wants Yenghuy to return quickly.'

The presence of tense generally correlates with the occurrence of control. The nominalizer -(u)m generally allows overt tense morphology. In contrast -ki allows overt tense morphology only in non-control contexts such as (64b):

(64)   a. 철수는 영희가 늦게 왔음이 싫다.

Chelswu=nun   Yenghuy=ka   nuckey   o-ass-um=i
Chelswu=TOP   Yenghuy=NOM   late   come-PAST-NOMNL=NOM
silh-ta.
dislike-PLN
'Chelswu dislikes that Yenghuy came late.'

b. 철수는 영희가 빨리 돌아왔기를 원한다.

Chelswu=nun   Yenghuy=ka   ppalli   tolao-ass-ki=lul
Chelswu=TOP   Yenghuy=NOM   quickly   return-PAST-NOMNL=ACC
wenha-n-ta.
want-PRES-PLN
'Chelswu wants Yenghuy to have returned quickly.'

6.4.2   *Complementizer:* kes

Descriptively, the bound noun *kes* heads clausal complements like *-(u)m* and *-ki*. Like *-(u)m* and *-ki*, because *kes* can be followed by case markers and postpositions, it is sometimes called a nominalizer. However the promiscuity of Korean case marking makes this a weak criterion. Unlike *-(u)m, kes* does not allow genitive to be assigned to the subject of its complement clause. *Kes* uncontroversially introduces complement clauses, so we will use the term complementizer for it. *Kes* is a very productive morpheme in this function. *Kes* must be preceded by an adnominalized form of the embedded predicate: *-nun* (present), *-(u)n* (past), or *-(u)l* (future).

(65)   Complementizer *Kes*
    a. 영희는 철수가 피자를 먹는것을 안다.

        Yenghuy=nun   *Chelswu=ka*   *phica=lul*   *mek-nun-kes=ul*
        Yenghuy=TOP   Chelswu=NOM pizza=ACC eat-PRES-NOMNL=ACC
        a-n-ta.
        know-PRES-PLN
        'Yenghuy knows that Chelswu eats pizza.'

    b. 영희는 철수가 피자를 먹은것을 안다.

        Yenghuy=nun   *Chelswu=ka*   *phica=lul*   *mek-un-kes=ul*
        Yenghuy=TOP   Chelswu=NOM pizza=ACC eat-PAST-NOMNL=ACC
        a-n-ta.
        know-PRES-PLN
        'Yenghuy knows that Chelswu ate pizza.'

    c. 영희는 철수가 피자를 먹을것을 안다.

        Yenghuy=nun   *Chelswu=ka*   *phica=lul*   *mek-ul-kes=ul*
        Yenghuy=TOP   Chelswu=NOM pizza=ACC eat-FUT-NOMNL=ACC
        a-n-ta.
        know-PRES-PLN
        'Yenghuy knows that Chelswu will eat pizza.'

Although *kes* clauses require adnominal morphology, as complements their syntactic properties differ from those of relative clauses. For example, scrambling is possible out of a *kes* complement clause:

(66)   피자를 영희는 철수가 먹는것을 안다.
    Phica=lul   *Yenghuy=nun* *Chelswu=ka*   *mek-nun-kes=ul*
    pizza=ACC   Yenghuy=TOP Chelswu=NOM eat-PRES-NOMNL=ACC
    a-n-ta.
    know-PRES-PLN
    'Pizza, Yenghuy knows that Chelswu eats.'

6.5   Numerals

Numerals include cardinal numbers, ordinal numbers and their classifiers. As we observed in Chapter 5, Korean has in common use native Korean numerals for one through ninety-nine, and Sino-Korean numerals spanning zero to infinity. In this section we also discuss the morphosyntax of numeral classifiers, which varies depending on the identity of the NP being quantified, as well as which system of numerals is used.

6.5.1   Cardinal Numbers

Native Korean cardinals are listed in (67).

(67)   Native Korean cardinal numbers
      a. 1–10
         hana, twul, seys, neys, tases, yeses, ilkop, yetepl, ahop, yel
      b. 11–19
         yel hana, yel twul, yel seys, yel neys, yel tases, yel yeses, . . ., yel ahop
      c. 20, 30, 40, 50, 60, 70, 80, 90
         sumwul, selun, mahun, swin, yeyswun, ilhun, yetun, ahun

The native Korean cardinals include one through ten (67a), and ten plus one through nine (67b). There are also native numerals for the multiples of ten (67c). This makes it possible to count to ninety-nine using native numerals alone.

(68)   Sino-Korean cardinal numbers
      a. 0–10
         yeng or kong, il, i, sam, sa, o, yuk, chil, phal, kwu, sip
      b. 11–19
         sip il, sip i, sip sam, sip sa, sip o, sip yuk, sip chil, sip phal, sip kwu
      c. 20, 30, 40, 50, 60, 70, 80, 90
         i sip, sam sip, sa sip, o sip, yuk sip, chil sip, phal sip, kwu sip
      d. 100, 1000, 10000, 100000, 1 million, 10 million
         payk, chen, man, sip man, payk man, chen man
      e. 100 million, 1 billion, 10 billion, 100 billion, 1 trillion
         ek, sip ek, payk ek, chen ek, co

The Sino-Korean numerals are phonologically similar to Chinese and Sino-Japanese since, like Sino-Japanese numerals, they were borrowed from Middle Chinese. There are two Sino-Korean terms for zero, *yeng* (< 零MC *leŋ* 'zero') and *kong* (< 空 MC *kʰuŋ* 'empty'). The teens are again additive: ten plus one, two, and so on (68b). The multiples of ten are multiplicative: two times ten, three times ten, and so on (68c). The SK system then has borrowed terms for 100 and its multiples: *payk* 100, *chen* 1,000, and *man* 10,000 (68d). *Man* 10,000 is the base for higher multiples, as in Chinese: 10 times 10,000 *sip man*, 100 times 10,000 *payk man*, and 1,000 times 10,000 *chen man*, as in (68d). *Ek* is 100 million and *co* is 1 trillion. The major difference between English and Korean numbers is that the former has a named unit every three digits and the latter every four digits.

For numbers 100 and up, the numeral terms can be composed including SK 100 (and up) and SK 1–99, or SK 100 (and up) combined with native Korean 1–99 as in (69).

(69)   Cardinal numbers 100 and up
        a. 158
           payk osip phal, payk swin yetelp
        b. 2639
           i chen yuk payk sam sip kwu, i chen yuk payk selun ahop
        c. 47625
           sa man chil chen yuk payk i sip o, sa man chil chen yuk payk sumwul tases

6.5.2   Ordinal Numbers

Ordinal numbers denote the position of the element in a sequence such as 'first', 'second', 'third' and so on in English. Once again, Korean has native Korean ordinals made up of the native cardinal followed by *ccay* '-th', and Sino-Korean preceded by *cey* 'number (in a sequence)', from Middle Chinese 第 *dei^H*.

(70)   Native Korean ordinals
        a. 1–10 (i.e., 1st–10th)
           ches ccay, twul ccay, seys ccay, neys ccay, tases ccay, . . .
        b. 11–19
           yel han ccay, yel twul ccay, yel seys ccay, yel neys ccay, yel tases ccay, . . .
        c. 20, 30, 40, 50, 60, 70, 80, 90
           sumwu ccay, selun ccay, mahun ccay, swin ccay, . . .

(71)   Sino-Korean ordinals
        a. 1–10
           cey il, cey i, cey sam, cey sa, cey o, cey yuk, cey chil, cey phal, cey kwu, cey sip
        b. 11–19
           cey sip il, cey sip i, cey sip sam, cey sip sa, cey sip o, cey sip yuk, cey sip chil, cey sip phal, cey sip kwu
        c. 20, 30, 40, 50, 60, 70, 80, 90
           cey i sip, cey sam sip, cey sa sip, cey o sip, cey yuk sip, cey chil sip, cey phal sip, cey kwu sip

6.5.3   Numeral Classifiers

A numeral classifier is a word or morpheme that combines with numerals quantifying NPs whose shape is dependent on the semantic properties of the NP. For instance, "three students" in a language with numeral classifiers will be expressed as "student(s) + number + classifier" where the classifier typically is one used for NPs denoting humans. Some Korean classifiers combine with native Korean numerals, some combine with Sino-Korean numerals, and some classifiers combine with both native Korean and Sino-Korean numerals.

The first type of classifier, combining with native Korean numbers, includes counting units for clothing, shoes, animals, nonhuman objects such as pencils and bottles, and time expressions such as hours and months.

(72)   Native Korean classifiers

벌	*pel*	clothing
켤레	*khyeylle*	shoes
마리	*mali*	animals
사람	*salam*	people
개	*kay*	objects
잔	*can*	glasses
필	*phil*	horses
시간	*sikan*	duration of an hour
달	*tal*	duration of a month
번	*pen*	times
대	*tay*	vehicles
장	*cang*	paper

The second type of classifier, combining with Sino-Korean numbers, includes counting units for money, floors, lessons, and time expressions such as year, month, week, date, minute, and second.

(73)   Sino-Korean classifiers

원	*won*	money (Korean)
불	*pwul*	money (American)
년	*nyen*	years
월	*wel*	months
일	*il*	days
분	*pwun*	minutes
초	*cho*	seconds

The third type, combining with either native Korean or Sino-Korean numerals, includes units for books, people, and units of measure.

(74)   Classifiers with either native Korean or SK numerals

권	*kwen*	volumes
명	*myeng*	people
병	*pyeng*	bottles
층	*chung*	floors
과	*kwa*	lessons
주	*cwu*	weeks

The syntax of numeral classifiers has already been mentioned in Sections 6.1.1 and 6.1.2, where we discussed nominative and accusative case spreading with floated numeral quantifiers, in examples like (23a). The three basic patterns for NP + numeral + classifier are shown in (75):

(75)   a. Floated quantifier
         철수가 고기를 어제 열마리(를) 먹었다.
         Chelswu=ka   koki=lul   ecey   yel mali(=lul)   mek-ess-ta.
         Chelswu=NOM fish=ACC   yesterday ten CLSF(=ACC) eat-PAST-PLN
         'Chelswu ate ten fish yesterday.'
         b. Postnominal quantifier
         철수가 어제 고기 열마리를 먹었다.
         Chelswu=ka   ecey   koki yel mali=lul   mek-ess-ta.
         Chelswu=NOM yesterday fish ten CLSF=ACC eat-PAST-PLN
         'Chelswu ate ten fish yesterday.'
         c. Prenominal quantifier
         철수가 어제 열마리(의) 고기를 먹었다.
         Chelswu=ka   ecey   yel mali(=uy)   koki=lul   mek-ess-ta.
         Chelswu=NOM yesterday ten CLSF (=GEN) fish=ACC eat-PAST-PLN
         'Chelswu ate ten fish yesterday.'

In (75a) the quantifier phrase, made up of numeral plus classifier, is "floated" away from the NP it quantifies, as shown by the intervention of the time adverb *ecey* 'yesterday' between them. There are various analyses of this pattern, including ones where the NP is moved out of a larger expression originally containing both NP and quantifier phrase, and ones where NP and quantifier phrase are separate from the beginning. In (75b), NP and quantifier phrase form a single constituent, with the NP coming first. In (75c), quantifier phrase and NP again form a single constituent, but the quantifier phrase precedes.

6.5.4   Plurality

Crosslinguistically, plurality is often marked by adding an inflectional morpheme. For example, *-s* or *-en* in English indicate more than one object or person as in *apples* or *children*. The plural clitic =*tul* in Korean is superficially similar, but its distribution is remarkably different: =*tul* attaches not only to nouns and pronouns (so-called "intrinsic" =*tul*), but to other parts of speech that are not normally thought to have a [±count] feature (so-called "extrinsic" =*tul*).

(76)   =*Tul* with [±count] nouns ("intrinsic" =*tul*)
         a. 학생들이 열명(이) 왔어요.
         Haksayng=tul=i   yel myeng(=i)   o-ass-eyo.
         student=PL=NOM   ten CLSF(=NOM) come-PAST-POL
         'Ten students came.'
         b. 아이들이 공부한다.
         Ai=tul=i   kongpwuha-n-ta.
         child=PL=NOM   study-PRES-PLN
         'Children study.'

   c. 사과들이 많이 달렸다.
     Sakwa=tul=i   manhi   tally-ess-ta.
     apple=PL=NOM a lot   hang-PAST-PLN
     'There are a lot of apples.'

(77)   *=Tul* with pronouns
   a. 우리들은 매일 공부한다.
     Wuli=tul=un   mayil   kongpwuha-n-ta.
     we=PL=TOP   every day   study-PRES-PLN
     'We study every day.'
   b. 너희들은 학교에서 뭐하니?
     Nehuy=tul=un   hakkyo=eyse mwe-ha-ni?
     you=PL=NOM   school=LOC   what-do-Q
     'What do you do at school?'
   c. 이 일은 자네들이 하지.
     I   il=un   caney=tul=i   ha-ci.
     this   work=TOP you=PL=NOM   do-COM
     'You please do this work.'

As shown in (77), *=tul* attaches to pronouns that are lexically plural. But *=tul* may also attach to lexically singular pronouns as well as proper names. In this case, N=*tul* derives what is called an associative meaning: "N and N's group."

(78) Associative *=tul*
   a. 너희들은 한겨레 신문을 발행한다.
     Nehuy=tul=un   Hankyeley   sinmwun=ul   palhayngha-n-ta.
     you=PL=TOP   Hankyoreh   newspaper=ACC publish -PRES-PLN
     'You ('you and your group') publish the Hankyoreh newspaper.'
   b. 철수들이 피자를 먹는다.
     Chelswu=tul=i   phica=lul   mek-nun-ta.
     Chelswu=PL=NOM   pizza=ACC   eat-PRES-PLN
     'Chelswu and his group eat pizza.'

Finally, *=tul* may attach to nonsubstantives, as in (79).

(79)   *=Tul* with nonsubstantives ("extrinsic" *=tul*)
   a. 우리가 빨리들 식당에들 가서 국들을 마셨다.
     Wuli=ka   ppalli=tul siktang=ey=tul   ka-se   kwuk=tul=ul
     we=NOM   quickly=PL restaurant=LOC=PL go-CON soup=PL=ACC
     masy-ess-ta.
     drink-PAST-PLN
     'We went quickly to the restaurant and drank soup.'

b. *우리 선생님이 식당에서들 국들을 마셨다.

*Wuli sensayngnim=i   siktang=eyse=tul kwuk=tul=ul
we teacher=NOM   restaurant=LOC=PL soup=PL=ACC
drink-PAST-PLN
masy-ess-ta.
'Our teacher drank soup in the restaurant.'

c. 남선생님이 학생들을 집들로 보냈다.

Nam sensayngnim=i haksayng=tul=ul cip=tul=lo   ponay-ss-ta.
nam teacher=NOM   student=PL=ACC   home=PL=DIR send-PAST-PLN
'Teacher Nam sent the students home.'

d. 학생들이 로봇들을 만들었다.

Haksayng=tul=i lopos=tul=ul mantul-ess-ta.
student=PL=NOM robot=PL=ACC make-PAST-PLN
'The students made robots.'

The examples in (79) demonstrate the essential properties of "extrinsic" =tul.
As a rule, extrinsic =tul attaches outside case markers and postpositions, like
directional =ey in (79a). But it may attach inside the case marker when associated
with a [-count] NP like kwuk 'soup' in (79a). Extrinsic =tul must be c-commanded
by a plural NP inside the same minimal clause, like wuli 'we' in (79a).
The sentence in (79b) is unacceptable because wuli does not c-command =tul.
The c-commanding plural NP may be a non-subject, like haksayng 'student' in
(79c) if that NP is the subject of a semantic predication; in (79c) ponay- 'send' can
be decomposed to mean 'cause students to go home'. It is sometimes claimed that
extrinsic =tul marks a distributive or pluractional meaning, but (79d) shows that
this is not so: =tul can be associated with a single event, where the students build
one robot together. Instead, as argued by An (2008), extrinsic =tul seems to be
similar to the English floated plural quantifiers all or both in examples like (80):

(80)   a. The students probably all will have all built the robot.
        b. The students will both probably have both built the robot.

The effect of iterated all or both is **maximalizing**: it emphasizes that the
predicate at the point where all or both is introduced in the structure holds
for all or both individuals denoted by the subject. On this view, English all and
both behave like adverbs of quantification. The semantic effect of Korean
extrinsic =tul is similar, but as a phonologically dependent element, it cliticizes
to the closest phrase on its left.

6.6   Outstanding Issues

In this section, we will explore four major outstanding issues relating to
structural case in Korean. The first issue is the classification of multiple

nominative and accusative constructions. The second is the subject status of nominative-marked NPs in multiple nominative constructions. The third is the nature of case assignment in double object constructions. Finally, related to each of these issues, we look at the so-called case-stacking phenomenon in Korean.

6.6.1   Types of Multiple Nominative or Accusative Constructions

Multiple case constructions (MCCs), have been classified in terms of the properties of the outer (leftmost) NP as well as the semantic (or pragmatic) relations between the two adjacent NPs (Youn 1990, O'Grady 1991, Yoon 2004, Kim and Sells 2007). Three types of multiple case constructions can be distinguished based on the properties of the outer NP: possessive, dative, and adjunct patterns. Among the possessive patterns (Payne and Barshi 1999, Yeon 2010), three types of multiple nominative constructions (MNCs) have been distinguished: inalienable, alienable, and kinship patterns. The examples in (81) exemplify the inalienable pattern: (81a) a base genitive construction, (81b) the corresponding double nominative construction, (81c) the base genitive construction for an object, and (81d) the corresponding double accusative pattern. In the (81a) and (81c) examples, clausal adverbs may not intervene between the possessor and possessee NPs, but in (81b) and (81d) they may. This shows that the genitive and double nominative/accusative patterns have different structures: in the genitive pattern, both NPs are contained in a larger NP, but this is not the case in the double nominative/accusative patterns.

(81)   Possessive MCC (Inalienable)
    a. 철수의 (*언제나) 머리가 길다.
       Chelswu=uy (*enceyna) meli=ka kil-ta.
       Chelswu=GEN (*always)   hair=NOM long-PLN
       'Chelswu's (*always) hair is long.'
    b. 철수가 언제나 머리가 길다.
       Chelswu=ka   (enceyna) meli=ka kil-ta.
       Chelswu=NOM   (always)   hair=NOM long-PLN
       'Chelswu's hair is (always) long.'
    c. 나는 철수의 (*어제) 머리를 잡았다.
       Na=nun   Chelswu=uy (*ecey)   meli=lul cap-ass-ta.
       I=TOP   Chelswu=GEN (*yesterday) hair=ACC catch-PAST-PLN
       'I grabbed Chelswu's (*yesterday) hair.'
    d. 나는 철수를 (어제) 머리를 잡았다.
       Na=nun   Chelswu=lul (ecey)   meli=lul cap-ass-ta.
       I=TOP   Chelswu=ACC (yesterday) hair=ACC catch-PAST-PLN
       'I grabbed Chelswu by the hair yesterday.'

Researchers have observed that the double accusative pattern (81d) is semantically distinct from the corresponding genitive pattern (81c). The former entails that I grabbed not only Chelswu's hair but also Chelswu; that is, I grabbed Chelswu by the hair. The latter has no such entailment; it could be used in a context where Chelswu's hair has been cut off and is lying on the table. The constraint that both accusative-marked NPs must be **affected** in the double accusative pattern leads to ungrammaticality when the possession relation is alienable, as we see in (82). Crosslinguistically, patterns similar to Korean possessive-type double nominative and double accusative constructions are sometimes called "possessor raising" constructions; the idea is that the possessor, normally marked genitive, is "raised" to object status in the main clause. The contrast between the (81–82) (c) and (d) examples shows that this cannot be quite right, because the double accusative pattern has a different meaning, and in the case of (82d), a different level of acceptability.

(82)   Possessive MCC (Alienable)
    a. 철수의 (*아주) 차가 멋있다.
        Chelswu=uy   *(*acwu)*   *cha=ka*   *mesiss-ta.*
        Chelswu=GEN   (*very)   car=NOM   cool-PLN
        'Chelswu's (*very) car is cool.'
    b. 철수가 (아주) 차가 멋있다.
        Chelswu=ka   *(acwu)*   *cha=ka*   *mesiss-ta.*
        Chelswu=NOM   (very)   car=NOM   cool-PLN
        'Chelswu's car is (very) cool.'
    c. 나는 철수의 (*어제) 차를 보았다.
        Na=nun   *Chelswu=uy*   *(*ecey)*   *cha=lul*   *po-ass-ta.*
        I=TOP   Chelswu=GEN   (*yesterday)   car=ACC   see-PAST-PLN
        'I saw Chelswu's (*yesterday) car.'
    d. *나는 철수를 차를 보았다.
        *Na=nun   *Chelswu=lul*   *cha=lul*   *po-ass-ta.*
        I=TOP   Chelswu=ACC   car=ACC   see-PAST-PLN
        'I saw Chelswu's car.'

Crosslinguistically, kinship relations sometimes pattern with inalienable possession, and Korean too allows the double nominative construction in (83b). But the double accusative pattern in (83c) is unacceptable because catching Chelswu's brother does not entail catching Chelswu; in other words, affectedness is the crucial condition for possessive-type double accusatives.

(83)   Possessive MCC (Kinship)
    a. 철수의 동생이 크다.
        Chelswu=uy   *tongsayng=i*   *khu-ta.*
        Chelswu=GEN   brother=NOM   tall-PLN
        'Chelswu's brother is tall.'

b. 철수가 동생이 크다.

Chelswu=ka   tongsayng=i khu-ta.
Chelswu=NOM   brother=NOM   tall-PLN
'Chelswu's brother is tall.'

c. *나는 철수를 동생을 잡았다.

*Na=nun   Chelswu=lul   tongsayng=ul cap-ass-ta.
I=TOP   Chelswu=ACC   brother=ACC   catch-PAST-PLN
'I caught Chelswu's brother.'

Multiple nominative constructions in Korean exemplify the crosslinguistic phenomenon of noncanonical or "quirky" case marking. Example (84a) shows "canonical" marking of the arguments of a stative predicate with a dative marking of the experiencer NP and nominative marking of the theme, whereas (84b) shows that the experiencer argument can also be marked nominative. But some speakers also allow the pattern described as "case stacking" in (84c), where both dative and nominative occur on the same NP (Youn 1990, Schütze 2001, Yoon 2004).

(84)   Experiencer multiple nominative and "case stacking" constructions
a. 나에게 그 여자가 좋다.

Na=eykey   ku   yeca=ka   coh-ta.
I=DAT   that   woman=NOM   like-PLN
'I like that woman.' (Lit. 'That woman is good to me.')

b. 내가 그 여자가 좋다.

Nay=ka ku   yeca=ka   coh-ta.
I=NOM   that woman=NOM   like-PLN
'I like that woman.'

c. 나에게가 그 여자가 좋다.

Na=eykey=ka ku   yeca=ka   coh-ta.
I=DAT=NOM   that woman=NOM   like-PLN
'(It is) I (that) like that woman.'

The usual description of case stacking in Korean observes that structural case is realized outside the lexical or semantic case. In the analysis we developed in Chapter 5, the case-stacking phenomenon is not surprising at all. We analyze dative =*eykey* as a postposition. We already saw in Section 6.1.3 that structural case can be assigned to PPs in Korean. Understood this way, case stacking can be analyzed much like the phenomenon of "quirky case" in languages like Icelandic. A marker associated with the semantic role of the NP, an oblique case such as dative in Icelandic or a dative postposition in Korean, is assigned in the position where the NP originates. The dative-marked NP then moves into a position where nominative is normally assigned. In Icelandic this manifests itself in the form of the subject properties of the quirky case-marked NP. In Korean it may manifest itself in the form of the canonical subject case, nominative, appearing outside the postposition. In the adjunct MNC pattern, the locative postposition on the outer NP in the base construction (85a) appears with nominative in the MNC (85b). This pattern also allows case stacking for some speakers in the order =Locative=Nominative (85c). Once again we see that the innermost case postposition reveals the case marking in the (85a) base pattern.

(85)   Adjunct MCC
        a. 서울에 사람이 많다.

        Sewul=ey   salam=i   manh-ta.
        Seoul=LOC   people=NOM   a lot-PLN
        'There are a lot of people in Seoul.'
        b. 서울이 사람이 많다.

        Sewul=i   salam=i   manh-ta.
        Seoul=NOM   people=NOM   a lot-PLN
        'There are a lot of people in Seoul.'
        c. 서울에가 사람이 많다.

        Sewul=ey=ka   salam=i   manh-ta.
        Seoul=LOC=NOM   people=NOM   a lot-PLN
        'There are a lot of people in Seoul.'

Youn (1990) points out the existence of whole–part or metonymic MCCs such as (86). Unlike possessive MCCs, no corresponding genitive pattern exists.

(86)   Double case construction (whole–part)
        a. 꽃이/*의 장미가 아름답다.
        Kkoch=i/=uy   cangmi=ka   alumtap-ta.*
        flower=NOM/*=GEN   rose=NOM   pretty-PLN
        'Roses are pretty among flowers.'
        b. 철수가 꽃을/*의 장미를 샀다.
        Chelswu=ka   kkoch=ul/=uy   cangmi-lul   sa-ss-ta.*
        Chelswu=NOM   flower=ACC/*=GEN   rose=ACC   buy-PAST-PLN
        'Chelswu bought roses among flowers.'

Youn (1990) includes among MCCs the "case spreading" context for nominative and accusative marking of floated quantifiers that we saw in Sections 6.1.1 and 6.1.2. As we saw there, these pattern with case spreading to adverbs. Youn also includes the MCC pattern with verbal nouns we saw in (18–19). Youn points out that passivizing the verbal noun construction can produce a double nominative (87a), while causativizing it produces a double accusative (87b):

(87)   Passive/causative double case constructions
        a. 도시가 파괴가 되었다.
        Tosi=ka   phakoy=ka   toy-ess-ta.
        city=NOM   destroy=NOM   become-PAST-PLN
        'The city was destroyed.'

b. 철수가 도시를 파괴를 시켰다.

> Chelswu=ka   tosi=lul phakoy=lul sikhye-ss-ta.
> Chelswu=NOM   city=ACC destroy=ACC make-PAST-PLN
> 'Chelswu made the city get destroyed.'

Finally, Youn includes among MNCs nominative marking on the predicate nominal with the negated copula which we saw in (15). Youn's broader classification brings us back to the question of the relationship between case and grammatical relation: which nominatives in MNCs are subjects, and which accusatives in multiple accusative constructions are objects?

6.6.2   Subjecthood

We saw in Section 6.1 that both the inner and outer nominative-marked NPs in genitive-type MNCs can pass subjecthood tests. This is a prima facie argument against the view that only the inner NP is a subject (Yoon 1986, Schütze 2001), or alternatively that only the outer NP is a subject (Chun 1985, Youn 1990), and in support of the view that in at least some cases both the outer and inner NPs can be subjects (Heycock 1993, Yoon 2015). The subjecthood tests we used in Section 6.1.1, subject honorification and anteceding reflexive *caki*, are difficult to apply to location or adjunct-type MNCs, but Yoon (2015) points out that this type of "major" subject passes another subjecthood test, ability to undergo raising to object (88c).

(88)   Adjunct MNC

a. 시골에 부모님이 많이 산다.

> Sikol=ey   pwumonim=i manhi sa-n-ta.
> country=at   parents=NOM a lot live-PRES-PLN
> 'A lot of parents live in the country.'

b. 시골이 부모님이 많이 산다.

> Sikol=i   pwumonim=i manhi sa-n-ta.
> country=NOM   parents=NOM a lot live-PRES-PLN
> 'A lot of parents live in the country.'

c. 나는 시골을 부모님이 많이 사신다고 생각한다.

> Na=nun sikol=ul   pwumonim=i manhi sa-si-n-ta-ko
> I=TOP   country=ACC parents=NOM a lot live-HON-PRES-PLN-COMP
> sayngkakha-n-ta.
> think-PRES-PLN
> 'I think that many parents live in the country.'

The examples in (88) show subject properties on both the inner ("major") and outer ("minor") subjects: the former undergoes subject-to-object raising in (88c), while the latter triggers honorific agreement.

The third approach taking both the outer and inner NPs to be subjects originates with Heycock's (1993) analysis of Japanese MNCs. In this approach, the constituent demarcated by the inner subject is taken to be a clausal predicate of the outer or major subject. Since predication in formal syntax and semantics is represented as a variable binding relationship, this requires that a pronoun (null or overt), or a trace of movement in the clausal predicate, be bound by the major subject. Yoon (2015) shows that in genitive-type MNCs the inner ("minor") subject may contain an overt pronoun bound by the major subject:

(89)   ?철수ᵢ가 그ᵢ의 어깨의 오른쪽의 윗부분이 아프더라.
         ?Chelswuᵢ=ka [kuᵢ=uy ekkay=uy   olunccok=uy wis-pwupwun]=i
         Chelswu=NOM he=GEN shoulder=GEN right=GEN   upper-part=NOM
         aphu-te-la.
         hurt-I.hear
         'I heard that the top part of Chelswu's right shoulder hurts.' (Yoon 2015: 83)

However, this is not generally possible; for example in (90), where there is only one level of embedding, the overt bound pronoun is not acceptable:

(90)   철수ᵢ가 (*그ᵢ의) 키가 크다.
         *Chelswuᵢ=ka   (*kuᵢ=uy) khi=ka   khu-ta.*
         Chelswu=NOM   (he=GEN) height=NOM tall-PLN
         'Chelswu is tall.'

As Yoon points out, the pronominal possessor in (89) is deeply embedded in the left branch of an NP, a position from which movement is usually blocked. This is exactly the behavior we would expect of resumptive pronouns in a movement context: the variable required for clausal predication is produced by movement where it can be, but otherwise by a pronoun, overt or null.

Under the clausal predicate analysis, adjunct MNCs like (88) must be derived by movement of the adjunct from the clausal predicate into a position where nominative is assigned, as shown in (91):

(91)   [시골ᵢ =이 [t ᵢ 부모님이 많이 산다]].
         [Sikol ᵢ =i [t ᵢ pwumonim=i manhi sa-n-ta]].
         country=NOM parents=NOM a lot   live-PRES-PLN
         'A lot of parents live in the country.'

On this view, adjunct major subjects can be generated in the normal way, for adjuncts, adjoined to the VP or the underlying clause. From this position, they are moved into major subject position. This kind of process is not unique to Korean; a similar process is involved in the English locative inversion construction in (92a). Like the Korean adjunct MNC, locative inversion passes at least one subjecthood test, raising to a higher subject position (92b):

(92)   English locative inversion
         a. In the country live many parents.
         b. In the country are thought to live many parents.

In generative grammar, subjects are defined as the specifiers of the clausal categories, S, or in more recent theories T(ense)P. Korean has the salient typological property that there can be more than one specifier of this type. One way to think about this, suggested by Whitman (2001), is that the subject case clitic =*i/*=*ka* is itself the head of the clausal category, or one type of clausal category, in Korean. In this approach, the outermost specifier or adjunct of the lower clause moves up to the specifier of =*i/*=*ka*, as shown in (93).

(93)

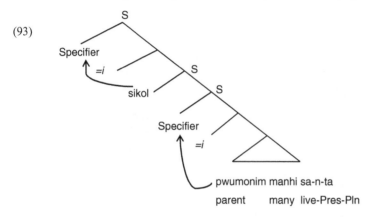

This approach predicts that the number of nominative-marked NPs in an MNC is limited only by the number of possessors and adjuncts available. Yoon (2015) gives an example with four, based on a Japanese example due to Kuno (1973):

(94)   남반구가 문명국가가 남자가 평균 수명이 짧다.
         Nampankwu=*ka*   *mwunmyeng-kwukka*=*ka*   *namca*=*ka*
         south hemisphere=NOM   civilized-countries=NOM   males=NOM
         phyengkywun   *swumyeng*=*i*   *ccalp-ta.*
         average   lifespan=NOM   short-PLN
         'It is the southern hemisphere where it is in the civilized countries where it is the men whose lifespan is short.' (Yoon 2015: 80)

6.6.3   Objecthood (Case Assignment)

There are two salient issues regarding multiple accusative constructions: whether both accusative-marked NPs in a double accusative construction are "real" objects; and what the mechanism for accusative case assignment is. We saw in example (20) in Section 6.1.2 that both the indirect and direct object in a ditransitive double-accusative construction (DAC) with *cwu-* 'give' can be passivized (that is, gain subject status as the result of the passive operation). Earlier researchers have used passivization as well as other movement operations, relativization, and topicalization, to test the objecthood of both NPs. These tests were interpreted to show that only the outer NP is a "true" object, while the inner NP is not. But this interpretation was based on a misunderstanding of the nature of movement. For example, under passivization, either or both of the NPs in an inalienable possession DAC may gain subject status, as long as they maintain their underlying order, possessor–possessee (95a–d). If the possessee is passivized over the possessor, the result is ungrammatical.

(95)   Passivization
    a. 철수가 아이의 팔을 잡았다.

Chelswu=ka	*ai=uy*	*phal=ul*	*cap-ass-ta.*
Chelswu=NOM	child=GEN	arm=ACC	catch-PAST-PLN

       'Chelswu caught a child's arm.'
    b. 철수가 아이를 팔을 잡았다.

Chelswu=ka	*ai=lul*	*phal=ul*	*cap-ass-ta.*
Chelswu=NOM	child=ACC	arm=ACC	catch-PAST-PLN

       'Chelswu caught a child's arm.'
    c. 아이가 철수한테 팔을 잡혔다.

Ai=ka	*Chelswu=hanthey*	*pha=ul*	*cap-hi-ess-ta.*
child=NOM	Chelswu=DAT	arm=ACC	catch-PASS-PAST-PLN

       'A child had his arm caught by Chelswu.'
    d. *팔이 철수한테 아이를 잡혔다.

*Phal=i	*Chelswu=hanthey*	*ai=lul*	*cap-hi-ess-ta.*
arm=NOM	Chelswu=DAT	child=ACC	catch-PASS-PAST-PLN

       'A child had his arm caught by Chelswu.'

However, the unacceptability of (95d) is explained by independent principles. In order to derive this sentence, the NP *phal* 'arm' must be moved into subject position over another NP, *ai* 'child', but this is a violation of Relativized Minimality (Rizzi 1986), a principle which says that when movement may potentially target two or more NPs of the same type, it must move the NP closest to the landing site. Yoon (2015: 93) points out that whole–part DACs behave differently from possessor-type DACs with respect to the passivization test:

(96)   과일이 요즘 사과*를/가 많이 먹힌다.

Kwail=i	*yocum*	*sakwa*=lul/=ka*	*manhi*	*mek-hi-n-ta*
fruit=NOM	nowadays	apple*=ACC/=NOM	many	eat-PASS-PRES-PLN

       'Speaking of fruit, apples are eaten a lot these days.' (Yoon 2015: 93)

If anything, the fact that passivization of the second NP is obligatory in (96) suggests that it is an object. We will therefore not take a position on the issue of whether or not both NPs in a DAC are "true" objects, except to observe that tests purporting to show that only the first NP is an object are inconclusive.

Regarding the accusative case-marking mechanism in DACs, the majority position seems to be that case is assigned in a one-to-many fashion, either by the verb, or in more recent analyses, by a functional category selecting the verb phrase (Kang 1985, Yoon 1986, 2015, Maling and Kim 1992, O'Grady 1991, Park 2013). Although multiple nominative and multiple accusative assignment seem similar, there are basic differences. There are no multiple nominative counterparts of the multiple accusative constructions with manner and durational adverbs. Even unaccusative verbs do not assign nominative to adverbs in parallel contexts:

(97)   a. 철수가 삼일 동안(*이) 있었다.
         Chelswu=ka   *samil tongan(*=i)*   *iss-ess-ta.*
         Chelswu=NOM   three days duration(*=NOM) be-PAST-PLN
         'Chelswu was (there) for three days.'
    b. 철수가 빨리(*가) 죽었다.
         Chelswu=ka   *ppalli(*=ka)*   *cwuk-ess-ta.*
         Chelswu=NOM   quickly(*=NOM) die-PAST-PLN
         'Chelswu died quickly.'

This indicates that multiple accusative is truly a one-to-many relation, with a single head category (the verb or a functional head) assigning case to all categories in a specific domain.

6.7   Summary

In this chapter, we have dealt with the interface of morphology and syntax relating to NPs in Korean: case, postpositions, delimiters, and nominalization, together with the morphosyntax of numerals, and plural marking. There are three structural case clitics: nominative, accusative, and genitive. In Section 6.2, we surveyed the major types of postpositions: dative, locative, direction, goal, source, conjunctive, and disjunctive. In Section 6.3, we focused on the association-with-focus delimiters corresponding to 'only', 'too', and 'even'. In Section 6.4, we discussed two nominalization processes and the complementizer *kes*. In Section 6.5, we described the morphosyntax of numbers, including cardinal numbers, ordinal numbers, and classifiers, and plurality, including the so-called ubiquitous Korean plural marker *=tul*. In Section 6.6 we discussed three major issues involving double nominative and accusative constructions, including the issue of subjecthood and objecthood, and the nature of case assignment.

Further Readings

An, Young-Ran. 2008. Korean tul and English all. In Cedric Boeckx and S. Ulutas (eds.), *Proceedings of the 4th Workshop on Altaic Formal Linguistics* (WAFL4). MIT Working Papers in Linguistics, Vol. 55. Cambridge, MA: MITWPL.

Cho, Sungeun. 2003. A conditioning factor in possessor agreement constructions. In Pat Clancy (ed.), *Japanese/Korean Linguistics*, Vol. 11, 343–351. Stanford, CA: CSLI Publications.

Hong, Jongseon. 2004. Myengsahwa [Nominalizing]. *Say Kwuke Saynghwal* 14 (2): 167–185. National Institute of Korean Language.

Kang, Beommo. 2002. *Pemcwu munpep: Hankwuke-uy hyeongthaylon, thongsalon, thaip-nonlicek uymilon* [Categorial grammar: The morphology, syntax, and typological semantics of Korean]. Seoul: Korea University Press.

Kim, Young-Joo. 1989. Inalienable possession as a semantic relationship underlying predication: The case of multiple-accusative constructions. In Susumo Kuno et al. (eds.), *Harvard Studies in Korean Linguistics*, Vol. 3, 445–468. Seoul: Hanshin Publishing.

Ko, Young-Kun. 1995. *Tane, Mwuncang, Theyksuthu* [Word, Sentence, Text]. Seoul: Hankuk Publisher.

Nam, Ki-Shim and Young-Kun Ko. 2013. *Phyocwun Kwuke Mwunpeplon* [Grammar of Standard Korean], 3rd ed. Seoul: TOP Publisher.

Rhee, Seongha. 2011. Nominalization and stance markings in Korean. In Foong Ha Yap, Karen Grunow-Hårsta, and Jack Wrona (eds.), Nominalization in Asian Languages: Diachronic and Typological Perspectives, 393–422. John Benjamins.

Tomioka, Satoshi and Chang-Yong Sim. 2007. The event semantic root of inalienable possession. Unpublished manuscript, University of Delaware.

Yang, Dong-Whee. 1999. Case features and case particles. In Bird et al. (eds.), *West Coast Conference on Formal Linguistics* 18, 626–639. Somerville, MA: Cascadilla Press.

Yoon, Jong Yurl. 1989. On the multiple *ka* and *lul* constructions in Korean. In Yukinori Takubo et al. (eds.), *Japanese/Korean Linguistics*, Vol. 16, 64–83. Stanford, CA: CSLI Publications.

References

Chun, Sun-Ae. 1985. Possessor ascension for multiple case sentences. In Susumo Kuno et al. (eds.), *Harvard Studies in Korean Linguistics* Vol. 1, 30–39. Seoul: Hanshin Publishing.

Heycock, Caroline. 1993. Syntactic predication in Japanese. *Journal of East Asian Linguistics* 2: 167–211.

Jenny, Mathias and San San Hnin Tun. 2013. *Burmese: A Comprehensive Grammar.* Routledge.

Kang, Youngse. 1985. Korean syntax and universal grammar. Unpublished Ph. D. dissertation, Harvard University.

Kim, Jong-Bok and Peter Sells. 2007. Two types of multiple nominative construction: A constructional approach. In Stephen Muller (ed.), *Proceedings of the 14th International Conference on Head-Driven Phrase Structure Grammar*, Stanford Department of Linguistics and CSLI's LingGo Lab, 364–372. Stanford, CA: CSLI Publications.

Kuno, Susumo. 1973. *The Structure of the Japanese Language*. Cambridge, MA: MIT Press.

Lee, E. and M. Shimojo. 2016. Mismatch of topic between Japanese and Korean. *Journal of East Asian Linguistics* 25: 81.

Maling, Joan and Soowon Kim. 1992. Case assignment in the inalienable possession construction in Korea. *Journal of East Asian Linguistics* 1: 37–68.

O'Grady, William. 1991. *Categories and Case*. Amsterdam: John Benjamins Publishing.

Park, Chongwon. 2013. Metonymy in grammar: Korean multiple object constructions. *Functions of Language* 20: 31–63.

Payne, Doris and Immanuel Barshi. 1999. *External Possession*. Amsterdam: John Benjamins.

Rizzi, Luigi. 1986. Null objects in Italian and the theory of *pro*. *Linguistic Inquiry* 17: 501–555.

Schütze, Carson. 2001. On Korean case stacking: The varied functions of the particles *Ka* and *Lul*. *The Linguistic Review* 18: 193–232.

Whitman, John. 2001. Kayne 1994: p. 143, fn. 3. In G. Alexandrova and O. Artunova (eds.), The Minimalist Parameter, 77–100. Amsterdam: John Benjamins.

Yeon, Jae Hoon. 2010. Constraints on double-accusative external possession constructions in Korean: A cognitive approach. In J. Yeon and Jieun Kaiser (eds.), *Selected Papers of 2nd European Conference on Korean Linguistics*. Lincom Europa.

Yoon, James. 1986. Some queries concerning the syntax of multiple subject constructions in Korean. *Studies in Linguistic Science* 16: 215–236.

Yoon, James. 2004. Non-nominative (major) subjects and case-stacking in Korean. In Peri Bhaskararao and K. V. Subbarao (eds.), *Non-Nominative Subjects*, Vol. 2, 265–314. Berlin: Mouton de Gruyter.

Yoon, James. 2015. Double nominative and double accusative constructions. In Lucien Brown and Jaehoon Yeon (eds.), *The Handbook of Korean Linguistics*. Wiley-Blackwell.

Youn, Cheong. 1990. A relational analysis of Korean multiple nominative constructions. Unpublished Ph.D. dissertation, State University of New York at Buffalo.

7 Syntax

Syntax studies the ways in which human beings form the sentences of natural language. This chapter focuses on the syntax of the verb phrase and the clause, starting with the basic properties of verbal, adjectival, and copular predicates. Section 7.2 examines clausal embedding, including relative clauses and clausal complements and adjuncts. It also discusses word order and the phenomenon of scrambling. Section 7.3 turns to the topic of passive and causative constructions. Section 7.4 discusses three major controversies surrounding causative and passive constructions in Korean. Finally, Section 7.5 summarizes the chapter.

7.1 Formation of Inflecting Stems

In traditional Western grammar, every sentence can be partitioned into a subject and a predicate. As we saw in Chapter 4, clausal predicates in Korean are headed by inflecting stems: verbs, adjectives, or the copula accompanying a nominal predicate. This is a major difference between Korean and English: in Korean, both verbs and adjectives are inflecting stems, and thus function as stand-alone predicates without the copula.

7.1.1 Verbal Predicates

As in other languages, verbal predicates in Korean can be classified by the number of arguments they require. One-place (intransitive) predicates can be further divided into agent-subject (1) and theme-subject (2) predicates.

(1)   One-place (intransitive) verbs with agent subjects
    앉다   *anc-ta*   to sit
    뛰다   *ttwi-ta*   to run
    (잠)자다   *(cam)ca-ta*   to sleep
    웃다   *wus-ta*   to laugh

(2)   One-place (intransitive) verbs with theme subjects
오다   *o-ta*   to come
죽다   *cwuk-ta*   to die
나다   *na-ta*   to come out, to occur
남다   *nam-ta*   to remain
없다   *eps-ta*   to not exist

The sentences in (3) exemplify intransitives of both types:

(3)   One-place predicates
a. 철수가 책상위에 앉는다.
   Chelswu=ka   chayksang-wi=ey   anc-nun-ta.
   Chelswu=NOM   desk-above=LOC   sit-PRES-PLN
   'Chelswu sits on the desk.'
b. 철수는 영희하고 싸운다.
   Chelswu=nun   Yenghuy=hako   ssawu-n-ta.
   Chelswu=TOP   Yenghuy=and   fight-PRES-PLN
   'Chelswu fights with Yenghuy.'
c. 철수가 학교에 온다.
   Chelswu=ka   hakkyo=ey   o-n-ta.
   Chelswu=NOM   school=DIR   come-PRES-PLN
   'Chelswu comes to school.'

The predicates *o-, ssawu-,* and *anc-* require only one argument, which is realized as the subject, *Chelswu,* in these sentences. Adjuncts such as postpositional phrases may be selected but are not required by these verbs. However, theme-subject verbs like *o-* 'come' in (3c) show properties often associated with unaccusative verbs across languages. Unaccusatives (Perlmutter 1978, Burzio 1986) are intransitive verbs whose subjects show some object properties; from a semantic standpoint, their subjects are typically themes. The contrasting type of intransitives are unergatives, whose subjects are typically agents. One common crosslinguistic hallmark of the unaccusative/unergative contrast is auxiliary selection. Kim (1990) points out that selection of the perfective auxiliary V-*e iss-* 'have V-ed' can be a diagnostic for unaccusativity in Korean. The perfective is acceptable for the verbs in (3), as shown in (4), but less acceptable for many speakers for the intransitives in (5).

(4)   Unaccusatives with perfective
a. 와 있다   *o-a iss-ta*   has come
b. 죽어 있다   *cwuk-e iss-ta*   has died
c. 나 있다   *na iss-ta*   has come out

(5)   *Unergatives with perfective
a. ??싸워 있다   *ssaw-e iss-ta*   has fought
b. ??(잠)자 있다   *(cam)ca iss-ta*   has slept
c. ??웃어 있다   *wus-e iss-ta*   has laughed

(6)   a. 태민/꽃병이 책상위에 앉아 있다.
> *Thaymin/kkoch pyeng=i*   *chayksang-wi=ey*   *anc-a iss-ta.*
> Taemin/flower vase=NOM   desk-above=LOC   sit-INF be-PLN
> 'Taemin/the flower vase is (in the state of) sitting on the desk.'

  b. 태민/*꽃병이 책상위에 앉고 있다.
> *Thaymin/*kkoch pyeng=i*   *chayksang-wi=ey*   *anc-ko iss-ta.*
> Taemin/flower vase=NOM   desk-above=LOC   sit-PROG be-PLN
> 'Taemin/the flower vase is (in the process of) sitting on the desk.'

The subject of *anc-* 'sit' can be conceptualized as a theme or an agent, but progressive *-ko-iss-* is odd with a subject that can only be understood as a theme, like 'flower vase' in (6b).

A more reliable indicator of the unergative/unaccusative contrast is that the latter shows properties associated with transitive verbs; in fact, some linguists analyze unergatives as covert transitives (Hale and Keyser 2002). Thus unergatives such as (잠)자- *(cam)ca-* 'to sleep' (lit. 'sleep a sleep') appear with the cognate objects (잠) *(cam)* 'sleep' (noun), formed from the *-(u)m* nominalized form of the verb stem discussed in Chapter 6. But unaccusative verbs do not allow this cognate object pattern; thus *음오다 **om o-ta* 'come a come' is ill-formed.

We discuss Korean lexical passives in Section 7.3.1. Not surprisingly, passives pattern with unaccusatives in that they freely allow the perfective, as shown in (7b), where *mwulli-* 'be bitten, be caught' allows the perfective, but its transitive counterpart *mwul-* 'bite' in (7a) does not:

(7)   a. 태민이 손가락을 물고/*물려 있다.
> *Thaymin=i*   *sonkalak=ul mwul-ko/*-e*   *iss-ta.*
> Taemin=NOM   finger=ACC   bite-PROG/*-INF   be-PLN
> 'Taemin is sucking his thumb.'

  b. 태민 손가락이 문에 물려/*물고 있다.
> *Thaymin*   *sonkalak=i*   *mwun=ey*   *mwully-e/*-ko iss-ta.*
> Taemin   finger=NOM   door=LOC   bite-INF/*-PROG be-PLN
> 'Taemin's finger is stuck in the door.'

Transitive, or two-place predicates, require both a subject and an object. Underived transitives are shown in (8a). Lexical causatives, discussed in Section 7.3.2, provide a rich source of transitive verbs derived from intransitives (8b).

(8)   Two-place predicates (transitive verbs)
   a. Underived transitives
먹다	*mek-ta*	to eat
깎다	*kkakk-ta*	to discount
놓다	*noh-ta*	to put down
넣다	*neh-ta*	to put in

b. Derived transitives (causatives)

앉히다	*anc-hi-ta*	to make someone sit down
재우다	*caywu-ta*	to put someone to bed
남기다	*nam-ki-ta*	to leave something behind
웃기다	*wus-ki-ta*	to make someone laugh
죽이다	*cwuk-i-ta*	to make someone die

Examples of underived transitives and derived transitives are given in (9).

(9)   Two-place predicates (transitive verbs)
      a. Underived transitive
          철수가 가격을 깎았다.

Chelswu=ka	*kakyek=ul*	*kkakk-ass-ta.*
Chelswu=NOM	price=ACC	discount-PAST-PLN

          'Chelswu discounted the price.'
      b. Derived transitive (causative)
          철수가 영희를 테이블에 앉혔다.

Chelswu=ka	*Yenghuy=lul*	*theyibul=ey*	*anc-hi-ess-ta.*
Chelswu=NOM	Yenghuy=ACC	table=LOC	sit down-CAUS-PAST-PLN

          'Chelswu made Yenghuy sit down on the table.'

Three-place predicates require three arguments: a subject, an object, and an indirect object. These are called 'ditransitive' verbs, as in (10).

(10)   Three-place predicates (ditransitive verbs)
      a. 철수가 영희에게 책을 준다.

Chelswu=ka	*Yenghuy=eykey*	*chayk=ul*	*cwu-n-ta.*
Chelswu=NOM	Yenghuy=DAT	book=ACC	give-PRES-PLN

          'Chelswu gives a book to Yenghuy.'
      b. 철수가 선생님께 책을 드린다.

Chelswu=ka	*sensayngnim=kkey*	*chayk=ul*	*tuli-n-ta.*
Chelswu=NOM	teacher=DAT	book=ACC	give-PRES-PLN

          'Chelswu gives a book to the teacher.'
      c. 철수가 친구에게 편지를 보낸다.

Chelswu=ka	*chinkwu=eykey*	*phyenci=lul*	*ponay-n-ta.*
Chelswu=NOM	friend=DAT	letter=ACC	send-PRES-PLN

          'Chelswu sends a letter to a friend.'

A minority of Korean verbs have the same form for the transitive and intransitive, as in (11). Linguistic typologists call these 'labile' verbs.

(11)   Labile (neutral) verbs
      a. 태민이 차를 움직인다.

Thaymin=i	*cha=lul*	*wumciki-n-ta.*
Taemin=NOM	car=ACC	move-PRES-PLN

          'Taemin moves the car.'

b. 차가 잘 움직인다.
   Cha=ka   cal   wumciki-n-ta.
   car=NOM   well   move-PRES-PLN
   'The car moves well.'
c. 태민이 차를 멈춘다.
   Thaymin=i   cha-lul   memchwu-n-ta.
   Taemin=NOM   car=ACC   stop-PRES-PLN
   'Taemin stops the car.'
d. 차가 쉽게 멈춘다.
   Cha=ka   swipkey   memchwu-n-ta.
   car=NOM   easily   stop-PRES-PLN
   'The car stops easily.'

The same verbs *wumciki-* 'move' and *memchwu-* 'stop' are used in both transitive and intransitive sentences. Historically, both seem to be cases where the transitive (causative) form of the verb became neutral. Earlier Korean has intransitive *wumcuk-* 'move' (intransitive) and *wumcuki-* 'move it' (transitive), as well as *mec-* 'stop' (intransitive) and *mechwu-* 'stop it' (transitive). The original intransitive verbs have been lost and the transitive (causative) verbs extended to both uses.

7.1.2   Adjectival Predicates

The second major predicate type is adjectives. As we saw in Chapter 5, adjectives also have adnominal and adverbial derived forms, but here we focus on their predicative use.

(12)   Functions of Adjectives
        a. Predicate
           철수가 많이 기쁘다.
           Chelswu=ka   manhi kippu-ta.
           Chelswu=NOM   a lot   happy-PLN
           'Chelswu is very happy.'
        b. Adnominal
           많이 기쁜 철수.
           manhi   kippu-n   Chelswu
           a lot   happy-ADN   Chelswu
           'Chelswu who is very happy.'
        c. Adverbial
           철수가 많이 기쁘게 공부한다.
           Chelswu=ka   manhi kippu-key   kongpwuha-n-ta.
           Chelswu=NOM   a lot   happy-ADV   study-PRES-PLN
           'Chelswu studies very happily.'

Adjectives can be divided into experiencer and theme subject types. Experiencer adjectives can be divided into several subtypes, as in (13).

(13)   Experiencer adjectives
    a. Sensory (theme subject)
       달다   *talta*   to be sweet
       차다   *chata*   to be cold (to the touch)
    b. Psychological (experiencer subject)
       좋다   *cohta*   to be good
       싫다   *silhta*   to dislike
       무섭다 *mwusepta* to be scared

Coh- 'to be good, to like' and *silh-* 'to be hateful, to dislike' in (13b) are labile, that is optionally transitive adjectives, subject to the constraint that the experiencer subject must be a discourse participant. As discussed in Section 6.1.1, in this transitive pattern both the experiencer subject and the theme object are marked nominative.

We discussed differences between verbs and adjectives in Section 5.1.1. A fuller list of differences is given in (14).

(14)   Verbs and adjectives contrasted

	Verb	Adjective
Present	Y(es)	N(o)
Progressive	Y	N
Adnominal (Past)	Y	N
Propositive S	Y	N
Imperative S	Y	N
Adverbials	Y (non-degree)	Y (degree)
NP-*eyse*	Y	N

We saw in Section 5.1.1 that verbs may inflect with present tense *-nun-*, and progressive *-ko iss-*, but adjectives do not.

Another difference between verb and adjective is that verbs allow both propositives and imperatives, but adjectives tend to disallow both, although acceptability improves if the adjective can be construed as controllable.

(15)   Propositives
    a. Verb
       오늘은 피자를 먹자.
       Onul=un   *phica=lul*   *mek-ca.*
       today=TOP pizza=ACC   eat-PROP
       'Let's eat pizza today.'
    b. Adjective
       ?오늘은 행복하자.
       ?Onul=un   *hayngpokha-ca.*
       today=TOP   happy-PROP
       'Let's be happy today.'

(16)   Imperatives
    a. Verb
       오늘은 피자를 먹어라.
       Onul=un   phica=lul   mek-ela.
       today=TOP   pizza=ACC   eat-IMP
       'Please eat pizza today.'
    b. Adjective
       ?오늘은 행복해라.
       Onul=un   hayngpok-hayla.
       today=TOP   happy-IMP
       'Please be happy today.'

Verbs disallow degree adverbials such as *maywu* 'very' (17). The dynamic locative marker *=eyse*, is allowed only with verbs, not adjectives (18).

(17)   Degree adverbs
    a. Verb
       철수가 피자를 잘/*매우 먹는다.
       *Chelswu=ka   phica=lul   cal/*maywu   mek-nun-ta.*
       Chelswu=NOM   pizza=ACC   well/*very   eat-PRES-PLN
       'Chelswu eats pizza well.'
    b. Adjective
       철수가 매우-/*잘 행복하다.
       *Chelswu=ka   maywu/*cal hayngpokha-ta.*
       Chelswu=NOM   very/*well happy-PLN
       'Chelswu is very happy.'

(18)   NP=*eyse*
    a. Verb
       철수가 집에서 피자를 먹는다.
       Chelswu=ka   cip=eyse   phica=lul   mek-nun-ta.
       Chelswu=NOM   home=LOC pizza=ACC eat-PRES-PLN
       'Chelswu eats pizza at home.'
    b. Adjective
       *철수가 집에서 행복하다.
       **Chelswu=ka   cip=eyse   hayngpokha-ta.*
       Chelswu=NOM   home=LOC happy-PLN
       'Chelswu is happy at home.'

7.1.3   Nominal Predicates with the Copula

=*(i)-ta* 'to be' allows NPs to serve as predicates in tensed clauses. The allomorphy of =*i-ta* is dependent on the shape of the word it enclitizes to: if it ends with a consonant, the predicate is =*i-ta*, and if it ends with a vowel, it is =*ta*. =*(i)-ta* shows typical copula properties; in terms of category, it inflects like an adjective. Tensed nominal predicate clauses require =*(i)-ta* (19a), while tenseless nominal predicate clauses replace it with the instrumental particle = *(u)lo* (19c):

(19) Allomorphy of copula =*(i)-ta*
  a. 이것이 책이다.
     I kes=i   chayk=i-ta.
     this=NOM   book=be-PLN
     'This is a book.'
  b. 저것이 학교다.
     Ce kes=i   hakkyo-ta.
     that=NOM   school-PLN
     'That is a school.'
  c. 나는 이것을 책으로 생각한다.
     Na=nun   i kes=ul   chayk=ulo   sayngkakha-n-ta.
     I=TOP   this=ACC   book=INST   think-PRES-PLN
     'I think this to be a book.'

The copula =*(i)-ta* shows the morphological properties of an adjective, specifically in that it disallows the adnominal present (20b):

(20) a. 철수가 학생이다.
      Chelswu=ka   haksayng=i-ta.
      Chelswu=NOM   student=be-PLN
      'Chelswu is a student.'
  b. 학생인/*이는 철수
      Haksayng=i-n/=i-nun   Chelswu*
      student=be-ADN/*=be-PRESADN Chelswu
      'Chelwsu, who is a student'

Like copulas in other languages, =*(i)-ta* allows the predicate inversion pattern in (21b), although only when the set denoted by the predicate is plausibly included in the subject.

(21) a. 나는 학생이다.
      Na=nun   haksayng=i-ta.
      I=TOP   student=be-PLN
      'I am a student.'
  b. 학생이 나다.
      Haksayng=i   na-ta.
      student=NOM   I-PLN
      '(The) student is me.'
  c. 기린이 동물이다.
      Kilin=i   tongmwul=i-ta.
      giraffe=NOM   animal=be-PLN
      'A giraffe is an animal.'

d. #동물이 기린이다.
Tongmwul=i   kilin=i-ta.
animal=NOM   giraffe=be-PLN
'An animal is a giraffe.'

=*(i)-ta* also appears in noun predicate idioms:

(22)   Noun predicate idioms
    a. 철수가 기린이다.
       Chelswu=ka   kilin=i-ta.
       Chelswu=NOM   giraffe=be-PLN
       'Chelswu is a giraffe (figuratively tall).'
    b. 침묵은 금이다.
       Chimmwuk=un   kum=i-ta.
       silence=TOP   gold-be-PLN
       'Silence is golden.'

The range of possible NP predicates in Korean is quite broad, as shown by the examples in (23), some of which lack English counterparts. The interpretation of the (23a), (23c), and (23d) sentences is something like the (23b), (23d), and (23f) sentences respectively.

(23)   Broadly interpreted NP predications
    a. 철수가 거짓말이다.
       Chelswu=ka   kecismal=i-ta.
       Chelswu=NOM   lie=be-PLN
       'Chelswu is a liar.' (Lit. 'Chelswu is a lie.')
    b. 철수가 거짓말을 한다.
       Chelswu=ka   kecismal=ul   ha-n-ta.
       Chelswu=NOM   lie=ACC   do-PRES-PLN
       'Chelswu tells a lie.'
    c. 철수는 영문과다.
       Chelswu=nun   yengmwunkwa-ta.
       Chelswu=TOP   English Department-PLN
       'Chelswu is an English major.' (Lit. 'Chelswu is the English Department.')
    d. 철수는 영문과에 다닌다.
       Chelswu=nun   yengmwunkwa=ey   tani-n-ta.
       Chelswu=TOP   English Department=DIR   goes-PRES-PLN
       'Chelswu goes (to university in) the English Department.'
    e. 미국이 서쪽이다.
       Mikwuk=i   seccok=i-ta.
       America=NOM   west=be-PLN
       'America is in the west.' (Lit. 'America is the west.')
    f. 미국이 서쪽에 있다.
       Mikwuk=i   seccok=ey   iss-ta.
       America=NOM   west=LOC   be-PLN
       'America is in the west.'

7.1.4   Light Verbs, Control Complements, and Auxiliaries

As we have seen, lexical predicates include verbs, adjectives, and NP predicates combined with the copula. Korean also has a rich variety of verbs and adjectives which combine with other inflecting words. Typically, the first in a sequence of verbs bears the lexical meaning and selects arguments, while the last verb in the sequence is marked for tense, aspect, and mood. We distinguish three types of inflecting stems in the latter slot: auxiliaries, complementation verbs, and light verbs. An example of the light verb, *peli-* 'throw away, discard' is given in (24).

(24)   Light verb *peli-*
    a. 철수가 학교에 갔다.
       Chelswu=ka   *hakkyo=ey* *ka-ss-ta.*
       Chelswu=NOM   school=DIR go-PAST-PLN
       'Chelswu went to school.'
    b. 철수가 학교에 가 버렸다.
       Chelswu=ka   *hakkyo=ey*   *ka peli-ess-ta.*
       Chelswu=NOM   school=DIR   go discard-PAST-PLN
       'Chelswu went and went to school.'

The term "light verb" originates from Jespersen (1965), and was originally used to designate verbs like 'take' in 'John took a nap'. In this kind of pattern there is no literal "taking"; instead, 'take' fulfills a largely grammatical function. Similarly, in (24b) there is no actual "disposal"; instead, the light verb *peli-* contributes the sense that Chelswu completed the action, perhaps rashly or in a fashion that can't be undone. Verbs such as 'throw (away), discard' function as light verbs in many languages of South and Southeast Asia, as in the following example from Hindi.

(25)   Ruma   cit^{h}i-ṭa   lik^h-e   phello.
       Ruma.Nom   letter-Classifier   write-PerfPart   throw.3.Past
       'Ruma wrote the letter completely.' (Butt and Ramchand 2005: 145)

We define as auxiliaries nonlexical verbs whose semantic function is to indicate tense, aspect, mood, or negation. Light verbs add information more directly related to the lexical verb meaning, such as telicity in the case of Korean *peli-* in (24) or Hindi *phello* 'threw' in (25). Complementation verbs typically add an argument, such as the subject argument added by 'want' or the beneficiary argument added by 'do for the benefit of'. Many of these verbs are traditionally treated as control predicates (e.g. 'want') or raising predicates (e.g. 'become').

Nonlexical verb structures consist of a main verb (V1), an inflectional suffix (-X), and the nonlexical verb (V2), as schematized in (26), where the shape of -X is selected by V2 and morphophonologically conditioned by V1.

(26)   V1 (lexical) -X   V2 (nonlexical)
                      Infinitive -a/-e/hay
                      Gerund -ko
                      Suspective -ci

Infinitive -a/-e/hay is the most common inflectional form selected by all three types of V2, as shown in (27).

(27)   Shapes of V1 selected by V2
        a. Infinitive -a/-e/hay
              V2 is a light verb
                  버리다 *pelita* discard   놓다   *nohta*   put
                  두다   *twuta*   put   가다   *kata*   go
                  오다   *ota*   come   나다   *nata*   come out
              V2 is a control/raising predicate
                  주다   *cwuta*   give   드리다 *tulita* give (DEF)
                  보다   *pota*   see, try   지다   *cita*   become
              V2 is an auxiliary
                  있다   *issta*   be (PERF)
                  말다   *malta*   end up
        b. Gerundive -ko
              V2 is a light verb
                  나다   *nata*   go out
              V2 is a control/raising predicate
                  싶다   *siphta* want
              V2 is an auxiliary
                  말다   *malta*   don't do
                  있다   *issta*   be   계시다 *kyeysita* be (honorific)
        c. Suspective -ci
              V2 is an auxiliary
                  않다   *anhta*   NEG
                  말다   *malta*   don't do 못하다 *moshata* can't do

The allomorphs of the infinitive are the one remnant of vowel harmony in Korean, together with the historically related past tense. The infinitive is -a for V1 stems ending in /a/ or /o/; otherwise it is -e. *Ha-* 'do' exceptionally has the infinitive *hay*. The three allomorphs of the infinitive are shown in (28).

(28)   -X is the infinitive
        a. 철수가 학교에 가 봤다.
            Chelswu=ka   *hakkyo=ey ka-(a)*   *po-ass-ta.*
            Chelswu=NOM   school=DIR go-INF   see-PAST-PLN
            'Chelswu tried going to school.'
        b. 철수가 피자를 먹어 봤다.
            Chelswu=ka   *phica=lul   mek-e*   *po-ass-ta.*
            Chelswu=NOM   pizza=ACC   eat-INF   see-PAST-PLN
            'Chelswu tried eating pizza.'

c. 철수가 언어학을 공부해 봤다.
   Chelswu=ka   enehak=ul   kongpwu-hay po-ass-ta.
   Chelswu=NOM linguistics=ACC   study-INF   see-PAST-PLN
   'Chelswu tried studying linguistics.'

As we see in (29) Chelswu is not only the goer, but also the trier. This is usually expressed by representing the relation between the subject of 'try' and the subject of 'go' as a relationship of control: the subject of 'try' is coindexed with the silent category *PRO* as the subject of 'go':

(29)   철수$_i$가 [PRO$_i$학교에 가] 봤다.
        Chelswu$_i$=ka   [PRO$_i$ hakkyo=ey ka-(a)] po-ass-ta.
        Chelswu=NOM   school=DIR   go-INF see-PAST-PLN
        'Chelswu tried going to school.'

The use of the pattern 'see V' as a control structure meaning 'try to V' is common in the world's languages. The same pattern is found in Japanese and Burmese:

(30)   'See V' as the control structure 'try to V'
        a. *Kyaung=ko thwa   kyi. teh.*   (Burmese)
           school=to   go   look-DEC
           '(I) tried going to school.'
        b. *Gakkoo=e   it-te   mi-ta.*   (Japanese)
           school=to   go-ing see-PAST
           '(I) tried going to school.'

In contrast, the light verb pattern V1-*e/-a peli-* in (24) does not add an extra participant to the basic meaning of V1. Instead, it contributes a telic, or completive, interpretation of the clause. We can also find semantic and structural differences between V1-infinitive light-verb and V1-infinitive control-predicate patterns. For example, in the V1-*e/-a po-* 'try to V1' pattern, it is possible for negation to scope only over V1, as in (31):

(31)   나는 매일 아침에 커피를 마시는데, 오늘은 안 마셔 봤다.
        Na=nun   mayil   achim=ey   khephi=lul masi-nuntey
        I=TOP   everyday   morning=in coffee=ACC drink-but
        onul=un   an-masy-e   po-ass-ta.
        today=TOP not-drink-INF see-PAST-PLN
        'I drink coffee every morning, but today I tried not drinking it.'

In contrast, negation must scope over both V1 and the light verb in the V1-*e/-a peli-* construction. This suggests that the constituent containing V1 in the control construction has the status of a clause, which may be negated independently from V2.

Among the complementation predicates selecting the infinitive is one raising predicate, *ci-* 'become' (distinct from the suspective suffix *-ci*). *Ci-* derives passives with a transitive verbal V1, and inchoatives with an adjectival or intransitive unaccusative V1, as shown in (32):

(32)   a. 태민의 얼굴이 그려졌다.   (그리다 *kulita* 'to draw')
        Thaymin=uy   elkwul=i   *kuli-e-ci-ess-ta.*
        Taemin=GEN   face=NOM   draw-INF-become-PAST-PLN
        'Taemin's face was drawn.'

      b. 태민의 눈이 커졌다.   (크다 *khuta* 'to be big')
        Thaymin=uy   nwun=i   *kh-e-ci-ess-ta.*
        Taemin=GEN   eye=NOM   big-INF-become-PAST-PLN
        'Taemin's eye's got big.'

      c. 태민의 돈이 없어졌다.   (없다 *epsta* 'to not exist')
        Thaymin=uy   ton=i   *eps-e-ci-ess-ta.*
        Taemin=GEN   money=NOM   not.exist-INF-become-PAST-PLN
        'Taemin's money disappeared.'

With raising predicates, an argument that originates in a lower position raises to subject position. This is exactly what happens in passives. It is thus no accident that many languages use the lexical verb 'become' to function as a raising predicate in passive constructions. Examples include, in addition to Korean *ci-* and *toy-* 'become', German *werden* and Dutch *worden* 'to become'.

The final complementation V2 pattern selecting infinitive V1 involves the benefactive verbs *cwu-* 'give' and *tuli-* 'give' (deferential). These verbs add a benefactee argument:

(33)   철수가 어머니의 집에 가 주었다.
        Chelswu=ka   emeni=uy   cip=ey   ka-(a) cwu-ess-ta.
        Chelswu=NOM mother=GEN house=DIR go-INF give-PAST-PLN
        'Chelswu did someone the favor of going to his mother's house.'

While the intransitive verb *ka-* 'go' in (33) has just the single core argument 'Chelswu', the benefactive verb *cwu-* adds a beneficiary argument.

The gerundive suffix *-ko* may also be selected by a light verb, a complementation predicate, or an auxiliary. In (34), examples are given with the progressive auxiliary (V-*ko*) *iss-*, and the control predicate *siph-* 'want'.

(34)   V1-*ko* (Gerundive)
      a. 철수가 학교에 가고 있다.
        Chelswu=ka   hakkyo=ey   ka-ko   iss-ta.
        Chelswu=NOM   school=DIR go-GER   be-PLN
        'Chelswu is going to school.'

b. 철수가 피자를 먹고 싶다.

    Chelswu=ka   *phica=lul*   *mek-ko*   *siph-ta.*

    Chelswu=NOM   pizza=ACC   eat-GER   want-PLN

    'Chelswu wants to eat pizza.'

c. 철수가 행복하고 싶다.

    Chelswu=ka   *hayngpokha-ko*   *siph-ta.*

    Chelswu=NOM   happy-GER   want-PLN

    'Chelswu wants to be happy.'

The suspective suffix *-ci* is selected by negative auxiliaries:

(35)   V1-*ci* (Suspective)

    a. 철수가 학교에 가지 않았다.

       Chelswu=ka   *hakkyo=ey*   *ka-ci*   *anh-ass-ta.*

       Chelswu=NOM   school=DIR   go-SUSP   NEG-PAST-PLN

       'Chelswu did not go to school.'

    b. 철수가 피자를 먹지 않았다.

       Chelswu=ka   *phica=lul*   *mek-ci*   *anh-ass-ta.*

       Chelswu=NOM   pizza=ACC   eat-SUSP   NEG-PAST-PLN

       'Chelswu did not eat pizza.'

    c. 철수가 행복하지 않다.

       Chelswu=ka   *hayngpokha-ci*   *anh-ta.*

       Chelswu=NOM   happy-SUSP   NEG-PLN

       'Chelswu is not happy.'

Nonlexical V2s may select another nonlexical verb, resulting in long strings of nonfinite verbs (36a). However, the general order must be lexical verb, then light verb, then complementation predicate, then auxiliary, as shown by the unacceptability of (36b). Doubling light verbs is possible, even when their meaning is similar, as in (36c).

(36)   Sequences of more than one V2

    a. 나는 종이를 찢어 버리고 싶지 않았다.

       Na=nun   *congi=lul*   *ccic-e* *peli-ko*   *siph-ci*

       I=TOP   paper=ACC   rip-INF discard-GER   want-SUSP

       anh-ass-ta.

       NEG-PAST-PLN

       'I didn't want to rip the paper.'

    b. *나는 종이를 찢지 않아 버렸다.

       **Na=nun*   *congi=lul*   *ccic-ci*   *anh-a*   *peli-ess-ta.*

       I=TOP   paper=ACC   rip-SUSP   NEG-INF   discard-PAST-PLN

       'I didn't rip the paper.'

    c. 나는 종이를 찢어 버리고 말았다.

       Na=nun   *congi=lul*   *ccic-e* *peli-ko*   *mal-ass-ta.*

       I=TOP   paper=ACC   rip-INF discard-GER   end.up-PAST-PLN

       'I ended up ripping the paper.'

7.2   Sentence Structure and Clause Type

7.2.1   Basic Clause Structure

Traditional analyses of clause structure recognize as the immediate constituents of S a subject noun phrase (NP) and a verb phrase (VP). In Korean, as we have seen, the predicate occupies the final position in the sentence. Typologists refer to this word order as S(ubject) O(bject) V(erb). We have already seen examples of the basic order of intransitive (37a), transitive (37b), and ditransitive sentences (37c). In the latter, the order of IO (Indirect Object) and DO (Direct Object) is interchangeable.

(37)   Basic word order
   a. Intransitive (SV)
      나는 행복하다.
      Na=nun   hayngpokha-ta.
      I=NOM   happy-PLN
      'I am happy.'
      철수는 학교에서 논다.
      Chelswu=nun   hakkyo=eyse   no-n-ta.
      Chelswu=TOP   school=LOC   play-PRES-PLN
      'Chelswu plays at school.'
   b. Transitive (SOV)
      영희는 강남에서 피자를 먹는다.
      Yenghuy=nun   Kangnam=eyse phica=lul   mek-nun-ta.
      Yenghuy=TOP   Kangnam=LOC   pizza=ACC   eat-PRES-PLN
      'Yenghuy eats pizza at Kangnam.'
   c. Ditransitive (S IO DO V)
      철수가 영희에게 책을 준다.
      Chelswu=ka   Yenghuy=eykey   chayk=ul   cwu-n-ta.
      Chelswu=NOM   Yenghuy=DAT   book=ACC   give-PRES-PLN
      'Chelswu gives Yenghuy a book.'

In SOV languages like Korean, it is tricky to prove the existence of a constituent VP excluding the subject NP but including the verb and its arguments (cf. Saito 1985 for Japanese). One way to do this is through the process of VP fronting, shown in (38).

(38)   VP fronting
      피자를 먹기는 영희가 했다.
      Phica=lul   mek-ki=nun   Yenghuy=ka   hay-ss-ta.
      pizza=ACC   eat-NOMNL=TOP   Yenghuy=NOM   do-PAST-PLN
      'Eat pizza, Yenghuy did.'

In Korean, as we have seen, tense, aspect, and modality are usually realized on the rightmost verb, but if this is somehow blocked, TAM can be realized on the dummy verb *ha-* 'do'. Now, the fronted constituent can be made up of the

verb and its object, excluding the subject, as in (38), but it cannot be made up of
the verb and the subject, excluding the object:

(39)   *영희가 먹기는 피자를 했다.
        *Yenghuy=ka   mek-ki=nun   phica=lul   hay-ss-ta.
        Yenghuy=NOM   eat-NOMNL=TOP   pizza=ACC   do-PAST-PLN

Based on this evidence we conclude that Korean sentences contain a VP
excluding the subject but containing the verb and its arguments.

Korean morphologically distinguishes four major clause types: declarative,
interrogative, imperative, and propositive (also called hortative). Kwon (2011:
86–90) distinguishes these four sentence types in terms of two pragmatic
variables: (i) [±speaker request to hearer], and (ii) [± action required]. From
this standpoint, the [+speaker request] sentence types are interrogatives,
imperatives, or propositives, and the [−speaker request] type is declarative.
Interrogatives are [+speaker request], [−action required]. Imperatives are
[+speaker request], [+action required]. Propositives are also [+speaker
request], [+action required], but the target of [+action required] is both the
speaker and the hearer. This is schematized in (40).

(40)   The four clause types of Korean (Kwon 2011: 86–90)
                                    Speaker's request from a hearer
                                         −   +
        Action to be followed −   Declarative   Interrogative
                               +   Imperative (hearer)
                                                   Propositive (hearer and speaker)

We introduced the morphological distinctions of speech style in Chapter 5; we
discuss when and how the different styles are used in Chapter 10. Below we
reintroduce the twenty combinations of clause type and speech style in (41),
adding to Kwon's four main clause types suspective -지- -ci-.

(41)   The 20 combinations of clause type and speech style (cf. (52) in Chapter 5)

	Declarative	Interrogative	Propositive	Suspective	Imperative
Plain	다Tense-*ta*	니Tense-*ni*	자-*ca*	지-*ci*	라/어라 -*la/-ela*
Intimate	아/어/해 -*a/e/hay*	아/어/해 -*a/e/hay*	아/어/해 -*a/e/hay*	지-*ci*	아/어/해 -*a/e/hay*
Polite	아/어/해 요-*a/e/hay-* *yo*	아/어/해요 -*a/e/hay-yo*	아/어/해 요-*a/e/hay-* *yo*	지요-*ci-yo*	아/어/해 요-*a/e/* *hay-yo*
Deferential	ㅂ/습니 다-*(su)* *pnita*	ㅂ/습니까 -*(su)pnikka*	ㅂ/읍시다 (-*u*)*psita*	시지요 -(*u*)*siciyo*	ㅂ/으십시 오-*p/* *usipsio*

As we have seen, Korean is a predicate-final and verb-final language, and it is
also a suffixing language. Thus the morphology expressing clause type and

speech style is realized at the end of the clause. The examples below show the five clause types in plain speech style in (42), intimate style (43), polite style (44), and deferential style (45).

(42)   Clause types (Plain speech style)
    a. Declarative
       철수는 도서관에서 책을 읽는다.
       Chelswu=nun   *tosekwan=eyse chayk=ul ilk-nun-ta.*
       Chelswu=TOP   library=LOC   book=ACC read-PRES-PLN
       'Chelswu reads a book in the library.'
    b. Interrogative
       철수는 도서관에서 책을 읽니?
       Chelswu=nun   *tosekwan=eyse chayk=ul ilk-ni?*
       Chelswu=TOP   library=LOC   book=ACC read-Q
       'Does Chelswu read a book in the library?'
    c. Propositive
       도서관에서 책을 읽자.
       Tosekwan=eyse   *chayk=ul*   *ilk-ca.*
       library=LOC   book=ACC   read-PROP
       'Let's read a book in the library.'
    d. Suspective
       돈이 없지.
       Ton=i   *eps-ci.*
       money=NOM   not.exist-SUSP
       'There is probably no money.'
    e. Imperative
       도서관에서 책을 읽어라.
       Tosekwan=eyse chayk=ul   ilk-ela.
       library=LOC   book=ACC   read-IMP
       'Read a book in the library.'

(43)   Clause types (Intimate speech style)
    a. Declarative
       철수는 도서관에서 책을 읽어.
       Chelswu=nun   *tosekwan=eyse chayk=ul ilk-e.*
       Chelswu=TOP   library=LOC   book=ACC read-INT
       'Chelswu reads a book in the library.'
    b. Interrogative
       철수는 도서관에서 책을 읽어?
       Chelswu=nun   *tosekwan=eyse chayk=ul ilk-e?*
       Chelswu=TOP   library=LOC   book=ACC read-Q
       'Does Chelswu read a book in the library?'
    c. Propositive
       도서관에서 책을 읽어.
       Tosekwan=eyse   *chayk=ul*   *ilk-e.*
       library=LOC   book=ACC   read-PROP
       'Let's read a book in the library.'

d. Suspective (same as Plain style)
e. Imperative
도서관에서 책을 읽어.

Tosekwan=eyse   chayk=ul   ilk-e.
library=LOC   book=ACC   read-IMP
'Read a book in the library.'

(44)   Clause types (Polite speech style)

a. Declarative
철수는 도서관에서 책을 읽어요.
Chelswu=nun   tosekwan=eyse chayk=ul   ilk-eyo.
Chelswu=TOP   library=LOC   book=ACC   read-POL
'Chelswu reads a book in the library.'

b. Interrogative
철수는 도서관에서 책을 읽어요?
Chelswu=nun   tosekwan=eyse chayk=ul   ilk-eyo?
Chelswu=TOP   library=LOC   book=ACC   read-Q
'Does Chelswu read a book in the library?'

c. Propositive
도서관에서 책을 읽어요.
Tosekwan=eyse   chayk=ul   ilk-eyo.
library=LOC   book=ACC   read-PROP
'Let's read a book in the library.'

d. Suspective
돈이 없지요.
Ton=i   eps-ci-yo.
money=NOM   not.exist-SUSP-POL
'There is probably no money.'

e. Imperative
도서관에서 책을 읽어요.
Tosekwan=eyse   chayk=ul   ilk-eyo.
library=LOC   book=ACC   read-IMP
'Read a book in the library.'

(45)   Clause types (Deferential speech style)

a. Declarative
철수는 도서관에서 책을 읽습니다.
Chelswu=nun   tosekwan=eyse chayk=ul   ilk-supnita.
Chelswu=TOP   library=LOC   book=ACC   read-DEF
'Chelswu reads a book in the library.'

b. Interrogative
철수는 도서관에서 책을 읽습니까?
Chelswu=nun   tosekwan=eyse chayk=ul   ilk-supnikka?
Chelswu=TOP   library=LOC   book=ACC   read-Q
'Does Chelswu read a book in the library?'

    c. Propositive

        도서관에서 책을 읽읍시다.

Tosekwan=eyse	*chayk=ul*	*ilk-upsita.*
library=LOC	book=ACC	read-PROP

        'Let's read a book in the library.'

    d. Suspective (same as Polite style)

    e. Imperative

        도서관에서 책을 읽으시오.

Tosekwan=eyse	*chayk=ul*	*ilk-usio.*
library=LOC	book=ACC	read-IMP

        'Read a book in the library.'

Interrogative clauses can be differentiated into *yes–no* (polar) questions, *wh-* (content) questions, and tag questions. In *yes–no* questions, the sentence ends with an interrogative suffix in the plain and deferential speech styles and rising intonation in the intimate and plain styles. In contrast to English *wh*-questions, where a phrase containing a *wh*-phrase must be displaced to the front of the sentence, Korean interrogative pronouns stay in their base position in the sentence. Korean is thus what is called a *wh*-in-situ language. The *wh*-pronoun *mwues* 'what' stays in the object position in (46b), and *eti* 'where' stays in the position for locative adjuncts in (46d).

(46)   *Wh*-questions in Korean

    a. 철수는 피자를 원해.

Chelswu=nun	*phica=lul*	*wenha-y.*
Chelswu=TOP	pizza=ACC	want-PLN

        'Chelswu wants pizza.'

    b. 철수는 무엇을 원하니?

Chelswu=nun	*mwues=ul*	*wenha-ni?*
Chelswu=TOP	what=ACC	want-Q

        'What does Chelswu want?'

    c. 철수는 도서관에서 공부해.

Chelswu=nun	*tosekwan=eyse*	*kongpwuha-y.*
Chelswu=TOP	library=LOC	study-PLN

        'Chelswu studies in the library.'

    d. 철수는 어디에서 공부하니?

Chelswu=nun	*eti=eyse*	*kongpwuha-ni?*
Chelswu=TOP	where=LOC	study-Q

        'Where does Chelswu study?'

In contemporary standard Korean, the interrogative suffixes are the same for *yes–no* and *wh*-questions. But in Middle Korean and in modern dialects such as North Kyŏngsang, the two types of questions are morphologically distinguished. *Wh*-questions are marked with the interrogative suffix *-ko* (MK *-(k) wo*), while *yes–no* questions are marked with *-ka*.

(47)   *Wh*-questions in Kyŏngsang
        a. 니 학교 가나?
           Ni   *hakkyo*   *ka-na.*
           you.NOM   school   go-QYN
           'Do you go to school?'
        b. 니 어데 가노?
           Ni   *et=ey*   *ka-no?*
           you.NOM   where=DIR   go-QWH
           'Where do you go?'

An important feature of clause type marking in Korean is that Kwon's four
types of clauses are distinguished not just in main clauses, but in clauses
embedded under the suffixal complementizer *-ko*, as shown in (48).

(48)   Four clause types distinguished in embedded clauses
        a. Declarative
           태민은 [그의 친구가 도서관에서 책을 읽는다고] 생각했다.
           Thaymin=un   *[ku=uy chinkwu=ka   tosekwan=eyse*
           Taemin=TOP   he=GEN friend=NOM   library=LOC
           chayk=ul   *ilk-nun-ta-ko]*   *sayngkakhay-ss-ta.*
           book=ACC   read-PRES-PLN-COMP   think-PAST-PLN
           'Taemin thought that his friend read a book in the library.'
        b. Interrogative
           태민은 [그의 친구가 도서관에서 책을 읽느냐고] 물었다.
           Thaymin=un   *[ku=uy chinkwu=ka   tosekwan=eyse*
           Taemin=TOP   he=GEN friend=NOM   library=LOC
           chayk=ul   *ilk-nu-nya-ko]*   *mul-ess-ta.*
           book=ACC   read-PRES-Q-COMP   ask-PAST-PLN
           'Taemin asked if his friend read a book in the library.'
        c. Propositive
           태민은 [그의 친구와 도서관에서 책을 읽자고] 생각했다.
           Thaymin=un   *[ku=uy chinkwu=wa   tosekwan=eyse*
           Taemin=TOP   he=GEN friend=with   library=LOC
           chayk=ul   *ilk-ca-ko]*   *sayngkakhay-ss-ta.*
           book=ACC   read-PROP-COMP   think-PAST-PLN
           'Taemin thought let's read a book with his friend in the library.'
        d. Imperative
           태민은 [그한테 책을 읽으라고] 말했다.
           Thaymin=un   *[ku=hanthey   chayk=ul ilk-ula-ko]*   *malhay-ss-ta.*
           Taemin=TOP   he=DAT   book=ACC read-IMP-COMP   say-PAST-PLN
           'Taemin said to read a book to him.'

The four clause types are distinguished not just in direct discourse complements but in indirect discourse complements under a variety of higher verbs, as
the third person pronouns in (48) show. In many analyses, the clause type
marking suffixes are treated as complementizers, but the patterns in (48) show
that two positions must be distinguished, one for the clause type marker and one

for the embedding complementizer. We discuss *-ko* in greater detail in Section 7.2.3.

7.2.2   Basic Word Order and Scrambling

Crosslinguistically, the three most common word orders in descending order of frequency are SOV as represented by Korean and Japanese, SVO as represented by English and Chinese, and VSO as represented by Austronesian languages such as Tagalog and Celtic languages such as Welsh. All three of these word order patterns place the subject before the direct object; languages where the object precedes the subject, such as Malagasy, are much rarer. Since Greenberg (1966), it has been known that languages with VO word order are far more likely to have prepositions than postpositions. If a language has SOV word order, it is significantly more likely to have postpositions than prepositions. Languages with SOV order also more commonly place genitives before the noun they modify.

(49)   Crosslinguistic word order patterns (Greenberg 1966)

Phrase type	SVO	SOV
VP	verb–object	object–verb
NP	noun–genitive	adjective–noun
PP	preposition–NP	NP–postposition

Korean fits all of the patterns for an SOV language in (49). However Korean has relatively free word order in that virtually any order of subject, object, and other NPs and PPs is acceptable as long as the predicate is in final position in the sentence. Dislocation of NPs and PPs from their canonical position is known as scrambling, as in (50).

(50)   Scrambling word order
   a. 철수가 영희에게 책을 준다.

Chelswu=ka	*Yenghuy=eykey*	*chayk=ul*	*cwu-n-ta.*
Chelswu=NOM	Yenghuy=DAT	book=ACC	give-PRES-PLN

'Chelswu gives Yenghuy a book.'
   b. 철수가 책을 영희에게 준다.

Chelswu=ka	*chayk=ul*	*Yenghuy=eykey*	*cwu-n-ta.*
Chelswu=NOM	book=ACC	Yenghuy=DAT	give-PRES-PLN

'Chelswu gives Yenghuy a book.'
   c. 영희에게 철수가 책을 준다.

Yenghuy=eykey	*Chelswu=ka*	*chayk=ul*	*cwu-n-ta.*
Yenghuy=DAT	Chelswu=NOM	book=ACC	give-PRES-PLN

'Chelswu gives Yenghuy a book.'
   d. 영희에게 책을 철수가 준다.

Yenghuy=eykey	*chayk=ul*	*Chelswu=ka*	*cwu-n-ta.*
Yenghuy=DAT	book=ACC	Chelswu=NOM	give-PRES-PLN

'Chelswu gives Yenghuy a book.'

    e. 책을 철수가 영희에게 준다.
       Chayk=ul   *Chelswu=ka*   *Yenghuy=eykey*   *cwu-n-ta.*
       book=ACC   Chelswu=NOM   Yenghuy=DAT   give-PRES-PLN
       'Chelswu gives Yenghuy a book.'
    f. 책을 영희에게 철수가 준다.
       Chayk=ul   *Yenghuy=eykey*   *Chelswu=ka*   *cwu-n-ta.*
       book=ACC   Yenghuy=DAT   Chelswu=NOM give-PRES-PLN
       'Chelswu gives Yenghuy a book.'

Two subtypes of scrambling are exemplified in (50). Examples (50c–f) involve scrambling the indirect object (50c, d) or direct object (50e, f) to the immediate left of the subject. This is called intermediate scrambling. Examples (50b, f) involve scrambling the direct object over the indirect object. This is called short scrambling. Examples (50d, f) involve scrambling both the direct and indirect object over the subject. This is called multiple scrambling. The existence of scrambling is sometimes correlated with the presence of rich case-marking morphology. Languages with rich case marking like Korean, such as Russian and Japanese, also allow scrambling.

    It is reasonable to ask, why are the orders other than subject – indirect object – direct object called scrambling at all? What is the evidence that these orders are derived by dislocation from a fixed underlying order? Some evidence is provided by the phenomenon of quantifier float. As we have seen, in certain circumstances, numeral quantifiers in Korean may be separated from the NPs they quantify.

(51)   Scrambling and quantifier float
    a. 학생이 영희에게 책을 두권 주었다.
       Haksayng=i   *Yenghuy=eykey*   *chayk=ul*   *twu-kwen*
       student=NOM   Yenghuy=DAT   book=ACC   two-CLSF
       cwu-ess-ta.
       give-PAST-PLN
       'The student gave Yenghuy two books.'
    b. 책을 학생이 영희에게 두권 주었다.
       Chayk=ul   *haksayng=i*   *Yenghuy=eykey twu-kwen cwu-ess-ta.*
       book=ACC   student=NOM Yenghuy=DAT   two-CLSF   give-PAST-PLN
       'Books, the student gave Yenghuy two.'
    c. 학생이 두명 영희에게 책을 주었다.
       Haksayng=i   *twu-myeng*   *Yenghuy=eykey*   *chayk=ul*   *cwu-ess-ta.*
       student=NOM   two-CLSF   Yenghuy=DAT   book=ACC   give-PAST-PLN
       'Two students gave Yenghuy the book.'
    d. *학생이 영희에게 책을 두명 주었다.
       *Haksayng=i   *Yenghuy=eykey chayk=ul*   *twu-myeng*   *cwu-ess-ta.*
       student=NOM   Yenghuy=DAT   book=ACC two-CLSF   give-PAST-PLN
       'Two students gave Yenghuy the book.'

Sentence (51b) shows us an example of quantifier stranding. The quantifier *twu-kwen* 'two-CLSF (for books)' may be left behind when the direct object *chayk=ul* 'book=ACC' is scrambled to the front of the sentence. In (51d), however, the quantifier *twu-myeng* 'two-CLSF (for human beings)' may not be separated from the subject *haksayng=i* 'student(s)=NOM'. The reason is that the subject is not generated in the position to the right of the direct object. The location of the stranded quantifier shows us the underlying position of the NP, before scrambling. The underlying position of the direct object is to the immediate left of the verb, but the underlying position of the subject is at the beginning of the sentence.

The third type of scrambling is long-distance scrambling. NPs can be scrambled out of the clausal complement of "bridge" verbs such as *sayngka-kha-* 'think' or *malha-* 'say':

(52)   Long-distance scrambling
    a. 철수는 [태민이 피자를 먹었다고] 생각했다.
       Chelswu=nun [Thaymin=i   phica=lul mek-ess-ta-ko]
       Chelswu=TOP Taemin=NOM pizza=ACC eat-PAST-PLN-COMP
       sayngkakhay-ss-ta.
       think-PAST-PLN
       'Chelswu thought that Taemin ate pizza.'
    b. 피자를 철수는 [태민이 먹었다고] 생각했다.
       Phica=lul   Chelswu=nun [Thaymin=i   mek-ess-ta-ko]
       pizza=ACC Chelswu=TOP Taemin=NOM eat-PAST-PLN-COMP
       sayngkakhay-ss-ta.
       think-PAST-PLN
       'Pizza, Chelswu thought Taemin ate.'

However, there are restrictions on long-distance scrambling. Scrambling obeys well-known constraints on movement. For example, scrambling is possible within a relative clause, as in (53b), but it is impossible to scramble out of a relative clause, as shown in (53c). Thus scrambling obeys the Complex NP Constraint of Ross (1967).

(53)   Constraints on Scrambling
    a. 강남에서 나는 길거리에서 피자를 먹는 철수를 만났다.
       Kangnam=eyse   na=nun   [kil keli=eyse   phica=lul
       Kangnam=LOC   I=TOP   street corner=LOC pizza=ACC
       mek-nun   Chelswu=lul] manna-ss-ta.
       eat-PRESADN   Chelswu=ACC meet-PAST-PLN
       'In Kangnam I met Chelswu, who was eating pizza on a street corner.'
    b. 강남에서 나는 피자를 길거리에서 먹는 철수를 만났다.
       Kangnam=eyse   na=nun   [phica=lul   kil keli=eyse
       Kangnam=LOC   I=TOP   pizza=ACC street corner=LOC
       mek-nun   Chelswu=lul] manna-ss-ta.
       eat-PRESADN   Chelswu=ACC meet-PAST-PLN
       'In Kangnam I met Chelswu, who was eating pizza on a street corner.'

c. *피자를 강남에서 나는 길거리에서 먹는 철수를 만났다.

   *Phica=lul   Kangnam=eyse   na=nun   [kil keli=eyse
   pizza=ACC   Kangnam=LOC   I=TOP   street corner=LOC
   mek-nun   Chelswu=lul]   manna-ss-ta.
   eat-PRESADN   Chelswu=ACC   meet-PAST-PLN
   'Pizza, in Kangnam I met Chelswu, who was eating on a street corner.'

Scrambling is also generally unable to reorder two NPs with the same case
marking. This extends to multiple nominative (54b), multiple accusative (54d),
and nested locative patterns (54f).

(54)   Scrambling blocked across NPs with the same case marking
        a. 철수가 키가 크다.
           Chelswu=ka   khi=ka   khu-ta. (cf. Yeon 2015: 85)
           Chelswu=NOM   height=NOM   big-PLN
           'Chelswu is tall.'
        b. *키가 철수가 크다.
           *Khi=ka   Chelswu=ka   khu-ta.
           height=NOM   Chelswu=NOM   big-PLN
           'Height, Chelswu is tall.'
        c. 나는 철수를 손을 잡았다.
           Na=nun   Chelswu=lul   son=ul   cap-ass-ta.
           I=TOP   Chelswu=ACC   hand=ACC   catch-PAST-PLN
           'I caught Chelswu's hand.'
        d. *나는 손을 철수를 잡았다.
           *Na=nun   son=ul   Chelswu=lul   cap-ass-ta.
           I=TOP   hand=ACC Chelswu=ACC   catch-PAST-PLN
           'I caught Chelswu's hand.'
        e. 나는 학교에서 도서관에서 너를 기다렸다.
           Na=nun   hakkyo=eyse   tosekwan=eyse ne=lul   kitaly-ess-ta.
           I=NOM   school=LOC   library=LOC   you=ACC   wait-PAST-PLN
           'I waited for you at the school library.'
        f. *나는 도서관에서 학교에서 너를 기다렸다.
           *Na=nun tosekwan=eyse hakkyo=eyse ne=lul   kitaly-ess-ta.
           I=NOM   library=LOC   school=LOC   you=ACC wait-PAST-PLN
           'I waited for you at the school library.'

Both processing-related and syntactic accounts have been proposed for the
facts in (54). On the first approach, it could be claimed that since case
marking or postpositions give no clue as to the relation between the
arguments, speakers appeal to word order as a default strategy. This
view might get some support from example (55), where khi 'height' has
topic status. When fronted as a topic, rather than simply scrambled,
'height' acquires a different status from the nominative-marked NP it
has been moved over.

(55)   (그 팀에서는) 키가 누가 제일 크니?
    (Ku thim=eyse=nun)   khi=ka   nwu=ka   ceyil   khu-ni?
    (that team=LOC=TOP)   height=NOM   who=NOM   most   tall-Q
    '(On that team), speaking of height, who is the tallest?' (cf. Yeon 2015: 85)

7.2.3   Clausal Embedding

We can distinguish two major types of embedded clauses in Korean: verbal and nominal. Verbal embedded clauses can be further subdivided into finite and nonfinite categories. In nominal embedded clauses, we distinguish nominalizations in the narrow sense, introduced in Chapter 6, and adnominal clauses.

(56) Embedded clause types
    a. Verbal
      i. Tenseless
      ii. Tensed, including direct quotations
    b. Nominal
      i. Regular nominal
      ii. Adnominal (including relative clauses)

Two important criteria in the classification are possibility of tense in the embedded clause and the postpositions which can follow it. The periphrastic causative -*key* clause in (57a) and the desiderative -*ko* clause in (57b) disallow tense in the embedded clause.

(57)   Embedded clauses (verbal tenseless)
    a. 나는 [철수가 학교에 가/*갔게] 했다.
      Na=nun   Chelswu=ka   hakkyo=ey   ka-*ss-key
      I=TOP   Chelswu=NOM   school=DIR   go-*PAST-*KEY*
      hay-ss-ta.
      do-PAST-PLN
      'I made Chelswu go to school.'
    b. 나는 [학교에 가/*갔고] 싶다.
      Na=nun   hakkyo=ey   ka-*ss-ko   siph-ta.
      I=TOP   school=DIR   go-*PAST-COMP   want-PLN
      'I want to go to school.'

Although tense is disallowed in both complement clauses in (58), their status is different. The -*key* complement in the syntactic causative in (58) is a raising complement, while as we see below, as complements of verbs of saying or propositional attitude, -*ko* clauses bear tense and allow overt subjects.

(58)   나는 아이들을 더 잘 이해하게 되었다.
        Na=nun ai-tul=ul   te   cal   ihayha-key   toy-ess-ta.
        I=TOP   child-PL=ACC   more well understand-*KEY* become-PAST-PLN
        'I came to understand the children better.'

The point here is that the syntactic status of complement clauses in Korean is
not completely predictable from their morphology. The suffixal complementizer *-ko*, for example, attaches both to tensed finite and non-tensed control
complements. In order to understand the syntactic status of a clausal complement in Korean, we must look at both the morphology that marks it and the
higher verb that selects it. A second point is that the notion of finiteness is
problematic in Korean. Traditionally, clauses that may express tense, agreement, and a nominative-marked subject are considered finite. But examples like
(59a), with a nominative subject but no tense allowed, show us that these
notions must be decoupled in Korean.

The types of complement clauses we have looked at so far may be followed by
delimiters, but not by structural case markers. Most delimiters are possible after
the embedded clauses in (59) except *itunci* 'or', *pakkey* 'only', and *khenyeng*
'even'.

(59)   Embedded clauses (Verbal tenseless)
        a. 나는 [철수가 학교에 가게]*를/만 했다.
           Na=nun Chelswu=ka   hakkyo=ey ka-key=lul/=man*
           I=TOP   Chelswu=NOM   school=DIR go-*KEY* *=ACC/=only
           hay-ss-ta.
           do-PAST-PLN
           'I only made Chelswu go to school.'
        b. 나는 [학교에 가고]*를/만 싶다.
           *Na=nun   hakkyo=ey ka-ko=*lul/=man   siph-ta.*
           I=TOP   school=DIR go-COMP=*ACC/=only   want-PLN
           'I only want to go to school.'

Tensed verbal complement clauses involve the suffixal complementizer *-ko*,
which may be preceded by the clause type or mood markers shown in (60).
The embedded clause in this case is fully clausal; thus not only tense but
a clause type marker is required. The complementizer *-ko* derives complement
clauses interpreted as indirect quotations; *-lako* derives direct quotations.

(60)   Embedded *-ko* clauses (Verbal tensed)
        a. 나는 [철수가 학교에 간다]고 말했다.
           Na=nun Chelswu=ka hakkyo=ey ka-n-ta-ko
           I=TOP   Chelswu=NOM school=DIR go-PRES-PLN-COMP
           malhay-ss-ta.
           say-PAST-PLN
           'I said that Chelswu goes to school.'

b. 나는 [철수가 학교에 간다]라고 말했다.
   Na=nun   Chelswu=ka   hakkyo=ey   ka-n-ta-lako   malhay-ss-ta.
   I=TOP   Chelswu=NOM school=DIR go-PRES-PLN-QUOTE say-PAST-PLN
   'I said "Chelswu goes to school."'

c. 나는 [철수가 학교에 갔다]고 말했다.
   Na=nun   Chelswu=ka   hakkyo=ey   ka-ss-ta-ko
   I=TOP   Chelswu=NOM school=DIR go-PAST-PLN-COMP
   malhay-ss-ta.
   say-PAST-PLN
   'I said that Chelswu went to school.'

d. 나는 [철수가 학교에 갔다]라고 말했다.
   Na=nun   Chelswu=ka   hakkyo=ey   ka-ss-ta-lako   malhay-ss-ta.
   I=TOP   Chelswu=NOM school=DIR go-PAST-PLN-QUOTE say-PAST-PLN
   'I said "Chelswu went to school."'

Like tenseless verbal complements, *-ko* complements can be followed by delimiters but not by case postpositions.

(61)   a. 나는 [철수가 학교에 간다]고*를/만 말했다.
           Na=nun   Chelswu=ka   hakkyo=ey   ka-n-ta-ko=lul/=man*
           I=TOP   Chelswu=NOM school=DIR go-PRES-PLN-COMP*=ACC/=only
           malhay-ss-ta.
           say-PAST-PLN
           'I said only that Chelswu goes to school.'

        b. 나는 [철수가 학교에 간다]라고*를/만 말했다.
           Na=nun   Chelswu=ka   hakkyo=ey   ka-n-ta-lako=lul/=man*
           I=TOP   Chelswu=NOM school=DIR go-PRES-PLN-QUOTE *=ACC/=only
           malhay-ss-ta.
           say-PAST-PLN
           'I said only "Chelswu goes to school."'

Certain embedded clause types such as subjunctive or irrealis complements selected by verbs such as 바라다 *palata* 'want', 원하다 *wenhata* 'want', and 지지하다 *cicihata* 'support', as well as the "tough" predicates 쉽다 *swipta* 'easy' and 어렵다 *elyepta* 'difficult' select nominalized complements in *-ki*, while 알다 *alta* 'know' and 의미하다 *uymihata* 'mean' select nominalized complements in *-(u)m*.

In terms of their status in the matrix clause, these embedded clauses behave as nominals, as we might expect given the presence of the nominalizers *-m, -ki*. Tense occurs in S2, except *te* 'past' as in (62c) and (62d), and most particles appear at the end of S2 as in (62e) and (62f).

(62)   Nominalized *-(u)m* and *-ki* complements

   a. 나는 [철수가 학교에 감]을 알았다.

   Na=nun   Chelswu=ka   hakkyo=ey   ka-m=ul
   I=TOP   Chelswu=NOM   school=DIR   go-NOMNL=ACC
   al-ass-ta.
   know-PAST-PLN
   'I knew that Chelswu goes to school.'

   b. 나는 [철수가 학교에 가기]를 원한다.

   Na=nun   Chelswu=ka   hakkyo=ey   ka-ki=lul
   I=TOP   Chelswu=NOM   school=DIR   go-NOMNL=ACC
   wenha-n-ta.
   want-PRES-PLN
   'I want Chelswu to go to school.'

   c. 나는 [철수가 학교에 갔음]을 알았다.

   Na=nun Chelswu=ka   hakkyo=ey ka-ss-um=ul
   I=TOP   Chelswu=NOM school=DIR go-PAST-NOMNL=ACC
   al-ass-ta.
   know-PAST-PLN
   'I knew that Chelswu went to school.'

   d. 나는 [철수가 학교에 갔기]를 원한다.

   Na=nun Chelswu=ka   hakkyo=ey ka-ss-ki=lul
   I=TOP   Chelswu=NOM school=DIR go-PAST-NOMNL=ACC
   wenha-n-ta.
   want-PRES-PLN
   'I want Chelswu to have gone to school.'

   e. 나는 [철수가 학교에 감]만을 알았다.

   Na=nun Chelswu=ka   hakkyo=ey   ka-m=man=ul
   I=TOP   Chelswu=NOM school=DIR   go-NOMNL=only=ACC
   al-ass-ta.
   know-PAST-PLN
   'I only knew that Chelswu goes to school.'

   f. 나는 [철수가 학교에 가기]만을 원한다.

   Na=nun Chelswu=ka   hakkyo=ey ka-ki=man=ul
   I=TOP   Chelswu=NOM school=DIR go-NOMNL=only=ACC
   wenha-n-ta.
   want-PRES-PLN
   'I only want for Chelswu to go to school.'

As (62a–d) show, the type of nominalization in *-(u)m* and *-ki* differs: *-(u)m* allows genitive subjects, while *-ki* nominalizations do not.

   The third major pattern of clausal complementation in Korean involves a complex NP structure where a bound head nominal such as *kes* 'one, thing, fact, that . . .' is preceded by the embedded clause with adnominal morphology. Often the difference between bound and free head is subtle. Bound *cwul* 'fact' and free *sasil* 'fact' have similar meanings and distributions; their main difference is that *sasil* is an independent noun meaning 'fact'. We analyze *kes* as a nominal functional category, which we label C(omplementizer) when it is preceded by an adnominal clause, and D(eterminer) when it is preceded by adjectives, demonstratives, or other nominal modifiers. The adnominal suffixes on the embedded predicate are differentiated by tense: *-nun* (Present), *-(u)n* (Past), *-ten* (Retrospective), and *-(u)l* (Future). The examples in (63) show the tense variation in this pattern of complementation.

(63)   Complex NP complements
   a. 나는 [철수가 학교에 가는]것/줄을 알았다.
      Na=nun   Chelswu=ka   hakkyo=ey   ka-nun   kes/cwul=ul
      I=TOP   Chelswu=NOM   school=DIR go-PRESADN   C/fact=ACC
      al-ass-ta.
      know-PAST-PLN
      'I knew that Chelswu goes to school.'
   b. 나는 [철수가 학교에 간]것/줄을 알았다.
      Na=nun   Chelswu=ka   hakkyo=ey   ka-n   kes/cwul=ul
      I=TOP   Chelswu=NOM   school=DIR go-PSTADN   C/fact=ACC
      al-ass-ta.
      know-PAST-PLN
      'I knew that Chelswu went to school.'
   c. 나는 [철수가 학교에 갈]것/줄을 알았다.
      Na=nun   Chelswu=ka   hakkyo=ey   ka-l   kes/cwul=ul
      I=TOP   Chelswu=NOM   school=DIR go-FUTADN   C/fact=ACC
      al-ass-ta.
      know-PAST-PLN
      'I knew that Chelswu will go to school.'
   d. 나는 [철수가 학교에 가는] 사실을 알았다.
      Na=nun   Chelswu=ka   hakkyo=ey   ka-nun   sasil=ul
      I=TOP   Chelswu=NOM   school=DIR go-PRESADN   fact=ACC
      al-ass-ta.
      know-PAST-PLN
      'I knew the fact that Chelswu goes to school.'
   e. 나는 [철수가 학교에 간] 사실을 알았다.
      Na=nun   Chelswu=ka   hakkyo=ey   ka-n   sasil=ul
      I=TOP   Chelswu=NOM   school=DIR go-PSTADN   fact=ACC
      al-ass-ta.
      know-PAST-PLN
      'I knew the fact that Chelswu went to school.'
   f. 나는 [철수가 학교에 갈] 사실을 알았다.
      Na=nun   Chelswu=ka   hakkyo=ey   ka-l   sasil=ul
      I=TOP   Chelswu=NOM   school=DIR go-FUTADN   fact=ACC
      al-ass-ta.
      know-PAST-PLN
      'I knew the fact that Chelswu will go to school.'

The external syntax of complex NP complements is fully nominal, as we see
from the possibility of structural case marking in (64). Such complements can
also be marked with delimiters:

(64)　　a.　나는 [태민이 학교에 간]것만을 알았다.

　　　　　　Na=nun　Thaymin=i　　hakkyo=ey　ka-n　　　　　kes=man=ul
　　　　　　I=TOP　　Taemin=NOM　school=DIR　go-PSTADN　　C=only=ACC
　　　　　　al-ass-ta.
　　　　　　know-PAST-PLN
　　　　　　'I knew only that Taemin went to school.'

　　　　b.　나는 [태민이 학교에 간] 사실만을 알았다.

　　　　　　Na=nun　Thaymin=i　　hakkyo=ey　ka-n　　　　　sasil=man=ul
　　　　　　I=TOP　　Taemin=NOM　school=DIR　go-PSTADN　　fact=only=ACC
　　　　　　al-ass-ta.
　　　　　　know-PAST-PLN
　　　　　　'I knew only the fact that Taemin went to school.'

Kes is used in a very common complex NP complementation pattern, the
S *kes i-ta* 'it is that V' pattern, where S embedded under *kes* is predicated
of the matrix copula. As in many languages of East and Southeast Asia, this
pattern is used to present the embedded S as non-asserted information, for
instance as the presupposition in a focus pattern, such as the corrective
focus in (65). Suppose, for example that speaker A asserts that Taemin went
to the market. Speaker B might correct this in the following way in Korean,
Burmese, and Japanese:

(65)　　a.　아니, 학교에 간 것이다/거야.

　　　　　　Ani,　　hakkyo=ey　ka-n　　　　　kes=i-ta/keya.
　　　　　　no,　　school=DIR　go-PSTADN　　C=be-PLN/INT
　　　　　　'No, (he) went to SCHOOL.'

　　　　b.　*Ma houʔ,　tʃsáũ　Өwá tà.*　　　　　Burmese
　　　　　　no, he　　school　go C
　　　　　　'No, he went to school.'

　　　　c.　*Iie,　　gakkoo=ni　it-ta no　　　da yo.*　　　　Japanese
　　　　　　no,　　school=DIR　go-PAST C　　be-SUSP
　　　　　　'No, it's that he has gone to school.'

The clausal nominalization pattern with Korean S *kes=i-ta*, Japanese S *no da*,
and Burmese S *ta* (Burmese does not use an overt copula) gives S presupposed
status, except for the focused element. Speaker B shares the presupposition that
Taemin went somewhere, but strongly asserts that where he went was school, not
somewhere else. The S+C+copula pattern easily becomes grammaticalized to
become a simple declarative. This has happened with the Adnominal Future +
kes=i-ta, as shown in (66):

(66)   나는 학교에 갈 것이다/거야/게.
Na=nun hakkyo=ey ka-l   kes=i-ta/ke-ya/key.
I=TOP   school=DIR go-FUTADN C=be-PLN/INT
'I will go to school.'

In contemporary Korean, the V-*(u)l kes=i-ta* pattern has become a normal way of expressing future likelihood or intention, with no special presupposition.

7.2.4   *Sentential Coordination and Adjunction*

Aside from clausal complementation, Korean marks adjunct and coordinate clauses (S1, S2) using the marker that appears at the end of S1. Traditionally, coordinate clauses are considered to be parallel in syntactic and semantic terms, while adjunct clauses involve subordination.

In Korean, it is not always easy to distinguish sentential coordination and conjunction, since both are marked by connective suffixes on S1. Distinguishing them requires careful examination of the syntactic and semantic relation between the two clauses and the meaning of the connective marker. There are about sixty different connective markers in Korean. We can distinguish at least three different semantic relationships between S1 and S2:

(67)   Partial inventory of coordinate markers

    a. Enumeration

고	*-ko*	Gerund
으며	*-umye*	Conjunctive
으면서	*-umyense*	Conditional+Particle
고서	*-kose*	Gerund+Particle
아/어서	*-a/ese*	Infinitive+Particle

    b. Contrast

으나	*-una*	Adversative
어도	*-eto*	Infinitive+'even'
지만	*-ciman*	Suspective+'only'= 'but'
으되	*-utoy*	Concessive
건만	*-kenman*	Literary Concessive
느니	*-nuni*	'rather than'

    c. Disjunction

거나 거나	*-kena . . . -kena*	Tentative Adversative
든지 든지	*-tunci . . . -tunci*	'whether. . . or'

Among the enumerative patterns, infinitive+particle -아/어서 *-a/ese* does not permit tense on S1, and the tense on S2 is interpreted as ranging over the whole clause (68b). Infinitive+particle *-a/ese* occurs with the delimiter *=man* 'only' in

(68c) and permits the honorific marker -*usi*- in both S1 and S2, as in (68d). We gloss -*a/ese* in these examples as 'and', and analyze the pattern as VP coordination.

(68) Enumeration-type sentential coordination
  a. 철수는 강남에 가서 피자를 먹었다.
     Chelswu=nun *Kangnam=ey* *ka-se*   *phica=lul*   *mek-ess-ta.*
     Chelswu=TOP   Kangnam=DIR go-and pizza=ACC   eat-PAST-PLN
     'Chelswu went to Kangnam and ate pizza.'
  b. *철수는 강남에 갔어서 피자를 먹었다.
     **Chelswu=nun*   *Kangnam=ey*   *ka-ss-ese*   *phica=lul*
     Chelswu=TOP   Kangnam=DIR go-PAST-and   pizza=ACC
     mek-ess-ta.
     eat-PAST-PLN
     'Chelswu went to Kangnam and ate pizza.'
  c. 철수는 강남에 가서만 피자를 먹었다.
     Chelswu=nun   *Kangnam=ey* *ka-se=man*   *phica=lul*
     Chelswu=TOP   Kangnam=DIR go-and=only   pizza=ACC
     mek-ess-ta.
     eat-PAST-PLN
     'Chelswu only went to Kangnam and ate pizza.'
  d. 선생님이 강남에 가셔서 피자를 먹으셨다.
     Sensayngnim=i   *Kangnam=ey*   *ka-sye-se*   *phica=lul*
     teacher=NOM   Kangnam=DIR go-HON-and   pizza=ACC
     mek-usye-ss-ta.
     eat-HON-PAST-PLN
     'The teacher went to Kangnam and ate pizza.'

The contrastive coordinate patterns in adversative 으나 -*una*, and the semi-literary adversative 건만 -*kenman* allow tense, affixation of a delimiter, and honorifics in S1 (69).

(69) Contrastive sentential coordination
  a. 철수는 강남에 가나 피자를 안 먹었다.
     Chelswu=nun *Kangnam=ey* *ka-na*   *phica=lul*   *an*
     Chelswu=TOP   Kangnam=DIR go-but   pizza=ACC   NEG
     mek-ess-ta.
     eat-PAST-PLN
     'Chelswu went to Kangnam, but he didn't eat pizza.'
  b. 철수는 강남에 갔으나 피자를 안 먹었다.
     Chelswu=nun *Kangnam=ey* *ka-ss-una*   *phica=lul*   *an*
     Chelswu=TOP   Kangnam=DIR go-PAST-but   pizza=ACC   NEG
     mek-ess-ta.
     eat-PAST-PLN
     'Chelswu went to Kangnam, but he didn't eat pizza.'

c. 선생님은 강남에 가셨건만 피자를 안 먹으셨다.

Sensayngnim=un Kangnam=ey ka-sye-ss-kenman phica=lul an
teacher=TOP   Kangnam=DIR go-HON-PAST-even   pizza=ACC NEG
mek-usye-ss-ta.
eat-HON-PAST-PLN
'Even though the teacher went to Kangnam, he didn't eat pizza.'

The disjunction pattern in 든지 *-tunci* 'whether . . . or' does not allow tense in S1 or a delimiter, but allows S1 to contain an honorific, as in (70).

(70)   Alternative sentential coordination

a. 철수는 강남에 가든지 뉴욕에 가든지 항상 행복했다.

Chelswu=nun   Kangnam=ey ka-tunci   Nyuyok=ey   ka-tunci
Chelswu=TOP   Kangnam=DIR go-or   New York=DIR go-or
hangsang   hayngpokhay-ss-ta.
always   happy-PAST-PLN
'Whether Chelswu went to Kangnam or New York, he was always happy.'

b. *철수는 강남에 갔든지 뉴욕에 갔든지 항상 행복했다.

*Chelswu=nun   Kangnam=ey ka-ss-tunci Nyuyok=ey   ka-ss-tunci
Chelswu=TOP   Kangnam=DIR go-PAST-or New York=DIR go-PAST-or
hangsang   hayngpokhay-ss-ta.
always   happy-PAST-PLN
'Whether Chelswu went to Kangnam or New York, he was always happy.'

c. *철수는 강남에 가든지만 뉴욕에 가든지만 항상 행복했다.

*Chelswu=nun   Kangnam=ey   ka-tunci=man   Nyuyok=ey
Chelswu=TOP   Kangnam=DIR   go-or=only   New York=DIR
ka-tunci=man   hangsang   hayngpokhay-ss-ta.
go-or=only   always   happy-PAST-PLN
'Whether Chelswu only went to Kangnam or New York, he was always happy.'

d. 선생님이 강남에 가시든지 뉴욕에 가시든지 항상 행복하셨다.

Sensayngnim=i   Kangnam=ey ka-si-tunci Nyuyok=ey   ka-si-tunci
teacher=NOM   Kangnam=DIR go-HON-or New York=DIR go-HON-or
hangsang   hayngpokha-si-ess-ta.
always   happy-HON-PAST-PLN
'Whether the teacher went to Kangnam or New York, he was always happy.'

The occurrence of tense, particles, and honorifics in S1 is related to the question of whether S1 + S2 is to be analyzed as a true coordinate structure, or whether S1 is to be analyzed as an adjunct subordinate to S2. In (71) cases are presented in which the tense of S1 is prior to the tense of S2 (71a), the tense of S2 is prior to the tense of S1 (71b), and both are concurrent (71c).

(71)   Tense in coordinate clauses
        a. S1 prior to S2
            어서 *-ese*   INF+Particle   고서   *-kose*   GER+Particle
            자 *-ca*   PROP   어야   *-eya*   INF+Particle
        b. S2 prior to S1
            으러 *-ule*   PURP   게(끔)   *-key(kkum)* Adverbative
            고자 *-koca*   'wanting to'   으려(고) *-ulye(ko)*   INTEN (+GER)
            도록 *-tolok*   Projective   으라고   *-ulako*   Subjunctive
                                                                  Attentive+COMP
        c. S1 concurrent with S2
            으면서 *- umyense* Conditional+Particle 건대   *-kentay*   'when, since'
            다시피 *-tasiphi*   DEC+ADV   을수록 *-ulswulok* 'the
                                                                  more ...'

In (71a), where S1 is interpreted as prior to S2, as we saw in (68b), tense may
not be realized in S1. Syntactically and semantically, this indicates that S1 is
interpreted under the temporal scope of S2. This in turn suggests that S1 should
be analyzed as a clausal adjunct, along the lines of 'Chelswu, having gone to
Kangnam, ate pizza.' This in turn is consistent with the fact that delimiter
particles may attach after the S1 suffixes in (71a), since delimiters attach freely
to adjuncts.

S1 in (71b) involves irrealis clauses associated with purpose and intent.
Again, this is consistent with adjunct status, and delimiters are possible after
S1 in at least some contexts:

(72)   학교는 공부하러만 가는 곳이 아니다.
        Hakkyo=nun   kongpwuha-le=man   ka-nun   kos=i   an-i-ta.
        school=TOP   study-PURP=only   go-PRESADN place=NOM not-be-PLN
        'School is not a place to go only to study.'

S1 in (71c) involves control clauses whose temporal interpretation is the
same as the matrix clause. Once again delimiter particles are possible after the
S1 affix, suggesting a temporal adjunct clause under the scope of the matrix
subject.

(73)   연애를 하면서만 느낄 수 있는 행복이 있다.
        Yenay=lul   ha-myense=man   nukki-l   swu   iss-nun
        love=ACC   do-while=only   feel-FUTADN possibility be-ADN
        hayngpok=i   iss-ta.
        happiness=NOM be-PLN
        'There is a happiness that you can feel only while in a romantic relationship.'

The focus of the debate over coordination versus adjunction in these
patterns has been on clauses linked by gerundive -고 *-ko*. Yoon (1997)

argues that *-ko* joining a tensed S1 to a tensed S2 is true clausal coordination, while tenseless VP1-*ko* is adjunction. The evidence Yoon gives for this contrast includes the fact that extraction is possible out of S2 over adjunct VP1-*ko*, but not over coordinate S1-Tense-*ko*, as the latter would violate the Coordinate Structure Constraint (examples from Yoon 1997):

(74)   a. 무엇을$_i$ 존이 책을 읽고 t$_i$ 먹었니?
         Mwues=ul$_i$ John=i   chayk=ul ilk-ko   t$_i$ mek-ess-ni?
         what=ACC$_i$ John=NOM book=ACC read-GER   t$_i$ eat-PAST-Q
         'What did John read a book and eat t$_i$?'
      b. *무엇을$_i$ 존이 책을 읽었고 t$_i$ 먹었니?
         **Mwues=ul$_i$ John=i   chayk=ul ilk-ess-ko*   t$_i$ mek-ess-ni?*
         what=ACC$_i$ John=NOM book=ACC read-PAST-GER t$_i$ eat-PAST-Q
         'What did John read a book and eat t$_i$?'

Yoon points out that the adjunct/conjunct distinction is confirmed by the possibility of particles after gerundive *-ko*. The particle *-se* and the topic marker delimiter *-(n)un* are possible after adjunct V1-*ko*, but not after coordinate S1-Tense-*ko*:

(75)   a. 존이 밥을 먹고서/는 빵을 먹었다.
         John=i   pap=ul   mek-ko-se/=nun ppang=ul   mek-ess-ta.
         John=NOM   meal=ACC   eat-GER-PRT/=TOP bread=ACC   eat-PAST-PLN
         'John, after eating his meal, ate bread.'
      b. 존이 밥을 먹었고*서/*는 빵을 먹었다.
         John=i   pap=ul   mek-ess-ko-se/*=nun   ppang=ul*
         John=NOM   meal=ACC   eat-PAST-GER*-PRT/*=TOP   bread=ACC
         mek-ess-ta.
         eat-PAST-PLN
         'John ate his meal and (ate) bread.'

This is consistent with what we have seen above: attachability of delimiter particles is a diagnostic for adjunct status.

From a semantic standpoint, we can distinguish seven major adjunct clause types based on the semantic relationship between S1 and S2 (76). They are (i) cause/effect, translatable as 'S1 so S2' (77); (ii) condition, translatable as 'if S1 then S2' (78); (iii) purpose, translatable as 'in order to S1, S2' (79); (iv) evaluation, translatable as 'S1=as we know, S2' (80); (v) result, translatable as 'as a result of S1, S2' (81); (vi) concessive, translatable as 'even though S1, S2 (82); and (vii) scalar, translatable as 'the more (better) S1, the more (better) S2' (83).

(76)   Semantic classification of adjunct clause markers
        a. Cause/Effect
            으니   *-uni*   Sequential   으니까   *-unikka* Extended sequential
            어서   *-ese*   INF+particle   느라고   *-nulako* PROC adjunctive
        b. Condition
            으면   *-umyen* Conditional   거든   *-ketun* Provisional
            어야   *-eya*   INF+particle   ㄴ들   *-ntul*   Conditional
        c. Purpose
            으러   *-ule*   PURP   으려고   *-uleyko* INTEN+GER
            고자   *-koca*   'wanting to'
        d. Evaluation
            다시피   *-tasiphi* DEC+ADV   건대   *-kentay* 'when, since'
        e. Result
            게(끔)   *-key(kkum)* Adverbative   도록   *-tolok* Projective
            으라고   *-ulako* Subjunctive attentive+COMP
        f. Concessive
            듯이   *-tusi*   'as if'   자   *-ca*   PROP
            다가   *-taka*   Transferative   을수록   *-ulswulok* 'the more ...'
        g. Scalar
            고 고   *-ko -ko*   자 ... 자   *-ca ... -ca*
            다가 다가   *-taka taka*   으나 ... 으나   *-una ... -una*
            어도 어도   *-eto -eto*   으면...을수록   *-umyen ... -ulswulok*

(77)   Cause/Effect clauses
        a. 강남에 가니까 좋은 음식점이 많이 있다.
            Kangnam=ey ka-nikka   cohun   umsikcem=i   manhi iss-ta.
            Kangnam=DIR go-because good   restaurant=NOM a lot be-PLN
            'I go to Kangnam, so I see many good restaurants.'
        b. 강남에 가서 피자를 먹었다.
            Kangnam=ey ka-se   phica=lul mek-ess-ta.
            Kangnam=DIR go-so   pizza=ACC eat-PAST-PLN
            'I went to Kangnam, so I ate pizza.'

(78)   Conditional clauses
        a. 강남에 가면 좋은 음식점이 많이 있다.
            Kangnam=ey ka-myen cohun umsikcem=i   manhi   iss-ta.
            Kangnam=DIR go-if   good restaurant=NOM a lot   be-PLN
            'If (you) are going to Kangnam, there are a lot of good restaurants.'
        b. 강남에 가거든 서양 음식을 먹어라.
            Kangnam=ey ka-ketun seyang umsik=ul   mek-ela.
            Kangnam=DIR go-if   western food=ACC   eat-IMP
            'If (you) are going to Kangnam, please eat Western food.'

(79)   Purpose clauses
    a. 피자를 먹으러 강남에 갔다.
       Phica=lul   mek-ule   *Kangnam=ey   ka-ss-ta.*
       pizza=ACC   eat-in order to   Kangnam=DIR   go-PAST-PLN
       'In order to eat pizza, (someone) went to Kangnam.'
    b. 피자를 먹으려고 강남에 갔다.
       Phica=lul   mek-ulyeko   *Kangnam=ey   ka-ss-ta.*
       pizza=ACC   eat-in order to   Kangnam=DIR   go-PAST-PLN
       'In order to eat pizza, (someone) went to Kangnam.'

(80)   Evaluative clauses
    a. 너도 알다시피 강남에는 좋은 식당이 많다.
       Ne=to   *altasiphi*   *Kangnam=ey=nun*   *cohun   siktang=i*
       you=too   as you know   Kangnam=LOC=TOP   good   restaurant=NOM
       manh-ta.
       a lot-PLN
       'As you know too, there are a lot of good restaurants in Kangnam.'
    b. 내가 보건대 철수는 행복하다.
       Nay=ka   *po-kentey*   *Chelswu=nun   hayngpokha-ta.*
       I=NOM   see-as know   Chelswu=TOP happy-PLN
       'As I see it, Chelswu is happy.'

(81)   Result clauses
    a. 음식을 먹게끔 준비 해주세요.
       Umsik=ul   mek-keykkum   cwunpi   *hay-cwu-seyyo.*
       food=ACC   eat-as a result   preparation   do-AUX-IMP
       'In order for me to eat, please prepare.'
    b. 음식을 먹도록 준비 해주세요.
       Umsik=ul   mek-tolok   *cwunpi*   *hay-cwu-seyyo.*
       food=ACC   eat-as a result   preparation   do-AUX-IMP
       'Please prepare so that I can eat.'

(82)   Concessive clauses
    a. 철수를 설득해 보았자 아무 소용이 없어요.
       Chelswu=lul   *seltukhay-po-ass-ca*   *amwu*   *soyong=i*
       Chelswu=ACC   persuade-AUX-PAST-even   nothing   use=NOM
       eps-eyo.
       not have-POL
       'Even though you persuade Chelswu, there is no use.'
    b. 철수를 설득할수록 일이 잘 안된다.
       Chelswu=lul   seltukhal-swulok   *il=i*   *cal*
       Chelswu=ACC   persuade-as much   things=NOM   well
       an-toy-n-ta.
       NEG-become-PRES-PLN
       'As much as we persuade Chelswu, things will not go well.'

(83)   Scalar clauses
    a. 피자는 먹어도 먹어도 더 먹고 싶다.
       Phica=nun   mek-eto   mek-eto   te   mek-ko siph-ta.
       pizza=TOP   eat-more   eat-more   more eat-would like-PLN
       'No matter how much (I) eat pizza, (I) want to eat more.'
    b. 피자는 먹으면 먹을수록 더 맛있다.
       Phica=nun   mek-umyen   mek-ulswulok   te   masiss-ta.
       pizza=TOP   eat-more   eat-more   more delicious-PLN
       'The more (I) eat pizza, the more delicious it is.'

7.3   Passive and Causative

Passive and causative constructions involve changes in valency: causatives add an argument, while passives may remove one. In this section, we describe the basics, types, and major characteristics of the two constructions and show how they are interrelated to each other.

7.3.1   *Passives*

In classical transformational grammar, active and passive sentences are understood to be related by a rule that derives passives, such as *Pizza was eaten by Youngmee in Kangnam* from the corresponding active sentence *Youngmee ate pizza in Kangnam.*

    In English, the passive operation can be schematized by the rule in (84):

(84)   NP   V   NP
      1   2   3   →
      3   be 2 en by 1

Few linguists would posit such a simple formulation today, but there is consensus that crosslinguistically passives are characterized by non-assignment of the external theta role to the highest argument position in the clause, and typically, a failure to assign object (accusative) case. Korean passives show one or both of these properties, but Korean is first and foremost distinguished by its variety of morphological devices for passivization. Korean distinguishes three passive patterns: lexical, morphological, and syntactic. We begin with the first of these.

(85)   Lexical passive
    a. 그 일이 결정 되었다.
       Ku   il=i   kyelceng   toy-ess-ta.
       that   thing=NOM   decide   become-PRES-PLN
       'That matter was decided.'

b. 선생님께 많은 꾸중을 맞았다 (들었다).

Sensayngnim=kkey   manhun   kkwucwung=ul   mac-ass-ta (tul-ess-ta).
teacher=NOM   a lot   scolding=ACC   receive/hear-PAST-PLN

'A teacher received/heard a lot of scolding.'

The justification for considering examples like (85) passives is that they have corresponding actives formed from the same verbal noun (e.g. *kyelceng* 'decide/decision', *kkwucwung* 'scold/scolding') plus the light verb *ha-* 'do'. Verbs that can alternate with active *ha-* in this way include *toy-* 'become' and *mac-* 'receive, be met with'. These verbs may be analyzed as light passive verbs: in examples like (85), the main verbal meaning is contributed by the verbal noun, while the light verb contributes a passive-like valency by not assigning an agentive role to subject position. This pattern is lexical in the sense that the identity of the passive light verb is not completely predictable: *toy-* 'become' is widespread with Sino-Korean verbal nouns, but *mac-* 'receive, be met with' is common with native Korean verbal nouns.

Morphological passives involve a suffix which attaches to the verb stem. Its allomorphs, *-i-, -hi-, -ki-, -li-*, also occur in the morphological causative, and are conditioned by the shape of the stem final.

(86)   Allomorphs of the morphological passive

a. 이 *-i*   (following a vowel, /h-/, or /kk-/)

보이다	*poita*	to be seen	쓰이다	*ssuita*	to be used
섞이다	*sekkita*	to be mixed	놓이다	*nohita*	to be put
높이다	*nophita*	to be raised			

b. 히 *-hi* (following an oral stop or affricate)

잡히다	*caphita*	to be caught	밟히다	*palphita*	to be trampled
묻히다	*mwuthita*	to be buried	업히다	*ephita*	to be carried
얹히다	*enchita*	to be put			

c. 리 *-li* (following /l-/ or /lu-; in the latter case, /u/ drops)

물리다	*mwullita*	to be bitten	풀리다	*phwullita*	to be freed
들리다	*tullita*	to be heard	밀리다	*millita*	to be pushed

d. 기 *-ki* (following a nasal, /nh-/, or /s-/)

안기다	*ankita*	to be hugged	끊기다	*kkunhkita*	to be cut
감기다	*kamkita*	to be washed	벗기다	*peskita*	to be removed

(87)   Examples of morphological active/passive pairs

a. -이 *-i*

i. 나는 책상위에 책을 놓는다.

Na=nun   chayksang-wi=ey   chayk=ul   noh-nun-ta.
I=TOP   table-top=LOC   book=ACC   put-PRES-PLN

'I put a book on the table.'

    ii. 책이 책상위에 놓인다.
       Chayk=i   *chayksang-wi=ey*   *noh-i-n-ta.*
       book=NOM   table-top=LOC   put-PASS-PRES-PLN
       'A book is put on the table.'

b. -히 *-hi*
    i. 나는 동생을 업는다.
       Na=nun   *tongsayng=ul*   *ep-nun-ta.*
       I=TOP   brother=ACC   carry.on.back-PRES-PLN
       'I piggyback my brother.'
    ii. 동생이 나에게 업힌다.
       Tongsayng=i   *na=eykey*   *ep-hi-n-ta.*
       brother=NOM   I=DAT   put-PASS-PRES-PLN
       'My brother is piggybacked by me.'

c. -리 *-li*
    i. 개가 고양이를 문다.
       Kay=ka   *koyangi=lul*   *mwu-n-ta.*
       dog=NOM   cat=ACC   bite-PRES-PLN
       'The dog bites the cat.'
    ii. 고양이가 개한테 물린다.
       Koyangi=ka   *kay=hanthey*   *mwul-li-n-ta.*
       cat=NOM   dog=DAT   bite-PASS-PRES-PLN
       'The cat is bitten by the dog.'

d. -기 *-ki*
    i. 메리는 아기를 안는다.
       Meyli=nun   *aki=lul*   *an-nun-ta.*
       Mary=TOP   baby=ACC   hug-PRES-PLN
       'Mary hugs the baby.'
    ii. 아기가 메리에 의해서 안긴다.
       Aki=ka   *Meyli=ey uy hayse*   *an-ki-n-ta.*
       baby=NOM   Mary=by   hug-PASS-PRES-PLN
       'The baby is hugged by Mary.'

As we see in the examples above, animate agents, if realized, are marked by dative *=eykey* or by the complex postposition *=ey uy hayse*. If the agent (or instrument) is an inanimate noun, it is marked by directional 에 *=ey* (88d).

(88)   Inanimate by-phrases in passive/active pairs
    a. 내가 새를 잡았다.
       Nay=ka   *say=lul*   *cap-ass-ta.*
       I=NOM   bird=ACC   catch-PAST-PLN
       'I caught a bird.'
    b. 새가 나에게 잡혔다.
       Say=ka   *na=eykey*   *cap-hi-ess-ta.*
       bird=NOM   I=DAT   catch-PASS-PAST-PLN
       'A bird was caught by me.'

    c. 새가 나에 의해서 잡혔다.
       Say=ka   na=ey uy hayse   cap-hi-ess-ta.
       bird=NOM I=by   catch-PASS-PAST-PLN
       'A bird was caught by me.'
    d. 새가 그물에 잡혔다.
       Say=ka   kumwul=ey   cap-hi-ess-ta.
       bird=NOM net=by   catch-PASS-PAST-PLN
       'A bird was caught by/with a net.'

Morphological passive formation is not a completely productive process. The list in (89) gives transitive verbs that have no corresponding morphological passive.

(89)   Transitive verbs with no morphological passive counterpart

주다	*cwuta*	to give	드리다	*tulita*	to give
받다	*patta*	to receive	얻다	*etta*	to gain
잃다	*ilhta*	to lose	찾다	*chacta*	to seek
돕다	*topta*	to help	닮다	*talmta*	to resemble

The Korean syntactic passive is formed by attaching the suffix *-ci-* to the infinitive form of the verb. *-ci-* has been grammaticalized from an originally independent verb meaning 'become', and it retains this meaning in inchoatives derived from stative stems, such as *eps-e-ci-* 'become nonexistent' from *eps-* 'not exist', or *coh-a-ci* 'get better' from *coh-* 'good'.

(90)   Syntactic passives
    a. 태민의 얼굴이 철수에 의해서 그려졌다.
       Thaymin=uy   elkwul=i   Chelswu=ey uy hayse
       Taemin=GEN   face=NOM   Chelswu=by
       kuli-e-ci-ess-ta.
       draw-INF-PASS-PAST-PLN
       'Taemin's face was drawn by Chelswu.'
    b. 야채가 다 먹어졌다.
       Yachay=ka   ta   mek-e-ci-ess-ta.
       vegetable=NOM all   eat-INF-PASS-PAST-PLN
       'The vegetables were all eaten.'

In Section 7.4 we discuss some of the semantic differences between morphological and syntactic passives. The major syntactic difference between them is that syntactic passives in *-ci-* block assignment of accusative case. This means that while an "indirect" passive retaining accusative case on the direct object (91a) is possible with a morphological passive, such a pattern is not possible with a syntactic passive.

(91)   a. 태민이 도둑에게 지갑을 빼앗겼다.
         Thaymin=i   totwuk=eykey cikap=ul   ppayas-ki-ess-ta.
         Taemin=NOM   thief=by   wallet=ACC   steal-PASS-PAST-PLN
         'Taemin had his wallet stolen by a thief.'
        b. *태민이 얼굴을 철수에게 그려졌다.
         **Thaymin=i   elkwul=ul   Chelswu=eykey   kuli-e-ci-ess-ta.*
         Taemin=NOM   face=ACC   Chelswu=by   draw-INF-PASS-PAST-PLN
         'Taemin had his face drawn by Chelswu.'

The syntactic -*ci*- passive is also used in a construction with an interpretation
similar to an English middle.

(92)   Syntactic -*ci*- passives as middles
        a. 내가 글씨가/를 잘 써진다.
         Nay=ka   kulssi=ka/=lul   cal   ss-e-ci-n-ta.*
         I=NOM   writing=NOM/*=ACC   well   write-INF-PASS-PRES-PLN
         'The writing is well written by me.'
        b. 책이 잘 읽어진다.
         Chayk=i   cal   ilk-e-ci-n-ta.
         book=NOM   well   read-INF-PASS-PRES-PLN
         'The book reads well.'

As with -*ci*- passives in general, accusative case cannot be assigned in this
pattern. Like the English middle, the -*ci*- middle expresses a stable property of
the theme argument, but unlike English middles, the agent argument can be
expressed as a subject, as in (92a).

7.3.2   Causatives

Crosslinguistically, causative constructions introduce a new "causer" argument,
with consequences for the expression of the external or subject argument of the
base predicate (the "causee"), and in the case of transitives, for the direct object.
Korean causatives are particularly interesting because unlike many languages,
Korean allows multiple accusative patterns. Causatives are a construction where
we see multiple accusative marking come into play. As with passives, Korean has
three types of causative constructions: lexical, morphological, and syntactic
causative. We begin with lexical causatives in (93):

(93)   Lexical causatives
        a. 나는 철수에게 공부를 시킨다.
         Na=nun   Chelswu=eykey kongpwu=lul sikhi-n-ta.
         I=TOP   Chelswu=DAT   study=ACC   CAUS-PRES-PLN
         'I make Chelswu study.'

b. 민수ᵢ가 철수ⱼ를 자기ᵢ, ⱼ 집으로 보냈다.
   Minswuᵢ=ka Chelswuⱼ=lul cakiᵢ, ⱼ cip=ulo ponay-ss-ta.
   Minsu=NOM Chelswu=ACC self home=DIR send-PAST-PLN
   'Minsuᵢ sent Chelswuⱼ to selfᵢ, ⱼ's home.'

c. 민수ᵢ가 철수ⱼ를 자기ᵢ, *ⱼ의 지도 교수에게 소개했다.
   *Minswuᵢ=ka Chelswuⱼ=lul cakiᵢ, *ⱼ=uy cito kyoswu=eykey*
   Minsu=NOM Chelswu=ACC self=GEN adviser=DAT
   sokayhay-ss-ta.
   introduce-PAST-PLN
   'Minsuᵢ introduced Chelswuⱼ to selfᵢ, *ⱼ's adviser.'

The lexical causative in (93a), like the lexical passive, is formed from a transitive verbal noun plus the morphological causative of light *ha-* 'do'. Just as *toy-* 'become' behaves as a passive light verb corresponding to active *ha-*, so *sikhi-* 'cause, make do' fulfills the role of a causative light verb. The relationship of *sikhi-* to *ha-* is suppletive (there is no longer a phonologically regular morphological passive of *ha-*). The example of *ponay-* 'send' in (93b) is different: *ponay-* is a causative verb from the standpoint of lexical composition. Its meaning can be decomposed into 'cause to go (to some goal)'. The syntactic status of lexical decomposition is controversial, but verbs like *ponay-* in Korean give some evidence for a more complex structure at some level of representation. Reflexive *caki* 'self' can usually only be anteceded by subjects, as shown in (93c). But with *ponay-* 'send', the direct object can exceptionally antecede *caki*, as in (93b). This arguably justifies treating the direct object as a subject at some level of representation, as it would be in a causative structure.

Morphological causatives involve the same allomorphs as the morphological passive: *-i, -hi,- li,* and *-ki*, as well as the distinct causative suffixes *-wu, -kwu,* and *-chwu*.

(94)   Morphological causative allomorphs
    a. 이 *-i*

Base stem	Meaning	Causative	Meaning
높- *noph-*	high	높이- *nophi-*	heighten
녹- *nok-*	melt$_{intrans}$	녹이- *noki-*	melt$_{trans}$
죽- *cwuk-*	die	죽이- *cwuki-*	kill
속- *sok-*	be tricked	속이- *soki-*	deceive
줄- *cwul-*	decrease$_{intrans}$	줄이- *cwuli-*	decrease$_{trans}$

    b. 히 *-hi*

Base stem	Meaning	Causative	Meaning
좁- *cop-*	narrow	좁히- *cophi-*	narrow$_{trans}$
밝- *palk-*	light, bright	밝히- *palkhi-*	lighten
넓- *nelp-*	wide	넓히- *nelphi-*	widen
읽- *ilk-*	read	읽히- *ilkhi-*	make read
잡- *cap-*	catch	잡히- *caphi-*	make grab
앉- *anc-*	sit down	앉히- *anchi-*	seat

c. 리 -li

물- *mwul-*	bite	물리- *mwulli-*	make bite
울- *wul-*	cry	울리- *wulli*	make cry
날- *nal-*	fly	날리- *nalli-*	make fly
열- *yel-*	open_{intrans}	열리- *yelli-*	open_{trans}

d. 기 -ki

벗- *pes-*	remove	벗기- *peski-*	make remove
숨- *swum-*	hide_{intrans}	숨기- *swumki-*	hide_{trans}
웃- *wus-*	laugh	웃기- *wuski-*	make laugh
남- *nam-*	remain	남기- *namki-*	leave behind

e. 우 -wu

지- *ci-*	fall, disappear	지우- *ciwu-*	erase
깨- *kkay-*	awake	깨우- *kkaywu-*	awaken
비- *pi-*	empty	비우- *piwu-*	empty_{trans}
자- *ca-*	sleep	재우- *caywu-*	make sleep

f. 구 -kwu

솟- *sos-*	rise, sprout up	솟구- *soskwu-*	raise

g. 추 -chwu

낮- *nac-*	low	낮추- *nacchwu-*	lower
늦- *nuc-*	late	늦추- *nucchwu-*	make late

As (94) shows, the allomorphy of the morphological causative is less regular than the morphological passive. For example, an /s-/ final stem is followed by *-ki-* in *pes-ki-* 'make remove' (94d), but by *-kwu-* in *sos-kwu-* 'raise'. The irregularities reflect the fact that the morphological causative is the result of an older layer of derivation than the morphological passive; most scholars believe that the morphological passive is derived from the causative, following crosslinguistic trends. The relative regularity of the morphological passive can be seen in cases where the passive and causative approach homonymity: for example, passive *mek-hi-* 'be eaten' follows the regular rule, while causative *mek-i* 'feed, cause to eat' follows the idiosyncratic pattern for stem-final /k-/ in causatives only.

As many of the examples in (94) show, the morphological causative derives transitives from intransitives, including adjectival stems. In terms of case marking, the causee argument of a causativized intransitive is marked accusative (95a), while the causee of a causativized transitive may be marked dative, or, for most speakers in many contexts, accusative.

(95)   a. Morphological causative of intransitive
           i. 아이가 운다.
              Ai=ka   *wu-n-ta.*
              baby=NOM   cry-PRES-PLN
              'The baby cries.'

    ii. 철수가 아이를/*에게 울린다.

        Chelswu=ka   ai=lul/*=eykey   wul-li-n-ta.

        Chelswu=NOM baby=ACC/*=DAT   cry-CAUS-PRES-PLN

        'Chelswu makes the baby cry.'

  b. Morphological causative of transitive

    i. 철수가 피자를 먹는다.

        Chelswu=ka   phica=lul   mek-nun-ta.

        Chelswu=NOM   pizza=ACC   eat-PRES-PLN

        'Chelswu eats pizza.'

    ii. 나는 철수에게/를 피자를 먹인다.

        Na=nun   Chelswu=eykey/=lul phica=lul   mek-i-n-ta.

        I=TOP   Chelswu=DAT/=ACC pizza=ACC eat-CAUS-PRES-PLN

        'I make Chelswu eat pizza.'

As Song (2015: 111) points out, there is a semantic difference between dative and accusative marking on the cause in causatives of transitives such as *mek-i-* in (95bii). Accusative case marking is consistent with a situation where the causee has relatively little control, while dative case marking indicates a higher degree of control or volitionality on the part of the causee.

    The syntactic causative involves the adverbative suffix *-key* or the projective suffix *-tolok* followed by the higher verbs *ha-* 'do' or *mantul-* 'make' (96).

(96)   Syntactic causatives

    a. 나는 철수를 가게 하였다.

       Na=nun Chelswu=lul ka-key ha-yess-ta.

       I=TOP   Chelswu=ACC go-CAUS-PAST-PLN

       'I made Chelswu go.'

    b. 나는 철수를 가게 만들었다.

       Na=nun Chelswu=lul ka-key mantul-ess-ta.

       I=TOP   Chelswu=ACC go-CAUS-PAST-PLN

       'I made Chelswu go.'

    c. 나는 철수를 가도록 하였다.

       Na=nun Chelswu=lul ka-tolok ha-yess-ta.

       I=TOP   Chelswu=ACC go-CAUS-PAST-PLN

       'I made Chelswu go.'

    d. 나는 철수를 가도록 만들었다.

       Na=nun Chelswu=lul ka-tolok mantul-ess-ta.

       I=TOP   Chelswu=ACC go-CAUS-PAST-PLN

       'I made Chelswu go.'

The case-marking possibilities in syntactic causatives are freer than in morphological causatives. Thus the causee in syntactic causatives can be marked dative, nominative, or accusative, regardless of the transitivity of the base predicate.

(97)   Case marking in syntactic causatives

a. 철수가 운다.
   Chelswu=ka   wu-n-ta.
   Chelswu=NOM   cry-PRES-PLN
   'Chelswu cries.'

b. 영희가 철수를/에게/가 울게 한다.
   Yenghuy=ka   Chelswu=lul/=eykey/=ka   wul-key ha-n-ta.
   Yenghuy=NOM   Chelswu=ACC/=DAT/=NOM   cry-CAUS-PRES-PLN
   'Yenghuy makes Chelswu cry.'

c. 철수가 피자를 먹는다.
   Chelswu=ka   phica=lul   mek-nun-ta.
   Chelswu=NOM   pizza=ACC   eat-PRES-PLN
   'Chelswu eats pizza.'

d. 영희가 철수에게/를/가 피자를 먹게 한다.
   Yenghuy=ka   Chelswu=eykey/=lul/=ka   phica=lul
   Yenghuy=NOM   Chelswu=DAT/=ACC/=NOM   pizza=ACC
   mek-key ha-n-ta.
   eat-CAUS-PRES-PLN
   'Yenghuy makes Chelswu eat pizza.'

However, evidence from adverb interpretation indicates that the structural position of the nominative-marked causes and the dative/accusative-marked causes is different:

(98)   a. 내가 [허둥지둥 철수가 집에 돌아 가게] 했다.
   Nay=ka   [hetwung-citwung   Chelswu=ka   cip=ey
   I=NOM   helter-skelter   Chelswu=NOM   house=to
   tola ka-key]   hay-ss-ta.
   return go-ADV   do-PAST-PLN
   'I made Chelswu go back home helter-skelter.'

   b. 내가 허둥지둥 철수에게 [집에 돌아 가게] 했다.
   Nay=ka   hetwung-citwung   Chelswu=eykey   [cip=ey
   I=NOM   helter-skelter   Chelswu=DAT   house=to
   tola ka-key]   hay-ss-ta.
   return go-ADV   do-PAST-PLN
   'I made Chelswu go helter-skelter back home.'

In (98a), with the adverb to the immediate left of the nominative-marked causee, the adverb may be interpreted in the main clause or associated with the embedded predicate (indicated with brackets). In (98b) when the adverb occurs to the left of the dative-marked causee, it can only be construed with the higher predicate *ha-* 'do, cause', suggesting that the dative-marked causee is in the higher clause.

In the final part of this section, we describe the differences between morphological and syntactic causative patterns, summarizing results found by previous researchers as well as the data presented here.

(99)   Differences between morphological and syntactic causatives

	Morphological	Syntactic
Manner of causation	Direct	Indirect
Nominative case possible	No	Yes
Negation scope	Wide	Wide/Narrow
Adverbial modifiers	Wide	Narrow
Honorifics	One location	Two locations
Auxiliary verb	One location	Two locations

As pointed out by previous researchers (e.g. Song 2015: 104 and references cited there), morphological causative tends to imply direct causation, while the syntactic causative is consistent with indirect causation. As we discuss in Section 7.4, this contrast is not always clear, but the contrasting translations in (100a–b) are indicative of the contrast.

(100)   Causation: direct versus indirect
    a. Morphological: direct
       나는 철수에게 피자를 먹였다.
       Na=nun   Chelswu=eykey phica=lul   mek-i-ess-ta.
       I=TOP   Chelswu=DAT   pizza=ACC   eat-CAUS-PAST-PLN
       'I fed Chelswu pizza.'
    b. Syntactic: indirect
       나는 철수에게 피자를 먹게 했다.
       Na=nun   Chelswu=eykey phica=lul   mek-key hay-ss-ta.
       I=TOP   Chelswu=DAT   pizza=ACC   eat-CAUS-PAST-PLN
       'I made Chelswu eat pizza.'

We saw in (97) that syntactic causatives allow nominative marking of the causee, and related this pattern in (98) to a structure where there is a clause boundary between the causer and causee. The nominative cause pattern is impossible with morphological causatives:

(101)   a. 나는 철수에게/*가 책을 읽혔다.
       Na=nun Chelswu=eykey/=ka   chayk=ul   ilk-hi-ess-ta.*
       I=TOP   Chelswu=DAT/*=NOM   book=ACC   read-CAUS-PAST-PLN
       'I made Chelswu read a book.'
    b. 나는 철수에게/가 책을 읽게 했다.
       Na=nun Chelswu=eykey/=ka   chayk=ul   ilk-key hay-ss-ta.
       I=TOP   Chelswu=DAT/=NOM   book=ACC   read-CAUS-PAST-PLN
       'I made Chelswu read a book.'

The biclausal nature of syntactic causatives is confirmed by the ability of negation to appear either on the matrix causative predicate (102bii) or on the embedded predicate (102bi); in contrast, morphological causatives allow only one position for negation, and it cannot take embedded scope (102a).

(102)   a. 나는 철수에게 책을 읽히지 않았다.
           Na=nun   Chelswu=eykey   chayk=ul   ilk-hi-ci-anh-ass-ta.
           I=TOP   Chelswu=DAT   book=ACC   read-CAUS-NEG-PAST-PLN
           'I didn't make Chelswu read the book.'
       b. i. 나는 철수에게 책을 읽게 하지 않았다.
              Na=nun   Chelswu=eykey   chayk=ul   ilk-hi-ci-anh-ass-ta.
              I=TOP   Chelswu=DAT   book=ACC   read-CAUS-NEG-PAST-PLN
           'I didn't make Chelswu read the book.'
          ii. 나는 철수에게 책을 읽지 않게 하였다.
              Na=nun   Chelswu=eykey   chayk=ul   ilk-ci-anh-key ha-yess-ta.
              I=TOP   Chelswu=DAT   book=ACC   read-NEG-CAUS-PAST-PLN
           'I made Chelswu not read the book.'

We saw in (98) that adverbs may receive either a matrix or an embedded interpretation in syntactic causatives, depending on their placement and the case marking of the causee (103b), but in morphological causatives, the same adverbs are construed only as matrix modifiers (103a).

(103)   a. 나는 철수에게 책을 많이 읽혔다.
           Na=nun   Chelswu=eykey   chayk=ul   manhi   ilk-hi-ess-ta.
           I=TOP   Chelswu=DAT   book=ACC   a lot   read-CAUS-PAST-PLN
           'I often made Chelswu read books.'
       b. 나는 철수에게 책을 많이 읽게 하였다.
           Na=nun   Chelswu=eykey   chayk=ul   manhi   ilk-key   ha-yess-ta.
           I=TOP   Chelswu=DAT   book=ACC   a lot   read-ADV do-PAST-PLN
           'I made Chelswu often read books.'

Further evidence for the biclausal nature of syntactic causatives comes from the placement of elements such as honorifics, auxiliaries, and light verbs. All of these may take matrix or embedded positions, or both in syntactic causatives (104b, c), but they may not be embedded under the causative suffix in morphological causatives (104a).

(104)   Honorifics
       a. 어머니께서 형님께 책을 읽히신다.
           Emeni=kkeyse   hyengnim=kkey   chayk=ul   ilk-hi-si-n-ta.
           mother=NOM   brother=DAT   book=ACC   read-CAUS-HON-PRES-PLN
           'Mother makes my brother read a book.'

b. 어머니께서 형님께 책을 읽게 하신다.

Emeni=kkeyse hyengnim=kkey chayk=ul ilk-key   ha-si-n-ta.
mother=NOM   brother=DAT   book=ACC read-ADV do-HON-PRES-PLN
'Mother makes my brother read a book.'

c. 어머니께서 형님께 책을 읽으시게 하신다.

Emeni=kkeyse hyengnim=kkey chayk=ul   ilk-usi-key
mother=NOM   brother=DAT   book=ACC   read-HON-ADV

ha-si-n-ta.
do-HON-PRES-PLN
'Mother makes my brother read a book.'

(105) Light verbs

a. 나는 철수에게 책을 읽혀 주었다.

Na=nun Chelswu=eykey chayk=ul ilk-hi-e   cwu-ess-ta.
I=TOP   Chelswu=DAT   book=ACC read-CAUS-INF   give-PAST-PLN
'I did Chelswu the favor of making him read a book.'

b. 나는 철수에게 책을 읽어 주게 하였다.

Na=nun Chelswu=eykey chayk=ul ilk-e   cwu-key hay-ess-ta.
I=TOP   Chelswu=DAT   book=ACC read-INF give-ADV do-PAST-PLN
'I made Chelswu do (someone) the favor of reading a book.'

c. 나는 철수에게 책을 읽게 해 주었다.

Na=nun Chelswu=eykey chayk=ul ilk-key   hay   cwu-ess-ta.
I=TOP   Chelswu=DAT   book=ACC read-ADV   do.INF give-PAST-PLN
'I did Chelswu the favor of making him read a book.'

These diagnostics show that syntactic causatives have biclausal structure. The size of the clause embedded under *-key* or *-tolok* must be large enough to contain negation, honorifics, light verbs and auxiliaries, as well as to host manner and temporal adverbs. On the other hand, it cannot host tense; once again we see in Korean that nominative case is licensed in a context where overt tense is not. An appropriate analysis of the embedded clause in syntactic causatives might be as a type of irrealis clause, similar to subjunctives in other languages. We examine the syntactic constituent associated with the root verb in morphological causatives in Section 7.4.

7.4   Outstanding Issues in the Analysis of Passives and Causatives

Korean causative and passive constructions have been the focus of a number of longstanding debates. In this final section, we focus on two issues: the interaction of passive and causative, and the debate over the supposed synonymity of morphological and syntactic causatives.

7.4.1   Passive–Causative Interaction

It is possible to form a syntactic passive of a morphological passive, but when
we do, not all expected derived patterns are acceptable:

(106)   Morphological causative + syntactic passive
   a. 어머니가 아이에게/를 밥을 먹인다.
      Emeni=ka   ai=eykey/=lul   pap=ul   mek-i-n-ta.
      mother=NOM   baby=DAT/=ACC   meal=ACC   eat-CAUS-PRES-PLN
      'The mother makes the baby eat a meal.'
   b. 밥이 어머니에 의해서 아이에게 먹여 진다.
      Pap=i   emeni=ey uyhayse ai=eykey   mek-i-e-ci-n-ta.
      meal=NOM   mother=by   baby=DAT   eat-CAUS-PASS-PRES-PLN
      'A meal is fed to the baby by the mother.'
   c. *밥이 어머니에 의해서 아이를 먹여 진다.
      **Pap=i   emeni=ey uyhayse ai=lul   mek-i-e-ci-n-ta.*
      meal=NOM   mother=by   baby=ACC   eat-CAUS-PASS-PRES-PLN
      'A meal is fed to the baby by the mother.'
   d. *밥이 어머니에 의해서 아이가 먹여 진다.
      **Pap=i   emeni=ey uyhayse ai=ka   mek-i-e-ci-n-ta.*
      meal=NOM   mother=by   baby=NOM   eat-CAUS-PASS-PRES-PLN
      'A meal is fed to the baby by the mother.'
   e. 아이가 어머니에 의해서 밥이 먹여 진다.
      Ai=ka   emeni=ey uyhayse pap=i   mek-i-e-ci-n-ta.
      baby=NOM   mother=by   meal=NOM   eat-CAUS-PASS-PRES-PLN
      'The baby has a meal be fed to it by the mother.'

Examples (106b, e) show that either the causee (106e) or the underlying direct
object (106b) may be passivized. The ungrammaticality of (106c) is explained by
the fact that syntactic -ci- passives disallow accusative case. The contrast between
(106d) and (106e), however, requires further explanation. One possible explanation
is that the multiple nominative pattern in (106e) is a "default" pattern that occurs
only when no other case marking is available. Since structural accusative is
unavailable for the direct object *pap* 'rice' in (106e), default nominative is assigned.
On the other hand, the causee argument *ai* 'child' can be marked dative, as in
(106b); given this possibility, default nominative is disallowed.

   However morphological passives suggest a different explanation of the same
paradigm (107):

(107)   a. 아이가 밥을 먹는다.
            Ai=ka   pap=ul   mek-nun-ta.
            baby=NOM   meal=ACC   eat-PRES-PLN
            'The baby eats the meal.'
         b. 어머니가 아이에게 밥을 먹인다.
            Emeni=ka   ai=eykey   pap=ul   mek-i-n-ta.
            mother=NOM   baby=DAT   meal=ACC   eat-CAUS-PRES-PLN
            'The mother makes the baby eat the meal/feeds the baby the meal.'

c. 일본에서, 밥이 잘 먹힌다.

Ilpon=eyse	*pap=i*	*cal*	*mek-hi-n-ta.*
Japan=LOC	meal=NOM	well	eat-PASS-PRES-PLN

'In Japan, meals are eaten well.'

d. 밥이 어머니에 의해서 아이에게 먹힌다.

Pap=i	*emeni=ey uyhayse*	*ai=eykey*	*mek-hi-n-ta.*
meal=NOM	mother=by	baby=DAT	eat-PASS-PRES-PLN

'The meal is fed to the baby by the mother.' (Not 'The meal is eaten to the baby by the mother'.

e. *밥이 어머니에 의해서 아이를 먹힌다.

**Pap=i*	*emeni=ey uyhayse*	*ai=lul*	*mek-hi-n-ta.*
meal=NOM	mother=by	baby=ACC	eat-PASS-PRES-PLN

'The meal was fed to the baby by the mother.'

f. *밥이 어머니에 의해서 아이가 먹힌다.

**Pap=i*	*emeni=ey uyhayse*	*ai=ka*	*mek-hi-n-ta.*
meal=NOM	mother=by	baby=NOM	eat-PASS-PRES-PLN

'The meal is fed to the baby by the mother.'

g. 아이가 어머니에 의해서 밥이 먹힌다.

Ai=ka	*emeni=ey uyhayse*	*pap=i*	*mek-hi-n-ta.*
baby=NOM	mother=by	meal=NOM	eat-PASS-PRES-PLN

'The baby has a meal fed to it by the mother.'

Example (107c) is the normal morphological passive *mek-hi* 'be eaten' of transitive *mek-* 'eat'. Example (107d) uses the same morphological passive marker -*hi*-, but syntactically and semantically this example is the passive not of the simple transitive (107a) but of the morphological causative (107b). It is often said that the morphological passive and causative in Korean is restricted in that the two suffixes cannot combine, in contrast to languages like Japanese where both passives of causatives and causatives of passives are possible. Examples like (107d–g) suggest that this restriction is purely morphological: a sequence such as **mek-i-hi-* 'be caused to eat' is morphologically ill-formed, but syntactically the passive causative construal of (107d) is not only possible but obligatory. Now, in (107e, f) we see that passivization of the direct object *pap* 'meal' over the causee *ai* 'child' is not permitted when the causee is marked with structural case: accusative (107e), or nominative (107f). We cannot account for (107e) in the same way as (106c) on the grounds that morphological passives allow assignment of accusative case, as we saw in (91a). Instead, the explanation for the ungrammaticality of (107e, f) must be Relativized Minimality, the generalization that one structurally case-marked NP may not be moved over another. Passivization of the direct object over the causee is possible only when the causee is marked with nonstructural dative case, as in (107d).

7.4.2 The Difference between Morphological and Syntactic Causatives Revisited

In Section 7.3.2 we touched on the syntactic and semantic differences between morphological and syntactic causatives. Following previous researchers, we characterized the difference between the morphological and syntactic causative in (100) in terms of directness of causation. But this distinction has been disputed by Yang (1974), who argues that morphological causatives like (100a) may also be used in cases of indirect causation, contra (Shibatani 1973) (see the summary of this debate in Song 2015). The crux of Yang's argument is that we find ambiguous interpretation of the adverb in examples like (108), due to Shibatani (1973), cited here from Song (2015: 106).

(108)   어머니가 아이에게 옷을 빨리 입혔다.
        Emeni=ka   ai=eykey os=ul   ppalli   ip-hi-ess-ta.
        mother=NOM child=DAT clothes=ACC quickly wear-CAUS-PAST-PLN
        'The mother quickly dressed the child.' OR
        'The mother made the child dress quickly.'

Song confirms Yang's judgment, contra Shibatani, that *ppalli* 'quickly' may be construed either with the base verb 'wear' or with the entire causative predicate 'make wear'. How are we to reconcile this ambiguity with the unambiguity of (103a), where the frequency adverb *manhi* 'often' can only be construed with the base verb *ilk-* 'read'? Song (2015) cites an additional example where an adverb modifies only the entire causative predicate:

(109)   경찰관이 살인범을 어렵게 죽였다.
        Kyengchalkwan=I salinpem=ul   elyepkey   cwuk-i-ess-ta.
        policeman=NOM   murderer=ACC with.difficulty die-CAUS-PAST-PLN
        'The policeman killed the murderer with difficulty.' NOT
        'The policeman caused the murderer to die in a difficult manner.'

The answer to this question has to do with the nature of the adverbs involved and the syntactic structure associated with morphological causatives. Whitman and Hahn (1988) argue that morphological causatives do involve an embedded structure, the smallest syntactic category compatible with the causee and other arguments of the base predicate. In the case of morphological causatives of transitives, this is the smallest category containing a VP and its agent argument, in modern syntactic terms, "small" *v*P. In the case of morphological causatives of intransitives, the embedded category may be simply VP. When we examine the base predicate in example (108), we see that it is transitive; the embedded category is thus *v*P, which is large enough to host a manner adverb such as *ppalli* 'quickly'. On the other hand, in (109) the base predicate is an unaccusative intransitive, so the embedded category is a minimal VP, too small to host even manner adverbs. Finally, in (103a), while the embedded category is again *v*P, frequentative adverbs such as *manhi* 'often' typically occupy a position associated with aspect above *v*P.

The upshot of this analysis is that morphological and syntactic causatives are structurally very different, but in specific cases such as (108), the syntactic domains involved may overlap enough to allow them to accommodate adverbs of the same type.

7.5   Summary

In this chapter, we have discussed inflecting stem formation, embedded clause types, and passive and causative patterns. For inflecting stem formation, we distinguished the properties of verbals, adjectivals and copular predicates. Among verbal predicates, we distinguished intransitive, transitive, and ditransitive verbs.

Adjectival predicates include both experiencer subject (psychological) and theme or location subject types. We discussed seven major differences between verbs and adjectives. With copular = *(i)ita* 'be' predicates, we found four basic patterns, depending on the relation between the surface subject and the nominal predicate. We also discussed auxiliary and light verb constructions.

In our discussion of matrix clause phenomena, we discussed the marking of basic clause types: declarative, interrogative, imperative, suspective, and propositive, as well as their pragmatic characterization. We also discussed the complex interaction of clause type marking and speech style marking; we saw that in Korean, there are twenty combinations of clause type and speech style, although in them we exemplified only plain speech style. The other three speech styles (intimate, polite and deferential) are discussed in more detail in Section 10.2. Finally, we discussed the patterns for *yes–no* questions and *wh*-questions, and we briefly introduced the basic properties of scrambling in Korean.

Embedded complement clauses, given the head-final nature of Korean, involve the embedding of S2 in S1. With respect to the form of S2, we distinguished verbal and nominal embedded clauses. Verbal embedded clauses include direct quotations as well as the complements of verbs or propositional attitude. Nominal embedded clauses are formed with nominalizers such as -*m* and -*ki*, while complex NP complements involve a bound or free head NP preceded by a clause in adnominal form. Adjunct and coordinate clauses are formed with two sentences (S1 and S2), where a morpheme appears at the end of S1 indicating its function. Coordinate clauses have three different types; enumerative, contrastive, and disjunctive. Adjunct clauses include cause and effect, condition, purpose, evaluation, result, scalar, and focus. Two variables, the possibility of tense in S1 and the possibility of particles following S1, were examined.

We described passive and causative constructions. In both constructions, we described the basic principles of forming the patterns, three types of patterns (lexical, morphological, and syntactic), and the major characteristics of each pattern. In the case of lexical passives, the lexical predicate by itself indicates a passive meaning. In morphological passives, the passive construction is a grammatical change, since the object in an active sentence is upgraded to a subject and the subject is downgraded to an object while adding a passive morpheme. There are four different passive morphemes, *-i, -hi, -li,* and *-ki,* and there are many exceptions to the rule that no passive counterpart of the active or no active counterpart of the passive sentence appears in this passive. Syntactic passives are formed with syntactic phrases, *-cita* and *-key toyta,* with similar exceptions that there is no passive or active counterpart generated from the corresponding active or passive construction. There are also four different "by phrases" in Korean that relate to the characteristics of the noun phrase formed with 'by'.

In causative constructions, a new subject is introduced and the original subject is downgraded, while the existing direct object stays as it is and a causative morpheme is added into the predicate. For lexical causatives, a lexical verb shows a causative meaning by itself. For morphological causatives, we introduced seven types with different causative morphemes, *-i, -hi, -li, -ki, -wu, -kwu,* and *-chwu.* For syntactic causatives, four types were introduced with four syntactic patterns, *-key ha-, -key mantul-, -tolok ha-,* and *-tolok mantul-.* Finally, we showed six major differences between morphological and syntactic causatives: causation and case change in the nominative marker, negation scope, adverbial modifier, co-occurrence with honorifics, and auxiliary predicates.

Further Readings

Kang, Hyun-Hwa. 1998. *Kwukeuy Tongsayenkeyl Kwusengey Kwanhan Yekkwu* [Research on Korean Verbal Connectives]. Seoul: Hankuk Publisher.

Ko, Yong-Kun and Ki-Sim Nam. 2003. *Phyocwun Kwuke Muspeplon* [Standard Korean Grammar]. Seoul: Thap Publishing.

Ko, Yong-Kun and Pon-Kwan Ku. 2008. *Wulimal Munpeplon* [Korean Grammar]. Phacwu-si: Cipmundang.

Lee, Ki-Gap. 1991. *Hankwuke Eswun Yeynkwusa* [Research on Korean Word Order]. Seoul: Seoul National University Press.

Nam, Ki-Shim. 2010. *Hyentay Kwuke Tongsalon* [Modern Korean Syntax], 4th ed. Seoul: Taehaksa.

Nam, Ki-Shim and Young-Kun Ko. 2013. *Pyocwun Kwuke Mwunpeplon* [Grammar of Standard Korean], 3rd ed. Seoul: TOP Publisher.

Park, Jeong-Woon. 1992. The Korean morphological causative and passive. *Korea Journal* 32 (3): 44–59.

..

Shibatani, Masayoshi. 1985. Passives and related constructions: A prototype analysis. *Language* 61: 821–848.

Siewierska, Anna. 1984. *The Passive: A Comparative Linguistic Analysis.* London: Croom Helm.

Sohn, Ho-min. 1999. *The Korean Language.* Cambridge University Press.

You, Hyun-Kyung. 1998. *Kwuke Hyengyongsa Yenkwu* [Research on Korean Adjectives]. Seoul: Hankuk Publisher.

References

Burzio, L. 1986. *Italian Syntax: A Government and Binding Approach.* Dordrecht: Reidel.

Butt, Miriam and Gillian Ramchand. 2005. Complex aspectual structure in Hindi/Urdu. In Nomi Ertishik-Shir and Tova Rappaport (eds.), *The Syntax of Aspect,* 117–153. Oxford: Oxford University Press.

Greenberg, Joseph. 1966. Some universals of grammar with particular reference to the order of meaningful elements. In J. Greenberg (ed.), *Universals of Language.* Cambridge, MA: MIT Press.

Hale, Kenneth and Jay Keyser. 2002. Prolegomenon to a Theory of Argument Structure, Vol. 39). Cambridge, MA: MIT Press.

Jespersen, Otto. 1965. *A Modern English Grammar on Historical Principles, Part VI: Morphology.* London: George Allen and Unwin.

Kim, Young-Joo. 1990. The syntax and semantics of Korean case: The interaction between lexical and syntactic levels of representation. Unpublished Ph. D. dissertation, Harvard University.

Kwon, Jae-Il. 2011. *Hankuke Tongsalon* [Korean Syntax], 5th ed. Seoul: Minumsa.

Perlmutter, D. 1978. Impersonal passives and the unaccusative hypothesis. In *Annual Meeting of the Berkeley Linguistics Society,* Vol. 4.

Rizzi, Luigi. 1986. Null objects in Italian and the theory of pro. *Linguistic Inquiry* 17: 501–555.

Ross, J. R. 1967. Constraints in variables in syntax. Unpublished Ph.D. dissertation, MIT.

Saito, Mamoru. 1985. Some asymmetries in Japanese and their theoretical implications. Unpublished Ph.D. dissertation, MIT.

Shibatani, Masayoshi. 1973. Lexical versus periphrastic causatives in Korean. *Journal of Linguistics* 9: 209–383.

Song, Jae Jung. 2015. Causatives. In Lucien Brown and Jaehoon Yeon (eds.), *The Handbook of Korean Linguistics,* 98–115. John Wiley and Sons.

Whitman, John and S. Hahn, 1988. Korean morphological passive/causatives. In Eung-Jin Baek (ed.), *Papers from the Sixth International Conference on Korean Linguistics,* 714–728. Seoul: Hanshin Publishing Company.

Yang, In-Seok. 1974. Two causative forms in Korean. *Language Research* 10: 83–117.

Yeon, Jaehoon. 2015. Passives. In Lucien Brown and Jaehoon Yeon (eds.), *The Handbook of Korean Linguistics,* 116–136. John Wiley and Sons.

Yoon, James. 1997. Coordination asymmetries. In S. Kuo et al. (eds.), Harvard Studies in Korean Linguistics, Vol. 7: 3–30.

8   Syntax–Semantics Interface

The interface of syntax and semantics is a vast area; in this chapter, we have chosen to focus on five issues: negation, information structure, tense/aspect/ mood (TAM), pronouns and anaphora, and zero anaphora.

Every language has a way to express negation, but they differ in the form and placement of negation. Korean is notable for having two types of syntactic negation, which differ in their semantic interpretation. It also has a rich inventory of negative polarity items (NPIs) licensed by lexical or syntactic negation in the sentence.

Information structure is the matter of topic and focus: their semantic interpretation and syntactic expression. While Korean is often grouped with Japanese, and both languages with Chinese as "East-Asian-style" topic-prominent languages, we focus on information structural differences with English, Japanese, and Chinese. We discuss prosodic and syntactic devices for marking focus and revisit the major differences between the subject marker =*i*/=*ka* and the topic marker =*un*/=*nun*.

There are outstanding debates as to the divisions and overlap between tense, aspect, and mood in Korean. We will explore the interaction of tense and aspect in Korean, and clarify the difference between mood and modality, which have frequently been used interchangeably in the literature. We show that some morphemes marking TAM have a discrete function, while others function as a type of portmanteau in the sense that they express more than one TAM category.

Turning to pronouns and anaphora, we describe personal pronouns across three dimensions of deixis: temporal, spatial, and discourse. We delay the discussion of social deixis, marked by honorifics, until Chapter 10. We also examine the behavior of reflexives and reciprocals. The discussion of pronouns and anaphora leads naturally to the topic of zero anaphora. In addition to NP zero anaphora, we examine predicate ellipsis and the related topic of particle drop.

8.1   Negation

Lexical negation in Korean is exemplified by negative verbs such as *eps-* 'not exist' and *molu-* 'not know', and the negative copula *ani-* 'be not', which is diachronically derived from fusion of the preverbal negation marker *an(i)* plus the copula *i-*:

(1)   Lexical negation

    a. 나는 돈이 없어요.

      Na=nun   ton=i   eps-eyo.

      I=TOP   money=NOM not have-POL

      'I do not have money.'

    b. 나는 이문제를 몰라요.

      Na=nun i mwuncey=lul   moll-ayo.

      I=TOP   this question=ACC not know-POL

      'I do not know (the answer to) this question.'

    c. 이 일은 아니에요.

      I   il=un   ani-eyyo.

      this thing=TOP not-POL

      'It is not this matter.'

Korean also has negative affixes of the type familiar from English *un-* in *unlikely* and *in-* in *inarticulate*. As in English, these prefixes are borrowed from a language with prefixal negation, in the case of Korean from Chinese. The Sino-Korean negative prefixes and their sources include *pi-* 非, *mi-* 未, *pwul-* and *pwu-* 不, *mwu-* 無, and *mol-* 勿. In general, the negative expression was borrowed as a unit, so the choice of prefix was determined by the Chinese source. For example, in *mikaypal* 'undeveloped' the negative prefix *mi-* 未, Middle Chinese *mɨi^H* 'not yet', was used because *mi-* 未 + *kaypal* 開發 'developed' means 'not yet developed'.

(2)   Sino-Korean negative prefixes

a.	비공개 *pikongkay*	unreleased	비무장 *pimwucang*	not armed
b.	미완성 *miwanseng*	incomplete	미개발 *mikaypal*	undeveloped
c.	불가능 *pwulkanung*	impossible	불필요 *pwulphilyo*	unnecessary
d.	무분별 *mwupwunpyel*	indiscreet	무작정 *mwucakceng*	unplanned
e.	부적응 *pwucekung*	maladjustment	부족 *pwucok*	lack
f.	몰상식 *molsangsik*	senseless	몰인정 *molinceng*	inhumanity

Although both the negative verbs in (1) and the Sino-Korean negative prefixes in (2) are forms of lexical negation, their syntactic and semantic status is very different. Negative verbs license negative polarity items in Korean, while negative prefixes do not:

(3)   Negative polarity licensing by negative verbs versus negative prefixes

    a. 나는 아무것도 몰라요.

      Na=nun amwukesto moll-ayo.

      I=TOP   anything   not know-POL

      'I don't know anything.'

b. *아무것도 부족해요.
   *Amwukesto   pwucokhay-yo.
   anything   lack-POL
   (Intended) 'Nothing is lacking.'

This contrasts with English, where even Latinate words with negative prefixes are syntactically and semantically negative, e.g. *unaware of any problem*.

Korean has two forms of syntactic negation: long-form negation appears postverbally and requires the dummy verb *ha-* 'do' to support tense and other verbal inflection, while short-form negation is preverbal with no *ha-* support, as in (4).

(4)   Syntactic negation
       a. Short-form: 아니/못 V   *an(i)/mos* V
       b. Long-form: V 지 않다/못하다 V-*ci anh-ta/mosha-ta*

Both negative particles are essentially proclitic-like, as nothing may intervene between them and the verb, although we follow convention here and represent them as independent words. Of the two negative particles, *an(i)* is nonmodal negation 'not', while *mos* expresses modal negation, usually translated as 'cannot'. Specialized forms for modal negation appear to be a Northeast Asian areal trait, as exemplified by Evenki *alba-* 'not be able' (Nedjalkov 1997: 97–98) and Nivkh *-jiki-* 'cannot' (Mattissen 2003). Both negative particles in Korean have a short-form and a long-form pattern. Nonmodal long-form negation surfaces in speech and writing in its contracted form as the negative verb *anh-*, although uncontracted *ani ha-* 'not do' is possible in both.

(5)   Nonmodal and modal syntactic negation
       a. 태호는 책을 읽는다.
          Thayho=nun   chayk=ul   ilk-nun-ta.
          Taeho=TOP   book=ACC   read-PRES-PLN
          'Taeho reads a book.'
       b. 태호는 책을 안 읽는다.
          Thayho=nun   chayk=ul   an   ilk-nun-ta.
          Taeho=TOP   book=ACC   NEG read-PRES-PLN
          'Taeho does not read a book.'
       c. 태호는 책을 읽지 않는다.
          Thayho=nun   chayk=ul   ilk-ci   anh-nun-ta.
          Taeho=TOP   book=ACC   read-SUSP   NEG-PRES-PLN
          'Taeho does not read a book.'

    d. 태호는 책을 못 읽는다.
       Thayho=nun chayk=ul mos ilk-nun-ta.
       Taeho=TOP   book=ACC cannot read-PRES-PLN
       'Taeho cannot read a book.'

    e. 태호는 책을 읽지 못한다.
       Thayho=nun chayk=ul ilk-ci mos ha-n-ta.
       Taeho=TOP   book=ACC read-SUSP cannot do-PRES-PLN
       'Taeho cannot read a book.'

There are a few restrictions on short-form negation. Adjectival predicates tend to disfavor short-form negation (6), although as we see in Chapter 9, there is regional variation with respect to this dispreference.

(6)   Short-form negation disfavored with adjectives

    a. *경치가 아주 안 아름답다.
       **Kyengchi=ka acwu an alumtap-ta.*
       scenery=NOM   really NEG pretty-PLN
       'The scenery is not really pretty.'

    b. *그 사람이 안 사랑스럽다.
       **Ku salam=i an salangsulep-ta.*
       that person=NOM NEG lovely-PLN
       'That person is not lovely.'

Another restriction on short-form negation applies to verbs with a prefixal element such as *hwi-kamta* 'entwined', *sel-ikta* 'half-cooked', and *ek-seyta* 'tough' (Chapter 5). Short-form negation is not allowed with these derived verbs, while long-form negation is possible.

(7)   Short-form negation restricted with prefixal verbs

    a. *나비는 실을 목에 안 휘감았다.
       **Napi=nun sil=ul mok=ey an hwikam-ass-ta.*
       Nabi=TOP   thread=ACC neck=LOC NEG reel-PAST-PLN
       'Nabi didn't wind thread around her neck.'

    b. 고구마가 설익었다.
       Kokwuma=ka selik-ess-ta.
       sweet potato=NOM half-cook-PAST-PLN
       'The sweet potato was half-cooked.'

    c. *고구마가 안 설익었다.
       **Kokwuma=ka an selik-ess-ta.*
       sweet potato=NOM NEG half-cook-PAST-PLN
       'The sweet potato was not half-cooked.'
       고구마가 설익지 않았다.

    d. *Kokwuma=ka selik-ci anh-ass-ta.*
       sweet potato=NOM half-cook-SUSP NEG-PAST-PLN
       'The sweet potato was not half-cooked.'

In contrast, V$_1$-*e/a* V$_2$ complexes such as *tul-e kayo* 'go in', from *tul-e* 'enter-INF' plus *ka-* 'go', allow both short-form and long-form negation (8a) and (8b). Syntactically derived forms such as passives or causatives also allow both short-form and long-form negation, as shown in (8c, d).

(8)   Short-form negation with V-V sequences and syntactically derived verbal forms

    a. 태민이 학교에 안 들어가요.
       Thaymin=i   hakkyo=ey an tuleka-yo.
       Taemin=NOM school=DIR NEG go in-POL
       'Taemin does not go into the school.'

    b. 태민이 학교에 들어가지 않아요.
       Thaymin=i   hakkyo=ey tuleka-ci anh-ayo.
       Taemin=NOM school=DIR go in-SUSP NEG-POL
       'Taemin does not go into the school.'

    c. 밥이 잘 안 먹혀요.
       Pap=i   cal   an   mek-hy-eyo.
       rice=NOM well NEG eat-PASS-POL
       'The rice is not eaten well.'

    d. 밥이 잘 먹히지 않아요.
       Pap=i   cal   mek-hi-ci   anh-ayo.
       rice=NOM well eat-PASS-SUSP NEG-POL
       'The rice is not eaten well (or often).'

In the verbal noun + light *ha-* 'do' pattern with short-form negation, it is generally preferred to place negation before *ha-* 'do', but younger speakers in casual speech may sometimes place the negative particle before the verbal noun.

(9)   Short-form negation with verbal nouns + light *ha-* 'do'

    a. %태민은 영어를 안 공부한다.
       Thaymin=un yenge=lul   an kongpwuha-n-ta.
       Taemin=TOP English=ACC NEG study-PRES-PLN
       'Taemin does not study English.'

    b. 태민은 영어를 공부 안 한다.
       Thaymin=un yenge=lul   kongpwu an ha-n-ta.
       Taemin=TOP English=ACC study   NEG do-PRES-PLN
       'Taemin does not study English.'

    c. %태민은 좋은 학생이 되려고 안 노력한다.
       Thaymin=un   cohun haksayng=i toy-lyeko   an
       Taemin=TOP   good student=NOM become-in order to NEG
       nolyekha-n-ta.
       effort-PRES-PLN
       'Taemin does not make an effort to be a good student.'

d. 태민은 좋은 학생이 되려고 노력 안 한다.

Thaymin=un cohun haksayng=i toy-lyeko nolyek an

Taemin=TOP good student=NOM become-in order to effort NEG

ha-n-ta.

do-PRES-PLN

'Taemin does not make an effort to be a good student.'

Syntactic long-form negation with *anh-* '(do) not' cannot be used with imperative and propositive mood. Instead, another negative auxiliary, *mal-* must be used in the long-form negation pattern in imperative or propositive sentences. Short-form negation is not acceptable in imperatives and propositives, as shown in (10a, b), nor is long-form negation with *anh-*, as shown in (10c, d); instead *mal-* must be used (10e, f).

(10)   a. *학교에 안 가라.

*Hakkyo=ey an ka-la.

school=DIR NEG go-IMP

'Don't go to school.'

b. *학교에 안 가자.

*Hakkyo=ey an ka-ca.

school=DIR NEG go-PROP

'Let's not go to school.'

c. *학교에 가지 않아라

*Hakkyo=ey ka-ci anh-ala.

school=DIR go-SUSP NEG-IMP

'Don't go to school.'

d. *학교에 가지 않자.

*Hakkyo=ey ka-ci anh-ca.

school=DIR go-SUSP NEG-PROP

'Let's not go to school.'

e. 학교에 가지 말아요.

Hakkyo=ey ka-ci mal-ayo.

school=DIR go-SUSP NEG-POL

'Don't go to school.'

f. 학교에 가지 말자.

Hakkyo=ey ka-ci mal-ca.

school=DIR go-SUSP NEG-PROP

'Let's not go to school.'

The issue of semantic scope with syntactic negation involves several distinct questions. First is the matter of association with focus. Both short-form and long-form negation allow negation to be associated with a constituent that is marked by intonational prominence. In (11a), intonational prominence on *Thaymin* generates a presupposition that someone didn't eat pizza, and that person is Taemin, while (11b) establishes a presupposition that Taemin ate something, and that thing is pizza. These readings are comparable to the focus readings on 'Taemin' in (11c) and 'pizza' in the pseudocleft constructions in (11d).

(11)   Association with focus marked by intonational prominence

    a. 태민이 피자를 안 먹었다.
       THAYMIN=I phica=lul an   mek-ess-ta.
       Taemin=NOM pizza=ACC NEG eat-PAST-PLN
       'TAEMIN did not eat pizza.'

    b. 태민이 피자를 먹지 않았다.
       Thaymin=i   PHICA=LUL mek-ci   anh-ass-ta.
       Taemin=NOM pizza=ACC   eat-SUSP NEG-PAST-PLN
       'Taemin did not eat PIZZA.'

    c. 피자를 먹은것은 태민이 아니다.
       Phica=lul mek-un-kes=un   Thaymin=i   ani-ta.
       pizza=ACC eat-PRENOM-NOMNL=TOP Taemin=NOM NEG-PLN
       'It is not Taemin who ate pizza.'

    d. 태민이 먹은것은 피자가 아니다.
       Thaymin=i   mek-un-kes=un   phica=ka   ani-ta.
       Taemin=TOP eat-PRENOM-NOMNL=TOP pizza=NOM NEG-PLN
       'It is not pizza that Taemin ate.'

The two types of negation show different scope interactions with quantifiers, as shown in (12). While short-form negation is generally held not to scope over a subject quantifier, as in (12a), long-form negation shows ambiguous scope, as in (12b).

(12)   Scope interaction of quantifiers and negation

    a. 모든 학생이 피자를 안 먹었다.
       Motun haksayng=i phica=lul an   mek-ess-ta.
       all students=NOM   pizza=ACC NEG eat-PAST-PLN
       'All students didn't eat pizza.' (all>not)

    b. 모든 학생이 피자를 먹지 않았다.
       Motun haksayng=i phica=lul mek-ci   anh-ass-ta.
       all students=NOM   pizza=ACC eat-SUSP eat-PAST-PLN
       'All students didn't eat pizza.' (all>not, not>all)

Addition of the topic marker *=un/=nun* produces a different information structural effect, one of contrast. Thus in (13a), the speaker asserts that Taemin did not eat the pizza, but the possibility is left open that he ate something else. The effect is comparable to English contrastive intonation with prominence on 'pizza' and negation. Example (13b) shows that attaching =*un*/ =*nun* to the suspective verb form makes the VP the target of contrast.

(13)   Contrastive =*un*/=*nun* with negation

    a. 태민이 피자는 안 먹었다.

       Thaymin=i   *phica=nun*   *an*   *mek-ess-ta.*

       Taemin=NOM   pizza=TOP   NEG   eat-PAST-PLN

       'Taemin DIDN'T eat PIZZA (maybe he ate something else).'

    b. 태민이 피자를 먹지는 않았다.

       Thaymin=i   *phica=lul*   *mek-ci=nun*   *anh-ass-ta.*

       Taemin=NOM   pizza=ACC   eat-SUSP=TOP   NEG-PAST-PLN

       'Taemin DIDN'T EAT THE PIZZA (maybe he did something else).'

Korean has a rich inventory of negative polarity items (NPIs). Four types of NPI are listed in (14): NP, adverb, prenominal, and exceptive.

(14)   Negative polarity item (NPI)

    a. NP

       아무도 *amwuto* no one   아무것도 *amwukesto* nothing

       하나도 *hanato* nothing

    b. Adverbs

       절대로 *celtaylo* absolutely   차마 *chama* to tolerate

       별로 *pyello* particularly   좀처럼 *comchelem* hardly

       여간 *yekan* normally   전혀 *cenhye* absolutely

       결코 *kyelkho* never   겨우 *kyewu* merely

    c. Prenominal

       아무 *amwu* no (o)ne   아무런 *amwulen* no/any

       별다른 *pyeltalun* not in particular

    d. Particle

       밖에 *pakkey* nothing but   커녕 *khenyeng* far from

We first discuss NPIs that require clausemate negation, that is, negation in the same minimal sentence that contains the NPI. The examples in (15) show NP, adverb, prenominal, and exceptive NPIs with clausemate negation.

(15)   NPIs licensed by clausemate negation

    a. 나는 아무것도 하지 않았다.

       Na=nun amwukesto ha-ci   *anh-ass-ta.*

       I=TOP   nothing   do-SUSP   NEG-PAST-PLN

       'I didn't do anything.'

    b. 이 일은 별로 힘들지 않다.

       I   *il=un*   *pyello*   *himtul-ci*   *anh-ta.*

       this thing=TOP particularly difficulty-SUSP NEG-PLN

       'This is not particularly hard to do.'

   c. 아무런 반응을 안 해요.
     Amwulen panung=ul   an   hay-yo.
     no   response=ACC NEG do-POL
     'There is no response.'

   d. 태민은 피자밖에 안 먹었다.
     Thaymin=un phica=pakkey   an   mek-ess-ta.
     Taemin=TOP pizza=other than NEG eat-PAST-PLN
     'Taemin ate nothing other than pizza.'

The examples in (16) show the same NPIs with negation in the immediately higher clause. These examples are completely unacceptable in Korean, in contrast with their English counterparts. While English allows NPIs to be licensed by negation in a higher clause, the Korean NPIs in (15–16) require clausemate negation.

(16)   NPIs not licensed by negation in the higher clause

   a. *나는 아무것도 한다고 말하지 않았다.
     *Na=nun amwukesto ha-n-ta-ko   malha-ci anh-ass-ta.
     I=TOP   nothing   do-PRES-PLN-COMP say-SUSP NEG-PAST-PLN
     (Intended) 'I didn't say that I would do anything.'

   b. *나는 이 일이 여간 힘들다고 말하지 않았다.
     *Na=nun i   il=i   yekan himtul-ta-ko   malha-ci
     I=TOP   this   thing=NOM a little difficult-PLN-COMP   say-SUSP
     anh-ass-ta.
     NEG-PAST-PLN
     'I didn't say that this will be a little difficult to do.' (Odd on NPI reading.)

   c. *나는 아무런 반응을 한다고 말 안 했어요.
     *Na=nun   amwulen panung=ul   ha-n-ta-ko   mal an
     I=TOP   any   response=ACC do-PRES-PLN-COMP say NEG
     hay-ss-eyo.
     do-PAST-POL
     (Intended) 'I didn't say there is any response.'

   d. *나는 태민이 피자밖에 먹는다고 말 안 했다.
     *Na=nun   Thaymin=i   phica=pakkey   mek-nun-ta-ko
     I=TOP   Taemin=NOM pizza=other than   eat-PRES-PLN-COMP
     mal   an   hay-ss-ta.
     say   NEG   do-PAST-PLN
     (Intended) 'I didn't say that Taemin eats anything other than pizza.'

The various positions for negation in Korean allow for the possibility of double negation. Double negation with *an(h)* 'not' combining short-form and long-form negation results in a strengthened affirmative with modal force, as in (17a). Double negation with the modal negative *mos* is not possible (17b, c).

(17)   Double negation

    a. 이번에는 네가 안 가지 않았다.

       I pen=ey=nun   ney=ka   an   ka-ci   anh-ass-ta.

       this time=LOC=TOP you=NOM NEG go-SUSP NEG-PAST-PLN

       'This time, you did not not go.'

    b. *이번에는 네가 못 가지 못했다.

       **I pen=ey=nun   ney=ka   mos   ka-ci   mos-hay-ss-ta.*

       this time=LOC=TOP you=NOM cannot go-SUSP cannot-do-PAST-PLN

    c. *이번에는 네가 못 가지 않았다.

       **I pen=ey=nun   ney=ka   mos   ka-ci   anh-ass-ta.*

       this time=LOC=TOP you=NOM cannot go-SUSP NEG-PAST-PLN

       *이번에는 네가 안 가지 못했다.

       **I pen=ey=nun   ney=ka   an   ka-ci   mos-hay-ss-ta.*

       this time=LOC=TOP you=NOM NEG   go-SUSP cannot-do-PAST-PLN

Combinations of double negation, one in a subordinate and one in a main clause, are possible as in (18a) and (18c). These combinations have the effect of strengthening their affirmative counterparts in (18b) and (18d).

(18)   Double negative = strengthened affirmative

    a. 이번에는 네가 가지 않으면 안된다.

       I pen=ey=nun   ney=ka   ka-ci   anh-umyen

       this time=LOC=TOP you=NOM go-SUSP   NEG-if

       an-toy-n-ta.

       NEG-become-PRES-PLN

       'This time, you must go (Lit. 'If you don't go, it won't do.').'

    b. 이번에는 네가 반드시 가야 한다.

       I pen=ey=nun   ney=ka   pantusi ka-ya-ha-n-ta.

       this time=LOC=TOP you=NOM always go-must-do-PRES-PLN

       'This time, you must go.'

    c. 나는 이 일은 하지 않을 수 없다.

       Na=nun i   il=ul   ha-ci   anh-ul swu-eps-ta.

       I=TOP   this thing=ACC do-SUSP NEG-must-NEG-PLN

       'I must do this thing (Lit. 'I cannot not do this thing.')

    d. 나는 반드시 이 일을 해야 한다.

       Na=nun pantusi i   il=ul   hay-ya-ha-n-ta.

       I=TOP   always this thing=ACC do-must-do-PRES-PLN

       'I must do this thing.'

8.2   Topic and Focus

The topic of a sentence is what is being talked about, and the focus (or comment) is what is being said about the topic. This is the classical, Praguean demarcation of information structure in a clause, but the actual strategy for marking topic and focus differs from language to language. Information structure may be marked by word order, intonation, specialized syntactic constructions, or morphological marking. Li and Thompson (1976), in an influential article, identified languages such as Mandarin as "topic-prominent" because of the absence of overt marking of subjecthood and the pervasiveness of patterns where the first NP in a sentence is the topic, rather than the subject. Li and Thompson identified languages like Korean and Japanese as subject and topic prominent, because of the presence of morphological marking for both subject and topic. Li and Thompson's full classification is given in (19).

(19)   Topic prominence versus subject prominence (Li and Thompson 1976)

Topic	+	−
Subject		
+	Japanese, Korean	English
−	Chinese	Tagalog, Ilokano

Languages like Korean have also been characterized as "discourse prominent," because focus marking also plays a prominent role. In this section we look at the interaction of information structural roles such as topic and focus, and grammatical relations such as subject.

In English, the subject is normally the same as the topic, but spoken English, for most speakers, also allows non-subject topics, as in (20b).

(20)   a Nayoung ate the pizza.
        b. The pizza, Nayoung ate.

These sentences have different topics. The first is about Nayoung, while the second is about the pizza. When we look more closely at the non-subject topic in (20b) we observe that its information structural status may differ, depending on factors like intonation and discourse context. For example, high pitch on the stressed syllable of *pizza* followed by a rapid fall may indicate contrast: the speaker commits to the proposition that Nayoung ate pizza but not to the proposition that Nayoung ate anything else. This may result in the implicature that Nayoung did NOT eat other items in the discourse context. Alternatively, (20b) may be used as an answer to the question 'What happened to the pizza?', although in this context, some English speakers might be more comfortable with the non-subject left-dislocation sentence 'Oh, the pizza, Nayoung ate it'. As we will see, topic marking in Korean has functions similar to these.

Focus is an information-structured category that determines which part of the sentence contributes new, nonpredictable information. Focus can be marked either prosodically, syntactically, or both, depending on the language.

In English (21), focus is marked phonetically by intonational prominence on *pizza* in (21a) and (21c), and syntactically by the *it*-cleft construction in (21b).

(21)   a. Nayoung only ate the PIZZA.
         b. It's the pizza that Nayoung ate.
         c. Nayoung ate the PIZZA.

The sentences in (21) exemplify two different notions of focus that are sometimes confused. Sentence (21a) is an example of association with focus, similar to what we briefly discussed in relation to negation in the Section 8.1. In this case the assignment of prosodic focus affects what semanticists call the truth conditional meaning of the sentence. For example, if (21a) is uttered in a context where Nayoung also ate the onion rings, the sentence is false. When we insert an element that associates with focus like *only* in the sentence, we set up a set of alternative things that Nayoung might have eaten (*eat the onion rings, eat the french fries, eat the pizza*, etc.). Prosodic prominence on *pizza* tells us that *eat the pizza* is the right choice and that Nayoung did NOT eat any of the other things. Therefore (21a) is not true if Nayoung happened to also eat the onion rings.

Example (21c) is a little different. We can utter (21c) in answer to the question 'What, if anything, did Nayoung eat?' Example (21c) answers this question, but it does not entail that Nayoung didn't eat anything else (although it may not be a very helpful answer if the speaker happens to know that Nayoung ate the onion rings too).

These two notions of focus can be distinguished as semantic focus and discourse focus. Semantic focus bears on the truth value of the sentence (what the sentence says about the true state of affairs in the world), while discourse focus has to do with what kind of information is new (or nonpredictable) and old (or predictable) in the discourse context. Now let's contrast all three sentences in (22) again:

(22)   a. Nayoung only ate the PIZZA. #She ate the onion rings too.
         b. It's the pizza that Nayoung ate. #She ate the onion rings too.
         c. Nayoung ate the PIZZA. She ate the onion rings too.

Most speakers of English would find the two sentences in (22a) to be a contradiction (this is indicated by the # mark before the second sentence). This seems to be true of the *it*-cleft sentence in (22b) too: most speakers find the second sentence to contradict something asserted by the first. But the sense of contradiction is not so strong in (22c), which involves discourse, not semantic focus.

We need to make one more distinction before going on to describe focus and topic in Korean. Intuitively, focus involves strengthening the assertion, by adding information, such as the entailment in (22a) or (22b) that not only did

Nayoung eat the pizza, she didn't eat anything else. This notion of "strengthening" must be distinguished from the kind of strengthening introduced by *really* or *sure* in a sentence like (23):

(23)   Nayoung really/sure ate the pizza.

Intensifiers such as *really* and *sure* also strengthen the assertion, but not in the same way as semantic or discourse focus do. Instead they may convey the speaker's surprise, pleasure, admiration, or displeasure at the event.

We are now ready to describe the formations and major characteristics of topic/focus structure in Korean. Like English, Korean can mark discourse focus with intonational prominence, as shown in (24). Here we mark intonational prominence with boldface.

(24)   Korean Focus (Prosodic)
        a. 나영은 먼 나라로 여행을 해요.
           Nayeng=un   **men~nala=lo**   *yehayng=ul hay-yo.*
           Nayoung=TOP   far~country=DIR travel=ACC   do-POL
           'Nayoung travels **to a far country**.'
        b. 나영은 피자를 먹는다.
           Nayeng=un   **phica=lul**   *mek-nun-ta.*
           Nayoung=TOP   pizza=ACC   eat-PRES-PLN
           'Nayoung eats **pizza**.'

Korean also uses both prosodic and lexical devices as intensifiers. For example, intensification of *men* 'far' in (24a) can be marked by lengthening the nuclear vowel. Intensification in (25b) is marked by the speaker-oriented adverb *celtaylo* 'absolutely', and this adjective may be further intensified by intonational prominence.

(25)   Intensification
        a. 나영은 먼:나라로 여행을 해요.
           Nayeng=un   *me:n nala=lo*   *yehayng=ul hay-yo.*
           Nayoung=TOP   far country=DIR travel=ACC   do-POL
           'Nayoung travels to a faaar-off country.'
        b. 나는 이 일을 절대로 안 해요.
           Na=nun   i   il=ul   *CELTAYLO an   hay-yo.*
           I=TOP   this thing=ACC   absolutely NEG do-POL
           'I absolutely do not do this.'

As the examples we have seen so far in English and Korean suggest, intensification is crosslinguistically associated with quantity: greater prosodic prominence (length, amplitude, or change in pitch) and greater lexical quantity. Thus in Korean another device for intensification is reduplication. The Korean mimetic stratum provides rich resources for reduplication that can be classified into the four major patterns in (26). Mimetic morphemes are in general uninflected. They may occur either as adverbs, as in (26a, b), or as clausal predicates in combination with the light verb *ha-* 'do'. The adverbial pattern in general requires reduplication, while reduplication in the light *ha-* pattern produces intensification. Examples such as (26a) involve quasi-mimetic uninflected morphemes: *cip* 'house' and *kos* 'place' are independent nouns, but in their reduplicated form they have a distinct meaning. Example (26a) exemplifies total reduplication, (26b) and (26c) two different forms of partial reduplication, and (26d) affixal reduplication, where only a difference in affix distinguishes the reduplicants. In (26d) the affixes are -디 *-ti* and -나 *-na*, suffixed after the first instance of the reduplicated adjective stem.

(26)   Korean reduplication

    a. Total
        집집   *cipcip*   everywhere/every household
        곳곳   *koskos*   everywhere
        강남에는 곳곳에 식당이 있다.
        Kangnam=ey=nun koskos=ey   siktang=i   iss-ta.
        Kangnam=LOC=TOP everywhere=LOC restaurant=NOM be-PLN
        'There are restaurants everywhere in Kangnam.'

    b. Partial (1)
        아사삭   *asasak*   sound of collapsing
        쿵작작   *khungcakcak*   sound of dumping
        건물이 아사삭 부서진다.
        Kenmwul=i   asasak   pwuse-ci-n-ta.
        building=NOM   sound of collapsing collapse-PASS-PRES-PLN
        'A building is collapsed.'

    c. Partial (2)
        울긋불긋   *wulkuspwulkus*   colorful
        얼룩덜룩   *ellwuktellwuk*   spotted
        가을에는 단풍이 울긋불긋하다.
        Kaul=ey=nun   tanphwung=i wulkuspwulkus-ha-ta.
        autumn=at=TOP maple=NOM   colorful-do-PLN
        'Maples are colorful in autumn.'

    d. Affixal
        차디차다   *chatichata*   very cold
        크나크다   *khunakhuta*   very big
        겨울에는 날씨가 차디차다.
        Kyewul=ey=nun nalssi=ka   chaticha-ta.
        winter=at=TOP   weather=NOM very cold-PLN
        'Winter is very cold.'

Korean also has a rich repertoire of morphological intensifiers involving prefixation, compounding, and sound symbolism. The intensifying prefixes in (27a) attach to unaccusative and stative predicates. Like the verb prefixes discussed in Chapter 5, some intensifying prefixes come from obsolete verbs; for example, *chi-* 'ascending' in (27a) comes from an obsolete verb meaning 'go up'. Compounding with the intensifying verbs *chi-* (probably from *chi-* 'to hit') and *noh-* 'to put down' derives the meaning 'to drop' (27b). The color adjectives *nolah-* 'to be yellow' or *kkamkkamha-* 'to be dark' are intensified, by raising the stem vowels in the first case and replacing the reinforced initial consonants with aspirates in the second (27c).

(27) Morphological (derivational) intensification

    a. Prefix

        짓밟다   *cispalpta*   step on
        시꺼멓다 *sikkemehta* pitch black
        치솟다   *chisosta*   gush out
        새가 하늘로 치솟는다.
        Say=ka   *hanul=lo*   *chisos-nun-ta.*
        bird=NOM sky=DIR   go up-PRES-PLN
        'Birds go up to the sky.'

    b. Suffix

        놓치다   *nohchita*   drop
        깨뜨리다 *kkayttulita* break
        나는 손에서 병을 놓쳤다.
        Na=nun   *son=eyse*   *pyeng=ul*   *nohchye-ss-ta.*
        I=TOP   hand=from bottle=ACC drop-PAST-PLN
        'I dropped the bottle from my hand.'

    c. Sound change

        노랗다   *nolahta*   → 누렇다 *nwulehta*   'yellow'
        깜깜하다 *kkamkkamhata* → 캄캄하다 *khamkhamhata* 'dark'
        하늘이 저녁에는 누렇다.
        Hanul=i   *cenyek=ey=nun nwuleh-ta.*
        sky=NOM   evening=at=TOP yellow-PLN
        'The sky is very yellow in the evening.'

Returning to the domain of focus proper, Korean also makes use of a variety of clause-final conjunctive endings to mark focus, with or without prosodic emphasis to mark a subclausal focused constituent. The conjunctive suffixes *-nikka* 'because', *-myense* 'while', and *-ko* '(saying) that' can be used in this function. Note that in all of the examples in (28), the verb occurs in its full declarative form with the plain declarative suffix *-ta*, the form that would be used in a quotation. These are examples of what Evans (2007) calls "insubordination," where a subordinate clause type surfaces as a matrix form with a specific function distinct from its subordinate interpretation. Prosodic prominence marks the focused constituent, in (28) the verb.

(28)   Korean conjunctive focus

    a. 철수가 학교에 갔다-니까.

      Chelswu=ka   *hakkyo=ey* **ka-ss-ta**-*nikka.*

      Chelswu=NOM   school=DIR go-PAST-PLN-SO

      'Because (I say) Chelswu **went** to school.'

    b. 철수가 학교에 갔다-면서.

      Chelswu=ka   *hakkyo=ey* **ka-ss-ta**-*myense.*

      Chelswu=NOM   school=DIR go-PAST-PLN-and so

      'While (I say) Chelswu **went** to school.'

    c. 철수가 학교에 갔다-고.

      Chelswu=ka   *hakkyo=ey* **ka-ss-ta**-*ko.*

      Chelswu=NOM   school=DIR go-PAST-PLN-and

      '(I say) Chelswu **went** to school.'

Because conjunctive suffixes in this function select the plain style declarative, they are ill-formed in combination with other sentence enders such as polite -*e/ayo* (29a), deferential -*supnita* (29b), or -*ney* (29c).

(29)   a. *나영이 학교에 갔어요-니까.

      **Nayeng=i*   *hakkyo=ey* *ka-ss-eyo-nikka.*

      Nayoung=NOM   school=DIR go-PAST-POL-SO

      'Nayoung went to school.'

    b. *나영이 학교에 갔습니다-면서.

      **Nayeng=i*   *hakkyo=ey* *ka-ss-supnita-myense.*

      Nayoung=NOM   school=DIR go-PAST-DEF-and so

      'Nayoung went to school.'

    c. *나영이 학교에 가네-고.

      **Nayeng=i*   *hakkyo=ey* *ka-ney-ko.*

      Nayoung=NOM   school=DIR go-*NEY*-and

      'Nayoung went to school.'

Finally, Korean has the pseudocleft construction, exemplified in (30). Korean pseudoclefts represent the presupposition in a clause headed by the bound noun or complementizer *kes* 'that, one' as in (30a), or in a relative clause headed by a noun such as *salam* 'person' (30b). With *kes*-headed presuppositions multiple foci are possible, as in (30c).

(30)   Korean pseudoclefts

    a. 나영이 어제 강남에서 먹은 것은 피자다.

      Nayeng=i   *ecey*   *Kangnam=eyse mek-un*   *kes=un*

      Nayoung=NOM yesterday Kangnam=in   eat-ADN   one=TOP

      phica=ta.

      pizza=be-PLN

      'What Nayoung ate in Kangnam yesterday is pizza.'

b. 피자를 먹은 사람은 나영이다.

Phica=lul mek-un   salam=un   Nayeng=i-ta.
pizza=ACC eat-ADN   person=TOP Nayoung=be-PLN
'The person who ate pizza is Nayoung.'

c. 나영이 피자를 먹은 것은   어제 강남에서이다.

Nayeng=i   phica=lul mek-un   kes=un   ecey
Nayoung=NOM pizza=ACC eat-ADN   one=TOP yesterday
Kangnam=in=be-PLN
Kangnam=eyse=i-ta.
'Where/when Nayoung ate pizza is yesterday in Kangnam.'

We have already seen several differences between the topic marker =un/
nun and the nominative or subject marker =i/ka. As we saw in Chapter 5,
=un/nun patterns as a delimiter, while we saw in Chapter 6 that =i/ka can
mark broad or narrow focus. Some of the commonly observed syntactic
and semantic differences between =un/nun and =i/ka are summarized
in (31).

(31)   Topic versus subject/focus

	=un/nun	= i/ka
Basic function	Topic	Subject/focus
Discourse status	Predictable	Unpredictable
Place allowed	Argument/Adjunct	Argument (subject)
Pragmatics	Contrast	Uniqueness
NP type	Generic	Specific
Embedded	No	Yes
Subset	Yes	No

Let us try to make these contrasting properties a bit more precise. A challenge
for any nonnative speaker learning Korean is that Korean must choose between
=un/nun and =i/ka in contexts where languages like English simply use
unmarked subjects. This is part of what Li and Thompson (1976) were getting
at when they described languages like Korean as "topic-prominent." This and
the fact that nominative can have a focus marking function has led other
researchers to label Korean a "discourse-configurational" language (Kiss
1995). At the same time, the properties of topic marking and nominative
marking for focus in Korean are not exactly the same as in languages which
share these two types of marking.

    First, consider discourse status. In (32), the nominative-marked subject of
the first sentence, *Taemin*, is not the topic of the current discourse, although as
a proper name, his identity is likely to be known to the hearer. *Nayoung* might
be the current discourse topic, and thus old information, or else the object of
contrast with *Taemin*.

(32)   태민이 학교에 갔다. 그리고 나영은 병원에 갔다.
       Thaymin=i   hakkyo=ey   ka-ss-ta.
       Taemin=NOM   school=DIR   go-PAST-PLN
       Kuliko   Nayeng=un   pyengwen=ey   ka-ss-ta.
       And   Nayoung=TOP   hospital=DIR   go-PAST-PLN
       'Taemin went to school. And Nayoung went to the hospital.'

It is not surprising that topics are predictable from preceding discourse, but Lee and Shimojo (2016) make this notion much more precise by contrasting topic and subject/focus marking in Korean and Japanese, another language that has overt topic marking focus readings associated with nominative subjects (33).

(33)   Korean and Japanese topic marking (adapted from Lee and Shimojo 2016, example [2])
       a. *Hwacangsil=i/*=un   eti=ey   iss-eyo?*   Korean
          restroom=NOM/*=TOP   where=LOC   exist-POL
          'Where is the restroom?'
       b. *Toire=wa/*=ga   doko=ni   arimasu ka?*   Japanese
          restroom=NOM/*=TOP   where=LOC   exist-POL
          'Where is the restroom?'

In public places such as restaurants and office buildings, it is predictable that there is a restroom, even though in most discourse contexts where one is asking the whereabouts of the restroom, the restroom is probably being mentioned for the first time. But Korean and Japanese treat this situation differently. Korean requires that an =*un/nun*-marked topic be mentioned in what Lee and Shimojo call the "current episode" of a discourse. Even if an entity has been mentioned in prior discourse, it is not enough to ensure that it will be marked with =*un/nun*, if, for example, another discourse topic has intervened. In Japanese, in contrast, it is enough for a speaker to infer the existence or relevance of an entity to mark it as topic. The result of this difference is that Japanese topic marking occurs with higher frequency than Korean topic marking with =*un/nun*, as Lee and Shimojo show.

   Another difference between topic marking =*un/nun* and nominative =*i/ka* is that the former can appear in a wider range of positions and mark a wider range of constituents than the latter. While subjects can be marked as topics or nominative (34a), objects of transitive verbs cannot be marked nominative regardless of where they occur (34b, c). Despite the existence of the multiple nominative constructions we saw in Chapter 6, adjuncts in general allow topic, but not nominative marking (34c, d).

(34)   Argument and adjunct topic versus nominative marking
       a. 태민은/이 강남에서 피자를 매일 먹는다.
          Thaymin=un/=i   Kangnam=eyse   phica=lul   mayil   mek-nun-ta.
          Taemin=TOP/=NOM   Kangnam=LOC   pizza=ACC   every day   eat-PRES-PLN
          'Taemin eats pizza in Kangnam every day.'

b. 피자는/*이 태민이 강남에서는 매일 먹는다.
   *Phica=nun/*i   Thaymin=i   Kangnam=eyse=nun   mayil*
   pizza=TOP/*NOM   Taemin=NOM   Kangnam=LOC=TOP   every day
   mek-nun-ta.
   eat-PRES-PLN
   'Taemin eats pizza in Kangnam every day.'

c. 태민이 강남에서 피자는/*이 매일 먹는다.
   Thaymin=i   Kangnam=eyse   phica=nun/=i   mayil*
   Taemin=NOM   Kangnam=LOC   pizza=TOP/*=NOM   every day
   mek-nun-ta.
   eat-PRES-PLN
   'Taemin eats pizza in Kangnam every day.'

d. 강남에서는/*가 태민이 피자를 매일 먹는다.
   Kangnam=eyse=nun/=ka   Thaymin=i   phica=lul   mayil*
   Kangnam=LOC=TOP/*=NOM   Taemin=NOM   pizza=ACC   every
   mek-nun-ta.
   day eat-PRES-PLN
   'In Kangnam, Taemin eats pizza every day.'

e. 태민이 강남에서는/*가 피자를 매일 먹는다.
   Thaymin=i   Kangnam=eyse=nun/=ka   phica=lul   mayil*
   Taemin=NOM   Kangnam=LOC=TOP/*=NOM   pizza=ACC   every
   mek-nun-ta.
   day eat-PRES-PLN
   'Taemin eats pizza in Kangnam every day.'

Example (35) contrasts with example (16c) in Chapter 6, repeated in a modified form below with the locative particle retained in the "case stacking" pattern:

(35)　　a. 서울에는 사람이 많다.
   Sewul=ey=nun   salam=i   manh-ta.
   Seoul=LOC=TOP   people=NOM   many-PLN
   'In Seoul, there are a lot of people.'

　　　b. 서울에가 사람이 많다.
   Sewul=ey=ka   salam=i   manh-ta.
   Seoul=LOC=NOM   people=NOM   many-PLN
   'It is Seoul that has a lot of people.'

The static locative expression 서울에 *Sewul=ey* 'in Seoul' may be followed by either the topic or nominative marker, although the meanings are different: (35a) marks (perhaps contrastive) topic, while (35b) marks focus. The contrast between (35b) and (34d, e) shows that nominative marking of locative expressions is generally allowed only with unaccusative or stative predicates, while topic marking has no such restriction.

Non-fronted topic-marked expressions generally receive, and fronted topics may receive, a contrastive interpretation. The contrastive interpretation associated with topic marking is distinct from the uniqueness interpretation associated with narrow-focus nominative marking. In response to A's question 'What do the people in this room do for a living?', B's reply (36Ba) with topic marking *=un/nun* contrasts Taemin with many people who may or may not be students. The reply (36Bb) with nominative marking imposes narrow focus, asserting that Taemin, and no one else, is the unique student.

(36)   Contrast with topic marking *=un/nun* versus uniqueness with nominative *=i/ka*

A: 이 방에 있는 사람들이 뭐 하는 사람들인지 아니?
   I pang=ey   iss-nun   salam-tul=i   mwe   ha-nun
   This room=LOC be-ADN person-PL=NOM what do-ADN
   salam-tul=in-ci   a-ni?
   person-PL=be-SUSP know-Q
   'Do you know what the people in this room do (for a living)?'

B: a. 많은 사람들이 있는데 태민은 학생이다.
   Manhun salam-tul=i   iss-nuntey Thaymin=un haksayng=i-ta.
   many person-PL=NOM be-but Taemin=TOP student=be-PLN
   'There are many people; I know Taemin is a student (but I have no idea about the others).'

   b. 많은 사람들이 있는데 태민이 학생이다.
   Manhun salam-tul=i   iss-nuntey Thaymin=i   haksayng=i-ta.
   many person-PL=NOM be-so Taemin=NOM student=be-PLN
   'There are lots of people, but it's Taemin who is a student.'

Generic NPs are marked with topic marking *=un/nun*, as in (37a), unless a narrow focus reading is intended. Example (37b) is odd because the uniqueness reading associated with narrow focus nominative *=i/ka* entails that only humans are animals.

(37)   Topic marking with generic NPs

a. 사람은 동물이다.
   Salam=un   tongmwul=i-ta.
   human=TOP animal=be-PLN
   'Humans are animals.'

b. #사람이 동물이다.
   #Salam=i   tongmwul=i-ta.
   human=NOM animal=be-PLN
   'It is humans that are animals.'

In embedded clauses, topic marking *=un/nun* is usually possible only on a contrastive reading. The narrow focus reading of nominative *=i/=ka* is also usually neutralized in these contexts.

(38) Topic marking in embedded clauses
나는 나영?은/이 쓴 책을 읽는다.

Na=nun   Nayeng?=un/=i   ssu-n   chayk=ul   ilk-nun-ta.
I=TOP   Nayoung?=TOP/=NOM   write-ADN   book=ACC   read-PRES-PLN
With *Nayeng=un*: 'I read the books that NAYOUNG writes (but not
necessarily others).'
With *Nayeng=i*: 'I read the books that Nayoung writes.'

Both nominative and topic marking are possible with the major subject in the
multiple-subject constructions we saw in Chapter 6, although, out of context,
speakers tend to find topic marking more natural, since the nominative-marked
subject may require a narrow-focus interpretation.

(39) Multiple subject constructions with topic and nominative marking
      a. 서울은 거리가 멋있다.
         Sewul=un   keli=ka   mes-iss-ta.
         Seoul=TOP   street=NOM pretty-be-PLN
         'As for Seoul, the streets are pretty.'

      b. 서울이 거리가 멋있다.
         Sewul=i   keli=ka   mes-iss-ta.
         Seoul=NOM   street=NOM   pretty-be-PLN
         'In Seoul the streets are pretty' (broad focus) OR
         'It is Seoul where the streets are pretty.'

There is, however, a class of "hanging topic" sentences where only topic, not
nominative, marking is possible.

(40)   범인은/*이 태민이 수상하다.
        Pemin=un/=i   Thaymin=i   swusangha-ta.*
        perpetrator=TOP/*=NOM Taemin=NOM suspicious-PLN
        'As for the perpetrator, Taemin is suspicious.'

Pemin 'perpetrator' in (40) is a "pure aboutness" topic, in that it introduces the
topic of the ensuing discourse, without being associated with an argument
position in the clause. This is impossible with nominative =*i*/=*ka*, even on
a narrow-focus reading.

8.3   TAM (Tense–Aspect–Mood)

Tense–Aspect–Mood (TAM) is the grammatical system in a language that
describes the expression of tense (location in time), aspect (spaciotemporal
flow in time), and mood (sentence type) or modality (speaker's psychological
attitude to the proposition). The three categories of TAM are often treated
together because (among other reasons) it is not always obvious that a given
form is strictly expressing only one of them.

8.3.1   Tense

Tense can be understood in terms of the relationship between utterance time and event time. In the case of present tense, utterance time is the same as the time of the occurrence of the event. With past tense, event time precedes utterance time, while with future tense, utterance time precedes event time. Tense can be expressed lexically, morphologically, or syntactically. Time adverbs such as *today, yesterday*, or *tomorrow* express tense lexically on their own.

(41)   Tense (Lexical)
   a. 나영은 오늘 강남에 간다.
      Nayeng=un   onul   Kangnam=ey   ka-n-ta.
      Nayoung=TOP today Kangnam=DIR go-PRES-PLN
      'Nayoung goes to Kangnam today.'

   b. 나영은 어제 강남에 갔다.
      Nayeng=un   ecey   Kangnam=ey   ka-ss-ta.
      Nayoung=TOP yesterday Kangnam=DIR go-PAST-PLN
      'Nayoung went to Kangnam yesterday.'

   c. 나영은 내일 강남에 갈 것이다.
      Nayeng=un   nayil   Kangnam=ey   ka-l kesi-ta.
      Nayoung=TOP tomorrow Kangnam=DIR go-FUT-PLN
      'Nayoung will go to Kangnam tomorrow.'

As the examples in (41) show, tense expressed lexically by temporal adverbs co-occurs with the appropriate tense expressed morphologically by verbal suffixes. Korean distinguishes main clause-final verbal suffixes and adnominal tense suffixes, shown in the paradigms in (42–43).

(42)   Adnominal tense suffixes
   a. Present 는 *-nun*
   b. Past ㄴ/은/던 *-n/-un-/ten*
   c. Future 르/을 *-l/-ul*

(43)   Main clause-final tense suffixes
   a. Present ㄴ/는 *-n/-nun*
   b. Past ㅆ/었/더 *-ss/-ess/-te*
   c. Future 겠/을 것이다 *-keyss/-(u)l kesita*

Examples of the adnominal tense suffixes are given in (44). As we saw in Chapter 2, these suffixes originally had a nominalizing function, but since Late Middle Korean they have been restricted to adnominal contexts such as NP modification in relative clauses like (44), or preceding bound nouns like *kes* 'one, that' in (45a, b) or *swu* 'possibility/ability' in (45c).

(44)   Adnominal tense preceding lexical nouns
         a. 나영이 먹는 사과는 크다.
            Nayeng=i   mek-nun   sakwa=nun   khu-ta.
            Nayoung=NOM eat-PRESADN apple=TOP   big-PLN
            'The apple that Nayoung eats is big.'
         b. 나영이 먹은 사과는 크다.
            Nayeng=i   mek-un   sakwa=nun   khu-ta.
            Nayoung=NOM eat-PSTADN apple=TOP   big-PLN
            'The apple that Nayoung ate is big.'
         c. 나영이 먹던 사과는 크다.
            Nayeng=i   mek-te-n   sakwa=nun   khu-ta.
            Nayoung=NOM eat-RET-PSTADN apple=TOP   big-PLN
            'The apple that Nayoung ate is big.'
         d. 나영이 먹을 사과는 크다.
            Nayeng=i   mek-ul   sakwa=nun   khu-ta.
            Nayoung=NOM eat-FUTADN apple=TOP   big-PLN
            'The apple that Nayoung will eat is big.'

Example (44c) involves two suffixes on the adnominal predicate *mek-te-n*
'eat-RET-PSTADN'. Retrospective *-te-* precedes adnominal tense affixes, so in
terms of its position, it is an aspectual suffix. However in terms of its
function, it is an evidential: it flags the way the speaker obtained the
information expressed in the sentence. Retrospective *-te-* in (44c) implies
that the speaker experienced Nayoung eating the apple through direct per-
ception, for example by being present at the scene. Retrospective is usually
incompatible with first-person subjects (since the experience must be external to the speaker), and it imparts a sense of "vividness" that is absent with
the plain past as in (44d).

(45)   Adnominal tense preceding bound nouns
         a. 나영이 사과를 먹은 것이 있다.
            Nayeng=i   sakwa=lul mek-un   kes=i   iss-ta.
            Nayoung=NOM apple=ACC eat-PSTADN   BNDN=NOM   exist-PLN
            'Nayoung has eaten an apple (has had the experience of eating an apple).'
         b. 나영이 사과를 먹는 것이 있다.
            Nayeng=i   sakwa=lul mek-nun   kes=i   iss-ta.
            Nayoung=NOM apple=ACC eat-PRESADN BNDN=NOM   exist-PLN
            'Nayoung eats apples (There are times when Nayoung eats apples).'
         c. 나영이 사과를 먹을/*는/*은 수 있다.
            Nayeng=i   sakwa=lul   mek-ul/-nun/*-un*
            Nayoung=NOM apple=ACC   eat-FUTADN/*-PRESADN/*-PSTADN
            swu   iss-ta.
            possibility   exist-PLN
            'Nayoung can eat apples (It is possible for Nayoung to eat apples).'

Experiential V-*(n)un kes=i iss-ta* allows either past, if Nayoung has had the experience of eating an apple in the past, as in (45a), or present, if there are multiple times when Nayoung eats apples. The abilitative bound noun *swu* must be preceded by the future adnominal, since potential events are events that have not yet occurred.

The matrix or main clause tense suffixes in Korean are all diachronically secondary. Present tense *-(nu)n* (46a) derives from the Middle Korean processive *-nu/o-* plus adnominal *-n-*. In other words, present tense *-(nu)n* was originally an adnominal form, and that is why it is identical to the present tense adnominal. Unlike the adnominal, however, matrix *-(nu)n* contracts to *-n-* after vowel stems (46b). Past *-e/ass-* derives historically from infinitive *-e/a-* plus *-iss-* 'exist, be', so it shows the same harmonic vowel alternations as the infinitive, but it contracts to *-ss-* after a vowel stem (46c). We discuss futures such as V-*(u)l kes=i-* in Section 8.3.3 as part of the discussion of modality.

(46)   Matrix tense suffixes

a. 나영이 사과를 먹는다.
   Nayeng=i   sakwa=lul mek-nun-ta.
   Nayoung=NOM   apple=ACC eat-PRES-PLN
   'Nayoung eats an apple.'

b. 나영이 강남에 간다.
   Nayeng=i   Kangnam=ey ka-n-ta.
   Nayoung=NOM   Kangnam=DIR go-PRES-PLN
   'Nayoung goes to Kangnam.'

c. 나영이 어제 강남에 갔다.
   Nayeng=i   ecey   Kangnam=ey ka-ss-ta.
   Nayoung=NOM   yesterday   Kangnam=DIR go-PAST-PLN
   'Nayoung went to Kangnam yesterday.'

d. 나영이 사과를 먹었다.
   Nayeng=i   sakwa=lul mek-ess-ta.
   Nayoung=NOM   apple=ACC eat-PAST-PLN
   'Nayoung ate an apple.'

Propositions which are eternally or analytically true are expressed by the present tense, as in (47).

(47)   a. 지구가 돈다.
            Cikwu=ka   to-n-ta.
            Earth=NOM   rotate-PRES-PLN
            'The Earth rotates.'

         b. 고래는 포유동물이다.
            Kolay=nun   phoyutongmwul=i-ta.
            whale=TOP   mammal=be-PLN
            'The whale is a mammal.'

8.3.2   Aspect

Aspect expresses the internal temporal properties of an action or state, for example whether it is ongoing or completed. Korean marks two aspects, progressive and perfective. To this may be added retrospective -te-, since it occurs before tense, although semantically -te-, as an evidential, has more in common with modals. As in many languages, morphological aspect is expressed closer to the verb stem than tense. The morphological progressive is realized by gerundive -ko plus iss- 'exist' (48a). A periphrastic progressive can be constructed by V-nun cwung i- 'be in the middle of' (48b).

(48)   Progressive
    a. 태민은 지금 피자를 먹고 있다.
      Thaymin=un cikum phica=lul mek-ko iss-ta.
      Taemin=TOP now pizza=ACC eat-GER be-PLN
      'Taemin is now eating pizza.'

    b. 태민은 지금 피자를 먹는 중이다.
      Thaymin=un cikum phica=lul mek-nun cwung=i-ta.
      Taemin=TOP now pizza=ACC eat-PRESADN middle=be-PLN
      'Taemin is now in the middle of eating pizza.'

Perfective aspect characterizes events that are seen as a complete whole. Such events are usually seen as complete at speech time, but future perfectives are also possible, where an event is characterized as complete at a future time. The basic auxiliary perfect is formed by infinitive -e/a plus iss- 'exist, be'. In addition there is an argument that past -e/ass- can function as a perfective in doubled -e/ass-e/ass- examples such as (49). In this pattern the first -e/ass- can be analyzed as perfective, and the second as past.

(49)   태민은 어제 강남에서 피자를 먹었었다.
      Thaymin=un ecey Kangnam=eyse phica=lul mek-ess-ess-ta.
      Taemin=TOP yesterday Kangnam=LOC pizza=ACC eat-PERF-PAST-PLN
      'Taemin had eaten pizza in Kangnam yesterday.'

The examples in (50) illustrate the difference between the perfective in -e/a iss- and the progressive in -ko iss-. The perfective (50a) views the event of sitting in the chair as a whole; there is no change of state. The progressive (50b) highlights an ongoing activity.

(50)   a. 태민은 의자에 앉아 있다.
      Thaymin=un uyca=ey anc-a iss-ta.
      Taemin=TOP chair=LOC sit-INF be-PLN
      'Taemin is seated in the chair.'

b. 태민은 의자에 앉고 있다.

Thaymin=un   uyca=ey   anc-ko iss-ta.
Taemin=TOP   chair=LOC   sit-GER be-PLN
'Taemin is (in the process of) sitting down in the chair.'

As we saw in Chapter 7, perfective *-e/a iss-* exists only for intransitives, largely unaccusatives, so **mek-e iss-* 'eat-INF be' and **twi-e iss* 'run-INF be' are ill-formed. Transitives that express a salient result state allow a resultative reading for *-ko iss-*, so that verbs like *ip-* 'wear' in (50a) are ambiguous. Previous researchers have related the resultative interpretation to the "reflexive" nature of verbs such as *ip-* 'wear', but Park (2014) points out that the ambiguity occurs more generally with verbs that allow both accomplishment (the progressive interpretation) and achievement readings (the resultative interpretation), as with nonreflexive *yel-* 'open' (transitive) in (51b).

(51)   a. 태민이 스웨터를 입고 있다.

Thaymin=i   suweythe=lul ip-ko   iss-ta.
Taemin=NOM sweater=ACC   wear-GER be-PLN
'Taemin is wearing a sweater.'

b. 태민이 가게의 문을 열고 있다. (Adapted from Park 2014)

Thaymin=i   kakey=uy   mwun=ul yel-ko   iss-ta.
Taemin=NOM   store=GEN   door=ACC open-GER be-PLN
'Taemin is opening the door of the store.'   (Progressive)
'Taemin has left the door of the store open.'   (Resultative)

Aside from resultative uses of *-ko iss-* like (51), the closest counterpart to a perfective for transitive and unergative verbs is simple past *-e/ass-*, where a perfective-like reading as in (52) can be enhanced by adverbs or clause-final modals.

(52)   a. 태민이 지금 피자를 먹었네.

Thaymin=i   cikum phica=lul mek-ess-ney.
Taemin=NOM now   pizza=ACC eat-PERF-APP
'Oh, Taemin has now eaten pizza.'

b. 태민은 지금 막 강남에 갔다.

Thaymin=un cikum mak Kangnam=ey ka-ss-ta.
Taemin=TOP now   right Kangnam=DIR go-PERF-PLN
'Taemin has just now gone to Kangnam.'

The perfective category of light verbs introduced in Chapter 5 also highlights the completive status of the action, often with a subject- or speaker-oriented evaluative overtone. For example, V-*e peli-* in (53a), by emphasizing the finality of Taemin's removal of the clothing, may indicate that the action involved some desperation, frustration, or anger on Taemin's part; similarly

V-*e chiwu-* in (53b) may express that the eating was done hurriedly, but again irreversibly.

(53)   Perfective light verbs

   a. 태민은 두꺼운 옷을 벗어 버렸다.
      Thaymin=un   twukkewun   os=ul   pes-e   peli-ess-ta.
      Taemin=TOP   thick   clothes=ACC remove-INF   discard-PAST-PLN
      'Taemin ended up taking off the heavy clothing.'

   b. 태민은 피자를 다 먹어 치웠다.
      Thaymin=un   phica=lul   ta   mek-e   chiwu-ess-ta.
      Taemin=TOP   pizza=ACC   all eat-INF remove-PAST-PLN
      'Taemin went and ate all the pizza.'

8.3.3   Modality and Evidentiality

Modality has to do with a speaker's attitude toward what she is saying: is she certain that it is true, or does she think it might be true but is unsure? Modals may overlap with tense, particularly in the case of futures. Modals may be broadly divided into epistemic modals, which have to do with whether and to what extent a proposition may be true, and deontic modals, which have to do with a speaker's judgment about whether an event should or should not happen, for example in a moral sense. Epistemic modals may be further divided into irrealis and realis. In realis clauses, the speaker commits to the truth of the proposition.

The examples of tense and aspect we have considered so far in this section all involved realis contexts. However, as in many languages, the Korean nonfinal future tense suffix *-keyss-* may be used not merely to indicate certainty about a future event, but to indicate the speaker's belief that an event is probable, regardless of its tense. Thus (54) has no future time reference at all; instead *-keyss-* indicates that the statement is conjectural. Preceding apperceptive *-nay*, *-keyss-* may appear with time adverbials denoting past, present, or future time:

(54)   태민은 어제 비행기로 가겠네.
         Thaymin=un   ecey   pihayngki=lo ka-keyss-ney.
         Taemin=TOP   yesterday   airplane=by   go-FUT-APP
         'Taemin will have gone by plane yesterday.'

With the adverb *ecey* 'yesterday', *-keyss-* obviously does not denote future time; instead, like English *will have* in the same context, it expresses the speaker's conjecture about a completed event. Similarly, in a context where the speaker is looking at a delicious-looking cake through a bakery window, (55) does not state that the cake will be delicious (the speaker may have no intention of buying), but her supposition that it is delicious.

(55)   맛있겠다. (Looking at a cake through a bakery window.)
       Mas iss-keyss-ta.
       taste exist-FUT-PLN
       'It must be delicious.'

The clearest evidence for the modal nature of *-keyss-* comes from "past–future" combinations where *-keyss-* follows past *-e/ass-*:

(56)   서울은 많이 변했겠지요. (Said after being away from Seoul for many years.)
       Sewul=un   manhi   pyenhay-ss-keyss-ci-yo.
       Seoul=TOP   much   change-PAST-FUT-SUSP-POL
       'Seoul must have changed a lot.'

Retrospective *-te-*, which we saw in an adnominal context in (43b), also indicates the speaker's epistemic stance, but it is more properly termed an evidential; it marks not only a high degree of certainty about the event, but how the speaker came about the information expressed in the sentence. When *-te-* occurs without tense markers, it indicates that the speaker directly witnessed the event, but is at temporal and/or spatial remove from the event at speech time (Chung 2006).

(57)   태민은 피자를 소스와 같이 먹더라.
       Thaymin=un phica=lul sosu=wa   kathi   mek-te-la.
       Taemin=TOP   pizza=ACC sauce=with   together   eat-RET-PLN
       'Taemin has eaten pizza with sauce.'

Chung points out that the temporal distance property of *-te-* explains why *-te-* is interpreted as indicating a past event in the absence of tense. When *-te-* is used in combination with a tense or modal affix, Chung observes that it functions as an inferential indirect evidential:

(58)   Tense/modal + evidential *-te-*

    a. 태민은 피자를 소스와 같이 먹었더라.
       Thaymin=un phica=lul sosu=wa   kathi   mek-ess-te-la.
       Taemin=TOP   pizza=ACC sauce=with   together   eat-PAST-RET-PLN
       'Taemin apparently ate pizza with sauce.'

    b. 태민은 피자를 소스와 같이 먹겠더라.
       Thaymin=un phica=lul sosu=wa   kathi   mek-keyss-te-la.
       Taemin=TOP   pizza=ACC sauce=with   together   eat-FUT-RET-PLN
       'Taemin must have eaten pizza with sauce.'

In (58a) the speaker has not directly witnessed the event, but is conjecturing with some certainty on the basis of Taemin's past behavior or other factors. With future *-keyss-* in (58b), the speaker is making a plausible conjecture about a past event based on salient evidence, such as that Taemin has sauce on his chin. Note that *-keyss-* in (58b) does not denote future time, but rather epistemic modality. Thus on purely morphological grounds, we are compelled to recognize -*te*- as an evidential, since it co-occurs with and is distinct from modal -*keyss*-. A similar argument can be made for the prospective assertive prefinal suffix -*(u)li*-, which like -*te*- follows tense and modal suffixes in non-adnominal contexts:

(59) Prospective assertive -*(u)li*-
    a. 태민이 피자를 먹으리라.
       Thaymin=i   *phica=lul* *mek-uli-la.*
       Taemin=NOM   pizza=ACC eat-CONJE-PLN
       'Taemin might/would eat pizza.'
    b. 태민이 피자를 먹었으리라.
       Thaymin=i   *phica=lul* *mek-ess-uli-la.*
       Thaymin=NOM   pizza=ACC eat-PAST-CONJE-PLN
       'Taemin might/would have eaten pizza.'
    c. 태민이 피자를 먹겠으리라.
       Thaymin=i *phica=lul* *mek-keyss-uli-la.*
       Taemin=NOM pizza=ACC eat-FUT-CONJE-PLN
       'Taemin might/would be going to eat pizza.'

8.4   Pronouns and Anaphora

After introducing the lexical inventory of pronouns in Korean, we discuss their deictic and anaphoric functions. We then explore the related issue of null anaphora and ellipsis processes in Korean.

8.4.1   *Pronominals*

A long tradition in linguistics distinguishes the pronouns designating discourse participants, first person (speaker) and second person (hearer), from third person pronouns which are subject to coreference restrictions within the clause. A further distinction opposes pronouns whose reference is determined by deixis – the speech context – from anaphoric pronouns. It is possible to impose the European categories of person, number, and even case and gender on the Korean pronoun system, but this involves a certain amount of artificiality, especially for the last two categories. A further distinction in Korean is between plain and humble/honorific forms.

    Korean first person distinguishes plain *na, nay* (nominative/genitive), *wuli* (plural) and humble *ce, cey, cehuy*. Second person has a parallel distinction between plain *ne, ney, nehuy* and honorific forms, *caney(tul), tangsin(tul), tayk(tul)*. Including third person in the same scheme, we can distinguish male, *ku, kui*, female *kunye*, and neutral *i, ce*, the latter derived from the proximal and distal demonstratives. For convenience we have also included the interrogative human pronoun *nwukwu* 'who' and the negative pronoun *amwu* 'no (any) one' with their plural counterparts. A summary of the personal pronoun system is given in (60).

(60)   Personal pronouns

			Nom/Gen		Plural	
a. First person	Base		Nom/Gen		Plural	
Plain	나	*na*	내	*nay*	우리	*wuli*
Non-honorific	저	*ce*	제	*cey*	저희	*cehuy*
b. Second person	Base		Nom/Gen		Plural	
Regular	너	*ne*	네	*ney*	너희	*nehuy*
Honorific	자네	*caney*	당신	*tangsin*		*-tul*
	댁	*tayk*	여러분	*yelepwun*		*-tul*
c. Third person	Base		(Nom)			
Male	그	*ku*	그이	*kui*		*-tul*
Female	그녀	*ku nye*				*-tul*
d. Interrogative	누구	*nwukwu*				*-tul*
e. Negative	아무	*amwu*				*-tul*

A number of features distinguish first-person *na* (plain) and *ce* (humble), and second person *ne* and *caney* as true pronouns: the first three inflect for case, distinguishing nominative/genitive from other cases; they disallow the regular nominal pluralizer *-tul*; and *ce* and *ne* have distinctive plural forms in *-huy*. Humble first-person *ce* is thought to originate from the Chinese reflexive 自, Middle Chinese *dzi^H*, modern Sino-Korean *ca*. It is used when speaking to a person who has a higher status in age, social rank, or profession.

(61)   Personal pronoun (first person singular)

a. 나는/내가 어제 학교에 갔다.
   Na=nun/nay=ka   ecey   hakkyo=ey ka-ss-ta.
   I=TOP/I=NOM   yesterday school=DIR go-PAST-PLN
   'I went to school yesterday.'

b. 저는/제가 어제 학교에 갔다.
   Ce=nun/cey=ka   ecey   hakkyo=ey ka-ss-ta.
   I=TOP/I=NOM   yesterday school=DIR go-PAST-PLN
   'I (humble) went to school yesterday.'

First person plural can be indicated by plain *wuli* and humble *cehuy*. Unlike the singular first person, *wuli* patterns like a common noun in that it can be marked by the plural suffix *-tul, wuli-tul* 'we-PL'. It also shows a broader range of meaning: *wuli* can be either inclusive (including the hearer) or exclusive, while for many speakers *cehuy* is used only exclusively. Distinguishing inclusive and exclusive first-person pronouns is another Northeast Asian regional feature, found for example in Manchu exclusive *be* 'we' (speaker but not hearer) and inclusive *muse* 'we' (speaker and hearer).

(62)   Personal pronouns (first person plural)

a. 우리는 오늘 수업이 있어요. (Inclusive/Exclusive)
Wuli=nun onul   swuep=i   iss-eyo.
we=TOP   today   class=NOM have-POL
'We have a class today.'

b. 저희는 오늘 수업이 있어요. (Exclusive)
Cehuy=nun   onul   swuep=i   iss-eyo.
we=TOP   today   class=NOM have-POL
'We (speaker and her group, not hearer) have a class today.'

c. 우리 모두 좋은 일을 합시다. (Inclusive)
Wuli motwu   cohun il=ul   ha-psita.
we   all   good   deed=ACC do-PROP
'Let us all do a good deed.'

d. *저희 모두 좋은 일을 합시다. (Exclusive)
**Cehuy motwu   cohun il=ul   ha-psita.*
we   all   good   deed=ACC do-PROP
'Let us all do a good deed.'

Sentence (62d) is ill-formed because propositive *-psita* requires that the action be performed by the speaker and hearer, but this is incompatible with exclusive *cehuy*. An anonymous reviewer points out to us that the exclusive property of *cehuy* may be due to the intrinstic humble nature of *ce*: it would be rude to include the hearer in most contexts in a group with an explicitly humble designation.

The common noun properties of *wuli* 'we/us' enable it to be used to indicate the speaker's in-group broadly, ranging from the entire nation in (63c) to the speaker in (63a, b).

(63)   Singular/in-group denoting use of *wuli* 'we/us'

a. 우리 어머니께서는 항상 가족을 돌보신다.
Wuli emeni=kkeyse=nun   hangsang kacok=ul   tolpo-si-n-ta.
we   mother=NOM.HON=TOP   always   family=ACC care-HON-PRES-PLN
'My mother always takes care of the family.'

b. 우리 이모가 도와 주셨다.
Wuli imo=ka   towa-cwu-si-ess-ta.
we   aunt=NOM   help-AUX-HON-PAST-PLN
'My aunt helped.'

c. 축구경기에서 우리나라가 이겼다.
Chwukkwu kyengki=eyse wuli nala=ka   ikye-ess-ta.
soccer   game=at   we country=NOM win-PAST-PLN
'My (our) country won the soccer game.'

The second-person pronouns also distinguish plain and honorific forms. Singular *ne* distinguishes *ney* for nominative/genitive. *Caney* and *tangsin* are both honorific forms; the former is native Korean while *tangsin* is Sino-Korean from Chinese 當身 'the current body'. Both have common noun properties, as they are pluralized with *-tul*.

(64)   Personal pronoun (second person)

    a. 너는 어제 어디에 갔니?

       Ne=nun ecey   eti=ey   ka-ss-ni.

       you=TOP yesterday where=DIR go-PAST-Q

       'Where did you go yesterday?'

    b. 네가 그 일을 해라.

       Ney=ka ku   il=ul   hay-la.

       you=NOM that thing=ACC do-IMP

       'You do that.'

    c. 자네가 이 일을 해야지.

       Caney=ka i   il=ul   hay-ya-ci.

       you=NOM this thing=ACC do-must-SUSP

       'You must do this.'

    d. 당신이 학교에 가세요.

       Tangsin=i hakkyo=ey ka-sey-yo.

       you=NOM school=DIR go-HON-POL

       'You must go to school.'

    e. 너희가 이 일을 해라.

       Nehuy=ka i   il=ul   hay-la.

       you-PL=NOM this thing=ACC do-IMP

       'You do this.'

The second person plural pronoun *nehuy* 'you-PL' may also be used for singular denotation, or to denote the hearer's in-group.

(65)   Singular use of *nehuy*

    a. 너희 어머니께서는 항상 가족을 돌보신다.

       Nehuy emeni=kkeyse=nun hangsang kacok=ul   tolpo-si-n-ta.

       you   mother=NOM=TOP always   family=ACC care-HON-PRES-PLN

       'Your mother always takes care of the family.'

    b. 많은 토론을 하셨는데 너희 의견을 들어 봅시다.

       Manhun   tholon=ul   ha-si-ess-nuntey nehuy   uykyen=ul

       much   discussion=ACC do-HON-PAST-SO you-PL opinion=ACC

       tule-pop-si-ta.

       listen-AUX-HON-PLN

       'There has been a lot of discussion, so why don't we listen to your opinion?'

The third person pronouns *ku* (male) and *kunye* (female) are both derived from the mesial demonstrative *ku* 'that (close to hearer)'. It is usually claimed that these pronouns were developed in the early modern period to translate third-person pronouns in Western languages. This is transparently so in the case of *kunye*, which is a blended native + Sino-Korean compound made up of *ku* 'that' and *nye* (Sino-Korean *nye* 女) 'woman'. The same native + Sino-Japanese combination was used to form Japanese *kanojo* 彼女, but the demonstrative element *ka* used in Japanese is distal rather than mesial.

(66)   Personal pronoun (third person)

    a. 존은 그의 학교를 갔다.
      Con=un   ku=uy   hakkyo=lul   ka-ss-ta.
      John=TOP   he=GEN   school=ACC   go-PAST-PLN
      'John went to his school.'

    b. 메리는 그녀의 학교를 갔다.
      Meyli=nun   kunye=uy=uy hakkyo=lul   ka-ss-ta.
      Mary=TOP   she=GEN   school=ACC   go-PAST-PLN
      'Mary went to her school.'

In addition, there exist two more pronouns, the interrogative/indeterminate pronoun, *nwu(kwu)* 'who', and the negative polarity pronoun *amwu(to)*.

(67)   Interrogative/indeterminate and negative pronouns

    a. 누가 피자를 먹어요?
      Nwu=ka   phica=lul   mek-eyo.
      who=NOM   pizza=ACC   eat-POL Q
      'Who eats pizza?'
      'Does someone eat pizza?'

    b. 아무도 피자를 안 먹어요.
      Amwuto   phica=lul an   mek-eyo.
      no one   pizza=ACC NEG eat-POL
      'No one eats pizza.'

Animate *nwu(kwu)* 'who' belongs to the inventory of indeterminate/interrogative pronouns including *mwues* 'what' and *eti* 'where'. The label "indeterminate" refers to the fact that in context, these pronouns may be interpreted either as interrogative (the 'Who eats pizza?' interpretation of [67a]) or existential (the 'Does someone eat pizza?' interpretation of [67a]). These interpretations are distinguished by intonation, as we see in Section 8.5.

While first- and second-person pronouns pick up their reference from the pragmatic context – specifically, the identity of the speaker and hearer – third-person pronouns are subject to antecedence or other licensing conditions that constrain their reference. NPIs such as *amwuto* require negation in the same minimal clause, as in (67b). The third person pronoun *ku* is usually held to be unable to occupy a higher position in the clause than its antecedent. In (68a), ku_i cannot be coreferent with $Thaymin_i$ (coreference is indicated by subscripting). But in (68b), although ku_i precedes $Thaymin_i$, coreference is possible, because ku_i is embedded: it does not occupy a higher position in the clause.

(68)   a. *그ᵢ가 [태민ᵢ이 바보라고] 생각한다.

      Ku_i=ka [*Thaymin_i=i*   *papo=la-ko*]   *sayngkakhan-ta.*
      he=NOM   Taemin=NOM   fool=be-COMP   think-PLN
      'He_i thinks [Taemin_i is a fool].'

    b. [[그ᵢ를 아는 사람들이] 태민ᵢ이 바보라고] 생각한다.

      [[*Ku_i=lul a-nun*   *salam-tul=i*]   *Thaymin_i=i*   *papo=la-ko*]
      he=NOM   know-ADN person-PL=NOM Taemin=NOM fool=be-COMP
      sayngkakhan-ta.
      think-PLN
      '[People who know him_i] think that Taemin_i is a fool.'

8.4.2   Reflexives and Reciprocals

Reflexives are pronouns that obligatorily get their meaning from another NP. Generative grammarians group reflexives in a larger class of anaphors, items that must get their reference from an antecedent, usually in some restricted syntactic or discourse context. English anaphors include reflexive pronouns formed from pronoun + *-self*, and reciprocal pronouns such as *each other* and *one another*. Korean anaphors include the reflexives *caki* 자기 and *casin* 자신 'self' and reciprocal *selo* 서로. In addition Korean, like English, allows *casin* to follow the personal pronouns, deriving complex pronouns like *na casin* 'I myself, myself' in (69a). Interestingly, pronouns such as *na* 'I' (plain) and *ce* 'I' (humble), which alternate between the base form *na/ce* and the nominative/genitive form *nay/cey*, optionally allow the latter when followed by *casin*:

(69)   Personal pronoun + reflexive

    a. 나/내 자신이 어제 학교에 갔다.

      Na/nay casin=i   *ecey*   *hakkyo=ey ka-ss-ta.*
      I self=NOM   yesterday school=DIR go-PAST-PLN
      'I myself went to school yesterday.'

    b. 저/제 자신이 어제 학교에 갔다.

      Ce/cey   *casin=i*   *ecey*   *hakkyo=ey ka-ss-ta.*
      I (humble) myself=NOM yesterday school=DIR go-PAST-PLN
      'I (humble) myself went to school yesterday.'

Similar formations occur with the other personal pronouns. The personal pronoun determines the interpretation of the pronoun + reflexive compound: thus while *wuli casin* has both inclusive and exusive interpretations, humble *cehuy casin* has only the exclusive use and does not allow the inclusive use for speakers who observe this distinction for bare *cehuy*, as shown in (70b).

(70)   Personal pronoun + reflexive (first person plural)

    a. 우리 자신 모두 좋은 일을 합시다. (Inclusive)

      Wuli casin   *motwu*   *cohun il=ul*   *ha-psita.*
      ourself   all   good deed=ACC do-PROP
      'Let's we ourselves all do a good deed.'

b. *저희 자신 모두 좋은 일을 합시다. (Exclusive)
*Cehuy casin motwu   cohun il=ul   ha-psita.
ourself   all   good   deed=ACC do-PROP
'Let's we ourselves all do a good deed.'

As we see from this example, in personal pronoun + reflexive combinations, the pronoun determines the interpretation and behavior of the whole. Thus these combinations are not, strictly speaking, reflexives, but personal pronouns with an emphatic reflexive element, much like English *we ourselves, you yourself*. Again as in English, the same emphatic function can be seen when *casin* follows a proper name, e.g. *Thaymin casin* 'Taemin himself'.

Three items count as true reflexives in Korean, *caki* 자기 (自己), *casin* 자신 (自身), and *caki casin* 자기 자신. All three are Sino-Korean in origin and are already attested in LMK. All three allow an antecedent in the same simplex clause, in contrast to the third person pronoun *ku*.

(71)   Reflexives versus pronouns in a simplex clause
       a. 태민ᵢ은 자기ᵢ /자신ᵢ /자기 자신ᵢ을 미워한다.
          Thaymin$_i$=un caki$_i$/casin$_i$/caki casin$_i$=ul miweha-n-ta.
          Taemin=TOP   self=ACC   hate-PRES-PLN
          'Taemin$_i$ hates himself$_i$.'

       b. *태민ᵢ은 그ᵢ를 미워한다.
          Thaymin$_i$=un ku$_i$=lul   miweha-n-ta.
          Taemin$_i$=TOP him$_i$=ACC hate-PRES-PLN
          'Taemin$_i$ hates him$_i$.'

Caki differs from reflexives in English in that it can take a long-distance antecedent; that is, its antecedent can be in a higher clause:

(72)   태민ᵢ은 [철수ⱼ가 자기ᵢ, ⱼ를 미워한다고] 믿는다.
       Thaymin$_i$=un Chelswu$_j$=ka   caki$_{i, j}$=lul miweha-n-ta-ko
       Taemin$_i$=TOP Chelswu$_j$=NOM self$_{i, j}$=ACC hate-PRES-PLN-COMP
       mit-nun-ta.
       believe-PRES-PLN
       'Taemin$_i$ believes that Chelswu $_j$ hates self$_{i, j}$.'

In the English counterpart of (72), *Taemin believes that Chelswu hates himself, himself* can only refer to its local antecedent, *Chelswu*, but Korean *caki* may be coreferent with the local antecedent *Chelswu* or with *Taemin*, the antecedent in the higher clause. In contrast many Korean linguists have suggested that with *casin*, there is a preference for the local antecedent, as in (73).

(73)   태민ᵢ은 [철수ⱼ가 자신ᵢ < ⱼ을 미워한다고] 믿는다.
       Thaymin$_i$=un Chelswu$_j$=ka   casin$_{i < j}$=ul miweha-n-ta-ko
       Taemin$_i$=TOP Chelswu$_j$=NOM self$_{i < j}$=ACC hate-PRES-PLN-COMP
       mit-nun-ta.
       believe-PRES-PLN
       'Taemin$_i$ believes that Chelswu $_j$ hates self$_{i < j}$.'

Kang (1998) provides statistical support for this claim based on a study of a five million word corpus extracted from the KOREA-1 corpus. Kang found that while *caki* is slightly more likely to take a long-distance antecedent than a local one, *casin* is more than twice as likely to take a local antecedent. This contrast becomes almost categorical with the complex reflexive *caki casin*, which many linguists have claimed allows only local antecedents:

(74)   태민ᵢ은 [철수ⱼ가 자기 자신*ᵢ, ⱼ을 미워한다고] 믿는다.
         *Thaymin*ᵢ=*un Chelswu*ⱼ=*ka   caki casin**ᵢ, ⱼ=*ul miweha-n-ta-ko*
         Taemin ᵢ=TOP Chelswu ⱼ=NOM self*ᵢ, ⱼ=ACC   hate-PRES-PLN-COMP
         mit-nun-ta.
         believe-PRES-PLN
         'Taemin ᵢ believes that Chelswu ⱼ hates self*ᵢ, ⱼ.'

This behavior of the Korean reflexives is consistent with the crosslinguistic generalization (Pica 1987) that complex reflexives such as *him*+*self* or *caki*+*casin* tend to require local antecedents, while monomorphemic reflexives such as *caki* may take long-distance antecedents. This generalization receives further confirmation from the behavior of the complex reflexive *ku*+*casin*, which has the exact composition of *him*+*self*. It too allows only local antecedents:

(75)   태민ᵢ은 [철수ⱼ가 그 자신*ᵢ, ⱼ을 미워한다고] 믿는다.
         *Thaymin*ᵢ=*un   Chelswu*ⱼ=*ka ku casin**ᵢ, ⱼ=*ul miweha-n-ta-ko*
         Taemin=TOP   Chelswu=NOM himself=ACC   hate-PRES-PLN-COMP
         mit-nun-ta.
         believe-PRES-PLN
         'Taemin ᵢ believes that Chelswu ⱼ hates himself*ᵢ, ⱼ.'

The hybrid behavior of bare *casin* can be explained by the data we have already seen. We saw in (69–70) and (74–75) that *casin* can follow another pronominal element, forming a complex reflexive. But we saw in (71) that *casin* can also appear on its own, behaving like a monomorphemic reflexive. Kang's (1998) data shows that *casin* takes a long-distance antecedent, but less often than *caki*. This mixed behavior can be explained if we hypothesize that there are two kinds of *casin*: a monomorphemic reflexive [*casin*], structurally identical to [*caki*], and complex reflexive [*pro casin*], with an unpronounced pronominal element (*pro*). We will see more evidence for Korean *pro* in Section 8.5.

     The Korean reciprocal *selo* also differs from its English counterpart *each other* in allowing long-distance antecedents.

(76)   Reciprocal *selo*
         a. 나영과 태민은 서로를 사랑한다.
            Nayeng=*kwa Thaymin*=*un selo*=*lul   salangha-n-ta.*
            Nayoung=and Taemin=TOP each other=ACC love-PRES-PLN
            'Nayoung and Taemin love each other.'

b. 나영과 서연은 [태민이 서로를 사랑한다고] 믿는다.

Nayeng=kwa   Seyen=un   Thaymin=i   selo=lul
Nayoung=and   Seoyeon=TOP   Taemin=NOM   each other=ACC
salangha-n-ta-ko   mit-nun-ta.
love-PRES-PLN-COMP   believe-PRES-PLN

(i) 'Nayoung believes that Taemin loves Seoyeon, and Seoyeon believes that Taemin loves Nayoung.'

(ii) 'Nayoung$_i$ believes that Taemin loves her$_i$, and Seoyeon$_j$ believes that Taemin loves her$_j$.'

(iii) '[Nayoung and Seoyeon]$_i$ believe that Taemin loves them$_i$.'

English *each other* allows only the short-distance pattern in (76a), but Choi (2004) points out that *selo* also permits three distinct long-distance readings in (76b). Choi suggests that the hybrid short- and long-distance behavior of *selo* can be accounted for by positing an unpronounced *pro* that combines with *selo*, somewhat as we suggested for *casin*. Without going into the details, we observe that the juxtaposition of two elements, *each* and *other*, does seem to be responsible for the short-distance behavior of *each other* in English (77a). When *each* and *other* are separated, the long-distance interpretation corresponding to (76bi) becomes possible, although not the readings corresponding to (76bii) and (76biii).

(77)   a. *Nayoung and Seoyeon believe that Taemin loves each other.

        b. Nayoung and Seoyeon each believe that Taemin loves the other.
           = (76bi)

8.4.3   Deixis and Deictic Pronouns

Deixis has to do with linguistic elements that must be understood contextually, usually with reference to the pragmatic or speech-act context. The first- and second-person pronouns we saw in Section 8.4.1 are examples of such deictic elements: to identify first person, we must know who is speaking, and to identify second person we must know who is being addressed in a specific speech-act context. We can distinguish personal, temporal, spatial, and social deixis. The first-person pronouns 'I' and 'you' exemplify personal deixis, time adverbs like 'now' exemplify temporal deixis, and 'here' exemplifies spatial deixis. In this section we describe how these three kinds of deixis are realized in Korean. Social deixis relating to honorifics is discussed in Section 10.3.

Demonstrative pronouns are a basic locus of deixis. Korean has a three-term demonstrative system: **proximal** (near speaker), **mesial** (near hearer) and **distal** (near neither speaker nor hearer). Proximal *i* indicates 'this', 'here', 'now'; mesial *ku* 'that', 'there', 'past'; and distal *ce* 'that over there', '(relatively) remote distance', and 'remote past'. A summary of the Korean deixis system as realized by the demonstratives is given in (78); for completeness we have also included the corresponding indeterminate/interrogative pronouns for the personal/adnominal, demonstrative pronoun, spatial, and temporal dimensions.

(78)   Korean demonstratives and deixis

	Proximal	Mesial	Distal	Indeterminate
a. Personal	이 *i*	그 *ku*	저 *ce*	누구*nwukwu*
b. Demonstrative	이것 *i kes*	그것 *ku kes*	저것 *ce kes*	무엇 *mwues*
c. Spatial	여기 *yeki*	거기 *keki*	저기 *ceki*	어디 *eti*
d. Temporal	어제 *ecey*	그제 *ku cey*	저제 *ce cey*	언제 *encey*

As we saw in Section 8.4.1, the mesial demonstrative *ku* has been grammaticalized as the third-person pronoun. Proximal *i* can still be used for personal reference as in (79a), but otherwise the demonstratives must be combined with a [+human] noun such as *salam* 'person' or *pwun* '(honorific) person' to designate a human referent. Thus (79b) is acceptable without *salam* 'person', but only on the meaning 'Who is he?'

(79)   Personal deixis with demonstratives

    a. 이는 형님이다.

        I=nun   *hyengnim=i-ta.*

        this person=TOP   older.brother=be-PLN

        'This is my older brother'

    b. 그 (사람)이 누구니?

        Ku (salam)=i   nwukwu-ni?

        that person=NOM who-Q

        'Who is that (person)?'

    c. 저 (사람)이 누구니?

        Ce   salam=i   nwukwu-ni?

        that (distal) person=NOM who-Q

        'Who is that person over there?'

The substantive demonstrative pronouns are formed by combining demonstrative + the bound noun *kes* 'thing, one': 이것 *i kes* 'this', 그것 *ku kes* 'that', 저것 *ce kes* 'that over there'.

    Demonstratives typically have both an exophoric and anaphoric (sometimes called endophoric) function. The former function involves reference to objects in the pragmatic context, and is clearest when referring to spatial location, as in (79a–c). Demonstrative specification of spatial location, as in many languages, is extended to temporal location:

(80)   Temporal deixis

    a. 이때가 언제니?

        I   ttay=ka   encey-ni?

        this   time=NOM when-Q

        'When is this time?'

b. 그때가 언제니?
   Ku   ttay=ka   encey-ni?
   that time=NOM when-Q
   'When is that time?'

c. 저때가 언제니?
   Ce   ttay=ka   encey-ni?
   that   time=NOM   when-Q
   'When is that time (in the more distant past)?'

But the function of the demonstratives in (80) is more likely to be anaphoric: referring to a time that has been mentioned in prior discourse. In this function, mesial *ku* picks out information known both to speaker and hearer, and thus is the highest frequency demonstrative in texts, often serving, like definite determiners in other languages, to pick out information that is presupposed or present in prior discourse.

As we saw in Section 8.4.1, Korean indeterminate pronouns function in two ways: as interrogative pronouns and indefinite pronouns, interpreted as *somebody*, *something*, etc., as in (81b, d, f).

(81)   Interpretation of indeterminate pronouns
         a. 이 사람이 누구야?
            I   salam=i   nwukwu-ya?
            this person=NOM who-Q
            'Who is this person?'

         b. 누가 왔네.
            Nwu=ka   o-ass-ney?
            somebody=NOM   come-PAST-APP
            'Somebody came.'

         c. 학교가 어디에 있어?
            Hakkyo=ka eti=ey   iss-e?
            school=NOM where=LOC   be-Q
            Where is the school?'

         d. 어디 가려고요.
            Eti   ka-lyeko-yo?
            somewhere   go-in order to-POL
            '(Somebody) wants to go somewhere.'

         e. 오늘은 무엇을 먹을까?
            Onul=un   [mwués=ul] [mek-úl-kka]?
            today=TOP what=ACC   eat-FUT-Q
            'What will you eat today?'

         f. 벌써 뭐 먹었어.
            Pelsse [mwe   mek-éss-e]?
            already something eat-PAST-INT
            '(I) already ate something.'

The interrogative and indefinite interpretations are disambiguated by intonation. Pronouns with the indefinite reading do not bear accent and do not form their own accentual phrase. Interrogative pronouns bear their own accent and form a separate accentual phrase, as indicated by the accents and bracketing in (81e, f). Interrogative *mwués=ul* 'what=ACC' in (81e) bears an accent and is phrased separately from the verb, while indefinite *mwues* 'what' in (81f) is unaccented and is phrased together with the verb.

8.5   Ellipsis and Unpronounced Elements

We have seen throughout this chapter (and indeed, throughout this book) examples where, in contrast to English and other languages that require a pronoun, Korean uses no phonological material at all. These included the reflexive *casin* 'self' in Section 8.4.2, which although consisting only of a reflexive element, behaves like pronoun+reflexive, like English *him/her+self*. This led us to suggest that *casin* might be analyzed as containing an unpronounced pronoun plus the pronounced element *casin*. In sentences like (81d) and (81f), the English translations contained the subject pronouns *someone* and *I*, but these pronouns are missing in the Korean examples. A traditional analysis is to posit an unpronounced pronoun, represented as *pro*, in subject position in such cases. In other words, we assume that Korean is a *pro*-drop language, a language which uses an unpronounced pronoun in contexts where non-*pro*-drop languages such as English must use overt pronouns.

In *pro*-drop languages such as Spanish and Italian, the person and number of subject *pro* is specified by agreement morphology on the verb. For example, in the following Italian sentence the verb ending indicates that the subject is first person singular.

(82)   *pro* [+1P, −PL] *ho*   *mangiato una pizza.* (Italian)
                      have.1SG eat   a   pizza
        'I ate a pizza.'

Korean verb inflection does not indicate the person or number of the unpronounced argument. Nevertheless, silent pronouns are very common in Korean. Kim (2000) shows that the incidence of null subjects in children acquiring Korean as a first language and in adult native Korean speakers is higher than in Chinese, another language with subject *pro* but no agreement morphology, and even slightly higher than in Italian. Linguistic context can help disambiguate the reference of *pro*; for example in a version of (57) with a *pro* subject:

(83)   피자를 소스와 같이 먹더라.
        pro phica=lul sosu=wa   kathi   mek-te-la.
        pro pizza=ACC sauce=with together eat-RET-PLN
        '*pro* has eaten pizza with sauce.'

We know that the subject in (83) cannot be first person, because the retrospective is incompatible with first person subjects. But in most cases, speakers must determine the reference of Korean *pro* by discourse or pragmatic factors, relying on such factors as the identity of the discourse topic or where the speaker is pointing. A rule of thumb is that *pro* is present where overt pronouns such as *ku* 'he' are possible, although in *pro*-drop languages such as Korean, speakers may prefer silent *pro* when focus prominence or other overt phonological material is not required. According to this rule of thumb, the gap represented as Ø in a simple monoclausal relative clause such as (84) is not an instance of *pro*, because it cannot be replaced by the pronoun *ku* in (84b):

(84)   a. Ø 피자를 먹는 아이
        Phica=lul mek-nun   ai
        pizza=ACC eat-PRESADN child
        'The child who ate the pizza'

    b. *그가 피자를 먹는아이
        **Ku=ka phica=lul mek-nun   ai*
        he=NOM pizza=ACC eat-PRESADN child
        'The child who he ate the pizza'

Instead, the missing subject of the relative clause must be some other kind of empty element related to the head of the relative clause, *ai* 'child'. But in certain other contexts the gap in a relative clause can be a pronoun. Consider (85), from Han and Kim (2004):

(85)   a. *[[[[Ø$_i$ Ø$_j$ 좋아하는] 강아지$_j$] 가 죽은] 아이$_i$]
        * [[[[Ø$_i$ Ø$_j$ *cohaha-nun*]   *kangaci$_j$]=ka cwuk-un*]   *ai$_i$*
        like-PRESADN   puppy=NOM   die-PSTADN child
        '[[the child$_i$ that [the puppy$_j$ that Ø$_i$ liked] Ø$_j$ died]'

    b. ??[[[[그$_i$가Ø$_j$ 좋아하는] 강아지$_j$] 가 죽은] 아이$_i$]
        [[[[*ku$_i$=ka* Ø$_j$ *cohaha-nun*]   *kangaci$_j$]=ka cwuk-un*]   *ai$_i$*
        he=NOM like-PRESADN   puppy=NOM die-PSTADN child
        '[[the child$_i$ that [the puppy$_j$ that he$_i$ liked] Ø$_j$ died]'

In (85a) the gap Ø$_i$ is inside the embedded relative clause, 'the puppy that Ø$_i$ loved'. As Han and Kim point out, crosslinguistically, relativization gaps are often disallowed in a position of this sort inside another relative clause, often referred to as syntactic "islands." Notice that this is the case with the English translation of (85a), where relativization is ungrammatical. Han and Kim point out that the acceptability of (85a) can be explained if the Ø$_i$ is not the result of relativization, but rather *pro*, the unpronounced pronoun. This view is supported by the fact that the overt pronoun *ku* 'he' is acceptable in the same position in (85b). Similarly, the English translation of (85b) also improves with an overt pronoun, although 'resumptive pronouns' of this sort are not perfect in

English. Thus we may conclude that Korean has at least two kinds of empty NPs, the one left behind "normal" relativization, as in (84a), and *pro*.

"Ellipsis" traditionally refers to contexts where constituents larger than an NP are missing. Linguists have distinguished four types of ellipsis in Korean (86).

(86)   Types of ellipsis

	Deletion	Remnant
a. VP ellipsis	VP	Subject (and verb)
b. Gapping	V	Subject and object
c. Sluicing	VP	*Wh*-words (and copula)
d. Stripping	VP	Subject or object

It is first of all important to distinguish ellipsis from single-constituent answers, as in (87):

(87)   VP ellipsis

   a. A: 누가 피자를 먹어?   B: 태민 (피자를 먹어)
     A: *Nwu=ka   phica=lul   mek-e?* B: *Thaymin (phica=lul mek-e).*
     who=NOM pizza=ACC eat-Q   Taemin (pizza=ACC eat-INT)
     'Who eats pizza? Taemin (eats pizza).'

   b. A: 어디서피자를먹었어? B: 강남에서 (피자를 먹었어)
     A: *Eti=se phica=lul mek-ess-e?* B: *Kangnam=eyse (pro phica=lul*
                                    mek-ess-e).
       where   pizza=ACC eat-PAST-Q   Kangnam=at (*pro* pizza=ACC eat-
                                        PAST-INT)
     'Where did *pro* eat pizza? In Kangnam (*pro* ate pizza).'

In (87), B answers A's questions with a single NP or PP. In such single-constituent answers, what is "omitted" does not correspond to a single constituent: instead it is the entire sentence minus the pronounced NP or PP. In contrast, in ellipsis a constituent is elided, or unpronounced. For example, in English VP ellipsis the VP is unpronounced, leaving auxiliaries behind:

(88)   VP ellipsis
    a. Nayoung likes anchovies, but Taemin doesn't [VP ~~like anchovies~~].
    b. Nayoung likes her puppy, and Taemin does [VP ~~like his/Nayoung's puppy~~] too.

Example (88b) shows a special property of VP ellipsis. We cannot say that the semantic content of the elided VP is exactly the same as the antecedent VP *likes her puppy*. That is because the elided VP can have what has been called the "sloppy identity" interpretation *likes his (Taemin's) puppy*, leading to the overall interpretation 'Nayoung likes her puppy, and Taemin likes his puppy'. Interestingly, we can produce the same interpretation in Korean with a sentence like (89):

(89)   Korean VP ellipsis
나영이 자신의 강아지를 좋아한다. 태민도Ø좋아한다.
Nayeng=i   casin=uy kangaci=lul cohaha-n-ta.   Thaymin=to
Nayoung=NOM self=GEN puppy=ACC like-PRES-PLN   Taemin=also
cohaha-n-ta.
like-PRES-PLN
'Nayoung likes self's puppy. Taemin does too.'

Like its English VP ellipsis translation, (89) allows two interpretations in
Korean: 'Taemin likes Nayoung's dog' or 'Taemin likes his (=Nayoung's)
dog'. The second is the "sloppy" interpretation we saw was associated with
VP ellipsis. Note that overt pronouns do not normally allow this sloppy
interpretation. If we replace the gap Ø with the overt pronoun *ku* in (89), the
sloppy reading disappears. *Ku* 'him' in (90) can only refer to Nayoung's puppy:

(90)   나영이 자신의 강아지를 좋아한다. 태민도 그를 좋아한다.
Nayeng=i   casin=uy   kangaci=lul   cohaha-n-ta.
Nayoung=NOM   self=GEN   puppy=ACC   like-PRES-PLN
Thaymin=to   ku=lul   cohaha-n-ta.
Taemin=also   *ku*=ACC   like-PRES-PLN
'Nayoung likes self's puppy. Taemin likes him too.'

This means, given our rule of thumb governing the distribution of *pro*, that the
gap Ø in (89) cannot be *pro*, since an overt pronoun cannot be used with the
same "sloppy interpretation." But then what is Ø? Ohtani and Whitman (1991)
suggest that it is a VP; that is, (88) is an example of VP ellipsis in Korean.
Ohtani and Whitman suggest that an empty VP can be created by raising the
overt verb *cohaha-* out of the VP, so the structure of (89) is as in (91):

(91)   Korean VP ellipsis
나영이 자신의 강아지를 좋아한다. 태민도 [VP Ø] 좋아한다.
Nayeng=i   casin=uy   kangaci=lul   cohaha-n-ta.
Nayoung=NOM   self=GEN   puppy=ACC   like-PRES-PLN
Thaymin=to   [VP Ø]   *cohaha-n-ta.*
Taemin=also   like-PRES-PLN
'Nayoung likes self's puppy. Taemin does too.'

V ellipsis deletes a verb with remnants in both the subject and object in
the second sentence of the conjunctive structure, as shown in (91).

Somewhat similar proposals have been made for the ellipsis process known
as gapping in English. Gapping occurs in sentences like *Taemin likes pizza, and
Nayoung Ø spaghetti*. Here it looks like just the second occurrence of the verb
likes has been elided. But it has been suggested that we can maintain the
generalization that ellipsis renders silent a phrasal constituent by hypothesizing
that in gapping, the object moves out of the second VP. Then the structure of
gapping in English would be another subtype of VP ellipsis: the object moves

out of VP, and the remaining material (the verb) is elided under identity with the verb in the antecedent VP: *Taemin likes pizza, and Nayoung [vp Ø] spaghetti.*

In Korean, gapping appears to elide not the first, but the second in a series of identical verbs:

(92)   Korean gapping
    나영은 피자를 먹고, 태민은 스파게티를 먹는다.
    Nayeng=un   phica=lul ~~mek-ko,~~ Thaymin=un suphakeythi=lul
    Nayoung=TOP pizza=ACC eat-GER   Taemin=TOP spaghetti=ACC
    mek-nun-ta.
    eat-PRES-PLN
    'Nayoung eats pizza and Taemin, spaghetti.'

This is a generalization about languages with object–verb order: while gapping in verb–object languages like English operates forward, gapping in verb-final languages like Korean operates backward. However, because backward gapping of the Korean type retains the shared constituent (in [92], the verb) on the far right of the clause, it has also been suggested that backward gapping is actually something completely different from English forward gapping: the Korean pattern is instead right-node raising, an operation that takes a constituent duplicated at the end of two coordinated clauses and places it at the end of the whole sentence. In Korean, since the verb comes at the end, the shared verb *mek-nun-ta* 'eats' is right-node raised, but in English other clause-final constituents undergo right-node raising, as in *Nayoung bought and Taemin ate the pizza.*

English has two types of ellipsis which have been claimed to elide an entire clause: sluicing and stripping. English sluicing retains only a *wh*-word, eliding the rest of the sentence under identity with an antecedent clause, as in *Nayoung ate something, but I don't know what ~~Nayoung ate~~*. Stripping elides all of the material in a clause identical to the antecedent before an element like *too*, as in *Nayoung ate the pizza, and the spaghetti ~~Nayoung ate~~ too*. The Korean patterns in (93) show a superficial resemblance to sluicing and stripping:

(93)   Korean pseudo-sluicing and stripping
    a. 나영은 무엇을 먹으나 나는 무엇인지 모른다.
       Nayeng=un   mwues=ul   mek-una na=nun mwues=i-n-ci
       Nayoung=TOP something=ACC eat-but I=TOP   what=be-PRES-SUSP
       molu-n-ta.
       not.know-PRES-PLN
       'Nayoung eats something, but I don't know what [s ~~Nayoung eats~~].'
    b. 나영은 피자를 먹고 스파게티도다.
       Nayeng=un   phica=lul mek-ko suphakeythi=to-ta.
       Nayoung=TOP pizza=ACC eat-GER   spaghetti=too-PLN
       'Nayoung eats pizza and spaghetti [s ~~Nayoung eats~~] too.'

In the English sluicing (93a) and stripping (93b) examples, the retained constituents are placed outside the elided clause. The Korean examples retain the same elements, but in each case they are accompanied by the copula (=*i*-), in (93a), or its allomorph (zero following a vowel before the plain suffix in [93b], which follows only verbs and adjectives). Because of this difference, it has been argued that apparent Korean sluicing is in fact a copular construction interpretable as 'Nayoung eats something but I don't know what it is' (Nishiyama, Whitman, and Yi 1996). The presence of copular morphology suggests a similar analysis for the apparent example of stripping in (93b).

The picture we are left with of Korean is that while null *pro* is highly frequent, ellipsis phenomena may be more restricted than in languages like English. A final phenomenon where morphological material is absent in Korean is so-called case drop, where a case marker is omitted. Case drop is ubiquitous in spoken Korean. In general the topic marker and the structural case markers nominative and accusative can be dropped.

(94)   Case drop

   a. 태민(은) 피자(를) 먹고 나영(은) 스파게티(를) 먹었다.
      Thaymin(=un)   phica(=lul)   mek-ko   Nayeng(=un)
      Taemin=TOP   pizza=ACC   eat-and   Nayoung=TOP
      suphakeythi(=lul) mek-ess-ta
      spaghetti=ACC   eat-PAST-PLN
      'Taemin ate pizza, and Nayoung ate spaghetti.'

   b. 태민(이) 학교(에/를) 갈 것이다.
      Thaymin(=i)   hakkyo(=ey/=lul)   ka-l kes=i-ta.
      Taemin=NOM   school=DIR/=ACC   go-FUTADN-COMP=be-PLN
      'Taemin will go to school.'

In (94a) the topic and accusative markers have been dropped, while in (94b) the nominative marker is dropped. It may also appear that the directional postposition =*ey* has been dropped in (94b), but *hakkyo* 'school' in this sentence may also be marked accusative, so we may maintain the generalization that only structural case markers are droppable. Where only a postposition is possible, it cannot be dropped, as shown in (95):

(95)   태민(은) 강남(*에서) 피자(를) 먹었다.
         Thaymin=un   Kangnam(=eyse)   phica(=lul)   mek-ess-ta.*
         Taemin=TOP   Kangnam=in   pizza=ACC   eat-PAST-PLN
         'Taemin ate pizza in Kangnam.'

8.6   Summary

In this chapter we surveyed Korean negation, information structure, tense, aspect, and mood (TAM), anaphors and pronouns, and ellipsis. We saw that there are three ways of forming Korean negation: lexical, morphological, and syntactic. Korean has two patterns of syntactic negation, each of which includes both modal ('cannot') and plain negation. Short-form negation places the negative morpheme preverbally, while long-form negation places the negative morpheme postverbally with *ha*-support. However, there are many deviations in short-form and long-form negation from this canonical type. Long-form negation includes patterns with *mal-* in imperative and propositive sentences, suppleting for *anh-*. We saw that short-form negation is not allowed with descriptive predicates, and certain derived and compound verbs. We also examined the semantic scope of negation in the two basic patterns. We examined the syntactic restrictions on negative polarity items (NPIs). We saw that Korean allows double negation with *an* 'not', but not with *mos* 'cannot'.

We examined the ramifications of Li and Thompson's classification of Korean as a topic- and subject-prominent language, and explored the realization of topic and focus in Korean. We introduced prosodic, morphological, and syntactic means of marking focus. We summarized the differences between *=un/nun* (topic) and *=i/ka* (focus) marking. In Section 8.3, we described tense, aspect, and mood. Korean has a three-way tense distinction: present, past, and future. We discussed the two major types of aspect: progressive and perfective. We introduced the three major mood patterns: indicative, retrospective, and prospective assertive, and discussed the evidential properties of retrospective *-te-*.

We examined the relationship between pronouns and deixis. Personal pronouns have an inclusive/exclusive distinction in the first person plural. We discussed the long-distance anaphor *caki* and the local reflexive *caki casin*. We saw that demonstratives have a three-way deictic distinction, based on the distance from the speaker and hearer: near the speaker *i* 'this', near the hearer, *ku* 'that', and a great distance from both the speaker and the hearer, *ce* 'that over there'. In the final section, we discussed null *pro* and several types of actual and apparent ellipsis.

Further Readings

Choi, Young Sik. 2004. The structure of *selo* and its implication for binding theory. *Language Research* 40 (3), 681–694.

Chung, K. S. 2006. Korean evidentials and assertion. In D. Baumer, D. Montero, and M. Scanlon (eds.), *Proceedings of WCCFL 25*, 105–113. Somerville, MA, Cascadilla Press.

Evans, Nicholas. 2007. Insubordination and its uses. In Irina Nikolaeva (ed.), *Finiteness: Theoretical and Empirical Foundations*, 366–431. Oxford University Press: New York.

Kang, Beom-mo. 1998. Three kinds of Korean reflexives: A corpus linguistic investigation on grammar and usage. *Language, Information, and Computation (PACLIC12)*, 10–19.

Kim, Jong-Bok. 2000. *The Grammar of Negation: A Lexicalist Constraint-Based Perspective*. Dissertations in Linguistics. Stanford: CSLI Publications.

Kiss, Katalin É. 1995. Discourse configurational languages: Introduction. In Katalin É. Kiss (ed.), *Discourse Configurational Languages*, 3–27. Oxford: Oxford University Press.

Ko, Young-Kun. 2009. *Hanwkukeuy Sicey Sepep Tongcaksang* [Tense, Mood, Aspect in Korean], revised ed. Seoul: Taehaksa.

Lee, Eun Hee and Mitsuaki Shimojo. 2016. Mismatch of topic between Japanese and Korean. *Journal of East Asian Linguistics* 25: 81.

Merchant, Jason. 2001. *The Syntax of Silence: Sluicing, Islands, and the Theory of Ellipsis*. Oxford: Oxford University Press.

Merchant, Jason. 2012. Ellipsis. In Tobor Kiss and Artemis Alexiadou (eds.), *Syntax: An International Handbook of Contemporary Syntactic Research*. Berlin: Walter de Gruyter.

Nishiyama, Kunio, John Whitman, and Eun-Young Yi. 1996. Syntactic movement of overt wh-phrases in Japanese and Korean. *Japanese/Korean Linguistics*, Vol. 5, 337–351. Stanford: CSLI.

Park, Chongwon. 2014. The ambiguity and alternative construals of the [X-*ko iss-ta*] construction in Korean. *Korean Linguistics* 16 (1), 18–50.

Pica, Pierre. 1987. On the nature of the reflexivization cycle. In J. McDonough and B. Plunket (eds.), *Proceedings of the North Eastern Linguistics Society* 17, 483–499. Amherst, MA: GLSA.

Sells, Peter. 2001. Three aspects of negation in Korean. *Journal of Linguistic Studies* 6: 1–15.

Yoon, Pyung-Hyun. 2013. *Kwuke Uymilon* [Korean Semantics], 7th ed. Seoul: Youkrack.

References

Han, Chung-hye and Jong-Bok Kim. 2004. Are there "double relative clauses" in Korean? *Linguistic Inquiry* 35: 315–333.

Kim, Young-Joo. 2000. Subject/object drop in the acquisition of Korean: A cross-linguistic comparison. *Journal of East Asian Linguistics* 9 (4), 325–351.

Li, Charles and Sandra Thompson. 1976. Subject and topic: A new typology of language. In Charles Li (ed.), *Subject and Topic*, 457–489. New York: Academic Press.

Mattissen, Johanna. 2003. *Dependent-Head Synthesis in Nivkh: A Contribution to a Typology of Polysynthesis*. Amsterdam: John Benjamins.

Nedjalkov, Igor. 1997. *Evenki*. Routledge Descriptive Grammars. London and New York: Routledge.

Ohtani, Kazuyo and John Whitman. 1991. V-raising and VP ellipsis. *Linguistic Inquiry* 22 (2), 345–358.

Part III

Language in Context

9   Language and Society

In this chapter, we describe five areas of interaction between language and society: regional dialects and languages, speech style, honorifics, terms of address, and language policy. Korean is classified into five different dialects (plus one distinct language within Koreanic) based on geographical region, four of which are located in South Korea and two in North Korea. We specify the major characteristics of those six dialects with regard to lexicon, phonology, morphology, and syntax. Section 9.2 describes four different speech styles (deferential, polite, intimate, and plain) that are related to sentence types and honorifics, which we briefly mentioned in Chapters 5 and 7. Having different speech styles in Korean society is a noteworthy property of the Korean language that governs what forms speakers use and when they use them in specific social contexts. We also explore two archaic speech styles, familiar and semi-formal. Section 9.3 explains honorific subsystems that depend on the relationship between the speaker, the hearer, and the referent. There are three types of honorifics: subject honorifics, object honorifics, and hearer honorifics; all involve different variables to determine the correct honorific to use. Vertical variables, such as rank and age, and horizontal variables, such as intimacy and familiarity between the speaker and hearer, are discussed. We call the vertical among these 'power' variables, and the horizontal ones 'solidarity' variables, following Brown and Gilman's (1970) well-known distinction. We also discuss variations away from the canonical honorifics in so-called *Apjonpŏp* and indirect honorifics. Section 9.4 illustrates different types of terms of address: second-person pronouns, titles with names, and kinship terms. In particular, Korean kinship terms are determined by two variables: the power relationship between speaker and hearer, and the marriage status of the addressee. Section 9.5 discusses language policy.

9.1   Regional Varieties

Korean linguists do not agree on how many regional varieties of Koreanic exist in Korea, but we will classify them into six, as recognized by Lee (1967: 410). Four of these are located in the Republic of Korea: Central or Standard dialect,

Kyŏngsang, Chŏlla, and Cheju, which as we argued in Chapter 2 is widely recognized as having the status of a separate language within Koreanic. The Democratic People's Republic of Korea distinguishes two main varieties: Hamgyŏng and Pyŏngan. The distinctions between these regional varieties range over the lexicon, and phonological and grammatical structure. In this section, we will describe the distinguishing characteristics of these six varieties.

9.1.1   South Korean Regional Varieties

9.1.1.1   Central Dialect   The Central dialect, or Standard Korean, is spoken in the capital city of South Korea, Seoul, and the surrounding areas of Kyŏnggi, Ch'ungch'ŏng, Kangwŏn, and Hwanghae provinces. For the most part the phonology, morphology, and syntax of this region are the Standard Korean represented elsewhere in this book, but we note some regional differences in this section. The phonemic inventory of the Central dialect is the largest among the Korean regional varieties, with nineteen consonants, three semivowels and, among the most conservative speakers, ten vowels, subject to some variation in different regions. There is a three-way distinction (lax, aspirated, and tensed) for bilabials, alveolars, palatals, and velars, a two-way distinction (lax, tensed) for the fricatives /s/ and /ss/, three nasals, one glottal stop and one alveolar lateral. The vowel inventory for the most conservative speakers distinguishes ten vowels according to tongue height, backness, and roundness. Among most younger speakers of the Central dialect, only seven vowels are actually distinguished. While standard treatments distinguish four high and mid vowels by backness and roundness (Cho 2006: 237–239), most younger speakers do not distinguish /ey/ [e] and /ay/ [ɛ], while /wi/ [y~ɥi] and /oy/ [ø~we] are realized as the diphthongs [ɥi] and [we] respectively.

(1)   Phonemic inventory (Central dialect)
    a. Consonants (cf. Table 3.1)

p [p~b]	ㅂ	t [t~d]	ㄷ	c [tɕ~dz]	ㅈ	k [k~g]	ㄱ			
ph [pʰ]	ㅍ	th [tʰ]	ㅌ	ch [tɕʰ]	ㅊ	kh [kʰ]	ㅋ			
pp [p̚]	ㅃ	tt [t̚]	ㄸ	cc [t̚ɕ]	ㅉ	kk [k̚]	ㄲ			
		s [s]	ㅅ							
		ss [s̚]	ㅆ							
m [m]	ㅁ	n [n]	ㄴ			ng [ŋ]	ㅇ	h [h]	ㅎ	
		l [l~r]	ㄹ							
w [w~ɥ]		y [j]				u [ɯ]				

    b. Vowels (cf. Table 3.2)

i [i]	이	wi [y~ɥ]	위	u [ɯ]	으	wu [u]	우
ey [e]	에	oy [ø~we]	외			o [o]	오
ay [ɛ]	애	a [a]	아			e [ʌ]	어

There are many distinctive syntactic and morphological properties in the Central dialect beyond those identified as Standard Korean features. First, there are variant nominative markers, in addition to Standard $=i\sim=ka$, as in (2) and (3).

(2)   Central dialect nominative markers
=*i*   이
=*ka*   가
=*ke*   거
=*iki*   이기
=*ise*   이서
=*taka*   다가
=*takase*   다가서

Ke is used mainly in Kangwŏn province while *ise* is used with collective nouns and *taka/takase* is used with [+human] nouns. The former is probably derived from the bound noun *kes* 'thing, one', while *ise* most likely derived from the infinitive form of the MK existential verb *is-* 'be'.

(3)   Central dialect nominative marker examples
         a. 철수가 학교에 간다.
            Chelswu=ka   *hakkyo=ey*   *ka-n-ta.*
            Chelswu=NOM   school=DIR   go-PRES-PLN
            'Chelswu goes to school.'
         b. 철수거 밥을 먹는다.
            Chelswu=ke   *pap=ul*   *mek-nun-ta.*
            Chelswu=NOM   cooked rice=ACC   eat-PRES-PLN
            'Chelswu eats cooked rice.'
         c. 둘이서 공부한다.
            Twul=ise   *kongpwuha-n-ta.*
            two=NOM   study-PRES-PLN
            'Two people study.'
         d. 학생다가/다가서 뛰어 논다.
            Haksayng=taka/takase ttwi-e   *no-n-ta.*
            student=NOM   jump-INF   play-PRES-PLN
            'Students play around.'

Second, there are a variety of accusative markers, *el, lel, u, lu, l;* dative markers, *hanthey, hanthi, intey, inthey, tele, pokwu;* and locative markers, *i, ey, wu, u.* Of the accusative markers, *el* and *lel* are used in most of the central parts of the region while *u* and *lu* are used in Kangwŏn province. The dative marker *hanthi* derives through monophthongization of the second syllable in Standard *hanthey* and is used in Ch'ungch'ŏng namdo, while *intey/inthey* is used in Kangwŏn province. Of the locative markers, *i, ey, wu* are used in Kyŏnggi and Ch'ungch'ŏng province.

(4) Nonstandard case markers
   a. Accusative: 얼 =*el*, 럴 =*lel*, 으 =*u*, 르 =*lu*, ㄹ =*l*
   b. Dative: 한테 =*hanthey*, 한티 =*hanthi*, 인데 =*intey*, 인테 =*inthey*, 더러 =*tele*, 보구 =*pokwu*
   c. Locative: 이 =*i*, 에 =*ey*, 우 =*wu*, 으 =*u*

A nonstandard feature of the Central region is raising of /o/ in the polite suffix -*a/eyo* to -*a/eyu*, common especially in Ch'ungch'ŏng province (5).

(5)   Polite ending -*a/eyo* raised to -*a/eyu*
   a. 철수가 학교에 가유.
      Chelswu=ka   hakkyo=ey ka-yu.
      Chelswu=NOM   school=DIR go-POL
      'Chelswu goes to school.'
   b. 나는 피자를 먹어유.
      Na=nun   phica=lul   mek-eyu.
      I=NOM   pizza=ACC   eat-POL
      'I eat pizza.'

9.1.1.2 Kyŏngsang Dialect   The dialect known as Kyŏngsang or Tongnam is spoken in Kyŏngsangnamdo and Kyŏngsangbukdo provinces. This variety is traditionally considered to be descended from the language of the Silla dynasty in the Three Kingdoms period, described as Old Korean in Chapter 2. As we saw there, our records of Old Korean are too sparse to identify specific features that are retained in modern Kyŏngsang. But modern Kyŏngsang varieties do retain features of Middle Korean, in particular, lexical pitch accent.

Kyŏngsang varieties also share some innovations. Some varieties merge the front vowels 에 /*ey*/ and 애 /*ay*/, as among younger speakers of the Central variety, but some also merge the mid central vowels 으 /*u*/ and 어 /*e*/. Typically Kyŏngnam (the Pusan area) maintains the distinction between the front vowels while Kyŏngbuk (centered around Taegu) maintains the distinction between the mid central vowels. As for consonants, the coronal fricatives ㅅ /*s*/ and reinforced ㅆ /*ss*/ are not distinguished in some parts of the region. The coda consonant cluster simplification process we observed as optional in Chapter 5 has apparently resulted in reshaping of the roots with singleton consonant codas in some Kyŏngsang varieties.

(6)   Coda consonants simplification
   a. 값이 *kaps=i* → 갑이 *kap=i* value-NOM
   b. 돐이 *tols=i* → 돌이 *tol=i* one year birthday-NOM
   c. 넋이 *neks=i* → 넉이 *nek=i* life-NOM
   d. 닭이 *talk=i* → 닥이 *tak=i* chicken-NOM

As for suprasegmental features, most Kyŏngnam varieties distinguish two tones, while three tones are distinguished in Kyŏngbuk province. Regular correspondences between the placement of pitch accent in Kyŏngsang varieties and Middle Korean indicate that the pitch-accent system is a retention from Middle Korean, although the locus of accent has shifted. There are a couple of distinctive features in the syntax and morphology of this dialect. First, the two nominative markers (=*i* and =*ka*) can be stacked in Kyŏngbuk province after a consonant-final noun (7).

(7)   Nominative marker
  a. 준묵이가 가슴이 커요.
     Cwunmwuk=i=ka   kasum=i   khe-yo.
     Cwunmwuk=NOM   chest=NOM big-POL
     'Cwunmwuk's chest is big.'
  b. 용이가 하늘로 올라간다.
     Yong=i=ka   hanul=lo   ollaka-n-ta.
     dragon=NOM   sky=DIR   go up-PRES-PLN
     'A dragon goes up into the sky.'

Second, the possessive marker 의 *uy* is monophthongized as 으 *u* after a consonant and 이 *i* after a vowel, as in (8). The latter process is also attested in Middle Korean.

(8)   Possessive marker
  a. 철수가 도서관으 방에서 공부해요.
     Chelswu=ka   tosekwan=u   pang=eyse kongpwuhay-yo.
     Chelswu=NOM   library=POSS   room=LOC   study-POL
     'Chelswu studies in the room of the library.'
  b. 영희가 학교이 식당에서 밥을 먹어요.
     Yenghuy=ka   hakkyo=i   siktang=eyse   pap=ul
     Yenghuy=NOM   school=POSS restaurant=LOC   cooked rice=ACC
     mek-eyo.
     eat-POL
     'Yenghuy eats cooked rice at the restaurant of the school.'

Third, there are a variety of dative markers (한테 *hanthey*, 인데 *intey*, 더러 *tele*, 대고 *tayko*, 보고 *poko*, 손에 *soney*) and two comitative markers (하고 *hako*, 캉 *khang*) used in this dialect. Fourth, two unique final verb suffixes are common in this dialect, as we see in (9).

(9)   Predicate ending marker
  a. 철수가 학교에서 공부합니더.
     Chelswu=ka   hakkyo=eyse kongpwuha-mnite.
     Chelswu=NOM   school=LOC   study-POL
     'Chelswu studies at school.'

b. 영희가 식당에서 밥을 먹심더.

Yenghuy=ka   siktang=eyse   pap=ul   mek-simte.
Yenghuy=NOM restaurant=LOC cooked rice=ACC eat-POL
'Yenghuy eats cooked rice at the restaurant.'

Fifth, this dialect freely allows preverbal negation of adjectives, as shown in (10).

(10)   Negation
a. 영희가 안 예쁘다.

Yenghuy=ka   an   yeyppu-ta.
Yenghuy=NOM   NEG pretty-PLN
'Yenghuy is not pretty.'

b. 영희가 예쁘지 않다.

Yenghuy=ka   yeyppu-ci anh-ta.
Yenghuy=NOM   pretty-NEG-PLN
'Yenghuy is not pretty.'

In (10), both short-form and long-form negation are allowed with adjective stems; (10a) is allowed in this dialect, but not in Standard Korean. Lastly, *l*-irregular stems in Kyŏngsang varieties contract final /l/ and omit the infinitive suffix *-e/a* in serial verb constructions (V1 + V2) in (11).

(11)   Contraction of *l*-irregular verbs in serial verb contexts
a. 철수가 교실에 드가다.

Chelswu=ka   kyosil=ey   tu-ka-ta.
Chelswu=NOM   classroom=DIR in-go-PLN
'Chelswu goes into the classroom.'

b. 영희가 아침 8시에 인나다.

Yenghuy=ka   achim   yetelsi=ey   in-na-ta.
Yenghuy=NOM morning 8 o'clock=at get-up-PLN
'Yenghuy gets up at 8 o'clock in the morning.'

The serial verb patterns in other dialects corresponding to (11) are *tul-e-ka-ta* and *il-e-na-ta*. There are also many unique lexical items that are used only in Kyŏngsang varieties, some of which are listed in (12).

(12)   Lexical features of Kyŏngsang varieties (Standard forms in parentheses)
a. Verb

동개다 (포개다)	*tongkayta (phokayta)*	to fold
도딕키다 (훔치다)	*totikkhita (hwumchita)*	to steal
깝치다 (재촉하다)	*kkapchita (caychokhata)*	to hurry
까리비다 (꼬집다)	*kkalipita (kkocipta)*	to pinch

b. Noun

다황 (성냥)	*tahwang (sengnyang)*	match
짠지 (김치)	*ccanci (kimchi)*	kimchi
능가 (벼랑)	*nungka (byelang)*	cliff

c. Adverb
백지 (공연히) *paykci (kongyenhi)* vainly
맹 (역시)   *mayng (yeksi)*   of course
하마 (벌써)   *hama (pelsse)*   already

d. Time expressions
저아래 *cealay* 'two days before yesterday', 아래 *alay* 'the day before yesterday', 어제 *ecey* 'yesterday', 오늘 *onul* 'today', 내일 *nayil* 'tomorrow', 모레 *moley* 'the day after tomorrow', 저모레 *cemoley* (Kyŏngbuk/Kyŏngnam) 'two days after tomorrow', 그제 *kucey* 'two days before yesterday'

9.1.1.3 Chŏlla Dialect The Chŏlla dialect is also known as the Sŏnam (southwest) or Honam (Sino-Korean for 'south of the river') dialect. It is spoken in Chŏllanamdo and Chŏllabukdo provinces. In Chŏlla varieties 에 *=ey* is sometimes raised to /i/, diphthongs in some contexts are monophthongized, and ㅎ *h* may be deleted, as seen in the following examples.

(13)   Chŏlla monophthongization and /h/ deletion
        a. 싯 (셋)   *sis (seys)*   three
        b. 시상 (세상)   *sisang (seysang)*   world
        c. 고양 (고향)   *koyang (kohyang)*   hometown
        d. 저나 (전화)   *cena (cenhwa)*   telephone

In Chŏlla varieties we also find tense and aspirated consonants corresponding to Standard Korean plain consonants (14).

(14)   Phonology in Chŏlla
        Tensed consonants
        a. 까죽 (가죽)   *kkacwuk (kacwuk)*   leather
           깨구락지 (개구리)   *kkaykwulakci (kaykwuli)*   frog
           또랑 (도랑)   *ttolang (tolang)*   ditch
           때롱 (대롱)   *ttaylong (taylong)*   hollow tube
           빤듯하다 (반듯하다)   *ppantushata (pantushata)*   straight
        b. Aspirated consonants
           카만히 (가만히)   *khamanhi (kamanhi)*   calmly
           타레박 (두레박)   *thaleypak (twuleypak)*   kibble
           차꼬 (자꾸)   *chakko (cakkwu)*   frequently
           혼차 (혼자)   *honcha (honca)*   alone

As for syntax and morphology, Chŏlla has both short-form and long-form negation, like Standard Korean, but long-form negation has a different form: verb plus 도/든/들 *to/tun/tul* + 않다 *anhta*, instead of using the regular form of 지 않다 *ci anhta*, as in (15).

(15)   Negation in Chŏlla
    a. 가도 않다   *kato anhta*   not go
    b. 있도 없다   *issto epsta*   not have
    c. 알도 모르다   *alto moluta*   not know

Examples of distinctive Chŏlla morphology are shown in the following examples. Note especially the locative marker, the delimiter for 'even', and different verbal endings in (16).

(16)   a. 에 *ey* → 에가 *eyka*
       고향에가 나무가 많다.
       Kohyang=eyka   namwu=ka manh-ta.
       hometown=LOC   tree=NOM   a lot-PLN
       'There are a lot of trees in a hometown.'
    b. 조차 *cocha* → 할라 *halla*
       혈압할라 높은데 . . .
       Heylap=halla   noph-untey . . .
       blood pressure-even   high-and
       'Blood pressure is high and . . .'
    c. 요 *yo* → 라우 *lawu*
       서울 갔는디라우 . . .
       Sewul   ka-ss-nunti-lawu . . .
       Seoul   go-PAST-and-POL
       '(Someone) went to Seoul and . . .'
    d. 소 *so* → 게 *key*
       어서 오게.
       Ese   o-key.
       please   come-POL
       'Please come.'
    e. 누가 죽으까미?
       Nwu=ka   cwuk-ukkami?
       who=NOM   die-Q
       'Who has died?'

With regard to lexical features, Chŏlla uses distinctive nominalizers and verbalizers, listed in (17).

(17)   Nominalizers and verbalizers in Chŏlla
    a. Nominalizer

가심 *kasim*	짓가심	*ciskasim*	vegetable for kimchi
	골칫가심	*kolchiskasim*	trouble maker
거리 *keli*	땔거리	*ttaylkeli*	firewood
	샛거리	*sayskeli*	side
보 *po*	먹보	*mekpo*	eater
	대갈보	*taykalpo*	person with a big head

쟁이	*cayngi*	떼쟁이	*tteycayngi*	person who throws a tantrum to get what he wants
		싸납쟁이	*ssanapcayngi*	scoundrel
뱅이	*payngi*	껄떡뱅이	*kkelttekpayngi*	gag
		더듬뱅이	*tetumpayngi*	stutterer

b. Verbalizers

시롭	*silop*	어른시롭다	*elunsilopta*	adult-like
		귀찮시롭다	*kwichanhsilopta*	annoying
허니	*heni*	께끗허니	*kkeykkusheni*	clean
		미안허니	*mianheni*	sorry
		누러니	*nwuleni*	yellow

9.1.1.4 Cheju The Cheju variety – here, as in current UNESCO practice, recognized as a distinct language in its own right – is spoken by people on Cheju Island, which is located off the southern tip of the Korean peninsula. It is divided into two major areas, based on location relative to Halla-san, the large volcanic mountain in the center of the island: the Sanbuk dialect (north of the mountain) and Sannam (south of the mountain). Due to Cheju Island's isolation from the main body of the Korean peninsula throughout history, the Cheju variety is not mutually intelligible with mainland varieties, especially in terms of the lexicon. On the basis of the "dialect chain" criterion of mutual intelligibility, Cheju may be considered a separate language in the Koreanic family. In 2010, UNESCO officially declared Cheju to be a critically endangered language on the basis of the number of surviving native speakers, all elderly, and the fact that the language is not being transmitted to the younger generation.

The vowel inventory of Cheju contains nine monophthongs and fourteen diphthongs. The monophthongs include a ninth vowel not found in Standard Korean, the low back rounded vowel /ɒ/, which is a direct reflex of the Middle Korean vowel [ʌ], known as *alay-a* 'lower a' and written < • > in fifteenth-century Hangul materials. (The MK vowel is transcribed as /o/ in the Yale Romanization system for Middle Korean.) MK *alay-a* is usually held to have been unrounded, based on its description in the *Hunmin chŏng'ŭm* and its distribution in Sino-Korean, but the modern Cheju reflex is described as rounded. Thus Cheju has /sɒnai/ for MK /sonahi/ [sʌnahi] 'man', Standard Korean *sanay* 사내, or more commonly, Sino-Korean남자. Cheju does not retain /ɒ/ as the reflex of MK *alay-a* [ʌ] in every environment, however. In noninitial syllables the Cheju reflex of *alay-a* is typically /o/, a pattern Cheju shares with some Chŏlla varieties. Thus Cheju has *manong* for MK [manʌr] (Standard *manul*) 'garlic' (see [19]).

In terms of consonant phonology, like some mainland varieties, Cheju regularly palatalizes historical /k/ before high front vowels. Thus the word for woman, *cicippai* 지지빠이 (21b) from *kyeycip* 'woman' plus *ai* 'child', has developed through monophthongization of the first syllable's vowel followed by palatalization. Another distinctive feature of Cheju phonology is widespread tensification at compound boundaries, also a feature shared with Chŏlla varieties; however in the examples in (18), tensification extends to tense consonant spreading into the onset of a vowel-initial syllable.

(18)   Tense consonant spreading in Cheju compounds
    a. 한국음식 (한국끔식) *hankwuk umsik (hankwuk kkumsik)* Korean food
    b. 맏아들 (맏따들) *mat atul (mat ttatul)* first son
    c. 계집아이 (지지빠이) *kyeycip ai (cici ppai)* girl

Another notable property of Cheju is the occurrence of the velar nasal /ŋ/ in the coda, typically in root-final position where there is no corresponding consonant in Standard Korean. Examples are given in (19).

(19)   Coda /ŋ/ in *Cheju*
    a. 마농 (마늘) *manong (manul)* garlic
      바농 (바늘) *panong (panul)* needle
    b. 아방 (아버지) *apang (apeci)* father
      어멍 (어머니) *emeng (emeni)* mother
    c. 파랑허 (파랗다) *palanghe (phalahta)* blue
      빨강허 (빨갛다) *ppalkanghe (ppalkahta)* red
    d. 경허 (그렇다) *kyenghe (kulehta)* be like that
      영허 (이렇다) *yenghe (ilehta)* be like this

With regard to morphosyntax, there are many verbal endings that are unique to Cheju, as shown in (20).

(20)   Verbal endings in Cheju
    a. Past tense 암ㅅ/엄ㅅ *ams/ems*
      가이가 지금 질을 막암ㅅ쑤다.
      Kai=ka   cikum cil=ul   mak-ams-sswuta.
      boy-NOM   now   road=ACC block-PAST-PLN
      'A boy blocked the road.'
    b. Past tense 앗/엇 *as/es*
      난 아까 밥 먹엇쑤다.
      Nan akka   pap   mek-es-sswuta.
      I   earlier cooked rice eat-PAST-PLN
      'I ate cooked rice earlier.'
    c. Plain 으크/으쿠 *ukhu/ukhwu*
      그거 나가 먹으쿠다.
      Ku=ke   na=ka mek-ukhwuta.
      that=thing I=NOM eat-PLN
      'I eat that thing.'

d. Imperative 읍서 *upse*

이디서 질을 막읍서 (여기에서 길을 막으십시오).

Iti=se   cil=ul   mak-upse.
here=from   road=ACC   block-IMP
'Block the road from here.'

e. Imperative 으라 *ula*

이디서 질을 막으라 (여기에서 길을 막으라).

Iti=se   cil=ul   mak-ula.
here=from   road=ACC   block-IMP
'Block the road from here.'

The Cheju lexicon also contains many distinctive forms. Some of these, listed in (21), have archaic features. For example, 'tree' (Standard Korean *namwu* 나무) is reconstructed as pre-MK *namok. The Cheju form is derived by syncope of the second syllable vowel followed by assimilation: *namok > *namk > nang [naŋ].

(21)   Lexicon in *Cheju*

a. 하르방 (할아버지)   *halupang (halapeci)*   grandfather
   할망 (할머니)   *halmang (halmeni)*   grandmother
b. 사나이 (남자)   *sanai (namca)*   man
   지지빠이 (여자)   *cicippai (yeca)*   woman
   비바리 (처녀)   *pipali (chenye)*   unmarried woman
c. 강생이 (강아지)   *kangsayngi (kangaci)*   dog
   고냉이 (고양이)   *konayngi (koyangi)*   cat
   도새기 (돼지)   *tosayki (twayci)*   pig
   쳉이 (쥐)   *cweyngi (cwi)*   mouse
d. 지실 (감자)   *cisil (kamca)*   potato
   감저 (고구마)   *kamce (kokwuma)*   sweet potato
   송키 (채소)   *songkhi (chayso)*   vegetable
   낭 (나무)   *nang (namwu)*   tree

9.1.2   North Korean Regional Varieties

9.1.2.1 Pyŏngan Dialect   The Pyŏngan dialect is spoken by people in the northwest region (Sŏbuk) of the Korean peninsula, particularly in Pyŏnganamdo and Pyŏnganbukdo provinces, including the capital city of the DPRK, P'yŏngyang, and part of Hwanghae province. Pyŏngan has an eight-vowel system. The dialect is characterized by retention of /t/ before high front vowels. Another well-known feature is that /l/ and /n/ appear in onset position in contexts where they have been lost in Standard Korean. The high front vowel /i/ becomes a mid central /u/ [ɯ] before *s, p,* or *ch,* as shown in (22).

(22)   Pyŏngan phonetic/phonological features
      ㄷ *t* Palatalization
- a. 디다 (지다)　　*tita (cita)*　　　go down
    티다 (치다)　　*thita (chita)*　　hit
    ㄹ/ㄴ *l/n* in initial position
- b. 리씨　　　　　*lissi*　　　　　　Mr. Lee
    류씨　　　　　*lyussi*　　　　　Mr. Yoo
    님재래 (임자가)　*nimcaylay (imcaka)*　darling
    녑구리 (엽구리)　*nepkwuli (yepkwuli)*　shoulder
    너느 (어느)　　*nenu (enu)*　　　which
    녯날 (옛날)　　*neysnal (yeysnal)*　old days
    이 *i* → 으 *u* before ㅅ *s*, ㅂ *p*, ㅊ *ch*
- c. 승겁다　　　　*sungkepta*　　　insipid
    슳다　　　　　*sulhta*　　　　　dislike
    즐다　　　　　*culta*　　　　　watery
    듬승　　　　　*tumsung*　　　　beast
    츩　　　　　　*chulk*　　　　　arrowroot
    츠다　　　　　*chuta*　　　　　hit

The nominative marker 레 *ley* is used, instead of the Standard Korean nominative markers, *i* or *ka*, as shown in (23).

(23)   Nominative marker in Pyŏngan
- a. 내레 점적해서 못 가것다.
    Nay=ley cemcekhay-se mos ka-kes-ta.
    I=NOM   shy-because   NEG go-FUT-PLN
    'I will not go, due to shyness.'
- b. 내레 어지께 그러디 아난?
    Nay=ley ecikkay   kuleti   anan?
    I=NOM   yesterday   that way NEG say
    'How is it that I didn't say it yesterday?'
- c. 학교레 멀어서 댕기기 힘들다.
    Hakkyo=ley mel-ese   tayngki-ki himtul-ta.
    school=NOM far away-because go-NOMNL hard-PLN
    'School is far away, so it is hard for me to go.'
- d. 그 문데는 어려워서 풀수레 없다.
    Ku mwuntey=nun elyew-ese   pwulswu=ley eps-ta.
    that question=NOM difficult-because solve=NOM NEG-PLN
    'That question is difficult, so (I) cannot solve it.'

In terms of morphology and syntax, there is a distinctive marker for past tense, 아시/앗 *asi/as*, 어시/엇 *esi/es*, 가시/갓 *kasi/kas*. This is derived from a contraction of MK infinitive *-a/e* plus *isi-* 'be, exist'.

(24)   Past tense marker in Pyŏngan
- a. 내레 고기를 잡아시오/잡앗어요.
    Nay=ley koki=lul cap-asi-o/cap-as-eyo.
    I=NOM   fish=ACC catch-PAST-POL
    'I caught a fish.'

b. 덤심을 먹어시오/먹엇어요.
Temsim=ul   mek-esi-o/mek-es-eyo.
lunch=ACC   eat-PAST-POL
'(I) ate lunch.'

c. 학교에 가시시오/가갔어요.
Hakkyo=ey   ka-sisi-o/ka-kass-eyo.
school=DIR   go-PAST-POL
'(I) went to school.'

d. 내레 먹가시오/먹갓어요.
Nay=ley   mek-kasi-o/mek-kas-eyo.
I=NOM   eat-PAST-POL
'I ate.'

Pyŏngan has dialect-specific lexical items (25). *Ssata* 'expensive' means 'inexpensive' in Standard Korean (25a).

(25)   Lexicon in Pyŏngan
  a. 싸다 (비싸다)   *ssata (pissata)*   inexpensive
  b. 큰아바지 (할아버지) *khun apaci (halapeci)* grandfather
  c. 맏아바지 (큰아버지) *mat apeci (khun apeci)* father's older brother
  d. 큰마니 (할머니)   *khun mani (halmeni)*   grandmother
  e. 맏오마니 (큰어머니) *mat omani (khun   wife of father's older
                                   emeni)*   brother

9.1.2.2 Hamgyŏng Dialect The Hamgyŏng dialect is spoken in Hamgyŏngnamdo and Hamgyŏngbukdo provinces, which are located in the northeast (Tongbuk) of the Korean peninsula, as well as in the adjacent areas of the Yanbian Korean Autonomous Prefecture in the People's Republic of China. These varieties are associated with the historical *Yukchin* (six garrisons) settlement, located near Tuman River.

Hamgyŏng retains the palatal glide /y/ attested in earlier stages of Korean after the affricates /c/ (Standard Korean [tɕ]), /ch/ (Standard /tɕʰ/), and /cc/ (Standard [tɕ]). The realization of the affricates themselves is as alveolar sibilant affricates: /ts/, /tsʰ/, /ts̬/.

(26)   Hamgyŏng phonetics and phonology
  a. Retention of /y/ after affricates
     따르다 (짧다)   *ttyaluta (ccalpta)*   follow
     됳다 (좋다)   *tyohta (cohta)*   like
     뎌것 (저것)   *tye kes (ce kes)*   this thing
  b. *i* 이 insertion
     치마 (치매)   *chima (chimay)*   skirt
     장가 (장개)   *cangka (cangkay)*   marriage
     장수 (장시)   *cangswu (cangsi)*   business man

In terms of syntax and morphology, this dialect has its own nominative markers and dative markers.

(27)   Nominative and dative markers in Hamgyŏng
    a. Nominative:
        냉기 nayngki, 잘기 calki, 이가 ika
    b. Dative:
        낭그 nangku, 잘그 calku

Hamgyŏng has the passive suffix -ki- and the causative morpheme -wu-. Thus, ccalkita has the passive meaning 'to be cut', which is realized as ccallita in other dialects, as shown in (28a).

(28)   Passive and causative in Hamgyŏng
    a. 기 ki after any consonants except ㅂ p, ㄱ k, ㅈ c

짤기다 (짤리다)	ccal-ki-ta (ccallita)	to be cut
닫기다 (닫히다)	tat-ki-ta (tathita)	to be closed
듣기다 (들리다)	tut-ki-ta (tullita)	to be heard

    b. 우 wu

놀래우다	nollay-wu-ta	to make surprised
얼리우다	elli-wu-ta	to make frozen
소기우다	soki-wu-ta	to make deceived
빠지우다	ppaci-wu-ta	to make fall

This dialect has special connective morphemes as shown in (29).

(29)   Connective endings in Hamgyŏng
    a. 길래 killay   because
    b. 자구 cakwu   in order to
    c. 래르 laylu   in order to
    d. 랴르 lyalu   in order to

There are three types of speech styles relating to honorifics; honorific, regular and half-talk (panmal). These vary depending on the clause type: affirmative, interrogative, imperative, or propositive.

(30)   Honorifics in Hamgyŏng
    a. Affirmative
        a. Honorific 읍/습 꾸미 up/sup kkwumi
                     읍/습꿔니 up/sup kkweni
        b. Regular   오/소 o/so
        c. Half-talk   다 ta
    b. Interrogative
        a. Honorific 읍/습 둥(두) up/sup twung (twu)
        b. Regular   오/소 o/so
        c. Half-talk   니 ni, 냐 nya, 은냐 unnya

    c. Imperative
        a. Honorific 읍/습 쇼 *up/sup syo*
        b. Regular 오/소 *o/so*
        c. Half-talk 아/어라 *a/ela*
    d. Propositive
        a. Honorific 깁소 *kipso*, 겝소 *keypso*, 꽈니 *kkwani*
        b. Regular 기오 *kio*, 게오 *keyo*
        c. Half-talk 쟈 *cya*

Below are some distinctive lexical items in the Hamgyŏng dialect.

(31)   Lexicon in Hamgyŏng
    a. 가매치 (누룽지)   *kamaychi (nwulwungci)*   burned rice
       겡게 (감자)   *keyngkey (kamca)*   potato
       동심 (겨울)   *tongsim (kyewul)*   winter
    b. Lexical items with meanings distinct from Standard Korean
       닦다 (볶다)   *takkta (pokkta)*   cook
       마누래 (천연두)   *manwulay (chenyentwu)*   smallpox
       바쁘다 (어렵다, 힘들다) *papputa (elyepta, himtulta)* difficult
       분주하다 (시끄럽다)   *pwuncwuhata (sikkulepta)* noisy
       삐치다 (참견하다)   *ppichita (chamkyenhata)*   meddle
       소나기 (우레)   *sonaki (wuley)*   thunder
       싸다 (사다)   *ssata (sata)*   buy
    c. Kinship terms: no difference between mother's side and father's side
       아재 (고모, 이모)   *acay (komo, imo)*   mother's sister
       맏아바니 (큰아버지, 큰이모부) *matapani (khun apeci, khun imopwu)*
                                              father's older brother
    d. Loanwords from Chinese, Russian, and Manchu
       광차이 (삽)   *kwangchai (sap)*   shovel
       다두배채 (양배추)   *tatwupaychay (yangpaychwu)* cabbage
       빙고 (썰매)   *pingko (sselmay)*   sleigh
       가름다시 (연필)   *kalumtasi (yenphil)*   pencil
       마선 (재봉틀)   *masen (caypongthul)*   sewing machine
       비지깨 (성냥)   *picikkay (sengnyang)*   match
       삭개 (모자)   *sakkay (moca)*   hat
       마우래 (모자)   *mawulay (moca)*   hat
       쿠리매 (외투)   *khwulimay (oythwu)*   coat

9.2   Speech Style

Speech style refers to a speaker's linguistic stance toward the hearer. There are six different speech styles in contemporary Korean, including two which are now largely archaic. Speech styles are used in combination with different sentence patterns and honorifics. This section describes the relationship between speech styles and sentence patterns.

As we have seen in earlier chapters, Korean linguists distinguish four major main clause types: declarative, interrogative, imperative, and propositive. Following Kwon (2011: 86–90), these four sentence types can be distinguished according to two variables: (i) whether a speaker requests something from a hearer, and (ii) whether action is to be taken. If a speaker asks something of a hearer, the sentence type is either interrogative, imperative, or propositive, but if a speaker does not ask anything of a hearer, it is declarative. An interrogative sentence involves a request to a hearer, but it does not require any action to be taken. On the other hand, an imperative sentence involves a speaker's request to a hearer and it requires taking action on the part of the hearer. Similarly, a propositive sentence involves a speaker's request to a hearer, but it requires action taken by both the speaker and the hearer, as schematized in (32).

(32)   Sentence types (Kwon 2011: 86–90) (Reintroduced from (40) in Chapter 7)

		Speaker's request from a hearer	
		−	+
Action to be followed	−	Declarative	Interrogative
	+		Imperative (hearer)Propositive (hearer and speaker)

There is disagreement on how many speech styles there are in Korean, depending upon whether or not we include the two archaic styles. Here we will introduce the four major contemporary styles, listed in (33).

(33)   Speech style
  a. Deferential
  b. Polite
  c. Intimate
  d. Plain

People use the deferential speech style to show respect to a hearer; this is considered to be the highest speech style and is used in formal settings, such as when giving a speech. The polite speech style is used with strangers and shows a lesser degree of respect than deferential; it is the most widely used speech style. The intimate speech style is used with those younger than the speaker and is known as *panmal* (literally, "half-talk"). The plain speech style is used by close friends and children, but also in certain formal occasions as a spoken form and to a general audience in written form. There are also two archaic speech styles: (i) familiar (네/게, -*ney*/-*key*) and (ii) semi-formal (오/소, *o/so*). As they are archaic, these will not be discussed in detail here. There are many factors that decide which speech style one has to use, and because they relate to when to use honorifics, we will discuss those factors in Section 9.3. Twenty combinations of sentence patterns are generated from five sentence types and four speech styles (34).

(34)   20 combinations of sentence type and speech style (Reintroduced
       from [52] in Chapter 5 and [41] in Chapter 7)

	Declarative	Interrogative	Propositive	Suspective	Imperative
Plain	ㄴ/는다	니	자	지	라/어라
	Tense-*ta*	Tense-*ni*	-*ca*	-*ci*	-*la*/-*ela*
Intimate	아/어/해	아/어/해	아/어/해	지	아/어/해
	-*a/e/hay*	-*a/e/hay*	-*a/e/hay*	-*ci*	-*a/e/hay*
Polite	아/어/해요	아/어/해요	아/어/해요	지요	아/어/해요
	-*a/e/hay-yo*	-*a/e/hay-yo*	-*a/e/hay-yo*	-*ci-yo*	-*a/e/hay-yo*
Deferential	ㅂ/습니다	ㅂ/습니까	ㅂ/읍시다	시지요	ㅂ/으십시오
	-*(su)pnita*	-*(su)pnikka*	(-*u*)*psita*	-(*u*)*siciyo*	-*p/usipsio*

Note that the plain style sentences in (35) are infelicitous with subjects requiring deference, as in (35b) and (35d).

(35)   Plain speech style
       a. 철수가 학교에 간다.
          Chelswu=ka   hakkyo=ey   ka-n-ta.
          Chelswu=NOM   school=DIR   go-PRES-PLN
          'Chelswu goes to school.'
       b. *아버지는 학교에 가니?
          **Apeci=nun   hakkyo=ey   ka-ni?*
          father=NOM   school=DIR   go-Q
          'Does father go to school?'
       c. 학교에 가자.
          Hakkyo=ey   ka-ca.
          school=DIR   go-PROP
          'Let's go to school.'
       d. *아버지가 밥을 먹어라.
          **Apeci=ka   pap=ul   mek-ela.*
          father=NOM   cooked rice=ACC   eat-IMP
          'Father, eat cooked rice!'

9.3   Honorifics

Honorifics are considered to be part of Korean culture, showing respect to the subject, the object, and the hearer. In this section, we describe what they are, when and how to use them with different variables, and departures from canonical honorific usage such as indirect honorifics and *Apjonpŏp*.

Honorifics show a speaker's attitude toward the clausal subject, object/indirect object, or hearer. A subject honorific is used to show respect to the subject. It can be formed lexically, morphologically, syntactically, or in some combination of these, as summarized in (36), with the corresponding sentence patterns in (37).

(36)   Subject honorific
         a. Lexical:
            i.   잡수시다   *capswusita*   eat
            ii. 계시다   *kyeysita*   be
            iii. 주무시다   *cwumwusita*   sleep
            iv. 돌아가시다   *tolakasita*   die
            v.   진지   *cinci*   cooked rice
         b. Morphological:
            i.   N +께서 *kkeyse*
            ii. N + 님 *nim*
         c. Syntactic
            i.   V + (으)시 *(u)si*

The following subject-honorific sentences show that if the subject is denoted by a title or kin term indicating a person worthy of deference, it should be marked by the honorific suffix *-nim*, while in general NPs denoting such referents take the nominative marker *=kkeyse,* and the sentence should also have the subject-honorific verbal suffix *-(u)si*. The sentences in (37) demonstrate the varying degrees of honorifics with (37a) being the least honorific and (37d) the most honorific.

(37)   Subject honorific
         a. 할아버지가 밥을 먹는다.
            Halapeci=ka   *pap=ul*   *mek-nun-ta.*
            grandfather=NOM   cooked rice=ACC   eat-PRES-PLN
            'Grandfather eats cooked rice.'
         b. 할아버지가 밥을 먹으신다.
            Halapeci=ka   *pap=ul*   *mek-usi-n-ta.*
            grandfather=NOM   cooked rice=ACC   eat-HON-PRES-PLN
            'Grandfather eats cooked rice.'
         c. 할아버님께서 밥을 먹으신다.
            Halape-nim=kkeyse   *pap=ul*   *mek-usi-n-ta.*
            grandfather-HON=NOM   cooked rice=ACC   eat-HON-PRES-PLN
            'Grandfather eats cooked rice.'
         d. 할아버님께서 진지를 잡수신다.
            Halape-nim=kkeyse   *cinci=lul*   *capswu-si-n-ta.*
            grandfather-HON=NOM   cooked rice=ACC   eat-HON-PRES-PLN
            'Grandfather eats cooked rice.'

There are two different ways to make object/indirect object honorifics: lexical and morphological. Some verbs and nouns have honorific counterparts, some of which are listed in (38a). When the object is an honorable person, it takes the honorific indirect object marker *kkey* after the morpheme *nim* as in (38).

(38) Object honorific
    a. Lexical V
        a. 뵙다   *poypta*   see
        b. 모시다   *mosita*   treat
        c. 드리다/올리다/바치다 *tulita/ollita/pachita* give
        d. 여쭙다   *yeccwupta*   ask
        e. 말씀드리다   *malssumtulita*   speak
    b. Morphological
        a. N + 께 *kkey*
        b. N + 님 *nim*

The sentences in (39) show instances of object honorifics with the most honorific in (39a) and the least honorific in (39d). The honorific suffix *nim* and the indirect object marker *kkey* are added, which agrees with the lexical verbs, *tulinta* 'give' or *poyessta* 'see'.

(39) Object honorific
    나는 아버님에게 이 책을 준다.
    a. *Na=nun*   *ape-nim=eykey*   *i*   *chayk=ul* *cwu-n-ta.*
       I=NOM   father-HON=DAT   this book=ACC give-PRES-PLN
       'I give this book to my father.'
    나는 아버님께 이 책을 준다.
    b. *Na=nun*   *ape-nim=kkey*   *i*   *chayk=ul* *cwu-n-ta.*
       I=NOM   father-HON=DAT (HON) this book=ACC give-PRES-PLN
       'I give this book to my father.'
    나는 아버님께 이 책을 드린다.
    c. *Na=nun*   *ape-nim=kkey*   *i*   *chayk=ul* *tuli-n-ta.*
       I=NOM   father-HON=DAT (HON) this book=ACC give (HON)-PRES-PLN
       'I give this book to my father.'
    나는 부친을 찾아 뵈었다.
    d. *Na=nun*   *pwuchin=ul* *chac-a*   *poy-ess-ta.*
       I=NOM   father=ACC   seek-INF see (HON)-PAST-PLN
       'I saw my father.'

When the speaker shows respect to the hearer, the hearer honorific is used. There are three ways to make hearer honorifics: lexically with the humble pronoun *ce* 'I', morphologically with *nim*, and syntactically with the verbal ending form, *yo* in an informal setting and *p/sup nita* in a formal setting, as summarized in (40).

(40) Hearer honorific
    a. Lexical
        a. 저 *ce* 'I'
    b. Morphological
        b. N + 님 *nim*
    c. Syntactic
        i. V + 요 *yo* (informal)
        ii. V + ㅂ/습니다 *p/sup nita* (formal)

The sentences in the following example illustrate the first-person pronoun changing to the humble form in (41b) and the verbal ending changing to *p/ sup nita* in a formal setting in (41c) and (41d). Example (41e) demonstrates all the changes as an example of the most honorific sentence.

(41)   Hearer honorific sentences
    a. 나는 학교에 가요.
      Na=nun hakkyo=ey ka-yo.
      I=NOM   school=DIR go-POL
      'I go to school.'
    b. 저는 학교에 가요.
      Ce=nun hakkyo=ey ka-yo.
      I=NOM   school=DIR go-POL
      'I go to school.'
    c. 나는 학교에 갑니다.
      Na=nun   hakkyo=ey ka-pnita.
      I=NOM   school-DIR go-POL
      'I go to school.'
    d. 저는 학교에 갑니다.
      Ce=nun hakkyo=ey ka-pnita.
      I=NOM   school=DIR go-POL
      'I go to school.'
    e. 선생님께서 진지를 드십니다.
      Sensayng-nim=kkeyse   cinci=lul   tusi-pnita.
      teacher-HON=NOM (HON)   cooked rice=ACC eat (HON)-POL
      'A teacher eats cooked rice.'

There are two major conditions determining when we need to use honorifics. The first condition consists of three variables: the vertical variable 'power', the horizontal variable 'solidarity', and the speech style. Power is related to age, professional ranking, and the familial distance between the speaker and hearer, while solidarity is concerned with intimacy (or familiarity) between two speakers and their genders. The other condition for using honorifics has to do with the level of formality in speech style. The conditions and variables are summarized in (42).

(42)   Variables in honorifics (1)
    a. Power (vertical)
        Age, professional ranking, family distance
    b. Solidarity (horizontal)
        Intimacy (familiarity), gender
    c. Speech style
        Formality

But honorific usage is not completely mechanical or rule-governed. We need to consider yet another variable, the speaker's willingness to acknowledge the three factors in (42). This is summed up in (43).

(43)   Variables in honorifics (2)
     a. Speaker's willingness
     b. Situation in honorifics

In (44), the subject is a person worthy of deference, but speakers may opt to use a subject honorific or not, depending on their willingness to acknowledge the social and interpersonal situation.

(44)   Speaker's willingness
     a. 박 선생이 백화점에 갔다.
       Pak sensayng=i   paykhwacem=ey   ka-ss-ta.
       Park teacher=NOM department store=DIR go-PAST-PLN
       'Teacher Park went to the department store.'
     b. 박 선생님께서 백화점에 가셨다.
       Pak sensayng-nim=kkeyse   paykhwacem=ey   ka-si-ess-ta.
       Park teacher-HON=NOM (HON) department store=DIR go-HON-PAST-PLN
       'Teacher Park went to the department store.'
     c. 형이 도서관에 간다.
       Hyeng=i   tosekwan=ey   ka-n-ta.
       brother=NOM library=DIR   go-PRES-PLN
       'A brother went to the library.'
     d. 형님께서 도서관에 가신다.
       Hyeng-nim=kkeyse tosekwan=ey ka-si-n-ta.
       brother-HON=NOM library=DIR   go-HON-PRES-PLN
       'A brother went to the library.'

In a formal setting such as giving a speech or on a television broadcast, the utterance is either a plain sentence or an honorific sentence, which is a variable of 'situation in honorifics'. The subjects 'the President' or 'father' are normal targets of deference, but it is possible to have the two sentence types in (45).

(45)   Situation in honorifics
     a. 대통령이 교육 정책을 발표하였다. (Television broadcast)
       Taythonglyeng=i kyoyuk cengchayk=ul palpyoha-yess-ta.
       president=NOM   education policy=ACC present-PAST-PLN
       'The President presented an education policy.'
     b. 대통령께서 교육 정책을 발표하셨다.
       Taythonglyeng=kkeyse kyoyuk cengchayk=ul palpyoha-si-ess-ta.
       president=NOM (HON)   education policy=ACC present-HON-PAST-PLN
       'The president presented an education policy.'
     c. 아버지가 세미나에서 발표한다. (Television broadcast)
       Apeci=ka   seymina=eyse   palphyoha-n-ta.
       father=NOM   seminar=LOC   present-PRES-PLN
       'Father presents at the seminar.'

d. 아버님께서 세미나에서 발표하신다.

Ape-nim=kkeyse   seymina=eyse palphyoha-si-n-ta.
father-HON=NOM (HON) seminar=LOC   present-HON-PRES-PLN
'Father presents at the seminar.'

There are two aberrations from the canonical honorific patterns, *Apjonpŏp* or 'suppressed honorific usage' (SK壓尊法) and indirect honorifics. *Apjonpŏp* is defined as a case where an honorific might be expected, but cannot readily be used, because the hearer is older or higher ranked in social position than the referent, or because the referent is younger or lower ranked in social position than the speaker. Instances of *Apjonpŏp* are shown in (46b), (46d), and (46f), with the corresponding regular honorific sentences in (46a), (46c), and (46e). In these examples S designates the speaker, R the referent, and H the hearer.

(46)   *Apjonpŏp*
   a. 아버지께서 들어오셨니?

   Apeci=kkeyse   tul-e   o-si-ess-ni?
   father=NOM (HON)   enter-INF   come-HON-PAST-Q
   'Did Father come in?' (S older brother < R father > H younger brother)

   b. 아버지가 들어왔니?

   Apeci=ka   tul-e   wa-ss-ni?
   father=NOM   enter-INF come-PAST-Q
   'Did Father come in?' (*Apjonpŏp*: S grandfather > R father > H son)

   c. 이 책을 아버님께 드려라.

   I   chayk=ul   ape-nim=kkey   tulye-la.
   this   book=ACC   father-HON=DAT (HON)   give (HON)-IMP
   'Give this book to (your) father.' (S grandfather > R father > H ego)

   d. 이 책을 아버지한테 주어라.

   I   chayk=ul   apeci=hanthey   chwu-ela.
   this   book=ACC   father=DAT   give-IMP
   'Give this book to the father.' (*Apjonpŏp*: S grandfather > R father > H ego)

   e. 작은형, 큰형님께서 돌아오셨어요?

   Cakun hyeng,   khun hyeng-nim=kkeyse   tol-a
   younger brother, older brother-HON=NOM (HON)   return-INF
   o-si-ess-eyo?
   come-HON-PAST-POL
   'Second oldest brother, did the oldest brother come back?'
   (S ego < R oldest brother < H second-oldest brother (lit. 'little brother'))

   f. 할아버지, 큰형이 돌아왔어요.

   Halapeci,   khun hyeng=i   tol-a   wa-ss-eyo.
   grandfather   older brother=NOM return-INF come-PAST-Q
   'Grandfather, did the older brother come back?'
   (*Apjonpŏp*: S ego < R older brother < H grandfather)

Taking (46e, f) for example, in (46e) both speaker (perhaps the youngest brother) and hearer (the second-oldest brother) rank below the referent (oldest brother), so the speaker feels no conflict in using honorific language toward the referent. This contrasts with (46f), where the hearer (the grandfather) is higher in status than the referent (the older brother). In such a context the speaker cannot use the honorific language she or he might normally use toward a higher ranking referent, out of deference to the hearer. The *Apjonpŏp* phenomenon shows that the axes of referent and hearer honorifics are not completely independent; instead the speaker must engage in a calculus involving the relative status of hearer and referent.

Indirect honorifics involve a different kind of departure from canonical honorifics, taking as the target of honorification body parts, belongings, and thoughts of the person to be honored.

(47)   Indirect honorifics
         a. 교수님께서 생각이 많으시다.
            Kyoswu-nim=kkeyse   sayngkak=i   manh-usi-ta.
            professor-HON=NOM (HON)   thoughts=NOM   a lot-HON-PLN
            'A professor has a lot of thoughts.'
         b. 선생님께서 손이 크시다.
            Sensayng-nim=kkeyse   son=i   kh-usi-ta.
            teacher-HON=NOM (HON)   hand=NOM   big-HON-PLN
            'A teacher has a big hand.'
         c. 아버님께서 집이 머시다.
            Ape-nim=kkeyse   cip=i   me-si-ta.
            father-HON=NOM (HON)   home=NOM   far away-HON-PLN
            'A father has a home far away.'

9.4   Terms of Address

"Terms of address" are words or phrases that refer to the addressee of social communication. Selection of term of address can be extremely complicated in specific social contexts. This area of research has always been a central topic in sociolinguistics, because terms of address open communicative acts and set the tone for the interchanges that follow. In this section, terms of address include the second-person pronoun, names with titles, and related kinship terms.

9.4.1   Second-Person Pronouns

There are multiple ways to say 'you', depending on the given situation in Korean. One of the major differences between English and Korean second-person pronouns is that in English, 'you' can be used in any situation, but in Korean, second-person pronouns have limited usages. For example, second-person pronouns cannot be used in (48b) and (48d), whereas it is possible to use 'you' in English in the same situation.

(48)   Second-person pronoun
    a. 아버지, 어디 가세요?
       Apeci, eti   ka-seyyo?
       father where go-POL
       'Father, where do you go?'
    b. #아버지, 너 어디 가세요?
       #Apeci, ne eti   ka-seyyo?
       father you where go-POL
       'Father, where do you go?'
    c. 아버지, 이번에는 아버지가 하세요.
       Apeci, ipeneynun apeci=ka   ha-seyyo.
       father this time   father=NOM do-POL
       'Father, please do it this time.'
    d. #아버지, 이번에는 당신이 하세요.
       #Apeci, ipeneynun tangsin=i ha-seyyo.
       father   this time   you=NOM   do-POL
       'Father, please do it this time.'

As we saw in Chapter 8, there are a variety of forms of 'you', depending on the degree of respect to the hearer, and they each have their own unique meaning. The examples in (49) show the degree of respect in the second-person pronouns with the most respectful in (49a) and the least respectful in (49f).

(49)   Types of second-person pronouns
    a. 어르신 *elusin* 각하 *kakha*
    b. 댁   *tayk*
    c. 당신   *tangsin*
    d. 자네   *caney*
    e. 자기   *caki*
    f. 너   *ne*

In (50), 'you' co-occurs with a polite verbal ending in the first three examples, while it co-occurs with a *panmal* "half-talk" ending in the last three examples.

(50)   Types of second-person pronoun
    a. 이 일은 어르신께서 하세요.
       I   il=un   elusin=kkeyse ha-seyyo.
       this thing=NOM you=NOM (HON) do-POL
       'Please (you) do this thing.'
    b. 이 일은 댁이 하세요.
       I   il=un   tayk=i   ha-seyyo.
       this thing=NOM you=NOM do-POL
       'Please (you) do this thing.'

c. 이 일은 당신이 하세요.
   I   il=un   tangsin=i   ha-seyyo.
   this thing=NOM you=NOM   do-POL
   'Please (you) do this thing.'

d. 이 일은 자네가 해.
   I   il=un   caney=ka hay.
   this thing=NOM you=NOM   do (IMP)
   'Please (you) do this thing.'

e. 이 일은 자기가 해.
   I   il=un   caki=ka   hay.
   this thing=NOM you=NOM   do (IMP)
   'Please (you) do this thing.'

f. 이 일은 네가 해.
   I   il=un   ney=ka   hay.
   this thing=NOM you=NOM   do (IMP)
   'Please (you) do this thing.'

Among the different forms of 'you', *tangsin* has a special usage in advertisements, in newspapers or magazines, or when people argue. The two examples in (51) show that *tangsin* is used when people argue. It is also used in newspapers and advertisements showing some degree of respect as in (51c).

(51)   Usage of *tangsin*
   a. 당신, 왜 그래?
      Tangsin   way   kulay?
      you   why   do
      'How come you do that?'

   b. 이거 당신거요?
      I=ke   tangsin-ke-yo?
      this-thing   you-thing-Q
      'Is this yours?'

   c. 당신의 고민이 뭐에요?
      Tangsin=uy komin=i   mwe-eyyo?
      you=POSS   worry=NOM what-Q
      'What is your worry?'

Caney is more commonly used by male speakers, but is not necessarily inappropriate for females to use. In (52a), *caney* assumes either a male adult or a respected adult with authority, but the addressee cannot be a young woman as in (52b).

(52)   Usage of *caney*
   a. 자네 뭐 해?
      Caney   mwe   hay?
      you   what do-Q
      'What do you do?'

b. *자네 아름답군.
   *Caney   alumtap-kwun.
   you   pretty-EXCLAM
   'You are pretty!'

Caki 'self' as a second-person pronoun is used between a husband and wife, or between two people in a romantic relationship. In (53a), *caki* indicates either a husband or a wife; it is most likely not used by two aged people in the context of (53b).

(53)   Usage of *caki* 'self' as a second-person pronoun
        a. 자기, 이거 어때?
           Caki i-ke   ettay?
           you this-thing how (Q)
           'Honey, how is this?'
        b. 자기, 뭐 먹어?
           Caki   mwe   mek-e?
           you   what   eat-Q
           'Honey, what will you eat?'

9.4.2   Titles with Names

There are four suffixes used as titles in combination with names in Korean which vary in their usage. *Nim* is the most common for honoring a person, *ssi* is used with people's names, *kwun* is used with both males and females, and *yang* is used only for females.

(54)   Vocative suffixes
        a. 님   nim
        b. 씨   ssi   Mr./Ms.
        c. 군   kwun   Mr.
        d. 양   yang   Ms.

As a common honorific marker, *nim* is used with professional titles and kinship titles. The degree of honorifics, from most to least respectful, is as follows: the addressee's title with *nim*, last name with title and *nim*, last name only, and first name only, as listed in (55c).

(55)   Usage of *nim*
        a. Title + *nim*
             a. 사장님   sacang nim   company president
             b. 선생님   sensayng nim   teacher
             c. 총장님   chongcang nim   university president
             d. 감독님   kamtok nim   movie director
        b. Kinship title + *nim*
             a. 형님   hyeng nim   older brother
             b. 누님   nwu nim   older sister

    c. 아버님   *ape nim*   father
    d. 할아버님   *halape nim* grandfather
  c. Degree of deference
    a. Title + 님   사장님   *sacang nim*
    b. Last name + Title + 님 이 사장님 *i sacang nim*
    c. Last name + Title   이 사장   *i sacang*
    d. First name   순신   *swunsin*

However, the usage of *nim* is subject to restrictions, including cases where it is superseded by other specialized honorifics. Thus 'President' in (56a) takes its own professional title, *kakha*, while kin terms such as 'uncle' and 'older brother' do not allow *nim* as a title in (56b); at the same time *samo* 'teacher's wife' and *tolyen* 'husband's younger brother' should obligatorily be followed by *nim* as in (56c) and (56d).

(56)   *Nim* exceptions
    a. *대통령님   **taythonglyeng nim*   President
       대통령 각하   *taythonglyeng kakha*   President
    b. *삼촌님   *samchon nim   uncle
       *오빠님   *oppa nim   older brother
    c. 사모님   *samo nim*   teacher's wife
       *사모   *samo   teacher's wife
    d. 도련님   *tolyen nim*   husband's younger brother
       *도련   *tolyen   husband's younger brother

Ssi is used with a full name in a formal setting, a last name only in a sarcastic sense, and a first name only in an informal or intimate setting.

(57)   Usage of *ssi* with proper names
    a. 조성대씨 *cosengtay ssi* Jo Sengtay
    b. 조씨   *co ssi*   Mr. Jo
    c. 성대씨   *sengtay ssi* Sengtay

Kwun is used with a full name, a last name, or a first name, for both males and females. Unlike gender-differentiated terms such as English 'Mr.', *kwun* can be used when an older figure of higher status talks to a female.

(58)   Usage of *kwun*
    a. 조성대군 *co sengtay kwun* Jo Sengtay
    b. 조군   *co kwun*   Mr. Jo
    c. 성대군   *sengtay kwun*   Sengtay
    d. 혜경군   *hyeykyeng kwun* Heykyung

Yang is used for females as 'Mrs.', 'Ms.', or 'Miss' with a full name, a last name, or a first name.

(59)   Usage of *yang*
    a. 김혜경양   *kim hyeykyeng yang*   Kim Heykyung
    b. 김양   *kim yang*   Ms. (Miss) Kim
    c. 혜경양   *hyeykyeng yang*   Heykyung

9.4.3   Kinship Terms

Korean has a complicated kinship system, but it has three rules of thumb for the linguistic usage of kinship terms. The first rule (age) is that older people use first names when addressing younger people, and the second rule (ranking) is that higher-ranked people use kinship titles when addressing lower-ranked people in a family structure. The third rule (marriage) relates to the marital status of the person referred to, as summarized in (60).

(60)   Kinship term rules
    a. First name: From older person to younger person
    b. Kinship title: From higher ranking to lower ranking in a family structure
    c. Marriage: Terms will vary before and after marriage

However, an older person uses a kinship title without a first name in a special situation such as an old nephew, a married son, an old younger brother, or a daughter's husband. These special conditions relate to age. Thus the kinship title of a young person will be changed to *cokhanim* 'nephew', *apem* 'father', *tongsayng* 'younger brother', and *sawi* 'son-in-law' when the person gets older as in (61).

(61)   Kinship title with no first name
    a. 조카 *cokha* 'nephew' becomes 조카님 *cokhanim* when a nephew gets older.
    b. 아들 *atul* 'son' becomes 애비/아범 *aypi/apem* 'father' when a son gets married.
    c. First name becomes 동생 *tongsayng* 'younger brother' when a brother gets older.
    d. First name becomes 사위 *sawi* 'daughter's husband' when a man gets married.

'Mother' and 'older brother' are kinship terms used by a lower-ranked person to a higher-ranked person in a family structure as in (62a) and (62c), but as we have explained, this usage is asymmetric, so an older person addresses a younger relative by first name rather than use the kin terms in (62b) and (62d).

(62)   Kinship titles
    a. 어머니/엄마 *emeni/emma* mother
    b. #아들   *atul*   son
    c. 형   *hyeng*   older brother
    d. #동생   *tongsayng*   younger brother

The same person is called by different terms before marriage and after marriage in (63a) and (63b), and before and after having children in (63c) and (63d).

(63) Kinship title before/after marriage and before/after having children
- a. 삼촌   *samchon*   uncle
  작은 아버지   *cakun apeci*   uncle
- b. 도련님   *tolyennim*   husband's younger brother
  서방님   *sepangnim*   husband's younger brother
- c. 서방   *sepang*   son-in-law
  애비   *aypi*   son-in-law
- d. 아가   *aka*   daughter-in-law
  애미   *aymi*   daughter-in-law

9.5 Language Policy

In this section, we briefly describe policy, primarily in the ROK, on Hangul, language standardization, language purification, and romanization.

9.5.1 Hangul

As we saw in Chapter 3, Hangul were invented in 1443 by King Sejong with the assistance of his advisors. The policy for the use of Hangul was first promulgated in the *Hangŭl mach'umpŏp t'ongil an* of the Chosŏnŏ Hakhoe on October 9, 1933, as noted in Chapter 3. This was revised in 1946 by the newly formed South Korean government, with successive revisions since then. The most recent revision of this *Hangŭl mach'umpŏp* was in 1988. The regulations of Hangul usage consist of six sections with fifty-seven detailed sub-rules. The first section consists of three basic rules for writing Hangul. The first basic rule is to write the Standard Korean as it is pronounced. The second basic rule is to leave a space between words. The third basic rule has to do with writing foreign words. The second section shows lists of consonants and vowels with their names, and *patchim* (coda consonant) orthography rules. Section 3 is on phonology and consists of thirteen sub-rules. Section 4 is on morphology and consists of twenty-six sub-rules. Section 5 covers spacing and Section 6 contains the rest of the sub-rules that were not prescribed in the previous sections.

9.5.2 Standard Language

In the 1933 *Hangŭl mach'umpŏp t'ongil an*, Standard Korean was considered to be the language spoken by middle-class people in Seoul in 1933. Since 1933, this standard has changed to be the language spoken by the educated people in contemporary Seoul. This revised concept of Standard Korean has two meanings. First, it promotes the use of the Central dialect, which is the focal point of politics, economics, society, and culture in Korea. This is also tantamount to saying that the Seoul dialect is contrasted with dialects of different regions in Korea. Second, it is the language spoken by educated people, which means that it is contrasted not only with other regional varieties but with different socio-economic registers.

9.5.3   Language Purification Policy

There are two major languages that have influenced Korean during its history, Chinese and English. Policy on language purification is concerned with those two languages, starting with how much of the two languages Korean should use, and how to use them if necessary.

Koreans have been using Chinese characters for two millenia, but policy on using Chinese characters has recently changed in the ROK. There are pros and cons to using only native Korean or using both Chinese characters and native Korean together. The policy for using only native Korean originates from the well-known Korean linguist Hyŏnbae Choi, who argued that a Hangul-only policy would have the advantage of raising education levels, since there would be no need to learn difficult Chinese characters. The opposing policy, which promotes using both Hangul and Chinese characters together, is promoted by some academic associations, who argue that the mixed-use policy has many advantages in terms of its effect on education, learning Sino-Korean vocabulary, and understanding major East Asian countries. The current status of this policy is to use both native Korean and Chinese characters.

Policy restricting the use of foreign characters, including English, has been set up as one of four major rules on policy, despite the prevalence of English education in Korea, which begins as early as elementary school. Two major rules are: transcribe foreign characters within the combination of Korean consonants and vowels, and maintain only seven consonants in *patchim* position, ㄱ *k*, ㄴ *n*, ㄹ *l*, ㅁ *m*, ㅂ *p*, ㅅ *s*, and ㅇ *ng*.

9.5.4   Romanization

Romanization represents the language using Latin script. As we discussed in Chapter 3, the ROK has used three major romanization systems: McCune–Reischauer (MR, 1937), Yale (YR, 1942), and Revised Romanization of Korean (RR, 2000). The following comparison shows the similarities and differences of these three systems; see the discussion of these systems in Chapter 3.

(64)   Romanization
          a. Consonants

Hangul	Yale	MR	RR
ㄱ	k	g/k	g/k
ㄲ	kk	kk	kk
ㄴ	n	n	n
ㄷ	t	d/t	d/t
ㄸ	tt	tt	tt
ㄹ	l	r/l	r/l
ㅁ	m	m	m
ㅂ	p	b/p	b/p
ㅃ	pp	pp	pp
ㅅ	s	s	s/t
ㅆ	ss	ss	ss/t
ㅇ	ng	ng	ng
ㅈ	c	ch/j	j
ㅉ	cc	tch	jj
ㅊ	ch	ch'	ch/t
ㅋ	kh	k'	k
ㅌ	th	t'	t
ㅍ	ph	p'	p
ㅎ	h	h	h/t

          b. Vowels and diphthongs

Hangul	Yale	MR	RR
ㅏ	a	a	a
ㅐ	ay	ae	ae
ㅑ	ya	ya	ya
ㅒ	yay	yae	yae
ㅓ	e	ö	eo
ㅔ	ey	e	e
ㅕ	ye	yö	yeo
ㅖ	yey	ye	ye
ㅗ	o	o	o
ㅘ	wa	wa	wa
ㅙ	way	wae	wae
ㅚ	oy	oe	oe
ㅛ	yo	yo	yo
ㅜ	wu	u	u
ㅝ	we	wö	wo
ㅞ	wey	we	we
ㅟ	wi	wi	wi
ㅠ	yu	yu	yu
ㅡ	u	ŭ	eu
ㅢ	uy	ŭi	ui
ㅣ	i	i	i

The MR system was the first major Anglophone-centered romanization created and was the officially recognized system in the ROK from 1984 to 2000. One objection to MR is its use of diacritics, but it is still used internationally by Anglophone scholars of Korean literature and history, among other fields. Recognizing this usage, we have adopted MR for proper names in this book. The YR system has become the established standard romanization for Korean among linguists, and is the system used in this book for linguistic examples, with minor modifications. The RR system is now the most commonly used and widely accepted system of romanization for Korean in South Korea. It was promulgated with rules for both transcription and transliteration. South Korea now has officially used this system since 2000. Almost all road signs and names of railways and subway stations in the ROK have been changed to this system. RR is similar to MR, but uses neither diacritics nor apostrophes; this has helped it gain widespread acceptance on the Internet. Orthographic syllable boundaries are indicated by a hyphen in case of ambiguity.

The MR system and the RR system differ from each other mainly in how they do or do not correspond to Hangul orthography. Both are subphonemic systems, in that they attempt to represent pronunciation in context, so the same Hangul letters may be represented by different Roman letters, depending on their pronunciation in the given context. The Yale system, on the other hand, represents each Korean letter by the same Roman letter context-independently; it is thus primarily a phonemic representation of Korean, and in that sense closest to being a transliteration of Hangul.

9.6   Summary

In this chapter, we discussed regional varieites, speech style, honorifics, terms of address, and language policy. Six major regional varieties were described from lexical, phonological, morphological, and syntactic perspectives. Four of those varieties are spoken in South Korea, while two are spoken in North Korea and the People's Republic of China.

Among South Korean regional varieties, the Central dialect is considered Standard Korean, and is spoken in the surrounding areas of Seoul such as Kyŏnggi, Ch'ungch'ŏng, Kangwŏn, and Hwanghae provinces. In particular, there are nineteen consonants and twenty-one vowels and diphthongs, although some variation exists in different regions, since the Central dialect has the broadest area geographically. This dialect also features many unique case markers including nominative, accusative, dative, and locative markers, along with verbal endings. Kyŏngsang dialect is spoken in Kyŏngsang province, and its distinctive features include suprasegmental features such as tone patterns, nominative markers, possessive markers, dative markers, and comitative markers. There are also many unique lexical items used only in this area.

The Chŏlla dialect is spoken in Chŏlla province and is also called Sŏnam (more commonly Honam) dialect, since Chŏlla is located in the southwest of the Korean peninsula. In terms of syntax and morphology, Chŏlla has a unique long-form negation pattern as well as several distinctive markers and verbal endings. It is phonologically different from other dialects in its greater frequency of tensed and aspirated consonants. Lexically, the Chŏlla dialect features several distinctive nominalizers and verbalizers. The Cheju language is spoken by the people of Cheju Island, off the southern tip of the Korean peninsula. This variety also has many tensed consonants, a likely influence from the Chŏlla province, which is geographically close to Cheju Island. There are many unique vocabulary items used only in this area, some of which are not mutually intelligible with the rest of the Korean varieties.

In North Korea, two dialects are described, Pyŏngan and Hamgyŏng dialect. Pyŏngan dialect is spoken by people in Pyŏngan province, including P'yŏngyang, the capital city of North Korea, located in the northwest region. It has eight basic vowels and is characterized by palatalization of /t/ and initial l/ n that does not exist in South Korean dialects. In terms of syntax and morphology, Pyŏngan features unique nominative markers and past tense markers. This dialect also has its own lexical items. Hamgyŏng dialect is spoken by people in Hamgyŏng province, which is located in the northeast region of North Korea. This dialect retains palatal glides before /c/ and features unique nominative, dative, passive, and causative markers. In terms of the lexicon, many words are borrowed from Chinese, Russian, and Manchu.

This chapter identified four different speech styles: deferential, polite, intimate, and plain, the usage of which depends on who is talking to whom. They show respect to the hearer, listed from the highest degree of respect to the lowest degree of respect. More crucially, the usage of speech styles combines with sentence type to create the sixteen combinations of patterns illustrated in this chapter. Another major sociolinguistic topic in Korean is the honorifics system, which is a part of Korean culture that depends on the relationship between the speaker, the hearer, and the referent. We discussed three variables which condition the use of honorifics: power, solidarity, and formality of speech style. There are two exceptions to the canonical honorifics, *Apjonpŏp* and indirect honorifics. *Apjonpŏp* describes cases where an honorific might be expected but cannot be used due to the status ranking among the speaker, hearer, and referent. Indirect honorifics are honorifics used for the body parts, belongings, and thoughts associated with an honorable person.

"Terms of address" is a speech phenomenon that refers to the addressee of social communication, which can be extremely complicated to determine. We illustrated three areas in terms of address: second-person pronouns, titles with names, and kinship terms. In the final section, we presented four areas of language policy: Hangul, Standard language, language purification policy, and romanization. In particular, we scrutinized national policy on Hangul and foreign words including Chinese and English. We concluded with a discussion of the three major romanization systems, MR, YR, and RR, each of which has pros and cons.

Further Readings

Lee, Ik Seop. 2013. *Sahoy Enehak* [Sociolinguistics], 10th ed. Seoul: Minumsa.
Lee, Sang Kyu. 2008. *Kuke Pangenhak* [Korean Dialectology]. Seoul: Hakyunsa.
Min, Hyun Sik. 2011. *Korean Orthography*, 4th ed. Seoul: Taehaksa.
National Institute of Korean Language. 2007. Pangen Iyaki [The Story of Dialects]. Seoul: Taehaksa.

References

Brown, Roger and Albert Gilman. 1970. *The Pronouns of Power and Solidarity.* [Bobbs-Merrill Reprint Series in the Social Sciences, A-274]. Indianapolis: Bobbs-Merrill.
Cho, Sungdai. 2006. Linguistic structures of Korean. In Ho-min Sohn (ed.), *Korean Language and Culture in Society*, 236–248. University of Hawai'i Press.
Kwon, Jaeil. 2011. *Hankuke Tongsalon* [Korean Syntax], 5th ed. Seoul: Minumsa.
Lee, Swung Nyung. 1967. Hankwuk Pangensa [Korean Dialectology]. Korea University Press.

10   Language and Gender

Language and gender is an area of research that investigates how varieties of speech are associated with gender categories or how they reflect gendered social norms. In this chapter, we describe how gender influences speech variety in four major areas: lexicon, phonology, syntax, and discourse.

Although moves have been made toward gender parity, Korea is historically a highly patriarchal society, and negative attitudes toward women and rigid expectations about women's roles in society still linger. Despite efforts at reform, the language still reflects this background, and the differences in speech styles that are conventionally male and conventionally female indicate that men and women have developed different means of navigating the social world.

For example, to build social bonds, women use more exclamatory words to show attentiveness, while men use more slang expressions to signal in-group status. In the following sections, we will show how variation in written and spoken language illustrates the different means men and women use to navigate their social world.

10.1   Basics

Traditional assumptions about how speech style relates to social roles have resulted in many broad generalizations about the differences in the way Korean men and women speak. Because men are still predominant in business, political, economic, and financial sectors, they are frequently said to speak in an aggressive and direct manner. In contrast, because women have traditionally worked inside the home, they are often said to speak in a relatively reserved manner and convey their messages indirectly and with friendliness. In the long run, this "separate spheres" theory is unexplanatory and relies on unfounded stereotypes. What research on other languages has shown is that rather than gendered speech styles, what exists are different strategies for negotiating an interaction that can be used by both men and women depending on the discourse context.

10.2   Lexical Differences

The Korean lexicon illustrates the gendered history of Korea and the gendered expectations that are still rampant in the culture today. Many gender-related words are either male default but modifiable, female default but modifiable, mixed, or irrevocably male or female. The terms in (1) are all common Sino-Korean terms in which the specification 'female' requires the additional SK morpheme *ye* 'woman'.

(1)   Male default (Sino-Korean)
   - a. 시인   *siin*   poet
   - b. 여시인   *ye-siin*   female poet
   - c. 비서   *pise*   secretary
   - d. 여비서   *ye-pise*   female secretary
   - e. 대학교   *tayhakkyo*   college
   - f. 여자 대학교   *yeca-tayhakkyo* women's college

Most titles and occupational terms belong to this group of the lexicon, reflecting the still prevalent attitude that Korean society is divided into two sectors, men in the public sphere outside the home and women in the private sphere inside. Thus the default assumption would be that the occupational terms below refer to males.

(2)   Titles and occupational terms
   - a. 사장   *sacang*   company president
   - b. 교수   *kyoswu*   professor
   - c. 판사   *phansa*   judge
   - d. 의사   *uysa*   medical doctor
   - e. 회사원   *hoysawen*   company employee

A more emblematic indication of gender hierarchy inherited from Sino-Korean usage is the ordering of SK morphemes designating gender in dvandva compounds.

(3)   "Male" before "female" in SK dvandva compounds
   - a. 남녀   *nam nye*   boy and girl
   - b. 부모   *pwu mo*   father and mother
   - c. 자녀   *ca nye*   son and daughter
   - d. 부부   *pwu pwu*   husband and wife
   - e. 신사 숙녀 *sinsa swuknye*   gentlemen and ladies

As in many other languages, words that indicate a sexually active man are not inherently negative, while the parallel words designating women can be pejorative.

(4)   Sexually active men
        a. 늑대   *nuktay* wolf
        b. 마초   *macho* macho

Contrary to the occupational terms in (2), sex industry terms such as *chep* 'concubine' and *chang* 'prostitute' designate females unless specifically indicated. The prefix *nam* must be added if a male is performing this role.

(5)   Female default
        a. 첩   *chep*   female concubine
        b. 남첩   *nam chep*   male concubine
        c. 창   *chang*   female prostitute
        d. 남창   *nam chang* male prostitute

Other terms such as *paywu* 'actor' and *sengmi* 'beauty' do not have these gender biases. The male prefix *nam* is equally unmarked with these terms, as in (6).

(6)   Male and female terms
        a. 남배우   *nam paywu*   actor
        b. 여배우   *ye paywu*   actress
        c. 남성미   *nam sengmi* male beauty
        d. 여성미   *ye sengmi*   female beauty

As in other languages, there are gender-related terms, particularly among kin terms, that are used only for one gender or the other.

(7)   Male gender-asymmetric terms
        a. 남편   *namphyen*   husband
        b. 남정네   *namcengney* fellows

(8)   Female gender-asymmetric terms
        a. 여식   *yesik*   daughter
        b. 여급   *yekup*   waitress
        c. 여권신장   *yekwen sincang* feminism

Some lexical items referring to human physical characteristics are gender-biased, as in (9).

(9)   Female gender-biased terms (physical characteristics)
        a. 여태   *yethay*   feminine attitude
        b. 각선미   *kaksenmi*   leg line beauty
        c. 쭉쭉빵빵   *ccwukccwuk ppangppang* voluptuous

Many such terms based on metaphor or common social stereotypes are blatantly pejorative toward women, as in (10). Some of these involve animal metaphor stereotypes found in other languages, such as (10a, b). The term in (10c) uses the device of contraction of Sino-Korean words, so that *senghyeng* 'cosmetic surgery' plus *koymwul* 'monster' elides the second and fourth morphemes to produce *sengkoy* 'cosmetic surgery monster'.

(10)   Female gender-biased metaphorical and compound terms
    a. 암탉   *amthalk*   hen
    b. 불여우   *pwulyewu*   red fox
    c. 된장녀   *toyncangnye*   gold digger
    d. 강남성괴   *kangnam sengkoy*   a Kangnam cosmetic surgery monster
    e. 김여사   *kimyesa*   woman who drives with no manners, but blames other drivers

There are four types of kinship terms relating to gender, age, and marriage. Siblings refer to their brothers or sisters according to whether the speaker is male or female. A brother calls his older brother *hyeng* (originally a Sino-Korean word) and his older sister *nwuna*. A sister calls her older brother *oppa* and her older sister *enni*. However, both refer to their younger sibling as simply *tongsayng*, optionally adding a male/female prefix, *nam-tongsayng/ ye-tongsayng*. As we saw in Chapter 9, age plays a crucial role in the use of these sibling terms (11).

(11)   Siblings
    a. 형   *hyeng*   older brother
    b. 누나   *nwuna*   older sister
    c. 오빠   *oppa*   older brother
    d. 언니   *enni*   older sister
    e. (남)동생 *(nam)tongsayng* younger brother
    f. (여)동생 *(ye)tongsayng*   younger sister

There are two ways to refer to parents-in-law, one from a wife's perspective and another from a husband's perspective. A wife calls her father-in-law *si-apeci* and her mother-in-law *si-emeni,* indicating that *si* refers to parents-in-law from a wife's perspective in (12). A husband calls his father-in-law *cang-in* and his mother-in-law *cang-mo*, indicating that *cang* refers to parents-in-law from a husband's perspective in (12).

(12)   Parents-in-law
    a. 시아버지 *si-apeci* father-in-law
    b. 시어머니 *si-emeni* mother-in-law
    c. 장인   *cang-in* father-in-law
    d. 장모   *cang-mo* mother-in-law

Another set of gender-differentiated kinship terms concerns the family structure on the father's side and the mother's side. A grandfather and grandmother are called *hal-apeci* 'grand father' and *hal-meni* 'grand mother', but *oy* is added for maternal grandparents, creating *oy-hal-apeci* and *oy-hal-meni*. A paternal uncle is called *samchon*, and a maternal uncle is *oy-samchon*. However, a father's sister or a mother's sister is called *komo* or *imo* respectively, while *pwu* is added when referring to their husband.

(13)   Father's side and mother's side
         a. 할아버지   *hal-apeci*   grandfather
         b. 외할아버지   *oy-hal-apeci*   grandfather
         c. 할머니   *hal-meni*   grandmother
         d. 외할머니   *oy-hal-meni*   grandmother
         e. 삼촌   *samchon*   uncle
         f. 외삼촌   *oy-samchon*   uncle
         g. 고모(부)   *komo(pwu)*   aunt (her husband)
         h. 이모(부)   *imo(pwu)*   aunt (her husband)

The same person has two different kinship designations, depending on marriage status. An uncle is *samchon* before his marriage but becomes *cakun-apeci* 'little father' or *khun-apeci* 'big father' after his marriage. *Chon* is a unique aspect of Korean kinship that describes the distance between two family members. Sino-Korean numerals with *chon* indicates a distance relationship, *il-chon* 'one *chon*' between oneself and one's parent, *i-chon* 'two *chon*' between oneself and one's sibling, *sam-chon* 'three *chon*' between oneself and one's father's sibling, and *mwu-chon* 'no *chon*' between husband and wife.

(14)   Marriage
         a. 삼촌   *samchon*   uncle
         b. 작은 아버지   *cakun-apeci*   uncle (father's younger brother)
         c. 큰 아버지   *khun-apeci*   uncle (father's older brother)
         d. 일촌   *il-chon*   distance from parents (one)
         e. 이촌   *i-chon*   distance from siblings (two)
         f. 삼촌   *sam-chon*   distance from father's sibling (three)
         g. 무촌   *mwu-chon*   distance between husband and wife (zero)

In many contexts, especially stereotyped or artificial ones such as television dramas or comic books (*manhwa ch'aek*), women are portrayed as using more linguistic markers of exclamation than men. The discourse markers in (15), generally indicating surprise or excitement at the beginning of an utterance, are examples of these. Most speakers would identify the items in (15) as characteristic of women's speech.

(15)   Exclamation (woman)
         a. 어머머   *ememe*   oh
         b. 어머나   *emena*   oh
         c. 어쩜   *eccem*   what a surprise
         d. 아이 참   *ai cham*   ah
         e. 흥   *hung*   ah
         f. 피   *phi*   sigh

Women's speech is also often characterized as making more frequent use of contractions.

(16)   Common contractions (stereotypically associated with women's speech)
    a. 그렇지   그치   *kulehci*   *kuchi*   is that so?
    b. 그런데   근데   *kulentey*   *kuntey*   therefore
    c. 어쩌면   어쩜   *eccemyen*   *eccem*   maybe
    d. 지요   죠   *ciyo*   *cyo*   isn't it?
    e. 지 않아요   잖아요   *ci anhayo*   *canhayo*   isn't it?

10.3   Phonological Differences

There are some salient differences between men and women with respect to intonation patterns. Women speak in a rising intonation at 220 Hz, and men speak in a falling intonation at 120 Hz, with the normal frequency of speech assumed to be around 100–400 Hz. This intonation pattern relates to the friendliness between the speaker and hearer, with a rising intonation imparting more friendliness to the hearer. In addition, women used to occupy a lower position in society, so the rising intonation is used as a strategy to show themselves to the hearer and to secure their position in society. This has been claimed to be a crosslinguistic phenomenon (Trudgill 1983). Women also favor standard pronunciation over regional dialects, whereas men use more regional dialect forms, since the use of dialect shows their affinity to the group through covert prestige.

One phonological trait that has been associated with women's speech is the use of tensed or aspirated consonants instead of plain consonants, particularly in gradient terms such as quality adjectives and adverbs. The plain consonant *c* or *t* becomes a tensed consonant *cc* or *tt* in a woman's speech (17).

(17)   Plain consonants versus tensed or aspirated
    a. 조금   *cokum*   a little
    b. 쪼금   *ccokum*   a little
    c. 다른 것   *talun kes*   different thing
    d. 따른 것   *ttalun kes*   different thing

Along these same lines, the sound *l* is often geminated in women's speech. 'This thing' *yokelo* becomes *yokello* by adding *l*, and 'do it that way' *kulelakwu* becomes *kulellakwu* by adding *l* in a woman's speech in (18).

(18)   *L*-addition
    a. 요거로   *yokelo*   this thing
    b. 요걸로   *yokello*   this thing
    c. 그러라구   *kulelakwu*   do it that way
    d. 그럴라구   *kulellakwu*   do it that way

Although native speakers may have the reaction that these phonological traits are "childish" or "cute," thus buying in to gender stereotypes, note that from a phonetic standpoint, aspiration, tensification, and gemination are all forms of strengthening. This pattern thus runs counter to a simple characterization of the relation between sound symbolism and gender stereotypes.

10.4   Syntactic Differences

There are notable syntactic differences between men's and women's speech styles in Korean. It is often held that men use proportionally more declarative sentences and women more interrogatives. The deferential speech style, *-(su)pnita*, tends to be associated with male speech in highly formal situations, while women's speech is associated with the polite speech style, *-yo*, in declaratives, as in (19).

(19)   Types of declarative sentences
       a. ㅂ/습니다   *p/sup nita*
           철수가 학교에 갑니다.
           Chelswu=ka   hakkyo=ey ka-pnita.
           Chelswu=NOM   school=DIR go-DEF
           'Chelswu goes to school.'
       b. 요   *yo*
           철수가 학교에 가요.
           Chelswu=ka   hakkyo=ey ka-yo.
           Chelswu=NOM   school=DIR go-POL
           'Chelswu goes to school.'

Men and women also typically use different interrogative markers, *nya* for men and *ni* for women (20).

(20)   Types of interrogative sentences
       a. 냐?   *nya*
           철수가 학교에 가냐?
           Chelswu=ka   hakkyo=ey ka-nya?
           Chelswu=NOM   school=DIR go-Q
           'Does Chelswu go to school?'
       b. 니?   *ni*
           철수가 학교에 가니?
           Chelswu=ka   hakkyo=ey ka-ni?
           Chelswu=NOM   school=DIR go-Q
           'Does Chelswu go to school?'

Another common stereotype is that men proportionally use more commands, while women use more incomplete sentences. Incomplete sentences allow the hearer more freedom of action or "face." Because Korean sentences are typically truncated from the end, an incomplete sentence avoids commitment to a specific speech act, since speech-act markers come at the end of the clause.

A stereotypical men's speech style is represented in (21), where a command or assertion is uttered, while (22) represents incomplete utterances stereotypically associated with women, with the unspoken part in parentheses.

(21)   Command/assertion
    a. 학교에 가지.
       Hakkyo=ey   ka-ci.
       school=DIR   go-COM
       'Please go to school.'
    b. 이것을 먹읍시다.
       Ikes=ul   mek-upsita.
       this=ACC   eat-PROP
       'Let's eat this.'

(22)   Incomplete sentence
    a. 학교에 가려나, (그렇지)?
       Hakkyo=ey   ka-lyena   kulehci?
       school=DIR   go-INTEN   is that so
       'Someone goes to school, isn't that so?'
    b. 이것을 먹을까(요)?
       Ikes=ul   mek-ulkka(yo)?
       this=ACC   eat-shall
       'Shall we eat this?'

Third, men use active voice more, and women use the passive construction more. The active voice emphasizes the performer of the action, so the sentence is more dynamic and forceful, which coincides with male stereotypes. The passive voice minimizes the role of the person performing the action and softens or makes the message less personal. Thus its sentence is more evasive or passive, which coincides with female stereotypes of lack of confidence.

    Fourth, women use more tag questions, again a trait that has been observed crosslinguistically.

(23)   Tag question
    a. 응   *ung* 'yes'
       어제 학교에 갔어, 응?
       Ecey   hakkyo=ey   ka-ss-e   ung?
       yesterday school=DIR   go-PAST-INT is that so
       'You went to school yesterday, yes?'
    b. 안 그래   *an kulay* 'isn't that so?'
       여기가 맞지, 안 그래?
       Yeki=ka   mac-ci an kulay?
       here=NOM   right-Q is that right
       'Here is the right place, isn't that so?'

c. 그렇지 않니 *kulehci anhni* 'isn't that the case?'
날씨가 춥다, 그렇지 않니?
Nalssi=ka   chwup-ta   kulehci anhni?
weather=NOM   cold-PLN   isn't it true
'The weather is cold, isn't that the case?'

d. 그렇죠 *kulehcyo* 'right'
내가 만든 김치 맛있죠? 그렇죠?
Nay=ka   mantu-n   kimchi   masiss-cyo?   Kulehcyo?
I=NOM   make-PRENOM Kimchee delicious-Q   is that so
'The Kimchee that I made is delicious, right?'

Fifth, women's speech is sometimes associated with richer use of adverbials, including reduplicated adverbs as in (24b).

(24)   Adverbial use
a. 너무 *nemwu* 'too (much)'
이 강아지 너무 예쁘다.
I   kangaci nemwu yeyppu-ta.
this   puppy   too   pretty-PLN
'This puppy is too pretty.'

b. 너무너무 *nemwunemwu* 'too too (much)'
떡볶이 너무너무 맛있다.
Ttekpokki   nemwunemwu masiss-ta.
rice cake with a spicy sauce   too too   delicious-PLN
'The rice-cake with spicy sauce is too too delicious.'

c. 참 *cham* 'quite, really'
이 옷 참 좋다.
I . os   cham   coh-ta.
this clothes   really good-PLN
'These clothes are really good.'

d. 꼭 *kkok* 'surely'
우리 여기 꼭 다시 오자.
Wuli   yeki   kkok   tasi   o-ca.
we   here   surely again   come-PROP
'Let us surely come here again.'

Finally, women are held to use more deictic terms than men, often in discourse anaphoric contexts.

(25)   Deixis use
a. 요것 *yokes* 'that thing'
이거 다 먹을래, 요것 빼고?
I=ke   ta mek-ullay yo-kes   ppay-ko?
this=thing all eat-Q   that-thing except-and
'Do you want to eat all of these, except that one?'

b. 고걸   *kokel* 'that thing (Accusative)'
두번째 본 옷 고걸로 사자.
Twupenccay po-n   os   kokel=lo   sa-ca.
second   see-PRENOM cloth that thing=by buy-PROP
'The second piece of cloth that we see, let's buy it.'

c. 요길, 조길 *yokil, cokil* 'here (Accusative), there (Accusative)'
요길 봐도 조길 봐도 예쁘네.
Yokil   pwa=to   cokil   pwa=to   yeyppu-ney.
here   see=too   there   see=too   pretty-APP
'It is pretty, whether you look here or there.'

d. 요게   *yokey* 'this (Nominative)'
먹어 보니까 케익 중에 요게 제일 맛있어.
Mek-e   po-nikka   kheyik-cwungey yokey ceyil masiss-e.
eat-CAUS see-because cake-among   that   most delicious-INT
'Having eaten it, among the cakes that one is most delicious.'

10.5   Discourse Differences

Women's speech is also characterized by negative-face strategies of politeness. In particular, women are known for frequently using hedges, indirect requests, and cooperative markers, all of which put the speaker's contributions in the position of requiring evaluation by the interlocutor before they are accepted as true. As these are all straightforward politeness strategies, both men and women use them when it behooves them to be polite.

A hedge is an adjective, an adverb, or a phrase that softens an assertion or lessens its strength. Thus it functions as euphemism or vagueness, which are characteristic of women's speech style.

(26)   Hedges or blurring expressions
a. 글쎄   *kulssey*
오늘 뭐 해? 글쎄, 잘 모르겠는데.
A: Onul mwe hay? B: Kulssey cal   molukeyss-nuntey.
today   what do-Q   well   well   don't know-ENDER
A: 'What are you doing today?' B: 'Well, I don't really know.'

b. 그냥   *kunyang* 'like that'
뭐가 그렇게 좋아? 그냥.
A: Mwe=ka   kulehkey   coh-a?   B: Kunyang.
what=NOM   that way   like-Q   just
A: 'Why do you like it that way?' B: 'Just . . . (no reason).'

c. ~ ㄴ/ㄹ 지 모르겠다   *~n/l ci molukeyssta* 'not know if/what'
오늘 뭐 했는지 모르겠다.
Onul   mwe   hay-ss-nunci molukeyssta.
today   what   do-PAST   don't know
'I don't know what I did today.'

d. ~ ㄴ 것 같다   *~n kes kathta* 'be like ... '
    너무 좋은 것 같은데.

    Nemwu   cohu-n kes   kathuntey.
    very   good-like   look
    'It looks like it's TOO good.'

e. ~대로 하다   *~taylo hata* 'do as ... '
    이거 어떻게 할까? 좋은대로 해.

    A: Ike   ettehkey ha-lkka? B: Cohuntaylo hay.
    this   how   do-Q   as you like   do
    A: 'How should I do this?' B: 'As you like.'

It is often held that indirect speech, or more broadly what we identified in Chapter 8 as "insubordination" (the use of an embedded pattern in a main clause context), is another typical characteristic of women's speech style. Once again, these patterns suppress main clause speech act markers.

(27)   Indirect speech/insubordination
         a. 오늘 학교에 가요?

            Onul   hakkyo=ey ka-yo?
            today   school=DIR go-Q
            'Will you go to school, today?'

         b. 오늘은 안 가는데.

            Onul=un   an   ka-nuntey.
            today=TOP   not   go-ENDER
            'Today, I do not go.'

         c. 오늘 너무 바쁜데.

            Onul   nemwu   papp-untey.
            today really   busy-ENDER
            'Today, I am really busy.'

Cooperative expressions such as *ung* 'yes' serve to smooth out the relation between speaker and hearer.

(28)   Cooperative expressions
         a. 응   *ung*
            지금 밥 먹을래? 응 알았어.

            Cikum   pap   mek-ullay? Ung   al-ass-e.
            now   cooked-rice eat-Q   yes   know-PAST-PLN
            A: 'Do you want to eat cooked-rice now?' B: 'Ok, got it.'

         b. 그래   *kulay*
            도서관에 내일 갈까? 그래 그럴까?

            A: Tosekwan=ey   nayil   ka-lkka? B: Kulay kule-lkka?
            library=DIR   tomorrow   go-Q   yes   do-Q
            A: 'Shall we go to the library tomorrow?' B: 'Yes, shall we?'

c. 맞아   *maca*
내 말에 대해 어떻게 생각해? 네 말이 맞아.
A: Nay mal=ey tayhay ettehkey sayngkakhay? B: Ney mal-i   maca.
my speaking about how   think-do   your speaking-NOM right
A: 'What do you think of my speaking?' B: 'Your speaking is right.'

10.6   Summary

In this chapter, we have described major areas of difference between male and female styles in spoken and written Korean: lexical, phonological, syntactic, and discourse differences. In males' and females' use of the lexicon, five types of lexicons were specified: no male terms, no female terms, only male terms, only female terms, and terms for both male and female. In 'no male terms', male terms are unmarked as a default, and a female prefix is added to this default lexicon, including terms for titles and occupation. In 'no female terms', female terms are unmarked as a default, and a male prefix is added to this default lexicon, including most discriminatory terms for women. In 'only male' and 'only female', these lexicons indicate characteristics of males or females. In 'terms for both male and female', a male prefix *nam* or a female prefix *ye* is added to this lexicon. Some terms indicate negative views of women including ones related to sexuality. Kinship terminology is also related to different lexicons for males and females, based on age and marriage.

The second major difference in male and female style is phonological. Women use a rising intonation and standard variants, and tend to perform strengthening processes such as *L*-addition or tensification, whereas men use a falling intonation and are more likely than women to use dialect variants. With regard to syntactic differences between men and women, men use more declarative sentences and deferential speech style, while women use more interrogative sentences, polite speech style, tag questions, adverbials, and deixis. In terms of discourse differences between men's and women's style, women use more indirect speech, hedges, obscure expressions, and cooperative communication, while men use a more direct speech style due to women's traditionally weaker status in society.

Further Readings

Kang, Soyoung. 2013. *Ene wa Yeyseng* [Language and Women]. Seoul: Jisik kwa Kyoyang Press.
Koo, Hyun-Jung. 2009. *Taewhauy Kipep* [Conversation Skill]. Seoul: Kyungjin Press.

References

Trudgill, P. 1983. *On Dialect: Social and Geographical Perspectives*. Oxford: Basil Blackwell.

Index